Basic Skills in English

Purple Level

Yellow Level

Blue Level

Orange Level

Green Level

Red Level

Basic Skills in English

Yellow Level

Joy Littell, EDITORIAL DIRECTOR

McDougal, Littell & Company
Evanston, Illinois
New York   Dallas   Sacramento

AUTHORS

Joy Littell, Editorial Director, McDougal, Littell & Company

The Editorial Staff of McDougal, Littell & Company

Kraft and Kraft, Developers of Educational Materials, Stow, Massachusetts

CONSULTANTS

Carole B. Bencich, Coordinator of Secondary Language Arts, Brevard County School Board, Rockledge, Florida

Dr. Sheila F. S. Ford, Coordinator for Secondary Language Arts, Spring Branch Independent School District, Houston, Texas

Marietta H. Hickman, English Department Chairman, Wake Forest-Rolesville High School, Wake Forest, North Carolina

Mary Evans Roberts, Supervisor of English and Language Arts, Savannah-Chatham Public Schools, Savannah, Georgia

ISBN: 0-86609-502-0   TE ISBN: 0-86609-503-9

Acknowledgments

Simon & Schuster: for entries on pages 17, 27, 29, 30, 32, 33, 40, and 440 from *Webster's New World Dictionary,* Students Edition; copyright © 1981 by Simon & Schuster, Inc. Bryna Untermeyer: For "The Fox and the Grapes" by Joseph Lauren, from *Story Poems,* edited by Louis Untermeyer; copyright © 1957 by Simon & Shuster, Inc.

88 / 12 11 10 9 8 7 6

Composition

Handbook

Developing Your Vocabulary

Discoveries

Learning Word Meanings from Context

Here's the Idea English has a larger, more varied vocabulary than most other languages. It includes a total of about 600,000 different words. In everyday situations, you usually recognize from 30,000 to 40,000 words. In speaking and writing, you may use 10,000.

One way to develop your vocabulary continually is to examine words in context. **Context** is the words and sentences within which a given word appears. Clues in the context can help you to figure out the meanings of unfamiliar words.

When **definition** is used in context, the meaning of an unfamiliar word is stated directly. Here is an example.

> Jean is taking a *yoga* class at the YWCA. *Yoga* is a system of controlled breathing and exercises.

When **restatement** is used, the meaning of a new word is explained. Look for the key words *or, that is,* or *which is.*

> The City Council approved a three percent tax *rebate.* That is, taxpayers will receive a return equal to three percent of their taxes.

You may be able to understand the meaning of a word through **examples** given. Look for the key words *especially, like, other, this, such as, for example,* and *for instance.*

> *Pasta,* such as spaghetti and macaroni, makes a filling and inexpensive meal.

When **comparison** is used, one word is compared with a similar word. Look for the key words *as, like, in the same way,* and *similar to.*

Ralph's *astute* answer was as clever as the teacher's question.

When **contrast** is used, a word is compared with an opposite word. Look for the key words *although, but, unlike, while, on the contrary,* and *on the other hand.*

That perfume is *subtle,* but this one has quite a sharp scent.

Check It Out   Read the following sentences.

1. I didn't understand the speaker's *dialect.* A dialect is a form of a language with its own vocabulary and pronunciation.
2. Dan's latest *objective,* or goal, is to run two miles every day.
3. Radioactive elements, such as *uranium* and *radium,* must be stored safely.
4. This *minestrone* is similar to Grandma's vegetable soup.
5. Although I was *punctual,* Donna was late for our meeting.

- What is the meaning of each italicized word? What context clue is used in each sentence?

Try Your Skill   Choose four of these words: *artist, cashier, electrician, reporter, salesperson, secretary.* Write sentences that explain each word. Use key words as context clues.

Keep This in Mind

- Develop your vocabulary by examining unfamiliar words in context. Helpful context clues are definition, restatement, examples, comparison, and contrast.

Now Write   Copy five unfamiliar words used in a textbook. Use context clues to write a definition of each word. Check your meanings in a dictionary. Label your paper **Discoveries,** the title of this lesson. Keep your work in your folder.

Drawing Conclusions

Inferring Meaning from Context

Here's the Idea The meaning of an unfamiliar word is not always made clear through direct context clues. However, the surrounding sentences may help you make a good guess at the meaning of an unfamiliar word. You may be able to read between the lines and draw a conclusion about the meaning of the word. This process is called **inference.**

The main idea of a passage or an entire paragraph may be related to the meaning of an unfamiliar word. In the following paragraph, for example, try to *infer* the meaning of the word *serene.*

> Jill had managed to stay *serene* in spite of a trying day. In the morning she didn't panic when she discovered that her bicycle had a flat tire. At lunch, she was patient with the freshman who tipped over her soup. She even remained unruffled during our surprise quiz in math this afternoon.

From the clues supplied in this paragraph, you can infer that *serene* means "quiet, calm, undisturbed."

Check It Out Read the following paragraph.

> When I finish high school, I am going to become an *apprentice* in the printing industry. For three years I will work with a master typesetter to learn all the phases of typesetting and printing. I will become familiar with various kinds of presses and with other printing machinery. I will also receive a salary while I learn the business.

• What can you infer about the meaning of *apprentice?*

Try Your Skill   As you read these passages, try to infer the meanings of the italicized words. Write definitions for them.

1. My cousin's *dilapidated* car is as unsafe as it looks. The fenders are one color, the roof another, and the trunk a third. The tires are bald. Only one of the brake lights is working. Each visible part of the car is rusty, dented, or worn. It is impossible for me to imagine that this car was ever new.

2. Critics point out that one bad side effect of watching too much violent television is increased *irascibility* in young children. Preschoolers who watch more than three hours a day are more quick-tempered and irritable than those whose viewing is more limited.

3. The most *prodigious* tides in the world occur in the Bay of Fundy, between Maine and Nova Scotia. In most other places, the difference between high and low tide is only a few feet. However, near the narrow mouth of the Bay of Fundy, the tides rise more than fifty feet! Because of these awesome tides, these waters are considered quite dangerous.

4. Shoveling snow became a *lucrative* activity for me last winter. The heavy snowfalls set records. People in my neighborhood paid me extra money to shovel the large drifts that buried driveways, cars, and sidewalks. In fact, I made more money in one month than I had during the last three winters put together.

Keep This in Mind

- Inference is the process of using clues to draw a conclusion. Inferences about unfamiliar words can be drawn from the main ideas of paragraphs.

Now Write   Suppose that you want to write a description of a friend who is especially *thoughtful*. Write four or five sentences that suggest this quality without defining it directly. Label your paper **Drawing Conclusions** and put it into your folder.

The Heart of the Matter

Base Words

Here's the Idea Many of the longer words in English are made of more than one part. Some of these words may seem complicated and impossible to understand at first. If you know how to recognize the parts, however, you can take long words apart. You can separate one part from another. If you know the meanings of a number of word parts, you can often piece together a meaning for the whole word.

The three key word parts are base words, prefixes, and suffixes. A **base word** is a shorter English word around which a longer word is built. A **prefix** is a word part added at the beginning of a base word. A **suffix** is a word part added at the end of a base word.

Study this list of words that have been built from the base word *use*. How is the meaning of *use* included in the meaning of each longer word?

disuse	"lack of use"
misuse	"use improperly"
reuse	"use again"
us**able**	"that can be used; ready for use"
use**less**	"having no use"
use**ful**	"having many uses; helpful"
reus**able**	"that can be used again"

Notice that the spelling of the base word may change when an ending is added.

Check It Out Examine these words and their definitions.

distrust	"lack of trust; suspicion"
mistrust	"lack of trust; suspicion"

trustful "full of trust or confidence"
mistrustful "full of suspicion"
trusty "that can be trusted or relied upon"

- What is the base word in each longer word?
- What parts have been added in each word? Is each part a prefix or a suffix?
- How does the meaning of the longer word include the meaning of the base word?

Try Your Skill The words in each of the following groups have the same base word. For each group, write the base word.

1. discredit   noncredit   creditable
2. action   inaction   react   reaction
3. remove   movable   immovable   removable
4. conceivable   inconceivable   preconceived
5. construction   misconstruct   reconstruct
6. replace   displace   misplace   replaceable
7. incorrect   correctable   correction
8. disassemble   preassembled   reassemble   assembly
9. flexible   flexion   inflexible
10. dishonor   honorable   dishonorable

Keep This in Mind

- A base word is a word from which other words can be made by adding new parts.
- The new parts may be added at the beginning of the base word, at the end, or in both places.

Now Write Choose one word from each of the ten groups in **Try Your Skill.** Write the meaning of each word you choose. Then use each word in a sentence. Label your paper **The Heart of the Matter** and keep it in your folder.

A Word Divided

Recognizing Prefixes

Here's the Idea   Another good way to develop your vocabulary is to examine the parts of an unfamiliar word. In English, many words are made up of parts that work together. If you learn some of the most common word parts, you will be able to learn many new words.

A **prefix** is a word part with its own meaning that is added to the beginning of a base word. For instance, the prefix *sub-* means "under" or "less than." Once you know the meaning of this prefix, you will know that *subsoil* is "a layer of soil beneath the surface soil." You will also see that a *subcompact* is "a car that is smaller than a compact." Notice how the addition of the prefix affects the meanings of the base words *soil* and *compact*.

Study this list of common prefixes, their meanings, and examples of their use. Some prefixes have more than one meaning.

Prefix	Meaning	Example
dis-	"opposite of" or "away"	dishonest, displace
in- (also **il-, im-,** and **ir-**)	"not"	inability, illogical, immature, irreplaceable
mis-	"wrong, bad"	misbehavior
non-	"not"	nonfiction
pre-	"before"	prepay
re-	"again" or "back"	remarry, regain

Do not expect to find prefixes in all words. Check a word and its history in a dictionary to determine if the word has a prefix.

Check It Out   Examine these words and their definitions.

discomfort—"lack of comfort; distress"
disarm—"to take away weapons; to reduce forces"
inattentive—"not attentive; careless"
illimitable—"not limited; without bounds"
immobile—"not movable; motionless"
irrational—"not reasonable; absurd"
misfortune—"bad luck; trouble"
nonessential—"not essential; unnecessary"
precaution—"care taken beforehand"
rearrange—"to arrange again or differently"
repay—"to pay back"

- What is the prefix in each? What is the base word?

Try Your Skill   Twelve of the following words have prefixes. For each word that has a prefix, write the prefix and its meaning, plus the base word. For example, for the word *preview* you would write: pre (before) + view.

1. miscount	6. nonskid	11. disinterested
2. distrust	7. miserable	12. prepackage
3. pressure	8. reenlist	13. irresistible
4. redecorate	9. mispronounce	14. nonrestricted
5. incapable	10. preelection	15. distant

Keep This in Mind

- A prefix is a word part added at the beginning of a base word. A prefix has its own meaning. Learn the meanings of common prefixes.

Now Write   Use a dictionary to find six unfamiliar words containing each of the six prefixes that you have learned. List these words and define them. Finally, study them. Label your paper **A Word Divided** and keep it in your folder.

On End

Recognizing Suffixes

Here's the Idea A word part added at the end of a base word is called a **suffix**. Like a prefix, a suffix has a meaning of its own that changes the meaning of the base word. Also like a prefix, a suffix may have more than one meaning or more than one form. For instance, the suffix *-er* or *-or* means "a person or thing that does something." Thus, a *counselor* is "a person who counsels or advises."

Unlike prefixes, however, suffixes usually affect the spelling of the base words. Sometimes the final consonant is doubled. For example, *shop* becomes *shopper*. Sometimes the final letter is dropped. For example, *move* becomes *movable*. Sometimes the final letter of the base word is changed. For example, *penny* becomes *penniless*.

Study this list of common suffixes, their meanings, and examples of their use.

Suffix	Meaning	Example
-able or **-ible**	"can be, having this quality"	lovable, sensible
-less	"without"	thoughtless
-ful	"full of, having"	doubtful
-ous	"full of, having"	courageous
-ist	"a person who does something"	biologist
-ion	"act of, result of, condition of"	correction
-y	"tending to be, characterized by"	foggy

Check It Out   Examine these words and their definitions.

> sociable—"enjoying the company of others; friendly"
> permissible—"that can be permitted; allowable"
> artless—"lacking skill or art; simple; natural"
> pitiful—"deserving pity because it is sad or pathetic"
> spacious—"having more than enough space; large"
> naturalist—"a person who studies animals and plants"
> formation—"something formed, arranged, or positioned"
> faulty—"having faults; imperfect"

- What is the suffix in each? What is the base word?

Try Your Skill   Number your paper from 1 to 15. Find the suffix in each of the following words. Write the base word and the meaning of the suffix for each word. Check the spelling of the base word if necessary. For instance, for the word *typist* you would write: type + a person who does.

1. famous
2. homeless
3. violinist
4. taxable
5. reflection
6. delightful
7. convertible
8. noisy
9. mysterious
10. wavy
11. guitarist
12. priceless
13. cupful
14. reasonable
15. translation

Keep This in Mind

- A suffix is a word part added at the end of a base word. A suffix has its own meaning. Learn the meanings of some of the most common suffixes. Use a dictionary to check the spelling of a word when you add a suffix.

Now Write   Use a dictionary to help you find seven words, each containing a different one of the seven suffixes you have learned. List the new words. Define them and study them. Label your paper **On End** and put it into your folder.

The Root of the Matter

Using Roots from Latin

Here's the Idea   You have learned that a prefix, such as *dis-*, meaning "opposite," can be added to a base word, such as *loyal*. The word formed, *disloyal*, means "without loyalty, faithless." You have also learned that a suffix, such as *-y*, meaning "characterized by," can be added to a base word, such as *sleep*. The word formed, *sleepy*, means "likely to fall asleep, drowsy." In these examples, it is clear that base words are separate words with their own meanings.

Some words are formed from a different kind of word part, called a **root.** Usually, a root is not an English word by itself. Nevertheless, a root has a meaning of its own. Because so many of the words in English come from Latin, the most common roots also come from Latin.

Study these four common Latin roots, their meanings, and examples of words in which they appear.

Latin Root	Meaning	Example
cred	"believe"	*credit*, meaning "belief or trust; approval; confidence"
duc, duct, duce	"lead"	*introduction*, meaning "something that leads into or prepares the way for"
fac, fact	"make"	*factory*, meaning "a building in which things are made"
pos, pon	"place or set"	*position*, meaning "the place where a person or thing is, especially in relation to others"

Check It Out   Examine these words and their definitions.

> creed—"a brief statement of beliefs"
> incredible—"unbelievable"
>
> produce—"to lead or bring forth; to create"
> deduce—"to figure out by logical reasoning"
>
> factor—"any condition that makes something happen"
> manufacture—"to make goods, especially by machinery"
>
> positive—"definitely set; sure"
> impose—"to place something on, such as a burden, tax, or regulation"

- What is the Latin root in each example? How is the meaning of the root related to the meaning of the whole word?

Try Your Skill   Copy the following words, circling the Latin root in each. Use the meaning of the root to help you figure out the meaning of the word. Then check the history and the meaning of each word in a dictionary.

creditable	abduct	fact	posture
accredit	aqueduct	facility	compose

Keep This in Mind

- A root is a part of a word and has a meaning of its own. Many common roots come from Latin. Learn some of the Latin roots, and you will have a clue to the meaning of many unfamiliar words.

Now Write   Using a dictionary, find four new words containing each of the four Latin roots you have learned. List and define the new words. Finally, study the roots. Label your paper **The Root of the Matter.** Put it into your folder.

Through the Centuries

Combinations from Greek

Here's the Idea Like Latin, Greek has contributed many word parts to English. There are, for instance, several words made from the Greek root *micro*, meaning "very small."

You are probably familiar with a *micro*wave oven. You have used a *micro*scope in science class. You may have read *micro*film in your school library. You may listen to a pocket stereo made possible through *micro*miniaturization of electronic parts. The meaning "very small" is important in each of these words.

Study these six common Greek roots, their meanings, and examples of words in which they appear. Notice that the forms of some roots may change slightly.

Greek Root	Meaning	Example
micro	"small"	*microfiche*, a card with print too small to read without magnification
bio	"life"	*biosphere*, the part of the earth and its atmosphere where living things are found
chrono	"time"	*chronic*, lasting for a long time
ology	"science"	*biology*, the science that studies life
graph	"writing"	*graphite*, the material used to make pencils
metron	"measure"	*chronometer*, an extremely accurate timepiece

Check It Out   Examine these words and their definitions.

biography—"writing about a person's life"
chronology—"the study of time; a sequence of events"
chronograph—"a machine that keeps a written record of time"
microbiology—"the branch of biology that studies the smallest
living things"
micrometer—"a tool for measuring very small distances"

- What Greek root or roots are in each example? How is
the meaning of each Greek root related to the meaning
of the whole word?

Try Your Skill   Copy the following words, circling the Greek
root or roots in each. Use the meanings of the roots to help you
figure out the meaning of each word. Write what you think each
word means. Then check the history and the meaning of each
word in a dictionary.

microcircuit	micronutrient	biochemistry
biometrics	biosatellite	synchronize
anachronism	epigraph	symmetry

Keep This in Mind

- Many English words are made from Greek roots. If
you learn some of the Greek roots, you will have a
clue to the meanings of many unfamiliar words.

Now Write   Using a dictionary, find six new words containing
each of the six new Greek roots you have learned. List and
define the new words. Finally, study the words. Label your
paper **Through the Centuries.** Put it into your folder.

In the Right

Using Words Precisely

Here's the Idea If you use language carelessly, you run two risks. First, your writing may be dull or boring. Second, and more important, your ideas may be misunderstood. Thus, it is important to choose specific words that express the precise meaning you have in mind.

To use words precisely, you need to learn to choose among synonyms. **Synonyms** are words with nearly the same meaning. For example, the words *easy, effortless, smooth,* and *simple* are synonyms. The meanings of synonyms may be quite similar, but the differences are usually important. These important shades of meaning are often explained in a dictionary. A *synonymy* (si nän' ə mē) is the list of synonyms and their shades of meaning that is given at the end of some entries in a dictionary.

Synonyms are also given in another helpful reference book called a *thesaurus* (thi sôr' əs). A thesaurus gives many synonyms for each word or idea listed.

To use words precisely, you also need to learn to use antonyms. **Antonyms** are words with opposite meanings. For example, *find—lose, arrive—depart,* and *ancient—modern* are pairs of antonyms. Antonyms will help you to show contrasts. For example, you might write, "In Rome the remains of *ancient* buildings are an important part of the *modern* city." You will find antonyms given in some dictionaries and in a thesaurus.

Check It Out Look at the synonymy given at the end of a dictionary entry for *sad,* and then answer these questions.

- Which synonym for *sad* suggests discouragement?
- What are antonyms for *sad?*

SYN.—**sad** is the simple, general term, implying anything from a mild unhappiness that is over quickly to a feeling of great, deep grief; **sorrowful** implies a sadness caused by some specific loss, disappointment, etc. *[her death left him sorrowful]*; **melancholy** suggests a more or less continuing mournfulness or gloominess, or, often, merely a deep thoughtfulness *[a melancholy view of life and its misfortunes]*; **dejected** implies discouragement or a sinking of spirits, as because of frustration; **depressed** suggests a mood of worry and hopelessness, as because of feeling tired or useless *[the unhappy ending left him feeling depressed]*; **doleful** implies a mournful, often exaggerated, sadness *[the doleful look on a lost child's face]* —*ANT.* happy, cheerful

Try Your Skill   Choose the synonym that best fits each sentence. Use a dictionary or thesaurus to help you.

1. I couldn't risk driving far on these (bad, wicked, severe, defective) tires.

2. Dr. McKenna hoped that her patient would (reply, answer, respond, retort) to the bright light.

3. You can turn to your elders for (intelligent, clever, alert, smart) advice on many practical matters.

4. The youngest children (chuckled, laughed, snickered, guffawed) at the clown's wonderful, silly tricks.

Keep This in Mind

· Use a dictionary or thesaurus to check the meanings of words. Learn to use words precisely.

Now Write   Choose two of the synonyms and one antonym for *sad* shown in **Check It Out.** Use each correctly in a sentence that shows its precise meaning. Label your paper **In the Right** and put it into your folder.

Special Effects

Building a Vocabulary of the Senses

Here's the Idea Your five senses are constantly giving you specific information. Much of the time, you do not pay particular attention to sensory details. However, if you stop and focus on each of your senses, you will realize the variety of impressions that you are receiving. When you write, you can use these sensory details to describe an experience and bring it to life.

Through the use of sensory details you can make any experience vivid. For example, suppose that you were home alone during a power failure. Can you imagine that experience as you read the following paragraph?

> I felt the sudden silence. The radio stopped. The furnace ceased its steady rumbling. The refrigerator stopped its droning hum. The only sounds were those of the wind whistling and the creaking of the old house. As I sat in the silence, I felt a chilly draft. I shivered and moved toward the window. I watched the sky darken as the storm thundered into the valley.

To learn how to use sensory details effectively, you need to do three things. First, train yourself to be more aware of your senses. Notice the details of your surroundings. Second, build a vocabulary of the senses. Become familiar with the sensory words such as those listed on pages 20 and 21 at the end of this lesson. Finally, use your sensory vocabulary effectively. Select sensory words that describe your experience precisely.

Check It Out Look at these examples of sensory words.

    Sight: silver, curved, sparkling, massive
  Hearing: thud, whine, hiss, rustle, sigh
    Touch: lukewarm, spongy, wooly, waxy

Taste: bittersweet, mellow, medicinal, savory
Smell: earthy, pungent, briny, musty

- Which of these sensory words are new to you? What do they mean? Think of an object or place that might be described by each of these words.

Try Your Skill   Think of two specific places that fit any of the general categories below. Name the two places and then list as many sensory words as you can think of that describe each one. Be specific. Try to use all of your senses.

a museum	a gymnasium
a department store	a classroom
an amusement park	a room
a restaurant	a garage

Keep This in Mind

- Use your senses to learn about your surroundings. Build a vocabulary of the senses. When you write, use vivid sensory details that bring an experience to life.

Now Write   Think of a place where you go to rest or relax. List as many sensory details about the place as you can. Try to use all of your senses. Choose specific, precise words. You may want to refer to the sample lists on the following pages. Label your paper **Special Effects.** Keep it in your folder.

A List of Sight Words

colorless	round	dotted	tidy
white	flat	freckled	handsome
ivory	curved	wrinkled	tall
yellow	wavy	striped	lean
gold	ruffled	bright	muscular
orange	oval	clear	sturdy
lime	angular	shiny	healthy
green	triangular	sparkling	fragile
turquoise	rectangular	jeweled	pale
blue	square	fiery	sickly
pink	hollow	sheer	small
maroon	narrow	drab	large
lavender	crooked	dark	massive
purple	lumpy	old	immense
gray	swollen	worn	attractive
silver	long	messy	perky
hazel	wiry	cluttered	showy
black	shapeless	clean	shadowy

A List of Hearing Words

crash	squawk	crackle	chime
thud	whine	buzz	laugh
bump	bark	clink	gurgle
boom	bleat	hiss	giggle
thunder	bray	snort	guffaw
bang	blare	bellow	sing
roar	rumble	growl	hum
scream	grate	whimper	mutter
screech	slam	stammer	murmur
shout	clap	snap	whisper
yell	stomp	rustle	sigh
whistle	jangle	whir	hush

A List of Taste Words

oily	rich	bland	ripe
buttery	hearty	tasteless	medicinal
salty	mellow	sour	fishy
bitter	sugary	vinegary	spicy
bittersweet	crisp	fruity	hot
sweet	savory	tangy	burnt

A List of Smell Words

sweet	piney	acrid	sickly
scented	pungent	burnt	stagnant
fragrant	spicy	gaseous	musty
aromatic	gamy	putrid	moldy
perfumed	fishy	spoiled	dry
fresh	briny	sour	damp
earthy	sharp	rancid	dank

A List of Touch Words

cool	wet	silky	sandy
cold	slippery	velvety	gritty
icy	spongy	smooth	rough
lukewarm	mushy	soft	sharp
tepid	oily	wooly	thick
warm	waxy	furry	dry
hot	fleshy	feathery	dull
steamy	rubbery	fuzzy	thin
sticky	bumpy	hairy	fragile
damp	crisp	leathery	tender

Part 10

Satellites and Silicon

Language for Special Fields

Here's the Idea   Our world changes at a rapid pace. People the world over influence our lives. They invent new machines, new processes, new ways of working and living. The English language changes to keep up with the times.

As the world changes, English grows and changes to enable us to communicate with each other. New words are created. Old words are given new meanings. New terms may be created by combining words that already exist, either with other existing words or with new ones.

The computer industry, for example, has added a new vocabulary to English. Some computer words are just old words with new meanings. Do you know what these computer terms mean?

loop   menu   bit   scroll   crash   bug

Other computer terms are entirely new. Some are acronyms. Others are compounds. Still others started out as slang terms among computer designers and hobbyists (or "hackers"). How many of these terms can you define?

RAM   printout   software   byte   user-friendly

Other areas of science, technology, and medicine also add words to your language. Which of these words do you know?

interferon   fly-by   genetic engineering

As time passes, the world changes. To understand the changing world, you must keep up with changes in the language. Since many dictionaries do not include definitions of the newest terms, you must turn elsewhere. Ask teachers for explanations of terms in their fields. Look for a glossary of terms at the end of a recent book on the subject.

Check It Out   The following terms are all recent additions to English. They have specialized meanings in science, technology, or medicine. Some of them have older, more familiar meanings. Others are made up of two familiar words. Study them carefully. Find out what their meanings are.

cursor   gene splicing   chip   floppy disk
bubble memory   spacewalk   industrial robot

- Do you see how English words can take on brand new meanings to describe new ideas and inventions?

Try Your Skill   Look up each of the following words in a dictionary. Write one familiar meaning for each word. Then write each word's new meaning in the field of computers, space exploration, medicine, or technology.

mouse   scan   core   boot

Keep This in Mind

- As the world changes, the vocabulary of English changes. New words are added. New meanings are added to old words.
- Dictionaries may not include definitions of the newest terms. Ask teachers for explanations of terms in their fields. Look for glossaries in recent books.

Now Write   Label your paper **Satellites and Silicon.** During the next two days, make a list of new technological terms that appear in a local newspaper. By asking experts, determine the meaning of each term. Next to each term, write its meaning. Share your words with your classmates. Save your work in your folder.

Using a Dictionary

Words To Guide You

Using a Dictionary

Here's the Idea A dictionary is a useful reference book containing lists of words and information about the words. Whenever you use words, you will want to use a dictionary. When you read, you will see unfamiliar words or words used in unfamiliar ways. A dictionary will help you to understand the meanings of the words you see. When you write, you will be searching continually for the right words. A dictionary will help you to choose the right words and to use them correctly.

There are several kinds of dictionaries you might find helpful. Usually you will be able to find what you need in an abridged, or shortened, dictionary. Sometimes, however, you may need an unabridged dictionary. This contains nearly all of the words in a language, including those that are rare. There are also specialized dictionaries that include only words used with a single subject, such as music.

Become familiar with the dictionaries you use. You will find that every dictionary organizes information in its own way and uses its own symbols and abbreviations. Read the introduction to a dictionary for an explanation of its format.

All dictionaries list words in alphabetical order. In addition, all dictionaries have two guide words in large, bold print at the top of each page to help you locate words listed on the page. The left guide word is the same as the first word on the page. The right guide word is the same as the last word on the page. When you are looking for a word, flip through the dictionary until you find the page where your word comes alphabetically between the guide words.

Check It Out Look at the top portion of a dictionary page, on the following page.

Gan·y·mede (gan'ə mēd) *Gr. Myth.* a beautiful youth who was cupbearer to the gods

gaol (jāl) *n. Brit. sp. of* JAIL —**gaol'er** *n.*

gap (gap) *n.* [ON. < *gapa*, to yawn, GAPE] **1.** a hole or opening made by breaking, tearing, etc.; breach **2.** a mountain pass or ravine **3.** an empty space or time; blank **4.** a difference in ideas, natures, etc. **5.** *same as* SPARK GAP —*vi.* **gapped, gap'-ping** to come apart; open

gape (gāp) *vi.* **gaped, gap'ing** [< ON. *gapa*, to yawn < IE. base *ghe-*] **1.** to open the mouth wide, as in yawning **2.** to stare with the mouth open, as in wonder **3.** to open wide, as a chasm —*n.* **1.** an open-mouthed stare **2.** a yawn **3.** a wide opening **4.** *Zool.* the measure of the widest possible opening of a mouth or beak —**the gapes 1.** a disease of poultry and birds, causing them to gape **2.** a fit of yawning —**gap'er** *n.* —**gap'ing·ly** *adv.*

☆**gar** (gär) *n., pl.* **gar, gars:** see PLURAL, II, D, 2 [contr. < GAR-FISH] any of a group of freshwater ganoid fishes with long, narrow bodies, long, beaklike snouts, and many sharp teeth

G.A.R. Grand Army of the Republic

ga·rage (gə räzh', -räj'; *Brit.* gar'äzh) *n.* [Fr. < *garer*, to GUARD] **1.** a closed shelter for automobiles **2.** a business establishment where automobiles are repaired, stored, etc. —*vt.*

GAR
(to 10 ft. long)

gar·goyle (gär'goil) *n.* [< OFr. *gargouille:* see GARGLE] **1.** a waterspout, usually in the form of a carved fantastic creature, sticking out from the gutter of a building **2.** a person with very strange or grotesque features

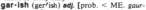
GARGOYLE

Gar·i·bal·di (gar'ə bôl'dē; *It.* gä rē bäl'dē), **Giu·sep·pe** (jōō zep'pe) 1807–82; It. patriot & general: leader in movement to unify Italy

gar·ish (ger'ish) *adj.* [prob. < ME. *gauren*, to stare] too bright or gaudy; showy —see SYN. at GAUDY —**gar'ish·ly** *adv.* —**gar'ish·ness** *n.*

gar·land (gär'lənd) *n.* [< OFr. *garlande*] a wreath of flowers, leaves, etc. —*vt.* to form into or decorate with a garland or garlands

Gar·land (gär'lənd) [after A. *Garland*, U.S. attorney general (1885–89)] city in NE Tex.: suburb of Dallas: pop. 81,000

gar·lic (gär'lik) *n.* [< OE. < *gar*, a spear (see GORE³) + *leac*, a leek] **1.** a bulbous plant of the lily family **2.** its strong-smelling bulb, made up of small sections called cloves, used as a seasoning —**gar'lick·y** *adj.*

gar·ment (gär'mənt) *n.* [< OFr. *garnement* < *garnir:* see GAR-NISH] **1.** any article of clothing **2.** a covering —*vt.* to clothe

gar·ner (gär'nər) *n.* [< OFr. < L. *granarium* < *granum*, GRAIN] **1.** a place for storing grain; granary **2.** a store of something —*vt.* **1.** to gather up and store in or as in a granary **2.** to get or earn [to *garner* praise] **3.** to collect or gather [to *garner* data]

- In what order are the words in each column listed? What special symbols are used? What are the guide words? Would you find the word *garden* on this page?

Try Your Skill
Look up each word in a dictionary and write the guide words for that page.

fireworks	synonym	phase	elegant
jackpot	atmosphere	century	limelight
kettle	typical	bouquet	carburetor

Keep This in Mind
- A dictionary is a reference book that lists words alphabetically and explains each word.

Now Write
In learning about governments you may see the following words: *aristocracy, communism, constitution, democracy, fascism, monarchy, nation,* and *republic.* Find each word in a dictionary and list the guide words on the page. Use four of the words in sentences. Label your paper **Words To Guide You** and put it into your folder.

In Search

Reading a Dictionary Entry

Here's the Idea   Each dictionary entry contains much more than the meaning of a word. It also has information to help you understand a word and use it correctly.

The **entry word** itself appears in bold print and is divided into syllables. The word *memorable,* for example, is entered as **mem·o·ra·ble.** Refer to the entry word whenever you need to divide a word at the end of a line of writing.

The **pronunciation** of a word is given in parentheses. Use the symbols and accent marks to help you sound out an unfamiliar word. The word *commercial,* for example, appears as (kə mʉr′shəl). Refer to the explanation of symbols often shown at the bottom of a page. You will usually find the complete explanation at the front of the dictionary.

The **part of speech** of a word is indicated by an abbreviation in bold print. *Noun,* for example, is abbreviated *n.* and *adjective* is *adj.* Refer to the complete list of abbreviations usually presented in the front of the dictionary. Some words can be used as more than one part of speech. If so, the other parts of speech will be indicated later in an entry.

If a word has **special forms** or **endings,** they will be included next in the entry. The entry for the irregular verb *see,* for example, includes the forms **saw, seen, seeing.** Plural endings of some nouns are also shown. For the noun *hero,* for example, the plural ending **-oes** is shown.

The **origin,** or **history,** of a word is given next, usually in brackets. The symbol < means "came from." Abbreviations, such as *Gr.* and *L.,* stand for the languages from which words came, such as Greek and Latin. Refer to the complete list of abbreviations used in your dictionary. This list is usually given at the front of the dictionary.

Definitions are given next. The most common definition of a word is often given first. When a word has a special meaning within a field, that meaning will be noted. One definition of *return*, for instance, says "*Sports* to hit, run, or throw back a ball."

Sometimes a word may have a special meaning in casual conversation and informal writing. This is called a *colloquial* meaning and is usually indicated in a dictionary. For instance, one definition of *character* is "[Colloq.] an odd or peculiar person." Slang—very informal, popular language—is also indicated in the dictionary. For instance, one definition of *charge*, as a noun, is "[Slang] a thrill."

Some dictionaries also list **synonyms** and **antonyms** at the ends of certain entries. A *synonymy* may explain a group of synonyms and their shades of meaning. For example, at the end of the entry for *sharp*, its synonyms *keen* and *acute* are also explained. *Dull*, an antonym for *sharp*, is also listed.

From all of these examples, you can see how much useful information is presented in an entry in a good dictionary.

Check It Out
Examine the dictionary entry below and then answer the questions at the top of page 30.

tune (to͞on, tyo͞on) *n.* [ME., var. of *tone,* TONE] **1.** a series of musical tones with a regular rhythm; melody; air **2.** the condition of having correct musical pitch, or of being in key; also, harmony; concord: now chiefly in phrases **in tune, out of tune** [a violin that is *in tune;* a person *out of tune* with the times] —*vt.* **tuned, tun′ing 1.** to adjust (a musical instrument) to some standard of pitch [to *tune* a piano] **2.** to adapt (music, the voice, etc.) to some pitch, tone, etc. **3.** to adjust (an electronics circuit, a motor, etc.) to the proper or desired performance —*vi.* to be in tune; harmonize —see SYN. at MELODY —**call the tune** to be in control —**change one's tune** to change one's attitude or manner: also **sing a different tune** —**to the tune of** [Colloq.] to the amount of —**tune in 1.** to adjust a radio or television receiver to a given frequency or channel so as to receive (a specified station, program, etc.) ☆**2.** [Slang] to become or make aware, knowing, etc. —**tune out 1.** to adjust a radio or television receiver so as to get rid of (interference, etc.) **2.** [Slang] to stop paying attention to, showing interest in, etc. — **tune up 1.** to adjust (musical instruments) to the same pitch **2.** to put (an engine) into good working condition

- How many syllables are there in *tune?* From what language did *tune* come? What parts of speech can *tune* be? Which definition is most familiar to you? Where would you find synonyms for *tune?* What informal expressions include *tune?*

Try Your Skill   Read this entry and answer the questions.

ice (īs) *n.* [OE. *is*]   **1.** water frozen solid by cold   **2.** a piece, layer, or sheet of this   **3.** anything like frozen water in appearance, etc.   **4.** coldness in manner or attitude   **5.** *a*) a frozen dessert, usually of water, fruit juice, and sugar   *b*) [Brit.] ice cream   ☆**6.** [Slang] diamonds —*vt.* **iced, ic′ing**   **1.** to change into ice; freeze   **2.** to cover with ice   **3.** to cool by putting ice on, in, or around [to *ice* a drink]   **4.** to cover with icing [to *ice* a cake]   **5.** *Ice Hockey* to shoot (the puck) from defensive to offensive territory —*vi.* to freeze (often with *up* or *over*) —**break the ice 1.** to make a start by getting over the first problems   **2.** to make a start toward getting better acquainted —☆**cut no ice** [Colloq.] to have no effect —☆**on ice** [Slang]   **1.** in readiness or reserve   **2.** sure to result in victory or success [this game is *on ice*] —**on thin ice** [Colloq.] in a risky situation

1. As what parts of speech can *ice* be used?
2. What endings does the verb *ice* have?
3. From what language does *ice* come?
4. State a specialized meaning of *ice*.
5. What informal expressions use the word *ice?*

Keep This in Mind

- A dictionary entry contains the meanings of a word and other useful information.

Now Write   Use a dictionary to find words with these characteristics. Each word should have one characteristic. Label your paper **In Search of** and put it into your folder.

1. two pronunciations
2. two parts of speech
3. has come from French
4. meaning in a special field
5. an informal meaning
6. an antonym

A Fitting Choice

Finding the Meaning of a Word

Here's the Idea   As you look through a dictionary, you will soon notice that many words have more than one meaning. Whenever you check a word in the dictionary, read all of its meanings. Find the meaning that fits the context in which you found the word or intend to use it.

For instance, the simple word *turn* has a surprising number of meanings. *Webster's New World Dictionary, Students Edition,* gives forty-three meanings for *turn* as a verb. The same entry gives sixteen meanings for *turn* as a noun, and sixteen phrases that include the word. In the following examples, notice how the context helps you determine the correct meaning.

   1. It was my *turn* to pitch the ball.
(In this context, *turn* means "the right or chance to do something, especially in regular order.")
   2. Marcia *turned* several plans over in her mind.
(Here, *turn* means "to think about, to ponder.")
   3. *Turn* your chair away from the window.
(Here, *turn* means "to change the position or direction of.")
   4. Hot weather will *turn* milk.
(Here, *turn* means "to make sour.")
   5. My sister Barbara just *turned* sixteen.
(Here, *turn* means "to reach or pass.")
   6. Grandpa was born at the *turn* of the century.
(Here, *turn* means "the time of change.")
   7. Her fall off the ladder gave us quite a *turn*.
(Here, *turn* means "a sudden, brief shock.")

From these few examples, it is clear how many meanings can be contained in a single entry.

Some words seem to be repeated in more than one entry. For

instance, you will find the word *lean* entered twice: *lean*[1], a verb, means "to bend from an upright position" or "to depend on for help"; *lean*[2], an adjective, means "thin, containing little or no fat." In each entry, *lean* has a different origin and different meanings. Such words are called *homographs*. Homographs have the same spelling, although they may have different pronunciations. Notice that each entry is not a shade of meaning of one word. It is actually a different word. When you notice a word with more than one entry, be sure to read all of the entries to find the meaning you want.

Check It Out   Read these dictionary entries.

match[1] (mach) *n.* [< OFr. *mesche*, prob. < L. *myxa*, lamp wick < Gr.] **1.** orig., a wick or cord prepared to burn at a uniform rate, used for firing guns or explosives **2.** a slender piece of wood, cardboard, etc. tipped with a composition that catches fire by friction, sometimes only on a specially prepared surface
match[2] (mach) *n.* [OE. (*ge*)*mæcca*, a mate < base of *macian*, MAKE] **1.** any person or thing equal or similar to another in some way; specif., *a*) a person, group, or thing able to cope with another as an equal *[*he met his *match* in chess when he played her*] b*) a counterpart or facsimile **2.** two or more persons or things that go together in appearance, size, etc. *[*a purse and shoes that are a good *match]* **3.** a contest or game; competition *[*a tennis *match]* **4.** a marriage or mating **5.** a person regarded as a suitable mate —*vt.* **1.** to join in marriage; mate **2.** to compete with successfully *[*he was able to *match* his opponent*] **3.** to put in opposition (*with*); pit (*against*) *[*to *match* one's strength against an enemy*] **4.** to be equal, similar, or suitable to *[*he could never *match* her in an argument*] **5.** to make, show, or get a competitor, counterpart, or equivalent to *[match* this cloth*] **6.** to suit or fit (one thing) to another **7.** to fit (things) together **8.** to compare ☆**9.** *a*) to flip or reveal (coins) to decide something contested, the winner being determined by the combination of faces thus exposed *b*) to match coins with (another person) —*vi.* to be equal, similar, suitable, etc. in some way —**match′a·ble** *adj.* —**match′er** *n.*

- Which definition of *match* fits the context of the sentence: My family came to my wrestling *match*?
- From what language is *match*[1]? *match*[2]? Which of the meanings of *match*[2] are most familiar to you?

Try Your Skill   Read the following dictionary entries and sentences. Determine which meaning of *pound* fits the context of each sentence and write your answer.

pound[1] (pound) *n., pl.* **pounds,** sometimes **pound** [OE. *pund* < L. *pondo,* abl. of *pondus,* weight, akin to *pendere:* see PENDANT] **1.** a unit of weight, equal to 16 oz. (7,000 grains) avoirdupois or 12 oz. (5,760 grains) troy: abbrev. **lb. 2.** *a)* the monetary unit of the United Kingdom (in full, **pound sterling**) equal to 100 (new) pennies or, in the earlier system, to 20 shillings: symbol £ *b)* the monetary unit of various other countries, as of Ireland, Israel, etc. See MONETARY UNITS, table

pound[2] (pound) *vt.* [OE. *punian*] **1.** to beat to a pulp, powder, etc. *[to pound corn into meal]* **2.** to strike or drive with repeated heavy blows *[to pound nails into a board]* **3.** to make by pounding *[he pounded a cabinet together]* —*vi.* **1.** to deliver repeated, heavy blows *(at* or *on* a door, etc.) **2.** to move with heavy steps, thumps, etc. *[he pounded down the hall]* **3.** to beat heavily; throb *[her heart pounded from the exercise]* —*n.* a pounding, or the sound of it —see SYN. at BEAT —☆**pound one's ear** [Slang] to sleep —**pound out 1.** to flatten, smooth, etc. by pounding **2.** to produce (musical notes, typed copy, etc.) with a very heavy touch —☆**pound the pavement** [Slang] to walk the streets, as in looking for work —**pound′er** *n.*

pound[3] (pound) *n.* [< OE. *pund-*] **1.** an enclosed place for keeping animals, esp. stray animals *[the city dog pound]* **2.** a place of confinement, as for arrested persons **3.** an enclosed area for catching or keeping fish

1. The almonds must be *pounded* into paste for the cake.
2. They found the lost dog at the city *pound.*
3. The bear *pounded* through the woods.
4. Have you ever seen a British *pound* note?
5. The mysterious noise caused my heart to *pound.*

Keep This in Mind

- When you look up a word in the dictionary, determine which meaning fits the context.
- Sometimes a word has more than one entry, with a different meaning and origin for each.

Now Write   Use a dictionary to find one example of a word with many different meanings and one example of a homograph. For each example, copy three definitions. Then write a sentence using each of the meanings you have written. Label your paper **A Fitting Choice** and put it into your folder.

The Right Language at the Right Time

Special Occasions

Standard and Nonstandard English

Here's the Idea Singers, dancers, and actors often wear special costumes when they perform. These costumes are appropriate for entertaining others. However, they are not appropriate for going to an interview or sitting in a classroom.

Similarly, some types of language are right only in certain situations. In this chapter you will learn about several types of language and when they are appropriate. Two common types of language are standard English and non-standard English. The following chart describes these two types of language.

Using Standard and Nonstandard English	
Definition and Use	**Examples**
Standard English is language that follows the rules of good grammar and usage. Standard English is acceptable in all situations.	1. I don't want anything. 2. Call Jim and me tonight. 3. I'm not going.
Nonstandard English is language that does not follow the rules of good grammar and usage. Nonstandard English should not be used in most situations, especially in discussions, in speeches, or in most kinds of writing.	1. I don't want nothing. 2. Call Jim and I tonight. 3. I ain't going.

Use standard English for speeches, class discussions, compositions, and reports. Use it on the job. Also use standard English when you meet new people. Always proofread your writing to avoid using nonstandard English.

Check It Out   Read the following sentences.

Standard English	Nonstandard English
1. The President himself signed the letter.	1. The President hisself signed the letter.
2. I told you about those others.	2. I told you about them others.
3. Susan doesn't work here.	3. Susan don't work here.
4. She and I are friends.	4. Her and me are friends.

- What is nonstandard about each second sentence?

Try Your Skill   From each pair, choose the sentence that is written in standard English.

1. Leave the dog run free.
   Let the dog run free.
2. Yolanda dances beautifully.
   Yolanda dances beautiful.
3. Them answers were right; I'm real sure.
   Those answers were right; I'm really sure.
4. It don't make no difference to Andy and me.
   It doesn't make any difference to Andy and me.

Keep This in Mind
- Standard English follows the rules of good grammar and usage.

Now Write   Write a paragraph telling what you hope to do after high school. Exchange papers with a classmate. Correct any examples of nonstandard English in your friend's paper.

One Way or Another

Formal and Informal English

Here's the Idea   Standard English is spoken and written in many different situations. Some of these situations are more formal than others. In order to suit your language to the occasion, you must understand how to use two different kinds of standard English. These kinds are called formal and informal English.

Formal English is language that is right for serious or important occasions. It is the language that is used in sermons and lectures. It is also used in reports, serious essays, and official documents. If you were asking the president of a company for a job interview, you would use formal English.

> Formal English: Mr. MacIntire, may I call your secretary for an appointment to talk to you about a job with your company? I will be graduating from high school next spring and have some ideas that may benefit both your company and me.

Informal English is the comfortable but correct language used in everyday situations. It is the language of conversations, letters, and informal talks. It is also the language of most newspapers and magazines. If you were talking to a friend about an upcoming interview, you would use informal English.

> Informal English: Hi, Jim! I got the interview. How about that! I'm going in tomorrow. I'll call you later and tell you all about it. Wish me luck—I'll need it.

Whenever you are speaking or writing, choose language that is right for the situation. If the situation is formal, use formal language. If the situation is informal, use informal language.

Check It Out   Read the following pairs of words.

children	kids
appropriate	okay
Wonderful!	Wow!
unfortunate	too bad
cannot	can't

- Which word in each pair would you use in a formal situation? Which would you use in an informal situation?

Try Your Skill   The following paragraph contains a mixture of formal and informal English. Revise the paragraph. Replace all informal language with language that is right for a report.

Some animals are highly social. Prairie dogs, for example, live in burrows placed a little way apart. These collections of burrows are really neat. They're like a little neighborhood or something. Furthermore, prairie dogs act much like human neighbors. They all do their share to keep their communities in good condition. They also warn one another if an enemy, such as a coyote, comes messing around looking for trouble. Prairie dogs are really something else!

Keep This in Mind

- Formal English is appropriate for serious or important occasions.
- Informal English is appropriate for conversations, letters, and informal talks.

Now Write   Imagine that you are the captain or manager of a sports team. You wish to congratulate a player on the team for his or her performance. Write a paragraph telling what you might say. Use informal English. Then, rewrite the paragraph for use in a formal speech at a sports banquet.

Far Out!

Using and Misusing Slang

Here's the Idea When using the dictionary, you may have noticed that some words are labeled "slang." Here is an example:

spiff·y (spif′ē) *adj.* **spiff′i·er, spiff′i·est** [< dial. *spiff*, well-dressed person] [Old Slang] neat and trim; smart or dapper

Slang is language made of fad words and phrases that are not accepted as standard English. Most slang is popular only for a short time. The word *spiffy*, for example, was extremely popular in the 1950's. Today, it is rarely used. Other slang terms that have now become outdated are the words *keen, marvy,* and *far out.* At different times, each of these slang terms has been used to mean "wonderful or interesting."

Slang is not considered standard English. It is also not always understood by everyone. Therefore, slang should never be used in compositions, reports, formal speeches, or business situations. It may be used in casual conversations, for informal talks, or in the dialogue of a short story.

Be especially careful not to use slang in formal writing. When you revise the work you do for school, always look for examples of slang. Replace any that you find. If you are unsure whether a given word is slang, look it up in a dictionary.

Check It Out The following slang terms all have the same or similar meanings. Read this list of terms.

shake a leg	get down	go to town
lean on it	hit it	pour it on

- What slang meaning is shared by these terms?
- How many of these terms have you heard before? How many are unfamiliar to you?

Try Your Skill   Identify the slang terms in the following sentences. Then, rewrite each sentence. Replace each slang term with a standard word or phrase.

1. Mark needs to mellow out a little; perhaps he should go on vacation.

2. His first film made big bucks, but his second was a real bust.

3. I saw a group of people protesting nukes.

4. If you forget your lines, you'll have to wing it.

5. My klutzy cat knocked a picture from the bookcase.

Keep This in Mind

- Slang, a type of nonstandard English, is made of fad words and phrases.
- Do not use slang in formal writing or speech.
- Use slang only in casual conversation or in the dialogue of a short story.

Now Write   The following paragraph from an old detective story contains many outdated slang words and phrases. Rewrite the paragraph. Replace the outdated slang with standard English.

What do I like about Rosie? Well, let me give you a for instance. Several years ago, she was all set to marry this palooka named Tommy Bayles. But old Tommy blew it when he said Rosie would have to quit this high-class, muckety-muck job she had downtown. When Rosie stopped laughing, she gave him the gate. Since then, lots of guys have thought Rosie was just the bee's knees, but old Rosie just ignores them. She's staying on the shelf and making her own way. I tell you, that Rosie has a mind of her own. I mean, she's got a real head on her shoulders. That's why she and I are pals.

Shop Talk

Using and Misusing Jargon

Here's the Idea   As you have already learned in this chapter, different occasions call for different types of language. For example, workers in many fields have special words and phrases that they use to describe their jobs. The words and phrases used to describe such specialized activities are called jargon. A farmer, for example, may use the following jargon to describe farm machinery:

baler	grub hook
binder	middlebreaker
combine	rotary plow
cultivator	snap machine
disk harrow	thresher

Farmers can use terms like these when talking to one another. This is because most farmers know the jargon of farming. However, most non-farmers do not understand such jargon. Therefore, a farmer who is talking to a non-farmer must either avoid these terms or define them as they come up in the conversation.

By using jargon, workers are able to communicate with one another quickly and easily. However, jargon must be used only with certain audiences. Whenever you write or speak about a specialized activity, first decide whether your audience is familiar with the jargon of that activity. If your audience is not familiar with the activity, use as little jargon as possible. When you do use a jargon word, define the word to avoid confusing your listeners or readers.

Check It Out   Read the following words from the jargon of railway workers.

gondola car   flat car   piggyback
roomette   cannonball   brakie

- Are you familiar with any of these words?
- Would you understand these words if a railway worker used them when speaking to you?
- Look up each word. Do any of these words have other meanings that are not related to railroads?

Try Your Skill   The following words are from the jargon of sports. Look up each word in a dictionary. Tell what the word means. Also tell what sport the word is used in. Then, use each word in a sentence.

1. icing
2. dribble
3. bunt
4. slalom
5. love

6. birdie
7. iron cross
8. knockout
9. snorkel
10. wicket

Keep This in Mind

- Words and phrases used to describe specialized activities are called jargon.
- Use jargon only when it is appropriate to your audience.

Now Write   Choose an activity with which you are very familiar. Make a list of the jargon words used by others who are familiar with this activity. Define each word.

On Location

Regional Language

Here's the Idea   The way you speak or write is the result of many influences. For example, people in different areas of the country speak and write differently. The types of language used in various parts of the country are called **regional dialects.**

Regional dialects differ in three ways. First, they differ in vocabulary. In the North and Midwest, for example, most people speak of *breakfast, lunch,* and *dinner.* In many areas of the South, these meals are called *breakfast, dinner,* and *supper.*

Second, regional dialects differ in pronunciation. In some areas of New England, for example, speakers often drop the *r* sound from some words and add it to other words.

> *Pahk* the *cah.*   What's the *idear?*

Third, regional dialects sometimes differ in grammar. For example, a speaker in the South or Midwest would say "Mr. Wilkes stood *in* line for three hours." Some speakers in the North would say "Mr. Wilkes stood *on* line for three hours."

Dialects add variety and interest to our language. Much outstanding writing uses various American regional dialects. However, dialects can also be a source of confusion. When writing or talking to one another, speakers of different dialects should try to use language that everyone will understand.

American dialects have become increasingly similar because of television, education, and travel. However, for years to come, you can expect that a person from Boston will not talk like a person from Charleston or Chicago.

Check It Out   The following are some words used in different areas of the country. The words in each group all have the same meaning. Read these words.

corn on the cob	veranda	stream
sweet corn	terrace	brook
table corn	stoop	branch
roasting ears	porch	creek

- Which of these words are used in your region?

Try Your Skill The following passage is about a family that has returned home after a flood. Find examples of dialect.

"The henouse is gone," sighed the woman.
"N the pigpen," sighed the man.
They spoke without bitterness.
"Ah reckon them chickens is all done drowned."
"Yeah."
"Miz Flora's house is gone, too," said the little girl.
They looked at the clump of trees where their neighbor's house had stood.
"Lawd!"
"Yuh reckon anybody knows where they is?"
"Hard t tell."
The man walked down the slope and stood uncertainly.
"There wuz a road erlong here somewheres," he said.
But there was no road now. Just a wide sweep of yellow, scalloped silt.
—RICHARD WRIGHT

Keep This in Mind

- The types of language used in various parts of the country are called regional dialects.
- Regional dialects differ in vocabulary, pronunciation, and grammar.

Now Write Watch two or three television programs that are set in different parts of the country. Make notes on any examples of regional dialect that you hear. Bring these notes to class.

Controlling Your Sentences

In the Clear

Using Sentences

Here's the Idea Individual words usually express parts of thoughts. A **sentence** is a group of words that expresses a complete thought.

Good sentences express complete thoughts clearly and directly. A good sentence has something to say. The idea that it expresses may be either humorous or serious, but it is always clear. A good sentence also expresses an idea in a direct and imaginative way.

Read these examples of effective, interesting sentences.

A light heart lives long. —WILLIAM SHAKESPEARE
A wise man will make more opportunities than he finds.
   —FRANCIS BACON
Remember, no one can make you feel inferior without your
   consent. —ELEANOR ROOSEVELT
The language of friendship is not words but meanings.
   —HENRY DAVID THOREAU
Please all and you please none. —AESOP

Each of these sentences has expressed one idea in a clear, direct, and original way. You can see how powerful a single sentence can be. When you write a sentence, use your senses and your imagination to express an idea in an effective way.

Check It Out Read the following sentences.

1. As Nancy raced to the exit, she searched the crowd for a police officer.
2. The patient's room was dark and smelled of antiseptic.
3. Homemade soup makes a light, tasty, and economical meal.

4. All citizens should participate in government by voting in elections.

5. Refugees are people who flee their homes or countries to seek safety during times of war and trouble.

- Does each sentence express a single, complete thought? Is each sentence clear and interesting?

Try Your Skill   Write one sentence in response to each of the following directions. Use real or imaginary details to make your sentences clear and effective.

1. Tell one thing that you usually do after school.
2. Describe something that you own.
3. Explain how to save money.
4. Explain why passengers should wear seat belts in cars.
5. Explain what a basketball is.
6. Describe your favorite meal.
7. Tell one event that happened to your family.
8. Explain what a doctor is.

Keep This in Mind

- A sentence is a group of words that expresses a complete thought. A good sentence is clear and interesting.

Now Write   Write five original sentences. One should tell part of a story. One should describe something. One should explain one step of a process. One should explain why something is useful. One should explain what something is.

Before you write, think about each sentence. Decide what point you are trying to make and how you can best make it. Be specific. Label your paper **In the Clear** and put it into your folder.

Beware of Detours

Keeping to the Point

Here's the Idea   A well-written sentence expresses one idea as clearly and directly as possible.

> The volleyball sailed over our heads.
> First prize in the poetry competition was awarded to Sandra.

Sometimes you may want to add details to a sentence to make it more interesting. Related details are those that support the main idea. By adding related details, you can add meaning to a sentence.

> The volleyball hit by Ms. Powers sailed over our heads.

Here, the added detail is related to the volleyball shot.

> First prize in the poetry competition was awarded to Sandra for her poem "Spring."

In this sentence, the added detail is related to the poem.

Whenever you include details in a sentence, be sure they are related to the main idea. Unrelated details will confuse the meaning of the sentence.

> The volleyball, which we also use for soccer, sailed over our heads.

The added detail is not related to the volleyball shot.

> First prize in the poetry competition was awarded to Sandra Morrison, who is six feet tall.

The added detail is about Sandra. However, the main idea of the sentence is the poetry prize.

Avoid using unrelated details in sentences that you write. Use only interesting and specific details that are related to the main idea. Be sure to keep to the point.

Check It Out Read the following sentences.

1. My locker, which I share with Dan, is on the third floor.
2. Maria's father, who was born in Mexico, works at city hall.
3. Barrel racing, a sport I've never tried, is popular in many Western states.
4. Open the green door, which used to be brown, at the end of this hallway and you'll see the office.

- In each sentence, what unrelated detail should be omitted? Are there any related details that you might add?

Try Your Skill Rewrite the following sentences, which contain unrelated details. Use related details.

1. Firefighters, who work long shifts, save many lives.
2. Mrs. Collins, who has two children, gives weekly quizzes.
3. You can park in the lot near the library, one of my favorite places to study.
4. An aunt of mine wrote a book, with her picture on the cover, about how to start a small business.
5. Hundreds of volunteers, mostly local college students, helped rescue birds hurt by the oil spill.

Keep This in Mind

- Use related details that add interest and meaning to the main idea of a sentence. Omit unrelated details that interrupt and confuse the meaning.

Now Write Write four sentences about subjects that interest you. Use related details that support the main idea of each sentence. Be sure that each sentence keeps to the point. Label your paper **Beware of Detours.** Keep it in your folder.

Empty-Handed

Avoiding Empty Sentences

Here's the Idea   Some sentences do not make a point either clearly or completely. They are called **empty sentences.**
One kind of empty sentence repeats an idea.

> The experiment failed because we were unsuccessful with it.

To fail at something means "to be unsuccessful," so the second part of the sentence is a useless repetition. You can see that this kind of sentence goes nowhere.

To improve this kind of empty sentence, you must avoid the repetition. Sometimes you may choose to make the sentence simpler. It is more likely, though, that you will choose to add related information.

> The experiment failed.
> The experiment failed because we tried to rush it.

There is also another kind of empty sentence. This second kind of empty sentence states a strong opinion. However, the opinion is not supported by facts, reasons, or examples.

> Radio talk shows are boring.

You can see that such a strong statement is empty of meaning to a reader unless it is explained. You can improve this kind of empty sentence by adding the supporting evidence necessary to complete the idea. Supporting evidence may be given in the same sentence or in another sentence.

> Radio talk shows are boring when their hosts are not well informed about the topics discussed.
> Radio talk shows are boring. Often their hosts are not well informed about the topics discussed.

Supporting evidence for such ideas might also be provided in paragraphs or compositions.

Check It Out   Read the following empty sentences.

1. Everyone should learn to drive.
2. Roller skating is popular now, and many people enjoy it.
3. Hockey is the most exciting sport.
4. I can't do this problem because it's too hard.
5. The team was exhausted, and the players needed rest.
6. The crumbling pavement on Maple Avenue needs repair.

- Which sentences repeat an idea? Which sentences state an unsupported opinion? How would you improve each of these empty sentences?

Try Your Skill   Rewrite each of these empty sentences.

1. Keeping wild animals as pets is cruel.
2. The team played so well that they were excellent.
3. People who won't change their opinions are annoying.
4. I find it hard to remember names because I'm forgetful.
5. Outdoor jobs are the most satisfying.

Keep This in Mind

- Sentences that repeat an idea or state an unsupported opinion are empty sentences. Improve a sentence that repeats an idea by simplifying it or by adding related information. Improve a sentence with an unsupported opinion by adding supporting evidence that explains the opinion.

Now Write   Label your paper *Empty Sentences*. Write, or find, three examples of each kind of empty sentences. Improve the sentences by avoiding repetition or by supplying facts or reasons. Write the improved sentences.

Stay Trim

Avoiding Padded Sentences

Here's the Idea   A **padded sentence** contains unnecessary words. The main idea of a padded sentence is smothered by extra words.

Several unnecessary phrases usually signal padded sentences and should be avoided.

in my opinion, I think	well
what I mean is that	you see
what I'm saying is	you know
the point is	due to the fact that
the thing is	because of the fact that
the reason is	on account of the fact that

You can usually improve a padded sentence simply by eliminating the useless expressions. Sometimes, however, you may need to revise the sentence totally.

Padded: What I mean is that winter is my favorite season.
Improved: Winter is my favorite season.

Padded: It is becoming easier all the time to take good pictures indoors owing to the fact that color film now available is very sensitive to light.
Improved: Since color film is now more sensitive to light, taking good pictures indoors is easier.

Many groups of words using *who is, which is,* or *that is* also pad sentences unnecessarily. Be sure to use such expressions only when they add to the meaning of a sentence.

Padded: The auto show, which is being held at the Civic Center, continues through next week.
Improved: The auto show at the Civic Center continues through next week.

Check It Out Read the following padded sentences.

1. Have you ever tried halvah, which is a kind of candy made with sesame seeds, nuts, and honey?

2. Well, Bonnie said that what she wanted was only a fair chance to audition for the part.

3. Hang gliding attracts people who like risk on account of the fact that it requires skill and luck.

4. The construction crew had to stop working until spring because of the fact that the ground became frozen.

5. I am going to write about careers in the field of communications, which includes jobs in TV production, you know.

• How would you improve each of these sentences?

Try Your Skill Rewrite the following padded sentences. Improve them by eliminating useless words or by revising a sentence completely.

1. On account of the fact that Saturn has rings, it is one of the most beautiful planets to observe.

2. Brian called Ramon, who is his best friend.

3. What I'm trying to say is what an exciting story you wrote.

4. The reason Dad becomes tired so easily is due to the fact that he has just recovered from the flu.

5. Kate tried on her new sweater, which is red.

Keep This in Mind

• Sentences that include unnecessary words are padded sentences. Improve a padded sentence by eliminating the useless expressions or by revising the sentence totally.

Now Write Label your paper *Padded Sentences*. Write, or find, five examples of padded sentences. Then improve the sentences. Eliminate an unnecessary expression or revise the sentence totally. Keep your paper in your folder.

Heavyweights

Avoiding Overloaded Sentences

Here's the Idea   There will be times when you need to express a complex idea in writing. However, you should not try to include too many ideas in a single sentence. Sentences having too many ideas are called **overloaded sentences.**

Overloaded sentences usually contain several thoughts loosely joined by *and*. The word *and* is used incorrectly when it is used to connect ideas that are not closely related.

> Our local radio station has a preference for fire stories, and every nightly newscast seems to include a story about a fire, and I have also noticed that other stations have their own favorite kinds of stories that are repeated often.

From this example, you can see how confusing an overloaded sentence is. Which is the main idea? It is impossible for a reader to know.

You can avoid such confusion. Separate an overloaded sentence into several shorter sentences.

> Our local radio station has a preference for fire stories. Every nightly newscast seems to include a story about a fire. I have also noticed that other stations seem to have their own favorite kinds of stories.

Whenever you write, make sure that each sentence contains only one main idea or related ideas.

Check It Out   Read this overloaded sentence.

Overloaded: Every year when safety inspections are required, I promise to take our car to be inspected early, and every year I promise, and yet I always find that I leave this task until the last possible day, and I have to rush around anxiously trying to have the inspection completed by the deadline.

Improved: Every year when safety inspections are required, I promise to take our car to be inspected early. Although I promise, I always find that I leave this task until the last possible day. Then I have to rush around anxiously trying to have the inspection completed by the deadline.

• How has this overloaded sentence been improved?

Try Your Skill   Improve these overloaded sentences.

1. It used to be that if you went to the movies you could choose from among many different films, and now there seem to be fewer movies playing, and they play for longer periods of time, and theaters in the same area will be showing the same films.

2. In my opinion, this country's lawmakers should resolve the question of whether an eighteen-year-old is a child or an adult, and the laws should be consistent, so that they are the same from state to state, and they will not be confusing as they are now.

3. As recently as 1979, the town of Kelso in California had no television at all because the mountains around this remote town interfered with TV reception, and it surprises me that no one has studied children who grew up there to see if they are different in any way from children who have watched TV.

Keep This in Mind

• Sentences containing too many ideas are overloaded sentences. Improve an overloaded sentence by separating it into shorter sentences.

Now Write   Label your paper *Overloaded Sentences*. Write, or find, four examples of overloaded sentences. Improve the sentences by separating the main ideas into several shorter sentences. Keep your work in your folder.

Sentence Combining

Join Forces

Combining Sentences

Here's the Idea   Whenever you write, you should try to show how your ideas are related to each other. Often you can do this by combining sentences that state similar ideas. Two sentences that state similar ideas of equal importance can usually be joined with a comma and the word *and*.

> Linda drew a picture of the school mascot. Geraldo printed the picture on the T-shirts.

> Linda drew a picture of the school mascot, **and** Geraldo printed the picture on the T-shirts.

Sometimes two sentences state contrasting ideas of equal importance. You can usually join these sentences with a comma and the word *but*.

> The hockey team won the regionals. It lost the state tournament.

> The hockey team won the regionals, **but** it lost the state tournament.

Finally, two sentences may offer a choice between ideas of equal importance. You can join these sentences with a comma and the word *or*.

> Were you able to buy tickets? Was the concert sold out?

> Were you able to buy tickets, **or** was the concert sold out?

Check It Out   Read the following sentences.

1. The sun was hot, and the hikers were thirsty.
2. Is Lake Mead a natural lake, or is it a reservoir?
3. The two cars collided, but no one was injured.

- Which sentence combines similar ideas of equal importance?
- Which sentence combines contrasting ideas of equal importance?
- Which sentence combines ideas of equal importance and offers a choice between them?

Try Your Skill   Combine each pair of sentences.

1. The mayor held a news conference. She did not announce plans to seek another term. (Join with **, but**.)

2. A surprise snowstorm hit Atlanta. Traffic slowed to a crawl. (Join with **, and**.)

3. Are you going to the speech club banquet? Do you have to work that evening? (Join with **, or**.)

4. People began lining up at dawn. By noon the line was two blocks long. (Join with **, and**.)

Keep This in Mind

- Use a comma and *and* to combine sentences that state similar ideas of equal importance.
- Use a comma and *but* to combine sentences that state contrasting ideas of equal importance.
- Use a comma and *or* to combine sentences that offer a choice between ideas of equal importance.

Now Write   Combine each pair of sentences using **, and** or **, but** or **, or.** Label your paper **Join Forces.** Save it in your folder.

1. Everyone grew silent. The President began to speak.
2. We followed the instructions. The experiment failed.
3. Is the amusement park open in the winter? Is it only open during the summer?
4. The airplane had engine trouble. It arrived safely.
5. Did you purchase this sweater? Was it given to you?

The Parts Department

Combining Sentence Parts

Here's the Idea   You have seen that you can join entire sentences. You can also join related sentence parts. If sentence parts state similar ideas of equal importance, you can join them with *and*.

> The gardener cleared the weeds. *The gardener* planted some tulips.
>
> The gardener cleared the weeds and planted some tulips.

Notice that when you combine sentence parts, you drop any repeated words. In the example above, these repeated words are shown in italics.

Sometimes two sentence parts state contrasting ideas of equal importance. You can usually join these sentence parts with *but*.

> Ants are attracted to sugar. *Ants are* repelled by cinnamon.
>
> Ants are attracted to sugar but repelled by cinnamon.

Sentence parts may also offer a choice between ideas of equal importance. Such parts can usually be joined with *or*.

> The director may choose the location. The producer *may choose the location.*
>
> The director or the producer may choose the location.

Check It Out   Read the following sentences.

1. Martha loves television. Martha hates the commercials.
Martha loves television but hates the commercials.
2. Henry wrapped the glasses in paper. Henry packed them into cartons.
Henry wrapped the glasses in paper and packed them into cartons.
3. Is the pool private? Is the pool open to the public?
Is the pool private or open to the public?

- Which sentence combines similar parts of equal importance?
- Which sentence combines contrasting parts of equal importance?
- Which sentence combines parts that offer a choice between ideas of equal importance?

Try Your Skill   Combine each pair of sentences by following the directions in parentheses. Leave out the italicized words.

1. The horses paraded around the circus ring. The bears *paraded around the circus ring.* (Join with *and.*)

2. The film was praised by the critics. *The film* didn't do well at the box office. (Join with *but.*)

3. The assembly hall is used for concerts. *The assembly hall is used for* basketball games. (Join with *and.*)

4. The squirrels ate the peanut butter. *The squirrels* wouldn't touch the crackers. (Join with *but.*)

Keep This in Mind

- Join sentence parts that state similar ideas of equal importance with *and.*
- Join sentence parts that state contrasting ideas of equal importance with *but.*
- Join sentence parts that offer a choice between ideas of equal importance with *or.*

Now Write   Combine each pair of sentences. Use *and, but,* or *or* to join sentence parts. Label your paper **The Parts Department.** Save it in your folder.

1. The directing in the movie was wonderful. The acting in the movie was wonderful.

2. My sister wants to be a dancer. My sister hates to practice.

3. Will the reporter submit the story? Will he file it away?

4. This shop sells makeup. This shop sells costume jewelry.

One at a Time

Combining by Adding Single Words

Here's the Idea Sometimes two sentences are very closely related. One sentence in the pair states a main idea. The second sentence adds only one important word to the idea. You may be able to combine such sentences by adding the one important word to the sentence that states the main idea.

> The street musicians wore costumes. *The costumes were* colorful.
> The street musicians wore colorful costumes.

Notice that the word *colorful* was added to the first sentence. The words in italics were dropped.

Occasionally you will have to change the form of a word when you add it to a sentence. You may have to change the ending of the word by adding *-ing, -ed,* or *-ly.*

> The ship rolled in the waves. *The waves* pounded *the ship.*
> The ship rolled in the pounding waves.
>
> Phil has been making pottery. *He* glazes *the pottery.*
> Phil has been making glazed pottery.
>
> Clara offered pointers to the other swimmers. *Clara was* patient.
> Patiently, Clara offered pointers to the other swimmers.

Check It Out Study the following examples.

1. The desk top is made of mahogany.
   The desk top has varnish *on it.*
   The desk top is made of varnished mahogany.
2. A storm beat against the windows of our cabin.
   The storm raged.
   A raging storm beat against the windows of our cabin.

3. The first baseman threw the ball to the shortstop.
The first baseman was quick.

   The first baseman quickly threw the ball to the shortstop.
4. Nancy bandaged her brother's knee.

   Nancy worked carefully.

   Nancy carefully bandaged her brother's knee.

- What words have been added to each sentence?

Try Your Skill   Combine each pair of sentences.

1. Put that plate on the bottom of the stack. *The plate has a crack.* (End the important word with **-ed.**)
2. The governor's aide arrived. *This happened* later.
3. In Yellowstone Park there are ten thousand hot springs. *They* bubble. (End the important word with **-ing.**)
4. We must act. *Our actions must be* immediate. (End the important word with **-ly.**)

Keep This in Mind

- Sometimes one sentence states a main idea and a second sentence adds one important word. Combine these sentences by adding the important word to the first sentence.
- When you add a word to a sentence, you may have to change the ending of the word to *-ing, -ed,* or *-ly.*

Now Write   Choose the important word from the second sentence in each pair. Add it to the first sentence. Remember that you may have to change the ending of the added word. Label your paper **One at a Time.** Save it in your folder.

1. Across the canal was a green light. The light flickered.
2. Today, shoppers fill the square. The shoppers are busy.
3. We ship the fresh fish in ice. We crush the ice.
4. A hawk circled overhead. The hawk circled lazily.

Group Effort

Adding Groups of Words

Here's the Idea   You learned that sometimes you can add a single word to a sentence. At other times you can combine sentences by adding a group of words.

> Edna was holding a kitten. *The kitten was* in her arms.
> Edna was holding a kitten in her arms.

The group of words may tell more about a person or thing. If so, add it near the words that name the person or thing.

> The students arrive today. *The students are* from Sweden.
> The students from Sweden arrive today.

The group of words may describe an action. If so, add it near the words that name the action.

> The students arrived last week. *The students arrived* from St. Louis.
> The students arrived from St. Louis last week.

The group of words may add information to the entire main idea of the other sentence. If so, you may add it at the beginning or at the end.

> The lute was a popular instrument. *The lute was popular* in the fifteenth century.
> The lute was a popular instrument in the fifteenth century.
> In the fifteenth century, the lute was a popular instrument.

Check It Out   Study the following examples.

> 1. I found an old letter. The letter was from my great-grandmother.
>   I found an old letter from my great-grandmother.

2. A candidates' debate will be held. The debate will be at the National Guard Armory.

A candidates' debate will be held at the National Guard Armory.

- What words were added to each sentence?
- What words were dropped?

Try Your Skill   Combine each group of sentences. Leave out the italicized words.

1. The Lakers took the lead. *The Lakers did this* with seconds left in the game.
2. The white house is ours. *The white house is* on the corner.
3. The jewelry was beautiful. *It was* at the crafts show.
4. The race car developed engine trouble. *The car developed trouble* on the last lap.
5. Many people are concerned. *Their concern is* about low-cost housing.

Keep This in Mind

- A sentence may contain a group of words that adds information to another sentence. Often you can combine the sentences by adding the group of words.

Now Write   Combine each group of sentences by adding a group of words to the first sentence. Leave out any unnecessary words.

1. Rarotonga is an island. It is in the South Pacific.
2. The pain began to go away. The pain was in my side.
3. The van delivered the ice. The van is from Gardner's Market.
4. We were ready to leave. We were ready before daylight.
5. Karen and Larry waited. Karen and Larry were at the subway entrance.

Winning Combinations

Using Combining Skills in Writing

Here's the Idea   By combining sentences, you can show how your ideas are related. You can also add variety to your writing. The following chart describes the many ways that you have learned to combine sentences.

Combining Ideas in Sentences

1. Use a comma and the words *and*, *but*, and *or* to combine related sentences.

2. Use *and*, *but*, and *or* to combine related sentence parts.

3. Add single words from one sentence to another. If necessary, change the forms of the words by adding *-ing*, *-ed*, or *-ly*.

4. Add groups of words from one sentence to another. Place the added words near the words that they describe.

Use your sentence-combining skills whenever you revise your writing. The new sentences make your writing clearer and more interesting to read.

Check It Out   Read the following paragraphs.

1. At ten o'clock, Nan was still waiting. The other hikers hadn't arrived. She sat on a log. She sat for a while. Sunlight fell through the leaves above. The sunlight flickered. Birds chirped in their nests. The birds were cheerful.

2. At ten o'clock, Nan was still waiting, but the other hikers hadn't arrived. She sat for a while on a log. Flickering sunlight fell through the leaves above. Cheerful birds chirped in their nests.

- In which paragraph are related ideas combined?
- How was each pair of sentences combined?

Try Your Skill Improve the following sentences by combining each pair. Leave out the italicized words.

1. Mardi Gras is a festival that is held each year in New Orleans. *The festival is* exciting. (Add the important word.)
2. During Mardi Gras, people wear masks. *People also wear* fancy costumes. (Join the sentence parts.)
3. Organizations called *krewes* hold parties. Their members dance through the streets. (Join the two sentences.)
4. The festival climaxes with a parade. *The parade is* grand. (Add the important word.)
5. Formal dances are held. *These take place* after the parade. (Add the group of words.)

Now Write Revise the following paragraph by combining the sentences. Label your paper **Winning Combinations.** Save it in your folder.

The drama club will begin its next production. This will happen soon. Ms. Sanchez will direct Kaufman and Hart's play *You Can't Take It with You.* The play is delightful. We need performers. We also need people for the technical crew. Auditions will be held on April 8. The auditions will be in the auditorium. If you want to try out, get a copy of the play. Get the copy from Ms. Sanchez. She will explain the audition procedures. She will also take the names of students who want to work backstage.

Examining the Paragraph

A Good Group

Defining a Paragraph

Here's the Idea You have examined words and sentences. Now you will examine paragraphs. A **paragraph** is a group of sentences dealing with one main idea. Notice how the sentences in each of these groups work together.

1   Nothing could have kept me there in the house that night. My mind held nothing but the driving desire to follow Shane. I waited, hardly daring to breathe, while Mother watched him go. I waited until she turned to Father, bending over him; then I slipped around the doorpost out to the porch. I thought for a moment she had noticed me, but I could not be sure and she did not call to me. I went softly down the steps and into the freedom of the night. —JACK SCHAEFER

2   There were no shops on the wide street that Billy Weaver was walking along, only a line of tall houses on each side, all of them identical. They had porches and pillars and four or five steps going up to their front doors. It was obvious that once upon a time they had been very elegant residences. Now, however, even in the darkness, Billy could see that the paint was peeling from the woodwork on their doors and windows. All of these handsome white houses were cracked and blotchy from neglect. —ROALD DAHL

3   Years ago, illiteracy was not as serious a handicap to employment as it is today. Society needed many unskilled workers. Today, however, it is very difficult for people who cannot read to find jobs. There are very few jobs that do not require at least some reading ability. For this reason alone, reading must be viewed as a valuable, practical skill.

Check It Out Examine the three groups of sentences above.

- Are these groups of sentences paragraphs? Does each group of sentences deal with one idea?

Try Your Skill One of the groups below is a paragraph. Two are not. For the paragraph, write the main idea. For the groups that are not paragraphs, explain why they are not.

1   In Lexington, Virginia, there is an odd Civil War relic— Stonewall Jackson's horse, which has been stuffed. The horse is displayed on the campus of the Virginia Military Institute. More women are now enrolling in military academies. Little Sorrel, Jackson's horse, still wears a saddle and bridle.

2   Day after day, Luis followed the same routine after school. He took a crosstown bus home, where he worked for two hours on his homework. He cooked dinner, so that it would be ready when his mother returned from work. Later, while she washed the dishes, Luis spread out his paints and materials on the kitchen table. He painted until he was too tired to work any more. Finally he went to bed. He dreamed of the day when his work would hang in a downtown art gallery.

3   Old buildings that once would have been torn down are now being restored. This nationwide trend is partly due to rising interest in the architecture of the past century or so. It is also due to rising building costs and the money saved in renovation. It is becoming more difficult for a person to purchase a home. People must come up with a big down payment and take a loan at high interest rates.

Keep This in Mind

- A paragraph is a group of sentences dealing with one main idea.

Now Write Rewrite those groups of sentences in **Try Your Skill** that are not paragraphs by changing or omitting sentences that do not belong. Label your paper **A Good Group.**

Of One Mind

Recognizing Unity in a Paragraph

Here's the Idea   Paragraphs are organized units of ideas. Each paragraph deals with one main idea. Every sentence in a paragraph should be related to that main idea. When all of the sentences work together, a paragraph has **unity.**

A unified paragraph follows a plan. Suppose that a paragraph deals with storms on the surface of the sun. Every sentence in that paragraph should include related information. Sentences about solar energy or sunny days would not belong in such a paragraph. They might be good sentences, but they would belong in other paragraphs.

Notice how these sentences relate to the idea of sand castle contests.

> Sand castle contests are attracting crowds on both the East and West coasts. Contestants use wet sand to build elaborate structures with high walls, towers, and moats. Some contestants use knives or sticks to carve the sand. Others use only their hands. The castles are soon demolished by the wind and waves. These unusual creations can usually be studied only in photographs.

Check It Out   Read the following paragraph.

> When you use yeast in baking, its temperature is very important. Yeast is alive, and cold temperatures stop its growth. Too much heat, on the other hand, kills it completely. Ideally, the liquid ingredients in which yeast is dissolved should be about 110 degrees. At this temperature, the liquid should feel warm but not hot to your touch. If the temperature is correct, you can be reasonably sure that the yeast will do its work.

- Do all of the sentences relate to one main idea? Does the paragraph have unity?

Try Your Skill Read the following paragraphs. Decide if each has unity. If a paragraph does not have unity, write the sentence or sentences that do not belong.

1 ESP is not confined to human beings. There are documented instances in which dogs and cats have shown remarkable psychic powers. Some animals have traveled to find their owners after the owners have moved hundreds of miles away. People should not leave pets without first making careful arrangements for them. Other animals have warned humans about earthquakes.

2 There are advantages to driving an older car. For one thing, you will probably worry less about the car being damaged or stolen. You will also find that many older models are easier for you to repair yourself. Finally, keeping an older car for several years will save you money.

3 It was a terrible sight. The force of the tornado had completely destroyed several buildings in the downtown area. Uprooted trees blocked the streets. Pieces of glass were scattered everywhere. The results of the damaging storm could be seen for miles. Tornadoes don't last very long. They are short-lived, though powerful.

Keep This in Mind

- All the sentences in a paragraph should relate to one main idea. Then a paragraph has unity.

Now Write Write the name of someone you admire. Write one sentence that sums up your thoughts about the person. Below that sentence, list five more sentences related to the main idea. Label your paper **Of One Mind.**

I Declare!

Using a Topic Sentence

Here's the Idea   A **topic sentence** states the main idea of a paragraph in a clear, direct way. A topic sentence is helpful to both readers and writers. It helps readers group related ideas together in their minds. It helps writers keep their ideas organized.

A topic sentence should also state an idea that can be developed by the other sentences in the paragraph. Suppose you were writing a paragraph about February. The sentence "February is the second month of the year" is too narrow to be a good topic sentence. It makes a statement of fact that cannot be developed. A better topic sentence might be "February contains two of my favorite holidays." This topic sentence offers an idea that promises more. It can be supported and developed by other sentences in the paragraph.

The topic sentence is often the first sentence in a paragraph. Used in this position, it prepares a reader for the statements that follow. However, the topic sentence may be used anywhere in a paragraph where it states the main idea most clearly.

Check It Out   Read the following paragraph.

My sister Mary is hard of hearing and needs to wear a hearing aid. Sometimes Mary uses her hearing problem to her own advantage. If we are having a disagreement and she wants to infuriate me, she can. She simply turns off her hearing aid. I find myself arguing emotionally, but Mary does not hear a word I say.

- Which is the topic sentence? Is it too narrow to be developed? State the main idea of this paragraph.

Try Your Skill   Read each paragraph below. Write the topic sentence. If the topic sentence is too narrow, label it *Narrow*. Then rewrite it so that it is a better topic sentence.

1   Ice fishing is not as rugged as it may appear to be. First of all, there are ways to fight the cold. This can be accomplished with warm clothing, portable shelters, and heaters. Second, portable radios and TV's help fishers pass the time on the ice. Third, a grateful family is likely to show its appreciation to the person who brings home fresh fish during the winter.

2   My birthday is July 12. To celebrate this year, I invited five friends to a cookout. Last year my family planned a special day's trip to Jones Beach. When I was younger, my favorite celebration was an afternoon of rides at a carnival.

3   Our dog Duke is a watchdog. Duke is always alert and on guard. Whenever a stranger approaches our house, Duke rises to meet him. The stranger cannot pass until Duke is assured by a family member that the person is a friend. We all feel safer knowing that Duke is around to protect us.

Keep This in Mind

- A topic sentence states the main idea of a paragraph. The sentence should deal with an idea that can be developed in a paragraph in a meaningful way.

Now Write   Think of three topics that you might develop into paragraphs. For each paragraph, write a topic sentence that states the main idea. Label your paper **I Declare!** and put it into your folder.

From the Ground Up

Ways of Developing a Paragraph

Here's the Idea   The main idea of a paragraph is stated in the topic sentence. The other sentences in the paragraph should develop and support that idea. You can develop a paragraph with sensory details, specific examples, facts and statistics, and incidents or anecdotes.

Sensory details tell how something looks, smells, tastes, feels, and sounds.

> The forest was engulfed in flames. Everywhere Jeff looked he saw sheets of orange-yellow fire. All he could taste was smoke. Around him, trees exploded in the intense heat. The suffocating smell of burning pine was everywhere.

Use **specific examples** to develop a general statement.

> The Indian tribes in North America used deer for almost everything. The flesh was used for food, the hide for moccasins and clothes, and the antlers for tool handles. The cords and sinews that connected the muscles of the deer to the bones were used for thread with which to sew clothing. The hooves were made into glue.—ROSEBUD YELLOW ROBE

Use **facts and statistics** to make an idea clear or to support an opinion.

> Amelia Earhart was the first woman to fly the Atlantic. In May, 1932, she made the solo flight in a single-engine Lockheed Vega. She was beset by bad weather. The wings of her plane coated with ice, forcing her to fly as close as seventy-five feet above the waves part of the time. Fifteen hours after her departure from Long Island, she landed in a farmer's pasture in Ireland.   —*The Women's Book of World Records and Achievements*

Incidents or anecdotes can help you to illustrate a point.

> My grandmother is a very patient woman. I remember a morning when she and I went fishing. For two hours we cast our lines with no success. I suggested leaving, but grandmother wouldn't hear of it. "The fish are here," she said. "They're just not ready to bite." Minutes later, I felt a tug on my line. Soon we had both caught our limit. "Patience," my grandmother reminded me later, "is a virtue."

Check It Out   Read the following paragraph.

> Second Street was peaceful. There was no traffic at that hour. Steve stood in the deserted street looking up at the rows of apartment windows with their shades still drawn. The sky was still dark, but the air was fresh. Steve began bouncing the basketball he had been carrying. A little later, he heard a shout from an eighth-floor window. "Be right down," Chris hollered.

- How is the topic sentence developed?

Try Your Skill   Copy the topic sentence in this paragraph. How is the main idea developed?

> <u>Ben struggled to climb the muddy trail</u>. His woolen shirt was not heavy enough to protect him from the sharp thorns. His compass and canteen hung from his belt and clanged against each other. His shoes were caked with mud.

Keep This in Mind

- The main idea of a paragraph can be developed with sensory details, specific examples, facts and statistics, or incidents or anecdotes.

Now Write   Take out the paper labeled **I Declare!** Choose one topic sentence. List three sensory details, three specific examples, three facts and statistics, or one incident or anecdote that would develop the main idea. Save your work.

What's Your Line?

Recognizing Three Kinds of Paragraphs

Here's the Idea Any paragraph you may write fits into one of three main categories. It might be a story, a description, or an explanation. Each kind of paragraph presents a topic in a different way.

A **narrative** paragraph tells a story or relates events. All events, real or imaginary, are usually told in the order in which they happened.

A **descriptive** paragraph is a word picture of an object, a scene, or a person. Its vivid sensory details usually create a certain mood.

A **explanatory** paragraph explains something. It may explain a process, state an opinion, or present a definition.

Check It Out Read the following paragraphs.

1   Willard Farquar felt his weight change the steps under his feet into an escalator. He cursed under his breath, but let them carry him. He was carried up to the tall, blue entrance doors, which silently parted when he was five meters away. The escalator changed to a slideway that carried him into a softly gleaming, high-domed room. "Martian peace to you, Willard Farquar," an invisible voice chanted.   —FRITZ LEIBER

2   One summer morning I lay on the sand after swimming in the small lake in the park. The sun beat down—it was almost noon. The water shone like steel. It was motionless except for the feathery curl behind a distant swimmer. From my position I was looking at a rectangle with sun, sand, water, a few solitary people, and around it all a border of dark, rounded oak trees. Ever since I had begun taking painting lessons, I had made small frames with my fingers, to look out at everything.   —EUDORA WELTY

3　　The term *checkmate* comes from the game of chess. It describes the situation in which a player attacks the opponent's king so that no defense or escape is possible. This is then the end of the game. The word *checkmate* comes originally from a Persian word *shāhmāt*, meaning "the king is dead." The word *checkmate* is now also used to mean "to defeat completely."

- Which paragraph is narrative? Which is descriptive? Which is explanatory?

Try Your Skill　As you read the following topic sentences decide what kind of paragraph they would most likely be part of. Write *Narrative, Descriptive,* or *Explanatory.*

1. The Golden Gate Bridge glowed in the brilliant orange light of the sunset.
2. One glance told me I had made a terrible mistake.
3. The Jerusalem artichoke is a vegetable that few people recognize.
4. Some old radio shows are still popular.
5. Gilbert seemed to be having a run of bad luck.

Keep This in Mind

- A narrative paragraph tells a story or relates events.
- A descriptive paragraph creates a word picture.
- An explanatory paragraph explains a process, states an opinion, or states a definition.

Now Write　Review your work labeled **From the Ground Up.** Write which of the three kinds of paragraphs you would use for this topic. Explain why this choice seems best. Label your paper **What's Your Line?** Keep your work in your folder.

Writing a Paragraph

Get in Step

Writing as a Process

Here's the Idea   To write a good paragraph, follow a step-by-step plan. This plan is called the process of writing. There are three stages: pre-writing, writing the first draft, and revising.

Pre-writing includes all the planning you do before you actually begin to write. Choosing a topic, narrowing it, gathering information, and organizing ideas are all parts of pre-writing.

Writing the first draft involves turning your pre-writing ideas into sentences and paragraphs. First, you write a topic sentence that states your main idea. Then you use your pre-writing notes to develop your subject. Don't be afraid to experiment.

Revising is the stage when you correct and improve your rough draft. You organize your ideas and proofread your writing.

Check It Out   Read the following note and paragraph.

General topic: Georgia

Narrowed topic: Savannah in the spring

Pre-Writing Notes: horse-drawn carriages, restored old buildings—tours, historical district, beautiful parks, flowers

First Draft and Revision:

Savannah Georgia is ~~nice~~ *magical* in the spring. Horses ~~go~~ *clip-clop* through the historical district. They pull ~~old~~ *antique* carriages ~~with tourists in them.~~ *loaded* ~~The~~ *In the* historical district ~~is where they have~~ *beautiful old* houses ~~that are fixed up~~ *have been restored* to look like they ~~used to.~~ *did before the Civil War.* These houses are ~~around~~ *surround* squares *filled* with ~~lots of flowers. Its no wonder it is~~ *azaleas and jasmine. Savannah is* called *rightly* the bell of the south.

- Explain how the writer followed each stage in the process of writing.

Try Your Skill   Make three columns on your paper. Title one column *Pre-Writing,* the second column *Writing the First Draft,* and the third column *Revising.* Put each of the following writing activities in the appropriate column.

changing general verbs to specific ones
writing a rough version of a paragraph
choosing a general subject
writing an ending

proofreading
gathering details
organizing ideas
narrowing a subject

Keep This in Mind

- The process of writing includes three main stages: pre-writing, writing the first draft, and revising.
- Pre-writing includes all of the planning you do before you write.
- Use the first draft to turn your ideas into sentences.
- When you revise your work, you can improve and correct your writing.

Now Write   Most experienced writers agree that one way to become a good writer is through practice. You can practice writing by keeping a journal. A journal is a notebook where you can record your thoughts, experiences, and reactions to the world around you. Keeping a journal allows you to practice your writing and at the same time build a rich storehouse of writing ideas.

Begin your journal today. On a piece of paper, write about an interesting event you experienced this week. You might also write about a conversation you had, or one you overheard. When you get a notebook for your journal, add this paper to it.

Your Choice

Pre-Writing: Choosing a Topic

Here's the Idea   The first step in writing a paragraph is to choose a topic. One way to do this is to examine your own interests, ideas, and opinions. What interests you? What things do you consider important? Answering these questions will help you find a topic that you will enjoy developing. Here are four other ways to find writing ideas for paragraphs:

Journal Writing   Keep a daily journal in which you record your experiences, thoughts, and feelings. Write in this journal as often as you can. Soon you will have collected many ideas that you can use for writing assignments.

Brainstorming   Another way to search for ideas is by brainstorming. Start with a general idea, such as *camping* or *football*. Then, in five or ten minutes, write down as many thoughts as you can about the subject. At the end of this time, you will have many possible ideas for writing.

Clustering   Clustering is a form of brainstorming. Write your general idea on a piece of paper and circle it. Then write a related idea, circle it, and connect it to the general idea. Continue in this fashion, writing down ideas connected to the general idea and to other related ideas.

Interviews and Discussions   Another source of writing ideas is other people. If you know someone who has an interesting hobby, you can interview him or her about it. Listen carefully and ask questions, and you will soon gather enough details for a paragraph. Class discussions or conversations with friends can also yield writing ideas. Again, listen carefully and ask questions.

Reading   Reading can be more than a source of knowledge and enjoyment. It can also be a source of new ideas. If a particular book, magazine article, or newspaper story interests you, make some general notes about it in your journal. You might also clip out interesting articles and save them.

Check It Out   Read these two entries from a journal:

April 10   My sixteenth birthday! Finally, I get to drive—*if* I pass the test. Mom has invited some of my friends for dinner tonight. It's supposed to be a surprise, but Willy let the cat out of the bag.

May 14   I found out today I got a summer job. I'll start work next month as a day camp leader. I'll be responsible for eight children with cerebral palsy. I hope I'll do okay. I'm kind of nervous.

• What writing ideas can you find in these journal entries?

Try Your Skill   Read the following list of general topics. With your classmates, pick out one general topic and discuss it for four or five minutes. See how many good topics you can find for paragraphs.

sports	music	school life
jobs	animals	summer

Keep This in Mind

• When choosing a topic to write about, consider what interests you and what is important to you.
• Five good ways to find subjects are journal writing, brainstorming, clustering, interviewing and discussing, and reading.

Now Write   Make a list of four or five topics that you would be interested in writing a paragraph about. Use one or more of the methods suggested in this lesson. Save your writing ideas in your folder.

Down to Size

Pre-Writing: Narrowing a Topic

Here's the Idea   Many topics, such as *music* or *school*, are too broad to be developed in a single paragraph. Such topics must be narrowed to make them more specific.

One good way to narrow a topic is to ask questions beginning with *who, what, when, where, why,* and *how.* For example, to narrow the broad topic *music,* you could begin with several *who* questions:

> Who is my favorite singer? instrumentalist?
> Who won this year's Grammy Award for best rock album?

You might also ask several *what* questions:

> What was the first concert I went to?
> What do I remember about my first guitar lesson?

Suppose you decided to write about the first concert you went to. You could continue to narrow this topic by asking questions like these:

> **Who?**   Michael Jackson
> **Where?**   Madison Square Garden, New York
> **Why?**   my favorite performer

Asking such questions will help you to find a topic that is narrow enough to be covered well in a paragraph. These questions will also help you to find specific details to include in your paragraph. The more specific you make your paragraph, the more interesting it will be to your readers.

Check It Out   Read the paragraph on the next page, and then answer the questions that follow.

I never would have discovered the flute if it hadn't been for my older sister, Lisa. Two years ago, she asked me to a concert by John Galway at Orchestra Hall. I wasn't very interested in the idea, but that soon changed. When I heard the first silvery notes from Galway's flute, I was in awe. From that moment, I knew I wanted to play the flute. Thanks to Lisa, I discovered the beauty of this musical instrument.

- What questions do you think this student might have asked to narrow her topic? How did she answer them?

Try Your Skill   Choose two of these general topics and write them on your paper. Narrow each topic by asking *Who? What? When? Where? Why?* or *How?*

animals   television   dreams   friends   games   future

Keep This in Mind

- Narrow a general topic by answering *who, what, when, where, why,* and *how* questions. Make sure that you have a specific topic that you can write about in an interesting and informative paragraph.

Now Write   Choose one of the general topics you listed in the **Try Your Skill** from the last lesson. Narrow the topic so that you can write an interesting and informative paragraph about it. Ask *who, what, when, where, why,* and *how* questions to help you. Write your narrowed topic on a piece of paper. Save it in your folder.

Improve Your Aim

Pre-Writing: Audience and Purpose

Here's the Idea   Suppose that a speaker from the auto industry were to give a talk at your school. What would you think if the speaker used many technical terms that only an expert would understand? How would you feel if the speaker just explained that cars come in different sizes, shapes, and colors? In both cases, you would probably be bored. The first talk would be too complicated. The second would be too simple. Neither talk would be right for its audience.

Before writing a paragraph, always ask these questions:

What is my purpose?
Who are the people in my audience?

The answers to these questions will help you to focus your ideas. They will also help you to suit your writing to your readers.

Your **purpose** is what you want to accomplish with your writing. To determine your purpose, think about why you have chosen your topic. Do you want to tell a story? Do you want to define your subject? to describe it? to compare or contrast it to something else? to analyze it? Also think about whether your aim is to inform, to persuade, or to entertain your readers.

The **audience** is all the people who will read your writing. You should consider the ages and interests of these people. You should also consider how much your readers already know about your subject. Suppose, for example, that you are writing a paragraph about how to throw a curve ball. You would write in one way for the members of your baseball team. You would write in another way for readers who know little about baseball.

Here is an example of how a writer's purpose and audience can help determine how a paragraph will be developed:

Topic: mountain climbing

Purposes: *to describe* my first experience as a climber
            to convince people that climbing is dangerous
            to explain the types of equipment needed

Audiences: experienced climbers
            beginning climbers
            people interested in outdoor sports

Check It Out   Read this paragraph.

From the first day Sluggo arrived at our house, he was boss. Our five-year-old cat Nancy took one look at the three-month-old kitten and ran for cover. The chase was on. Sluggo is always the chaser and Nancy the chased. In contrast to Sluggo's mad dashing from room to room, Nancy tiptoes silently. Sluggo wriggles away if I try to hold him. Nancy, on the other hand, loves to curl up in my lap, purring contentedly. Whoever thinks all cats are alike hasn't met my two furry friends!

• What is the purpose of this paragraph?

Try Your Skill   If the above writer had wanted to convince a cat hater that cats are loving, gentle pets, the details would have been different. List three or four details that might be included if that were the purpose of the paragraph.

> **Keep This in Mind**
>
> • Your purpose is what you want to accomplish with your writing. The audience is all of the people who will read your writing.
> • Identifying purpose and audience will help you to select details and suit your writing to your audience.

Now Write   On a sheet of paper, write the purpose of the paragraph you plan to write. Then write a brief description of the people who will read your paragraph. Save these notes.

Attention Please

Pre-Writing: Creating a Topic Sentence

Here's the Idea A good topic sentence will do several things. First, it should state the main idea of the paragraph clearly. That is, it should tell the reader what the paragraph will be about. Second, it should capture the reader's attention. If the topic sentence is not interesting, the reader may not want to finish reading the paragraph. The following rules will help you to accomplish these goals when writing topic sentences.

1. Make it informative. Stick to a single idea. Do not wander from your topic. Do not introduce unnecessary information. Avoid rambling, overloaded topic sentences such as the following:

> Paul Revere was a naval captain and patriot who was born in Boston, and he warned the colonists that the British were coming, and he was also an accomplished silversmith.

Instead, make a statement that introduces just one idea.

> Paul Revere, the Revolutionary War hero, was an accomplished silversmith.

2. Make it interesting. Try to find an unusual aspect of your subject to write about in your sentence. You can also add interest to your subject by approaching it in an unusual way:

> Paul Revere rode into the pages of American history.

3. Make it direct. Introduce the topic, not yourself. Do not begin with such phrases as *I think, I feel,* or *I believe.* Avoid wordy sentences such as the following:

> I want to write about the fact that Paul Revere actually made two famous rides, not one.

Instead, state your topic directly:

Paul Revere actually made two famous rides, not one.

Check It Out   Read the following topic sentences.

1. Friday the thirteenth was a lucky day for me.
2. If you ever see a mop wearing a blue bow, that's my dog Fluffy.
3. Amphibians are animals that are at home both on land and in water.
4. You can grow vegetables even if you live in an apartment.

- Is each of these sentences informative, direct, and interesting? Explain your answer.

Try Your Skill   Rewrite these sentences. Find a more informative, direct, and interesting way to state the same main ideas.

1. There are fifty states in the United States, but Alaska is the one I'm most interested in.
2. I guess if I put my mind to it I could tell you a thing or two about modern music.
3. Molly, who likes the spring season best, said that she was prepared for a long winter.
4. In biology, the day that students dissect an animal, which is usually a frog, is a memorable day.

Keep This in Mind

- Write a topic sentence that is informative, interesting, and direct.

Now Write   From your folder, take out the topic you chose and narrowed for your paragraph. Write several topic sentences that state the main idea of your paragraph. Experiment with your topic sentences. Try to express your main idea in several different ways. Make your sentences informative, interesting, and direct. Save your topic sentences in your folder.

Collecting Data

Pre-Writing: Developing a Paragraph

Here's the Idea   In Part 5 you learned how to write a topic sentence to express the main idea of a paragraph. Once you have written a topic sentence, you can then look for specific details to support and develop your main idea. The following types of details are helpful in developing different kinds of paragraphs.

sensory details	facts and statistics
specific examples	incidents or anecdotes

Always look for details that suit your purpose. If you want to write a descriptive paragraph, look for sensory details. These are details that tell how a subject looks, sounds, tastes, feels, and smells. If you want to express an opinion, look for facts and statistics to use as support. If you want to prove a point, you may consider telling an anecdote. If you want to explain or define a general idea, you may decide to give specific examples to make the idea clearer.

To gather the details you need, use any of the following methods: personal observation, brainstorming, interviewing, discussion, research, and general reading. Again, choose a method that suits your purpose. If you want to describe a scene in nature, go to the scene and make some personal observations. If you want to find facts to back up an opinion, do some research in such reference works as encyclopedias and almanacs. Choose the sources of information that are most likely to provide reliable information about your topic. For more information on choosing sources, see Critical Thinking, pages 273–291.

Check It Out   Read the following list of pre-writing notes.

Topic: The Grand Canyon

> 227 miles long, one mile deep, 18 miles wide in places
> Carved out by erosion—Colorado River, weather
> In deepest part, the stone is two billion years old
> Cliffs, hills, and slopes of many colors

- How do you think the writer gathered these details?

Try Your Skill What kinds of details might you use to develop each of the following topic sentences? How might you gather these details?

1. A rainy Saturday needn't be a washout.
2. Niagara Falls is an important source of energy.
3. I feel damp whenever I remember my ride on the "Maid of the Mist" at Niagara Falls.
4. Sixteen is not too young to drive.
5. Lion tamers go through intense training.

Keep This in Mind

- You can develop your paragraph with sensory details, facts and statistics, specific examples, or incidents or anecdotes.
- Gather details and ideas for your paragraph through personal observation, brainstorming, discussions, interviews, research, and general reading.
- Gather details and ideas that will support your purpose and appeal to your audience.

Now Write Read the topic sentence you wrote in the last lesson. Look over your notes on purpose and audience. Then decide what kinds of information you need to develop your paragraph. Use whichever method of gathering details will give you the kinds of details you need. Save your pre-writing notes.

One After Another

Pre-Writing: Organizing a Paragraph

Here's the Idea   Suppose that every time you took notes in class you simply jotted the notes onto pieces of scrap paper. You then shoved the papers into your book bag. What would happen when it came time to study for a test? Of course, your notes would be a mess. Only when information is organized logically can it be understood readily. The same is true when you are writing a paragraph. If your ideas are not organized logically, your readers may not understand what you are trying to say. Here are some methods you can use.

Chronological Order   Use chronological order when you are telling a story or explaining how something is done. Present the events in the order in which they occurred or should occur.

Spatial Order   Spatial order helps you to present the sensory details of a description. It allows your readers to see how the things you are describing are related in space to other things.

Order of Importance   Use this order when giving reasons, facts, or examples to support an opinion. Present each detail, in order, from least important idea to the most important.

General to Specific   Use this order to define an object or idea. Begin with a general statement. Then add specific details.

Most Familiar to Least Familiar   Use this order when defining or describing. Begin with details that are familiar to your readers. Then introduce less familiar ideas and details.

Comparison and Contrast   Comparison and contrast can help you to show the similarities and differences between two subjects. Begin by describing how the subjects are alike. Then, show how they are different. You can also do the reverse.

Check It Out   Read the following paragraph.

We walked down the quaint village street with a row of elms on each side of it. Just beyond were two ancient stone pillars, weather-stained and lichen-blotched, bearing upon their summits a shapeless something which had once been the rampant lion of Birlstone Manor. A short walk along the winding drive with such sward and oaks around it as one only sees in rural England, then a sudden turn, and the long, low house of dingy, liver-colored brick lay before us, with an old-fashioned garden of cut yews on each side of it. As we approached it, there was the wooden drawbridge and the beautiful, broad moat as still and luminous as quicksilver in the cold, winter sunshine.

—SIR ARTHUR CONAN DOYLE

- What is the purpose of this paragraph?
- What kind of organization has the writer used?

Try Your Skill   Below is a list of topics for a paragraph. For each topic, choose a good method of organization.

1. Waxing a car is a simple process.
2. The emu and the penguin are both flightless birds, yet they lead very different lives.
3. Perseverance is a special quality that is often defined in the motto, "If at first you don't succeed, try, try, again."
4. Toxic waste is a problem that deserves our attention.
5. Aunt Sarah's home is a beautiful, old Victorian house, filled with treasured antiques.

Keep This in Mind

- Organize the details of your paragraph in a clear, logical order.
- Choose an order that best suits the purpose of your paragraph.

Now Write   Take out your pre-writing notes and organize them. Choose a method of organization that suits the purpose of your paragraph. Save your organized notes in your folder.

Trial Run

Writing the First Draft

Here's the Idea When you have finished the pre-writing steps described in Parts 1–7, you should have a topic sentence and an organized list of details. The next step in the writing process is to turn your pre-writing notes into sentences. This step is called writing the first draft.

The main point of writing a first draft is to get all your ideas down in sentence form. Do not worry about the details of grammar, capitalization, punctuation, and spelling at this point. You will have time later to correct any mistakes you might make. Instead, concentrate on what you want to say. Feel free to change, take out, or add ideas as you write.

As you turn your ideas into sentences, try to make one sentence flow smoothly into the next. Use transitional words and phrases to help your readers understand the relationships between your ideas more easily.

In a paragraph that is organized in chronological order, use transitional words and phrases that express time. Examples include the words *first, next, then,* and *finally.*

In a paragraph that is organized in spatial order, use transitional words and phrases that relate to place or position. Some words and phrases that are useful in descriptive paragraphs are *next to, above, under, over, beside,* and *behind.*

A paragraph that is organized in some other way may use any of a great number of transitional words and phrases. Some words that are often used include *therefore, as a result, on the other hand, similarly,* and *in contrast.*

Check It Out Read this descriptive paragraph.

The fortune-teller sat in the shadows. In front of her was a deck of tarot cards and beside the deck was a crystal ball. On every finger of the gypsy's hands were large, flashy rings. A bright, flowered scarf was wrapped around her head. From her ears dangled huge hoop earrings that jingled like bells whenever she nodded her head.

- What transitional words and phrases did the writer use?

Try Your Skill Add transitional words and phrases to the following paragraph. Use transitions that help show the kind of order being used in the paragraph.

Carlos steadied himself in the starting blocks. He looked up at the track ahead of him. The gun went off. He jumped out of the blocks. He was running at an all-out sprint. He passed several runners. Two runners were still ahead of him. He passed one. He passed the other. His legs ached and his heart was pounding. He rounded the last turn in first place. He crossed the finish line. Carlos found out he had set a new school record.

Keep This in Mind

- The first draft is your first chance to put your ideas into sentence form.
- When writing a first draft, let your thoughts and ideas flow freely. Use transitional words and phrases to help make your ideas and organization clear.

Now Write Take out your topic sentences and your organized pre-writing notes. Choose the topic sentence that you like the best. Then, write the body of your paragraph. Use your organized notes to guide you. In the next lesson, you will write an ending for your paragraph. Save your first draft in your folder.

Top It Off

The First Draft: Ending a Paragraph

Here's the Idea   Have you ever seen a great television show that was spoiled by a bad ending? If so, you know how important a good ending is. This is why you must pay particular attention to the last sentence in every paragraph you write.

A good ending sentence sums up, or ties together, the ideas presented in the rest of the paragraph. An ending sentence may also explain the importance of these ideas. In either case, a good ending helps readers to make sense of what they have just read.

An ending sentence should not introduce any new information. It should make a clear, final statement that follows logically from the other sentences in the paragraph. In fact, an ending sentence may simply restate the idea of the topic sentence using different words.

A good ending sentence is also interesting. Whenever you write a paragraph, try to express your central idea in an ending sentence that your readers will want to remember.

Check It Out   Read this real-life account.

My adjustment to my new world was a very difficult one. I ran into problems with my classmates almost immediately after returning to school. Everything proceeded smoothly enough until the entire class was out on the playground during recess. A large group of children gathered around me the moment I finally reached the playground. "Hey, Harold," asked one of the boys, "what is it really like to be completely blind?"   —HAROLD KRENTS

- Does the ending sentence sum up the main idea of this paragraph? Does the ending capture your interest?

Try Your Skill Read these paragraphs and rewrite the poorly written endings. Try to make your concluding sentences interesting.

1   Levin Hutchins was a clockmaker who lived in Concord, New Hampshire. He was also a creature of habit. It was Hutchins's rule to get up at four o'clock sharp every day. He was upset with himself whenever he overslept. In 1787, when he was only twenty-six, Hutchins decided to attach a bell to the timing mechanism of one of his clocks. *Although he hadn't invented the first clock, which had been invented many years before, Hutchins invented the first alarm clock.*

2   Hercules was one of the most powerful heroes of Greek legends. He performed twelve impossible tasks. He killed two giant snakes when he was a baby. When he became a man, his weapon was a bow so big that no other person on earth could shoot an arrow with it. Hercules killed a huge, ferocious lion with his bare hands. He also won a battle against a nine-headed snake monster. *I like to read about heroes.*

3   You can create an inexpensive art object by using colored sand. First, buy several packages of sand in different colors. Next, find a clear glass container such as a vase, drinking glass, or jar. Then, carefully spoon one layer of sand at a time into your container. As the artist, you will choose the order of colors used and the thickness of the layers. *You can make many sand objects.*

Keep This in Mind

- A good ending sentence should sum up the main idea of a paragraph. It should also be interesting.

Now Write It is your turn to write a strong ending to your own paragraph. Read your first draft. Think about what you have written. Then write an ending that sums up the main idea in an interesting way. Save your completed first draft in your folder.

Just So

Revising a Paragraph

Here's the Idea   Revising is the final step in the process of writing. To revise a paragraph, you must read it carefully several times. As you read, look for ways to improve what you have written.

Begin by looking for ways to improve your **content.** The content includes all the ideas and details you have presented. First, make sure that your topic sentence is direct, interesting, and informative. Second, make sure that your paragraph has unity. A paragraph has unity if all its details are related to the single idea given in the topic sentence. Third, make sure that you have developed your main idea fully. If you need more details to support your main idea, add them.

Next, check the **presentation** of your ideas. Presentation refers to the way in which your ideas are organized. Make sure that your paragraph has coherence. A paragraph has coherence if its ideas are arranged in a clear, logical order. The ideas in the paragraph should flow smoothly from one to the other. The method of organization used should suit your purpose.

Then read your paragraph aloud to check its **style.** Style refers to the kind of language that you have used. Make sure that your words are right for your audience and your topic. Replace any dull or uninteresting language you find. Use strong, specific verbs, adverbs, and adjectives to make your writing come to life.

Now you must proofread your paragraph. Again, read your paragraph carefully. Look for and correct any errors in grammar, capitalization, punctuation, and spelling. When you have revised and proofread your paragraph, make a final copy of your work. Proofread this copy one last time, and correct any errors you find.

Check It Out   Read this partially revised paragraph.

You may have heard the expression "Time is money."
Did you know that
Food can be money. Edible money has been used from
^   ^, too?
Ancient Times up to the present Century. In ancient egypt
merchants paid their helpers with   *with*
~~people~~ ~~used~~ grain ~~for~~ ~~money~~. Roman solders was paid ~~in~~ salt.
valuable
Pepper was so ^good during the middle Ages that it was used
as currency   *Near the end of*
more often ~~to pay for things~~ than as a spice, In World War II

the germans, ^when there official currency became worthless
We should all be thankful
~~used coffee and sugar as money~~ Today we use credit cards for *that*
paper, coins, and
money. *It could get pretty sticky*
carrying jelly doughnuts in your wallet.

- What changes have been made to improve the content,
  presentation, and style of this paragraph?
- What revising step has not yet been done?

Try Your Skill   The paragraph in **Check It Out** has been revised for content, presentation, and style. However, it still has
errors in grammar and mechanics. Try your skill at finding and
correcting these errors.

Keep This in Mind

- Revise the first draft of your paragraph for content,
  presentation, and style. Then proofread it for errors
  in grammar and mechanics.

Now Write   Revise your paragraph, following the guidelines
in this lesson. When you are satisfied that your paragraph is the
best it can be, make a neat, clean final copy. Save your finished
paragraph in your folder.

The Process of Writing

The Process of Writing

Throughout the rest of this book, you will be learning about and practicing many different kinds of writing. You will write narratives, descriptions, explanations, and a research paper. Although the kind of writing you do will change, one aspect of your writing will remain the same. You will always use the three stages of the process of writing—pre-writing, writing the first draft, and revising—to plan, write, and improve your paragraphs and compositions.

Pre-Writing A football coach wouldn't send his team onto the field without a game plan. A builder wouldn't start digging the foundation for a skyscraper without an architect's plans. Careful planning is important to nearly all activities. It increases the odds that the outcome of the activity will be successful.

As a writer, you need to plan, too. The planning stage of the process of writing is called pre-writing. During pre-writing, you will complete the following activities.

1. **Choose and narrow a subject.** Look for a subject that interests you and that you know something about or want to learn about. You can find interesting writing ideas through brainstorming, clustering, reading, research, interviewing, discussing, and looking in your journal. Then narrow your subject so that it is specific enough to be covered well in a paragraph, a composition, or a research paper.

2. **Define your purpose.** Why are you writing? Do you want to tell a story, describe something or someone, explain a process, express an opinion, or define something? Knowing your purpose will help you to focus your writing.

3. **Identify your audience.** Who are your readers? What are their interests and opinions? How old are they? How much do they

know about your subject? If you know your audience, you can suit your writing to your readers.

4. Gather details. Look for details, ideas, and other information to support and develop your topic. You can use sensory details, specific examples, facts and statistics, or incidents or anecdotes. You can use the same techniques to gather information that you used to choose a topic.

5. Organize your information. You must arrange the details you have gathered into a logical order. Some methods of organization you can use are chronological order, spatial order, the order of importance, general to specific order, most familiar to least familiar order, and comparison and contrast. Whichever method you choose, be sure that it suits the type of writing you are doing.

Pre-Writing

You list possible topics and select one.	the hail storm — our cactus garden my new nephew — *my hospital experience* (circled) the Olympics — Mexico City
You identify your purpose and audience.	Purpose: to describe waking up in the hospital Audience: my classmates

① waking up, groggy ⑧ fine in a few days
~~sound of buzzer~~ ~~no clock~~
② white plaster cast ~~Memorial Hospital~~
④ dry throat ⑤ doctor enters
③ tube on arm ⑦ broken arm / concussion
⑥ moped accident

You list details, choose those that develop your topic, and organize them.

Writing the First Draft

When you have finished all of your planning, you are ready to write your first draft. A first draft is like the sketches an artist draws before he or she begins a painting. Like the artist, you want to see how well things fit, whether anything needs to be added, taken out, or moved.

When you write a first draft, concentrate on turning your details into sentences and paragraphs. Follow your organized pre-writing notes as you write, but don't be afraid to experiment with the order of your ideas. Let your ideas flow naturally as you write. Don't interrupt this flow by questioning your grammar, capitalization, punctuation, or spelling. You will have time later to correct any mistakes you make.

Writing the First Draft

You write a paragraph about your topic.	I woke up feeling funny. I heard voices. Slowly I opened my eyes. My left arm was in a cast. I was in a strange room. My right arm had a tube taped to it. My throat was sore. I was confused. Suddenly a door opened up. A doctor with her assistants said my name. She said that while riding my moped I had slipped on some oil. I broke my arm and got a concussion. She said I was okay. I could leave in a few days. I smiled and thanked her and fell asleep.

Revising

A first draft is just a rough version of your written work. During the third stage of the process of writing, called revising, you smooth out the rough edges. You work to improve what you have written, to make your writing the best it can be.

When you revise, you should pay attention to three important aspects of your writing: content, presentation, and style.

Content refers to the ideas and details you have presented. To check the content of your writing, ask yourself these questions.

1. Does each topic sentence express the main idea of a paragraph?
2. Do all of my details relate directly to my main idea?
3. Have I included enough details to develop my main idea fully?
4. Does my conclusion sum up my ideas?
5. Have I fulfilled my purpose?

Presentation refers to the way your writing is organized. The following questions will help you to check your presentation.

1. Does my writing have a clear beginning, middle, and ending?
2. Have I arranged my details in a logical order?
3. Does my method of organization suit the kind of writing I am doing?
4. Do my ideas flow smoothly from one to another?

Style refers to the way you have expressed yourself in your writing. Most writers have different styles. Still, there are some examples of good style that are common to all writers.

1. Is each topic sentence interesting enough to capture a reader's attention? Is each topic sentence direct, not wordy?
2. Have I used lively, vivid language?
3. Is my language well suited to my audience?
4. Have I included transitional words and phrases to help the reader see how my ideas are connected?

Proofreading When you are satisfied with the content, presentation, and style of your writing, proofread your work. Look for and correct any errors in grammar, capitalization, punctuation, and spelling. When you proofread, use a dictionary and the Handbook sections of this book to check your work.

As you revise your first draft, use the following proofreading marks to show your corrections and changes.

Proofreading Symbols

Symbol	Meaning	Example
∧	add	*have* would gone ∧
≡	capitalize	United states
/	make lower case	our club President
∼	reverse	th i e r
℘	take out	finished the the race
¶	make new paragraph	....be over. New ideas
⊙	period	....and stop Before we
⋏	add comma	Red, blue and green are

Revising

You rewrite. You express your idea in a different way.

(handwritten, revised paragraph:)

I woke up feeling funny. ~~dazed and groggy. In the distance,~~ I heard voices. Slowly I forced ~~opened~~ my eyes open. My left arm stretched out beside me, was in a cast. ~~I was in a strange room.~~ My right arm had a tube taped to it. ~~found myself~~ My throat felt parched and scratchy. ~~was sore.~~ I clear was confused. Suddenly a door opened up. A doctor accompanied by her assistants, ~~said~~ spoke my name. She told me ~~said~~ that while riding my moped I had skidded ~~slipped~~ on a patch of oil. I had broke ~~broke~~ my arm and suffered ~~got~~ a mild concussion. She said assured me that I was not in any danger and that ~~the hospital~~ was okay. I could leave in a few days. Smiling weakly, I ~~smiled and~~ thanked her and fell asleep. drifted off into a deep sleep.

Notice how the paragraph has been improved.

110

The Final Copy When you have finished revising and proof-reading your writing, copy it in its final form. Write carefully. Make your work as neat as possible. Proofread your final copy. Neatly correct any errors you find.

Final Copy

> I woke up feeling dazed and groggy. In the distance, I heard voices. Slowly, I forced my eyes open. I found myself in a strange room. My left arm, stretched out beside me, was wrapped in a white plaster cast. My right arm had a clear tube taped to it. My throat felt parched and scratchy. My mind was confused. Suddenly, a door opened. A doctor, accompanied by her assistants, spoke my name. She told me that while riding my moped, I had skidded on a patch of oil. I had broken my arm and suffered a mild concussion. The doctor assured me that I was not in any danger and that I could leave the hospital in a few days. Smiling weakly, I thanked her and drifted off into a deep sleep.

Now you are ready to begin learning and practicing different kinds of writing. Whenever and whatever you write, follow all the stages of the process of writing. Each time you write, you will be learning something about writing and about yourself.

The Narrative Paragraph

What's the Story?

Pre-Writing: Developing a Narrative

Here's the Idea A narrative paragraph is one that tells a story. You can write a narrative to describe an experience, provide an example, or entertain. A narrative paragraph may stand alone or it may be used as part of a speech, a composition, or a report.

To write a narrative paragraph, first choose a story that you want to tell. The story may be about a real experience such as something that happened to you while on vacation. The story may also be totally imaginary. In either case, the story must be a brief one. Otherwise, you will not be able to develop it fully in a single paragraph.

When you have chosen a general idea for a story, make your topic more specific. Do this by asking questions that begin with *who, what, when, where, why,* and *how.* The answers to these questions will help you to focus your ideas. The answers will also provide you with some details to tell your story.

When you have a more specific topic, make a list of every event that you want to include. Even a very short story may contain many separate events. Consider how the things in your story look, sound, feel, taste, and smell. Then, list the details that will appeal to the senses of your readers. Together these two types of details will help you to write a vivid narrative.

Check It Out Look at this list of details.

who:	Jeff and me
what:	grudge match in tennis
where:	school tennis court
when:	after school
why:	to prove girls are as good in athletics as boys
how:	won with self confidence

Now read the narrative.

Jeff was always bragging that boys were better athletes than girls. So I challenged him to a tennis match after school to prove that he was wrong. We each won one game and then I lost a game. Jeff was so pleased with his apparent victory that he started making mistakes. But, it hardly mattered. I was rushing every shot. I didn't feel I had control of the ball. I needed to relax. I decided to change racquets between sets for luck. I got my confidence back. I moved in after my serves and put his returns away. It worked—my game—and match!

- What separate events help to tell the story?
- What sensory details does the story include?

Try Your Skill Recall a particular situation in which you were frightened or taken by surprise. On your paper, list *Who? What? When? Where? Why?* and *How?* Recall and list sensory details about the situation.

Keep This in Mind

- A narrative paragraph tells a brief story. The story may be true or imaginary.
- Gather specific details for a narrative paragraph by asking *who, what, when, where, how,* and *why* questions.
- Develop a narrative paragraph with specific and sensory details.

Now Write Think about a brief story you would like to tell. The story may be true or imaginary. Make a list of the events that will tell your story. Save your pre-writing notes in your folder.

Moment to Moment

Pre-Writing: Using Chronological Order

Here's the Idea   Most stories are told in **chronological order.** In other words, the events are presented in the order in which they occurred. Notice the use of chronological order in the following example.

> When I was free for a few hours, I explored the foothills. I would leave the town and head toward the point of the foothills nearest my home. There I would test my legs and lungs against the hillside. It was hard work. At first, I ran two miles at the fast pace of perhaps five or six miles an hour. Then, I climbed a hillside of five hundred feet or more in elevation. At last, I returned to home and bed, dead tired, every muscle of my legs aching. Time and again I followed this routine.
>
> —WILLIAM O. DOUGLAS

Before writing a narrative paragraph, always organize the list of events you want to include. Arrange these events in the order that they occurred. By using chronological order, you will make it easier for your reader to follow what is happening in your story.

Check It Out   Now read this imaginary narrative.

> He was an old man who fished alone in a small boat in the Gulf Stream and he had gone eighty-four days now without taking a fish. In the first forty days, a boy had been with him. However, after forty days without a fish the boy's parents had told him that the old man was now definitely and finally un-lucky. At their orders, the boy had gone in another boat that caught three good fish the first week. It made the boy sad to see the old man come in each day with his boat empty, and he always went down to help him.   —ERNEST HEMINGWAY

- Are the events of this narrative in chronological order? Explain your answer.

Try Your Skill   Assume you are going to write a narrative paragraph about getting ready for school in the morning. Make a list of everything you do. Then arrange that list in chronological order.

Keep This in Mind

- The events of a narrative paragraph are organized in chronological order.

Now Write   Examine the pre-writing notes you made in the last lesson. Arrange the events and details in chronological order. You can add or take out details as you see fit. Save your organized notes in your folder.

Who Sees What?

Pre-Writing: Choosing a Point of View

Here's the Idea   Every narrative has an author. He or she is the person who *writes* the story. Every narrative also has a narrator. He or she is the person who *tells* the story. Sometimes the narrator is a character in the story. At other times, the narrator may be an outsider, someone who is not in the story at all. When you choose a narrator to tell your story, you are choosing a **point of view.** Point of view means the eyes and mind through which something is written.

Point of view is an important choice when you are writing a narrative paragraph. As a pre-writing step, you must decide which of the three different points of view you will use.

One point of view you may choose is the **first-person point of view.** When you use this point of view, you use the first-person pronoun *I*. The character *I* is the narrator. Your reader will know only what the narrator knows.

With **third-person point of view,** the third-person pronouns *he, she,* and *they* are used. Your story is told by an outsider. who cannot tell what any character is thinking or feeling. Thus, this point of view is called **third-person limited.**

A second type of third-person point of view is called **third-person omniscient.** *Omniscient* means "knowing all things." The pronouns *he, she,* and *they* are used. This narrator knows what each character is thinking and feeling.

Check It Out   Read the following two narrative paragraphs.

1   Once, while I was baby-sitting for Jim and Jenny Lee, I decided to take them shopping. As we entered Filene's, I saw my friend Maria and stopped to say hello. One minute the

twins were right next to me, but the next minute they had disappeared. At first, I was frantic. I ran up and down nearby aisles, calling their names. Finally, I had an inspiration—try the toy department!

2   Steve and Maria were delighted to run into each other in Filene's. Steve remembered how much fun they'd had last summer as lifeguards at Harbor Beach Park. As they chatted, Steve failed to notice that Jim and Jenny had drifted off. When the twins found the toy department, they broke into a run. Jim had never seen so many model trains before. Jenny couldn't wait to find out what was inside a huge box of building materials. By then, Steve was searching for the missing twins.

• What is the point of view of each paragraph?

Try Your Skill   Suppose that you arrive home to find that no one is there and you have forgotten your key. While you are trying to find a way in, a stranger appears on the scene. First, write several sentences that relate these events from the first-person point of view. Relate the same events from the third-person limited and the third-person omniscient points of view.

Keep This in Mind

- With the first-person point of view, the narrator, *I*, tells what the characters say and do.
- With the third-person limited point of view, the narrator is an observer.
- With the third-person omniscient point-of-view, the narrator is "all knowing." He or she tells everything—actions, thoughts, and feelings.

Now Write   Take out the pre-writing notes you organized in the previous lesson. Choose a point of view that seems suited to the story you have chosen to tell. Write down your choice in your pre-writing notes. Save your notes in your folder.

As Time Goes By

Writing the First Draft

Here's the Idea During the pre-writing stage of writing a narrative paragraph, you chose a group of events to tell about. You arranged these events in chronological order. You also chose a point of view from which to tell your story. Having done these things, you are now ready to write your first draft.

As you begin writing the first draft, remember that you are telling a story. Therefore, you do not have to begin with a topic sentence that states the main idea. Instead, you may write a sentence that sets the scene or that tells about the first event. The other events of the narrative should then follow in order.

There are many special words and phrases that you can use to make the order of events clear. These are called transitional words and phrases. They allow you to show how much time has passed between events in a narrative. Here is a list of useful transitional words and phrases:

first	now	when	at the same time
then	before	soon	by the time
next	earlier	suddenly	at the beginning
while	after	immediately	in the middle
last	later	finally	at the end

Notice that these words and phrases all deal with time. They tell the reader *when* each event in the story takes place. In addition to the transitional words and phrases above, you may want to use time words and phrases that are more specific. For example, you may need to write *after ten minutes, at noon,* or *in September.* Use a variety of transitional words or phrases to tell your reader exactly when each event takes place.

Check It Out Read this narrative paragraph.

We reached the beach late in the afternoon. The tide was high and the surf was heavy. I dived in and rode a couple of waves, but they had reached that stage of power in which you could feel the whole strength of the ocean in them. The second wave, as it tore toward the beach with me, spewed me a little ahead of it, encroaching rapidly; suddenly it was immeasurably bigger than I was, it rushed me from the control of gravity and took control of me itself; the wave threw me down in a primitive plunge without a bottom, then there was a bottom, grinding sand, and I skidded onto the shore. The wave hesitated, balanced there, and then hissed back toward the deep water, its tentacles not quite interested in me enough to drag me with it.
　　　　　　　　　　　　　　　　　　　—JOHN KNOWLES

- What transitional words and phrases has the author used in this paragraph?
- Do the transitional words and phrases help to show time and order?

Try Your Skill Look again at the narrative paragraph by William O. Douglas on page 116. Find and list the transitional words and phrases he used.

> **Keep This in Mind**
>
> - Transitional words and phrases that tell *when* help to show chronological order in a narrative paragraph.

Now Write Begin writing the first draft of your narrative paragraph. For now, just write to get your ideas into paragraph form. Let your thoughts and ideas flow freely. Don't hesitate to make changes as you write. Remember to include transitional words and phrases that tell *when*. Save your first draft in your folder.

Achieving Excellence

Revising Your Narrative Paragraph

Here's the Idea Revising is the last stage in the process of writing a narrative paragraph. When you revise, you change parts of your story to make it clearer and more interesting.

Here are some questions to ask yourself as you revise your narrative:

1. Have I included specific and sensory details in my narrative?
2. Have I arranged the events in chronological order?
3. Have I made the order of the events clear by using transitional words and phrases?
4. Have I used only one point of view?

When writing a narrative, always try to use language that is specific. This will make your story more vivid to your readers. Avoid such general verbs as *walk*. Replace any such verbs with ones that are more specific. For example, the verb *walk* could be replaced by *amble, tiptoe,* or *march.* Choose the verb that fits the particular action you are describing.

> The lazy boy *ambled* down the hall.
> Cautiously, Sarah *tiptoed* up the steps to the attic.
> Luis *marched* into the room with a scowl on his face.

Also avoid weak linking verbs. These include all forms of the verb *be*, such as *is, were*, or *had been.* Instead, use strong verbs that show action, such as *leap, dunked,* or *flew.*

Once you have checked the ideas, organization, and word choice in your paragraph, proofread it carefully. Find and correct any errors in grammar, capitalization, punctuation, and spelling.

Check It Out   Notice how the author has used strong and specific verbs in this paragraph.

Kino deftly slipped his knife into the edge of the shell. Through the knife he could feel the muscle tighten hard. He worked the blade lever-wise and the closing muscle parted and the shell fell apart. The lip-like flesh writhed up and then subsided. Kino lifted the flesh, and there it lay, the great pearl, perfect as the moon. It captured the light and refined it and gave it back in silver incandescence. It was as large as a sea-gull's egg. It was the greatest pearl in the world.

—JOHN STEINBECK

• Which verbs in particular make this paragraph come alive?

Try Your Skill   Replace the verbs in italics below with stronger, more specific verbs.

Jerome *ran* up the alley, terrified and nearly out of breath. He *ran* into a garbage can, which *made noise* as it *moved* along the pavement. Behind him, the huge dog was closing in. It *went* past the intersection and *came* into the alley at incredible speed. With one last, desperate effort, Jerome *put* himself through an open window in the house at the end of the alley. He *turned* and *shut* the window just as the snarling dog reached the house.

Keep This in Mind

• When revising a narrative paragraph, add strong and specific verbs to make the story come alive.

Now Write   Revise your first draft. Follow the guidelines in this lesson, adding strong, specific verbs where necessary. Proofread your paper for errors in grammar and mechanics. Then make a final copy of your narrative. Save it in your folder.

The Descriptive Paragraph

Making Sense

Pre-Writing: Gathering Sensory Details

Here's the Idea   A **descriptive paragraph** is like a painting. It presents a picture of a real or imaginary person, place, or thing. To make this picture live in the reader's mind, the writer of a descriptive paragraph uses sensory details. **Sensory details** describe things that can be *seen, heard, felt, smelled,* or *tasted.* Notice the use of sensory details in the following paragraph.

> From halfway down the block, Miss Strangeworth could catch the heavy scent of her roses, and she moved a little more quickly. The perfume of roses meant home, and home meant the Strangeworth House on Pleasant Street. Miss Strangeworth stopped at her own front gate, as she always did, and looked with deep pleasure at her house, with the red and pink and white roses massed along the narrow lawn, and the rambler going up along the porch; and the neat, the unbelievably trim lines of the house itself, with its slimness and its washed white look. Every window sparkled, every curtain hung stiff and straight, and even the stones of the front walk were swept and clear.   —SHIRLEY JACKSON

To write a descriptive paragraph, you must first choose a subject. Once this is done, you must gather sensory details to create a vivid picture for your reader. One way to gather sensory details is through observation. Suppose, for example, that you want to describe a crowd of fans at a football game. To do this, you could go to a game and take notes. Your notes would include the things that you could see, hear, touch, taste, and smell. Another source of sensory details is your memory. If, for example, you wanted to describe a scene from your childhood, you could simply picture the scene in your mind. However, your memory of the scene would have to be clear enough to provide all the details you need. Whenever you write a description, try to choose details that are specific enough to give your reader a clear picture of your subject.

Check It Out   Read the following description.

> The lamplight in the Store gave a soft make-believe feeling to our world that made me want to whisper and walk about on tip-toe. The odors of onions and oranges and kerosene had been mixing all night and wouldn't be disturbed until the wooden slat was removed from the door and the early morning air forced its way in with the bodies of people who had walked miles to reach the pickup place. —MAYA ANGELOU

   • What sensory details does this description use?

Try Your Skill   Read the following general topics. Choose one and narrow it so that it is more specific. For example, if you choose "a friend," narrow this topic to a specific friend. Then list as many sensory details as you can about your topic.

a kitchen	a friend	a traffic jam
a garden	a relative	a holiday celebration

Keep This in Mind

• Use sensory details to create a vivid description.
• Gather sensory details through observation or from your memory.

Now Write   Make a list of persons (an unusual neighbor, a bus driver), places (an abandoned house, a shopping mall), and objects (a painting, an exotic sports car) that you might want to describe.

Choose one of these subjects as a topic for your descriptive paragraph. Be sure your subject is narrow enough to be described well in just one paragraph. Make a list of sensory details that will help you to describe your subject. Save these notes.

Directional Signals

Pre-Writing: Using Spatial Order

Here's the Idea   As you learned in Part 1, a descriptive paragraph uses sensory details to create a vivid picture. These details are most effective when they are organized in a logical way.

The details in a description are often arranged according to spatial order. **Spatial order** shows how one detail in a description is related in space to other details. Using spatial order, you might describe a subject from top to bottom or from bottom to top. You might also describe it from left to right, from right to left, from near to far, or from far to near. Be sure to choose a pattern of spatial order that suits your subject. For example, you would be more likely to describe a tree from top to bottom than from near to far. Notice the use of spatial order in this description:

> Bonsai—the Oriental art of growing miniature trees—is my new hobby. My bonsai tree is prickly juniper, only eighteen inches high. I have carefully shaped my dwarf tree so that it resembles an umbrella. At the top, the spice-scented needles are tightly bunched. Below this cluster of needles, the tiny trunk is twisted and wrinkled. Below that, the roots of the juniper are covered with moss. The base of the bonsai tree is a shallow dish in which the tiny juniper is growing.

Sometimes it's difficult to arrange the details in a description according to spatial order. Suppose you were trying to describe the atmosphere at a rock concert or your feeling of exhilaration after winning a first place in a track meet. These descriptions are not well suited to spatial arrangement. Instead, you might arrange the details in whatever order you want the reader to notice them. Always arrange your details in an order that suits the kind of paragraph you are writing.

Check It Out Read this description.

Last weekend I helped my mother turn our once cluttered basement into a well-organized workroom for her new upholstery business. At the foot of the stairs we set up a display of fabric selections. Above the fabrics we stapled pictures of finished products. Along the wall to the left of the stairs we arranged samples of a variety of wood stains and varnishes. Beside this display, we set her sewing machine. On the adjoining wall we placed her workbench. Above the workbench, we hung her tools. Finally, we moved two newly reupholstered chairs against the fourth wall to show customers the end products of my mother's skills.

• How does this description use spatial order?

Try Your Skill Imagine that you have been asked to write a description of a street in your town. You might choose the street on which you live. You might also choose a street in the business district. Choose a street, and make a list of sensory details that you could use to describe it. Arrange your details according to spatial order.

Keep This in Mind

• Use spatial order or some other logical order to organize the details in your description.

Now Write Read your pre-writing notes from the last lesson. Arrange your details in a logical order. Save your organized notes in your folder.

Words Have Feelings

Pre-Writing: Creating Mood

Here's the Idea Have you ever wondered why people enjoy listening to music? The answer, of course, is that music stirs powerful feelings in people. Music can make you feel happy, sad, tender, peaceful, or excited. These feelings are called **mood.**

Mood is extremely important in a description. Before you begin writing, you must decide what mood you want your writing to suggest. Mood is suggested by the language a writer uses. Nouns, verbs, adjectives, and adverbs can all suggest mood. For example, suppose you were going to describe a beach scene. To create one kind of mood, one that suggested a positive feeling, you might choose words like these:

Nouns	Adjectives	Verbs	Adverbs
sea gulls	sunny	lapping	brightly
sand castle	sparkling	splash	contentedly
popsicles	breezy	laughing	softly

To suggest a very different mood about the beach, you might use words like these:

Nouns	Adjectives	Verbs	Adverbs
sand fly	crowded	crash	hotly
sunburn	blinding	scream	fiercely
litter	sticky	shatter	harshly

When you are planning your description, think about the feeling you want to suggest. Write lists of nouns, adjectives, verbs, and adverbs that will help you to create a specific mood.

Check It Out   Read the following paragraph.

When I think of the home town of my youth, all that I seem to remember is dust—the brown, crumbly dust of late summer—arid, sterile dust that gets into the eyes and makes them water, gets into the throat and between the toes of bare brown feet. I don't know why I should remember only the dust. Surely there must have been lush green lawns and paved streets under leafy shade trees somewhere in town; but memory is an abstract painting—it does not present things as they are, but rather as they *feel*. And so, when I think of that time and that place, I remember only the dry September of the dirt roads and grass-less yards of the shanty-town where I lived.

—EUGENIA COLLIER

• What words help to create the mood of this paragraph?

Try Your Skill   Assume you have been asked to write a description of a large sporting goods store on the first day of their annual "Half-Price Madness Sale." Write a brief statement indicating the mood you want to create. Then make a list of nouns, adjectives, verbs, and adverbs that will help you to suggest that feeling.

Keep This in Mind

• Mood is the feeling suggested by a piece of writing.
• Writers express mood through the language they use.

Now Write   Review the pre-writing notes you have made for your descriptive paragraph. What mood do you want to create in your description? Make a list of nouns, adjectives, verbs, and adverbs that will help you create that mood. Save your list in your folder. Use these words when you write your first draft.

Can You Place It?

Writing the First Draft

Here's the Idea When you write narrative paragraphs, you use transitional words and phrases to show *when* things occur. When you write descriptive paragraphs, you should use other transitions to show *where* things are. Here are some transitional words and phrases that help to show spatial order in descriptive paragraphs:

above	beside	in the center	over
against	between	near	side by side
ahead of	by	next to	south
alongside	down	north	throughout
at the end of	east	on	to the left
at the top	facing	on the bottom	to the right
around	in	on the corner	under
below	in back of	on the edge	up
beneath	in front of	outside	west

As you write the first draft of a descriptive paragraph, use transitions such as these. They will help your readers to understand where each item in the description is in relation to other items. You may place a transitional word or phrase at the beginning, in the middle, or at the end of a sentence, as follows:

Beside the curb sat a wet, shaggy dog.
Only the chimney could be seen *above* the flood waters.
The monkeys scurried in the trees *overhead*.

Check It Out Read this paragraph.

Until that year, Pompeii was a prosperous city of 25,000 people. Nearby was the Bay of Naples, an arm of the blue Mediterranean. Rich men came down from wealthy Rome, 125 miles to the north, to build luxurious seaside villas. Fertile farmlands occupied the fields surrounding Pompeii. Rising sharply behind the city was the 4,000-foot bulk of Mount Vesuvius, a grass-covered slope where the shepherds of Pompeii took their goats to graze. Pompeii was a busy city and a happy one. —ROBERT SILVERBERG

- What words and phrases in this paragraph tell *where?*

Try Your Skill The following paragraph contains blanks where transitional words and phrases should be inserted. Add transitional words and phrases to this paragraph. Use words from the list in this lesson or any others that tell *where.* Be aware that there are no right or wrong answers. Use any words or phrases you want to create a personal description. Compare your description with those of your classmates.

_____, a path wound its way through the forest. We decided to explore the path. _____, silver spruce trees pointed skyward. A narrow stream gurgled along _____. Red-winged blackbirds chattered _____ in the trees. _____, we spied a fawn. Its mother followed _____. _____, the forest was alive.

Keep This in Mind

- In a description, transitional words and phrases that tell *where* can be used to show spatial order.

Now Write Write the first draft of your descriptive paragraph. Follow your organized pre-writing notes as you write. Introduce the subject of your description in your topic sentence. Develop your description with sensory details in the body of your paragraph. Use transitional words and phrases to show the order of your details. Sum up your description in a strong ending sentence. Save your first draft in your folder.

Reviewing It

Revising Your Descriptive Paragraph

Here's the Idea   The first draft of your descriptive paragraph is just a rough version of what you want to say. It must be revised before it can be considered finished.

When you revise your paragraph, ask yourself these questions.

1. Is my topic sentence interesting? Is it informative?
2. Are the details in my description vivid? Can the reader see, hear, taste, smell, or feel what I am describing?
3. Did I include enough details to develop the description?
4. Are my details arranged in a logical order?
5. Have I used transitional words and phrases to show order? Do these words and phrases lead from one detail to the next?
6. Have I used specific language to suggest a particular mood?

When you have finished revising, check for errors in grammar, capitalization, punctuation, and spelling. Correct any errors that you find.

Check It Out   Read the following descriptive paragraph.

The professor had succeeded in making a French garden in Hamilton. There was not a blade of grass; it was a tidy half-acre of glistening gravel and glistening shrubs and bright flowers. There were trees, of course; a spreading horse-chestnut, a row of slender Lombardy poplars at the back, along the white wall, and in the middle two symmetrical round-topped linden trees. Masses of green-brier grew in the corners, the prickly stems interwoven and clipped until they were like great bushes. There was a bed for salad herbs. Salmon pink geraniums dripped over the wall. The French marigolds and dahlias were just now at their best—such dahlias as no one else in Hamilton could grow. —WILLA CATHER

- Does the topic sentence introduce the subject of the description?
- What sensory details does this description include? Are there enough details to develop the description?
- What mood does the description suggest? What words help to create that feeling?

Try Your Skill Proofread the following paragraph. You should be able to find and correct nine errors in grammar, usage, and mechanics.

The sleek Indy race car was fastened securely to the trailer. The nose of the car was fited with a wide, ground-effects spoiler. Gawdy product decals decorated the front end. Further back, a narrow plastic windscreen wrapped around the cockpit. Nestled in the rear of the car, was a awesome, chrome Turbocharged engine. A row of exhaust pipes were protruding from it. Above the engine, another spoiler was positioned to catch the wind and keep the car from flying off the track. Four fat black tires set at the corners of the car. With it's metallic silver paint and aerodynamic body, the car could have been mistaken for a starship from another galaxy.

Keep This in Mind

When revising your descriptive paragraph:
- Be sure to use specific sensory details.
- Arrange your details in a logical order.
- Use transitional words and phrases that tell *where*.
- Use specific nouns, adjectives, verbs, and adverbs that will suggest a particular mood.

Now Write Revise your descriptive paragraph, using the guidelines in this lesson. Then proofread your description for errors in grammar and mechanics. Correct any errors you find. Make a neat final copy and save it in your folder.

The Explanatory Paragraph

Explaining a Process

Let Me Tell You

Pre-Writing: Explaining a Process

Here's the Idea   Hardly a day goes by that you don't explain something to someone. You might explain how you made that delicious carrot cake, how your science experiment went, or how to get to the concert without fighting traffic. All of these are explanations of how to do something or how something happens or works.

You can develop a written explanation of a process by writing an explanatory paragraph. You could write an explanatory paragraph to explain how to paint a car, how to string a violin, or how earthquakes happen. When you choose your topic, be sure to choose one that interests you. Also, choose a topic that is narrow enough to be developed in just one paragraph.

After you have chosen your topic, you will have to list all the important steps of the process. For example, if you had chosen the topic "How to Make the Hottest Chili in Town," your notes would include everything from the purchasing of all the ingredients to the final seasoning just before serving.

When you write your pre-writing notes, be sure to include all the necessary steps of the process. If you leave any steps out, your readers may become confused. Write each step clearly and simply so that your explanation will be easy to understand.

Check It Out   Read the following explanatory paragraph that explains a process.

There is an art to taking a good photograph. The first step is to decide exactly what you want in the picture. This step is called "composing" the picture. When you have composed the picture the way you want it, your next step is to focus the subject. This requires turning the focusing ring on the lens until the image you see through the camera is crisp and sharply defined. The next step is to set the f-stop by turning the f-stop ring on the lens. This adjusts the amount of light entering the camera so that the picture will be properly exposed. Now you are ready to press the shutter release and take a beautiful photograph.

- What process is explained in this paragraph?
- Are all the steps included?
- Is each step explained simply and clearly?

Try Your Skill The first step in writing your explanatory paragraph about a process is choosing your topic. Take some time to think about processes that interest you and that you are familiar with. You can choose to explain how to do something, how something works, or how something happens. Make a list of six different processes that you could write an explanatory paragraph about. Be sure each topic is narrow enough to be covered well in a paragraph. Save your list in your folder.

Keep This in Mind

- An explanatory paragraph explains how to do something or how something works or happens.
- Include all the necessary steps of the process.
- Explain each step clearly and simply.

Now Write Look over the list of six topics you developed in **Try Your Skill.** Choose one topic for the explanatory paragraph you will write. Then make a list of all of the important steps involved in the process you have chosen to explain. Don't leave out any important steps. Save your pre-writing notes in your folder.

First Things First

Pre-Writing: Using Step-by-Step Order

Here's the Idea When a mechanic replaces the parts of a car, he or she must place the parts in the right order. Otherwise, the car will not run properly. When you write a paragraph, you must also place the parts in the right order. Otherwise, your readers will become confused.

In an explanatory paragraph that explains a process, information should be presented in **step-by-step order.** This is the order in which something happens or is done. To organize your explanation, begin with your pre-writing notes. These list every step in the process that you are writing about. Decide which is the first step in the process. Place this step first. Then, decide which is the second step. Place this step second. Continue in this way until you reach the last step. By placing each step in the proper order, you can make certain that your reader will understand the process from beginning to end.

Check It Out Read the following paragraph.

There's really nothing to painting a room. Of course, the first thing to do is buy paint. After buying the paint, open the paint and put the brush in. Start painting. Of course, you need to cover all the furniture when you get home. You must mask around areas you don't want painted, such as windows, trim, and light switch plates. Before you go and buy the paint, be sure you know exactly what color you want. It is helpful if you bring a piece of material from a couch or draperies so that the color of the paint will match. I mentioned earlier that it is important to cover the furniture. This should be one of the first things you do. Also, before you cover the furniture, it helps to move it all to the center of the room so it is not in the way when you paint. When you are all finished remember to put the brushes away. All brushes should be washed thoroughly before putting them away.

- What process is explained in this paragraph?
- Is this paragraph organized in step-by-step order? Explain your answer.

Try Your Skill Rewrite the paragraph in **Check It Out.** Place all of the steps in proper step-by-step order. If you feel any steps are missing, add them. Compare your rewritten paragraph with those of your classmates.

Keep This in Mind

- Step-by-step order is the order in which the steps of a process happen or are to be done.
- Use step-by-step order to organize the details in an explanatory paragraph explaining a process.

Now Write Organize your pre-writing notes from **Now Write** in the last lesson into step-by-step order. Be certain that all the necessary steps are included and are arranged in the order in which they happen or should be done. Save your organized notes in your folder.

Take One

Writing the First Draft

Here's the Idea The best way to begin the first draft of your explanatory paragraph is with a good topic sentence. This sentence should tell your readers exactly what process you intend to explain. It should also capture your reader's attention. Avoid dull topic sentences such as the following:

> In this paragraph I will explain how to throw a football properly.

This sentence lets the reader know what to expect. However, it is not very interesting. This topic sentence is much better:

> To throw a football properly, you have to know all the right moves.

After you have written your topic sentence explain, in order, all the steps in your process. Present each step in a separate sentence. Use transitional words and phrases to guide your readers from step to step. The following words and phrases are particularly useful in paragraphs that explain processes.

first	when	the next step	finally
second	afterwards	at the same time	then
third	later	while	next
as	after that	following that	at last
	at least	the last step	

Of course, you are not limited to these particular words and phrases. You may also use any other transitions.

Check It Out Read the following paragraph.

> An omelet is a quick and tasty breakfast. First, whisk together three eggs and a tablespoon of cream or milk until all is

well blended. Then prepare a filling. Chopped vegetables, shredded cheeses, and crumbled bacon or sausage are all delicious possibilities. As soon as the eggs and filling are ready, melt a tablespoon of butter in an omelet pan over medium heat. When the butter has melted, slowly pour in the eggs. Once the eggs on the bottom have set, lift the edge of the omelet with a spatula and tilt the pan so that the uncooked eggs on top will run under and cook. Now that the omelet is almost cooked through, sprinkle the filling over the top. Next, use your spatula to carefully fold the omelet in half. Cook the folded omelet for several minutes so that the filling heats through. Finally, slide the omelet onto a warm plate, garnish with a sprinkling of chopped parsley or some other herbs, and dig in!

- What process is explained in this paragraph?
- Are the steps arranged in proper step-by-step order?

Try Your Skill   Reread the paragraph in **Check It Out.** Make a list of all of the transitional words and phrases that have been used to lead the reader from one step in the process to the next step.

Keep This in Mind

- Begin an explanatory paragraph with an informative and interesting topic sentence.
- Use correct step-by-step order.
- Use transitional words and phrases to show step-by-step order and to help your readers move easily from one idea to the next.

Now Write   Write the first draft of your explanatory paragraph that explains a process. Follow your organized pre-writing notes which should include all of the necessary steps of the process you are explaining. Start with a good topic sentence and use step-by-step order. Save your first draft in your folder.

The Final Touch

Revising Your Explanatory Paragraph

Here's the Idea Every step in an explanatory paragraph should be explained clearly and completely. Nothing in the paragraph should keep the reader from understanding the process being explained. Therefore, you must revise your paragraph carefully. When you revise, read your rough draft several times. As you read, ask these questions.

1. Is the topic sentence interesting? Does it tell what process I am explaining?
2. Have I included all the important steps in the process?
3. Are the steps organized in the order in which they happen?
4. Is each step explained clearly and completely?
5. Do my transitions guide my reader from step to step?

Once you have revised your content, organization, and word choice, proofread the paragraph. Find and correct any errors.

Check It Out Read the following revised paragraph.

Teaching your dog to perform simple tricks can be a rewarding experience.
Most dogs enjoy performing tricks. You may want to teach your dog to shake hands. *First,* Decide what simple command you will use. *Second,* Call your dog by *its* name and make it sit in front of you. Keep *your dog's* its attention through constant eye contact. *Next,* Say the dog's name followed by the command. *At the same time,* Gently nudge the dog's paw. Repeat these steps until the first time your dog correctly responds to your command. *Then,* Immediately reward the dog with a dog biscuit and a great deal of praise.

- How has the writer improved the topic sentence?
- What transitional words have been added? How do they improve the paragraph?

Try Your Skill Examine the following explanatory paragraph. Revise it, paying particular attention to transitions and to providing a clear and interesting topic sentence.

You take a pail and add a mild soap and fill it with water. Bring it out to your car. Hose down the car with water. Using a soft sponge or towel, wet it with the soapy solution and begin washing your car. Start with the top. Don't wash the windows with soap or they will become smeary in the rain. Don't wash the entire car without rinsing it as you go along. Be sure to wash the hubcaps and the tires with a stiff brush. Dry the car. Move the car into the shade and apply a good paste wax. Let it dry to a haze before rubbing it off. Rub it off. Clean the windows inside and out. Vacuum the interior of the car. Your car is the cleanest on the block now!

Keep This in Mind

- Revise your explanatory paragraph so that it begins with an informative and interesting topic sentence.
- Include all the necessary steps of the process and order them in step-by-step order.
- Use transitional words and phrases to show the order of each step and to help your readers move easily from one idea to the next.
- Proofread your paragraph for errors in grammar and mechanics.

Now Write Using the questions in this lesson, revise your explanatory paragraph. Remember to proofread for errors in grammar and mechanics. When you have finished revising your paragraph, make a final copy. Save your work.

The Explanatory Paragraph

Presenting an Opinion

Mind and Matter

Pre-Writing: Developing an Opinion

Here's the Idea In the last chapter, you learned how to write an explanatory paragraph that tells how. Such paragraphs are used to explain processes. In this chapter, you will learn how to write an explanatory paragraph that tells why. Such paragraphs are used to express and support opinions.

Everyone has opinions. An opinion is a belief you hold. Your opinion might be a judgment, a prediction, or a statement of obligation. A judgment tells how you feel about something.

> Aerobic exercise is the best exercise of all.

A prediction tells what you think will happen in the future.

> During the next twenty years, computers will play an increasingly important role in everyday life.

A statement of obligation tells what you believe ought to be done about something.

> Governments should fund public transportation to reduce air pollution from cars.

Always begin your pre-writing notes for this explanatory paragraph by stating an opinion. This opinion can be the topic sentence of your paragraph. Try to write the opinion as simply and directly as possible.

The next step in developing your paragraph is to list reasons and facts that support your opinion. The reasons should be logical. The facts should be accurate and provable. Try to list enough supporting facts and opinions to convince your readers that your opinion is sound.

Check It Out Read the following statement of an opinion and the reasons and facts supporting it.

Opinion: All automobile drivers and passengers should be required to wear seat belts.
—lowers insurance costs due to decreased injuries
—lessens chance of injury in crash
—saves lives

- Is the opinion a judgment, a prediction, or a statement of obligation?
- Is the opinion supported with logical reasons and accurate facts?

Try Your Skill From the following list of opinions choose one you agree with. Support that opinion with four or five accurate facts or logical reasons. Save your work in your folder.

1. Women should receive equal pay for equal work.
2. Holidays have become too commercial.
3. Employers should not be allowed to pay teenagers less than the minimum wage.
4. Those people who are eligible to vote should use that right.
5. America should explore the use of solar power more extensively.

Keep This in Mind

- When you want to present your opinion about something, write an explanatory paragraph.
- Always support your opinion with accurate facts and logical reasons.

Now Write What do you feel strongly about? Spend time thinking about an issue or subject that interests you. Write a clear and direct sentence that states your opinion. Then, list accurate facts and logical reasons that support your belief. Save your pre-writing notes in your folder.

The Order of Things

Pre-Writing: Organizing an Opinion

Here's the Idea As you already know, the ideas in a paragraph should be organized logically. By following a logical order, you help your reader to understand how your ideas are related. When you write an explanatory paragraph in order to present an opinion, organize your ideas according to the **order of importance.** In other words, order your ideas from the least important to the most important.

Begin by stating your opinion. This will be your topic sentence. Then, organize the supporting ideas from your pre-writing notes. These will make up the body of your paragraph. Start with the least important of your supporting ideas. Place this idea first. Then, find the next most important supporting idea. Place this second. Continue in this way until you reach the most important supporting idea of all.

Suppose, for example, that you are writing about why students should become involved in local elections. You might organize your supporting ideas from most important to least important, as follows:

1. gives students something to do after school
2. helps students to learn about important local issues
3. teaches students how their political system works

Check It Out Examine the following pre-writing notes.

Opinion: more jobs should be available for teenagers

Reasons: want something to do
need to earn money
teenagers are good workers
need to learn responsibility

Now read the following paragraph.

More jobs should be made available for teenagers. First of all, teenagers want something to do other than just "hanging out." Like everybody else, teens want to feel as if they are contributing to society. Second, teenagers are good workers. They are energetic, and they are often willing to take jobs that older people don't want. More important, teenagers need to earn money. By the time a person is sixteen or seventeen years old, it's not right to expect Mom and Dad to pay for everything. Teens want to be able to pay their own share and to be able to buy for themselves the things that they want. Finally, working teaches reponsibility. Working teens learn to deal with money and with people. They also learn some important things about themselves. Providing more jobs for teens is a way for society to encourage self-sufficiency and responsibility among young people.

- Does the topic sentence state an opinion clearly?
- Are the supporting reasons in this paragraph arranged in the order of their importance? Explain your answer.

Try Your Skill   Look over the pre-writing notes you made in **Try Your Skill** in the last lesson. Organize them in the order of importance, from the least important to the most important.

Keep This in Mind

- Organize your facts and reasons in order of their importance, from the least important idea to the most important.

Now Write   Look at the pre-writing notes you made in the last lesson for your explanatory paragraph. Which of the reasons or facts you listed to support your opinion is the most important? Which is the next in importance? Examine your notes carefully. Arrange your reasons or facts from the least important idea to the most important. Save your organized pre-writing notes in your folder.

Here's Why

Writing the First Draft

Here's the Idea   When you write the first draft of an explanatory paragraph that presents an opinion, always keep your purpose in mind. Your purpose is to explain your opinion as convincingly as possible. The following guidelines will help you to present your opinions forcefully.

1. Make sure your topic sentence states your opinion directly. Avoid beginning your topic sentence with *I feel, I think, I believe,* or *In my opinion.* Such sentence openers will make your opinion sound weak. Compare the following topic sentences. Which sounds stronger?

> I feel that, perhaps, our school should start a summer theater program.
> Our school should start a summer theater program.

2. Use transitional words and phrases to connect your ideas. There are two kinds of transitions you can use. One kind introduces reasons or facts. *Because, so, since, if, therefore,* and *as a result* are transitions of this kind. Another useful type of transition shows order of importance. *First, second, more important, most important,* and *finally* are transitions of this kind.

3. End your paragraph with a strong concluding sentence. This sentence may restate your opinion in different words. It may also summarize the ideas you have given to support your opinion.

Check It Out   Read the following paragraph.

Every high school student should work for a candidate in a local election campaign. First of all, it is a public service to help candidates by stuffing envelopes and answering phones. More important, by becoming involved, the student will learn first-hand what issues are important to the community and how local government works. As a result, the student will be better prepared to participate as an informed citizen.

- Does the topic sentence state an opinion directly?
- Is the supporting evidence organized in order of importance? Which transitions are used?
- Does the concluding sentence sum up the argument?

Try Your Skill Reread the paragraph in **Check It Out.** Write two different ending sentences for this paragraph. Be sure each sentence sums up the opinion or the reasons that support it.

Keep This in Mind

- State your opinion clearly and directly in the topic sentence.
- Use transitional words and phrases to introduce your reasons and show the order of their importance.
- Write a strong concluding sentence to sum up your ideas.

Now Write Present your opinion by writing the first draft of your explanatory paragraph. Be sure to include a clear topic sentence, transitional words and phrases, and a strong ending sentence to conclude your paragraph and sum up your opinion and reasons. Save your first draft in your folder.

Last, But Not Least

Revising Your Explanatory Paragraph

Here's the Idea   When you have completed the first draft, you are ready to revise your paragraph. As when revising other types of paragraphs, read your paragraph over several times. Check your content and organization as you read. Ask yourself the following questions to identify possible areas of improvement.

1. Does your topic sentence state your opinion clearly and directly?

2. Is your paragraph unified? Have you supported your opinion with enough evidence? Are your facts accurate? Are your reasons logical?

3. Have you presented your supporting ideas in order from least important to most important?

4. Is your paragraph coherent? Have you used transitional words and phrases to show how your supporting ideas are related?

5. Does your paragraph end with a strong concluding sentence? Does this sentence restate your opinion or summarize your supporting ideas?

After you have made any necessary revisions, proofread your paragraph. Correct any errors in grammar, punctuation, capitalization, and spelling.

Check It Out   Notice how the following explanatory paragraph has been revised.

- How has this paragraph been improved through revision?

Everyone who wants to join a team should. *be allowed to. First of all,* Because every-
one needs ~~exersize~~ *exercise* and being on a team ~~helps.~~ *is an enjoyable way to work out.* A player could
and
~~still~~ not make a ~~teem~~ *team* if ~~everyone~~ *someone* else were better. And a player *Moreover,*
could enjoy a sport ~~and~~ *and* be very good at it. ~~Tryouts should not~~
~~be part of school team sports.~~ Also, *Finally,* school teams should not ~~just~~
be ~~there~~ to win games. *formed just* ~~You should learn~~ *ing* about a sport and how
to play it ~~in school.~~ *well is the most important part of school athletics.*

Try Your Skill   Revise this paragraph.

In my opinion, I think that automobile drivers and pasengers should be recquired to wear seat belts. Wearing a seat belt would lower the cost of insurance. If you have a seat belt on, you have a better chance of not being hurt in a crash. Seat belts save lives, too. That's my opinion.

Keep This in Mind

- State an opinion clearly and directly in an explanatory paragraph that presents an opinion.
- Use accurate facts and logical reasons to support the opinion.
- Make sure the supporting evidence is arranged in order of importance from the least important idea to the most important.
- Use transitional words and phrases to present reasons and facts and to show their order.
- End the paragraph with a strong concluding sentence that sums up your opinion.

Now Write   Revise the first draft of your explanatory paragraph presenting an opinion. Use the questions in this lesson to guide your revision. Make a final copy and save it.

The Explanatory Paragraph

Stating a Definition

On Your Terms

Pre-Writing: Learning About Definitions

Here's the Idea In the last two sections, you have learned to write paragraphs that explain processes and present opinions. Now you're going to write a third kind of explanatory paragraph—an explanatory paragraph that states a definition. What is defined may be a real object like a *bobsled* or *ozone*. What is defined may also be a term or an idea, like *food chain* or *leadership*.

A good definition does three things. First, it gives the subject to be defined. Next, it puts that subject in its general class. Then, by giving specific characteristics, it shows how the subject is different from all the other members of its class.

Imagine that you want to define a *zucchini*. First, you would write that a zucchini is a vegetable. That puts it in its general class. How is a zucchini different from other vegetables? A zucchini is a squash. However, because there are several other kinds of squash besides zucchini, you might add that a zucchini is a summer squash. Because there are many types of summer squash, you could add that a zucchini is shaped like a cucumber. Because there are other cucumber-shaped summer squashes, you can add that the zucchini has a smooth, dark green skin. Now you have a complete definition.

Your complete definition might be stated like this: A zucchini is a smooth-skinned, dark green, cucumber-shaped vegetable that belongs to the summer squash family.

When you have a one-sentence definition of your subject, you must gather details to expand and develop the definition. Choose facts and figures and specific examples as you gather your pre-writing notes. Gather facts and figures through research. Specific examples will come from your own experience.

When you are ready to write your paragraph, the one-sentence definition you have composed will become your topic sentence. The details you have gathered will make up the body of your definition.

Check It Out   Read these pre-writing notes.

Topic: Hang glider

Notes: an aircraft
     triangular sail; often bright, vivid colors
     frame measures about 18 feet
     no engine; powered by air currents
     pilot hangs underneath
     steers with a control bar
     first became popular in U.S. in 1970's

- To what general class does the hang glider belong?
- What features distinguish the hang glider from other members of its class?

Try Your Skill   Use the notes in Check It Out to write a one-sentence definition of a hang glider. The definition should give the word to be defined, its general class, and one or two distinguishing characteristics.

Keep This in Mind

- An explanatory paragraph can state a definition.
- A good definition puts a subject into its general class, then shows its particular characteristics.

Now Write   Think of a real object, a term, or an idea that you want to define. Write a one-sentence definition of the word. You may want to use a dictionary or an encyclopedia to help you. Then make a list of details that will help you to develop the definition of your subject. Save your notes in your folder.

All the Specifics

Pre-Writing: Organizing a Definition

Here's the Idea At this stage in the process of writing your explanatory paragraph, you should have all of the information you need to develop your definition. Before you can start writing, however, you have to organize your information.

A definition can be organized in a number of ways. Usually, a definition begins with a general statement. This general statement names the subject, its general class, and a few particular characteristics. The general statement is then followed by specific details that add to the reader's understanding of the subject. These details should be organized logically. If the subject is unfamiliar to your readers, or is a technical or scientific term, you may want to begin with the most familiar details. Then, as your reader's understanding grows, you can introduce less familiar details that further define your subject.

However you decide to organize your definition, be sure to choose a method that is well suited to your subject.

Check It Out Read this explanatory paragraph.

The guitar is a stringed musical instrument. Historians believe that the guitar was first developed in Egypt about 5,000 years ago. The modern guitar was created in the late 1800's in Spain. Made of a light wood, it has curved sides and is shaped somewhat like an hourglass. It is played by plucking the strings with the fingers or with a small, flat object called a *pick*. Guitars usually have six strings, although some have as many as twelve, and some have as few as four.

- How was this explanatory paragraph organized? Explain your answer.

Try Your Skill Write a one-sentence three-part general definition of each of these terms.

dictator   woodpecker
sailboat   tollway

Keep This in Mind

- An explanatory paragraph that states a definition should begin with a general statement. That statement should be followed by specific details.

Now Write Organize the pre-writing notes you have gathered for your explanatory paragraph. Choose a method that best suits the subject. Save your organized notes in your folder.

Exacting Work

Writing the First Draft

Here's the Idea A good beginning to any first draft is a strong topic sentence. Remember that in an explanatory paragraph that defines, your topic sentence must do three things. It must give the subject being defined, put the subject into its general class, and show some of the particular characteristics of the subject.

As you write your first draft, expand the one-sentence definition given in your topic sentence. Use the facts and statistics or specific details and examples you gathered and organized in prewriting to fully develop your definition.

Finish your paragraph with a strong ending sentence. Try to leave your readers with an interesting thought or detail about your subject.

Check It Out Read the following definition.

> A rival is a person or group who competes for the same goal as another person or group. A rival tries to equal or outdo his or her competition. My brother and his friend Don are now rivals for the position of school band leader. The football team from my school, North High, is always anxious to play its rival, the team from South High. My mother, who sells real estate, hopes to do as much business as her rivals. Friendly rivalry is a natural part of everyday life.

- Does each sentence expand the definition in the topic sentence? Explain your answer.

Try Your Skill Choose one of the words you defined in **Try Your Skill** in the last lesson. Make a list of several specific details you might use to expand the three-part general definition you wrote for that word.

Now Write   Write the first draft of your explanatory paragraph. Include a strong topic sentence that presents a good general definition of your subject. Write an ending sentence that leaves the reader with an interesting thought or detail about your subject. Save your paragraph in your folder.

Another Chance

Revising Your Definition

Here's the Idea   Your reader should have a perfectly clear understanding of the subject you have defined. Read your first draft thoroughly to be sure that the content and the presentation are absolutely clear. Be sure that your writing style suits your purpose and is appropriate to your audience. Answer these questions as you revise your paragraph.

1. Does my topic sentence give a clear three-part definition?
2. Have I included enough details to fully develop my topic?
3. Did I organize the details logically?
4. Have I used transitional words and phrases where needed?
5. Did I write a strong ending sentence?

After you have revised your paragraph, proofread it for errors in grammar, usage, and mechanics.

Check It Out   Notice how this paragraph was revised.

The papaya is a large *,melon-like* fruit that grows on *small* trees. *throughout Central America.* The papaya *varies* goes from yellow to orange *in color* and is shaped like a pear. *the fruit* *somewhat, only much larger.* *color of the* Its taste is like a cantaloupe. *reminds many people of* In central America *,the papaya* it is eaten as *enjoyed at* breakfast. And is also used for pies and sherberts. *It* *cooked into* *frozen in* *Unfortunately, the* It's too bad it *papaya* can't be shipped over long distances because of a space in its *the hollow cavity* middle. This space causes it to come apart when it is soft. That *cavity* *the fruit* *break down* *ripe* is why many people will never get to eat this fruit. *throughout the world* *enjoy* *a chance* *delicious*

164

- How has this paragraph been improved through revision?

Try Your Skill Revise the following paragraph. Compare your revision with those of your classmates.

A wolf looks like a German shepherd dog. They avoid human beings. It is very powerful, and can run for hours in search of prey. Some people think that wolfs live only in Canada. But they also live in Europe, Asia and in Northern United States. It has a long bushy tail and ears, that are always standing up. Farmers and ranchers used to offer rewards for wolf skins because wolfs sometimes steal livestock. And many people fear them. They seldom attack people. Most male wolves weigh over 100 pounds. Females are lighter. They can be white, black, gray, or brown, and there fur is very valuable because it is so beautiful. But I think wolfs should be protected.

Keep This in Mind

- Revise your explanatory paragraph to be sure it is clear and exact. The development of the definition should be well organized.

Now Write Revise your explanatory paragraph that states a definition, following the guidelines in this lesson. When you are satisfied that your ideas are clear and well organized, and that you have chosen interesting and suitable language, proofread your paragraph for errors in grammar, usage, and mechanics. Then make a final copy of your paragraph. Save your revised paragraph in your folder.

Writing a Composition

Three-Part Harmony

What Is a Composition?

Here's the Idea   A **composition** is a group of paragraphs dealing with a single main idea. A composition, like a paragraph, can be a narrative, a description, or an explanation. It also has a definite beginning, middle, and end. These parts are called the introduction, the body, and the conclusion.

The **introduction** is a single paragraph. It presents the topic of the composition. It also captures the interest of the audience.

The **body** is made up of several paragraphs. These paragraphs support and develop the main idea presented in the introduction. The body may contain the events of a story or the sensory details of a description. It may also contain the step-by-step details of a process or a group of facts used to support an opinion.

The **conclusion** is the last part of the composition. The conclusion gives the reader the feeling that the composition is over. It often restates the main idea of the composition. It may also summarize or draw a lesson from the ideas in the body.

Check It Out   Read this composition.

An Unusual Trip

Last summer, I was a ranch hand at the Lazy K, and my girlfriend Janie was waitressing ninety miles away. We wrote or phoned each other almost every day, but I still missed Janie. Early one morning, my boss said that I could have the day off.

I did not have a minute to spare, so I saddled up Panhandler and raced him to Seven Corners. I was told at the bus station that the bus had come through town just moments before I had. Luckily a rancher driving a load of hogs into the city said that I was welcome to ride along if I didn't mind riding with his livestock. I hopped in among the pigs, and off we went.

Two hours later, I caught sight of Janie's restaurant. Then I saw Janie coming up the street.

"Janie!" I shouted.

"Willie! What are you doing here? I'm on my way to the bus stop," Janie replied. "My boss gave me the afternoon off, so I planned to take a little trip."

"Where?" I asked miserably.

"Some ranch called the Lazy K," she teased, grabbing my arm and tugging me along behind her.

- What kind of composition is this? How do you know?
- Does the introduction capture your interest?
- Does the conclusion signal an end to the composition?

Try Your Skill   Which part of a composition does this paragraph come from? Write a brief explanation for your answer.

We are living in the age of the computer. Computers are used in every area of life from big business to small business, from supermarkets to super trains, from space stations to the home. To help young people cope with this new technology, computer science must become an important part of the course of studies in every high school.

Keep This in Mind

- A composition is a group of paragraphs that present and develop one main idea.
- A composition has an introduction, a body, and a conclusion.
- A composition may be narrative, descriptive, or explanatory.

Now Write   Read a brief article in one of your favorite magazines. Notice that it has an introduction, a body, and a conclusion. On a piece of paper, write the title of the article. Tell whether it is narrative, descriptive, or explanatory. Write the sentence that serves as the topic sentence. Save your work.

The Main Idea

Pre-Writing: Choosing a Topic

Here's the Idea Good compositions are full of details that appeal to the senses and interests of readers. Finding enough details to fill a composition will be easier if you choose a topic you already know something about.

To choose a good topic, think about the important people, places, things, and events in your life. What sports, hobbies, or other activities do you enjoy? Who are the most interesting people you've met? What people or events have influenced you most? What opinions, beliefs, or values do you have? What subjects in school do you find most interesting? Asking such questions will help you to find a topic you will enjoy.

You can also arrive at a topic by looking through your journal, watching television, or reading magazines, newspapers, and books. Brainstorming, clustering, class discussions, and interviews are also excellent sources of topics.

Once you choose a topic, narrow it to fit your composition. In other words, if your topic is very general, make it more specific. Do this by asking questions about the topic. Begin these questions with *who, what, where, when, why,* or *how.* For more information on narrowing a topic, see pages 88–89.

Check It Out Read the following list of topics:

a description of a football
the Civil War
learning to drive a car
New York City
how to apply for a job

a definition of *triangle*
the blue whale
a history of the Marine Corps
why seat belts should be
    mandatory
marine life of the Pacific

- Which of these topics are too broad for a five-paragraph composition? too narrow? just right? Explain your answers.

Try Your Skill Below is a list of general subjects. Choose one that interests you. Ask *who, what, where, when, why,* and *how* questions about it. Narrow the general subject until you have a specific topic that you could cover well in a five-paragraph composition. Write whether your composition would be a narrative, a description, or an explanation.

sporting events	brothers and sisters
July 4th	acts of courage
biology class	city adventures
the beach	hobbies

Keep This in Mind

- Choose a topic that you know something about and that interests you.
- Discover topics by reading your journal, books, magazines, and newspapers. Also try brainstorming, clustering, class discussions, and interviews.
- Narrow your topic to make it more specific.

Now Write Follow the guidelines in this lesson as you choose and narrow a topic. Be sure your topic is specific enough to be covered well in several paragraphs. You may want to use the topic you developed in **Try Your Skill.** Save your topic in your folder.

Picking up the Pieces

Pre-Writing: Organizing Your Ideas

Here's the Idea   The first step in writing a composition is to choose and narrow a topic. The next step is to select details to develop that topic. You may gather sensory details, specific examples, facts and statistics, or incidents or anecdotes.

The type of details you gather will depend upon the type of composition you are writing. For example, you could gather facts and statistics if you were writing a composition to support an opinion. If you were writing a descriptive composition, you would gather mostly sensory details. Sometimes you will gather more than one kind of detail to support and develop a topic.

Once you have gathered the details you will use in your composition, you must organize these details logically. Begin by getting rid of any details that are not related to your main idea. Then, decide which of the remaining details go together. Try to discover two or three major ideas to which the other details are related. Group your details around each of these major ideas. If you do not have enough information to support or develop a major idea, gather more details. Each of these groups of details will become a paragraph in your final composition.

The next step is to organize the idea groups and the details within each group. Do this as you would for any paragraph. Use any of the following methods of organization.

chronological order   spatial order
order of importance   general to specific order
most familiar to least   comparison and contrast
  familiar order

For more information about methods of organization, see pages 96–97.

Check It Out Read these notes for a descriptive composition.

Topic: the old Marine and Hardware Store
Details: kitchen items, straw brooms
fishing lures (feathers, brightly colored thread)
fishing rods/tackle boxes
sail cloth—white, yellow, blue
muffin tins (black, cast iron)
fishers/boaters paradise
row boats—small electric motors
hardware for do-it-yourselfers
shiny copper food molds
hammers, nails, screwdrivers, saws
bright-orange life preservers
plumbing supplies, fix-it manuals

- What kinds of details has the writer gathered?

Try Your Skill Group the pre-writing notes in **Check It Out** around three main ideas.

Keep This in Mind

- Gather specific examples, sensory details, facts and statistics, or incidents or anecdotes to support and develop the main idea of a composition.
- Group similar details around several main ideas.
- Organize main ideas and the details grouped around them into one of the following orders: chronological, spatial, order of importance, general to specific, most familiar to least familiar, or comparison and contrast.

Now Write Gather details to support and develop the topic you have chosen. Organize your details into idea groups. Arrange the idea groups and the details within them into an order that suits the purpose of your composition. Save your notes.

Explorations

Writing the First Draft

Here's the Idea   Writing the first draft of a composition is a process of exploration and discovery. At this stage you should not worry about the details of grammar, punctuation, capitalization, and spelling. Simply follow your organized list of pre-writing notes, and get your ideas down on paper.

Remember that your composition must have three parts: an introduction, a body, and a conclusion. When writing the introduction, be sure to state your topic clearly and directly. Try various ways of introducing the composition until you hit upon one that will capture the attention of your readers.

When writing the paragraphs of the body, make sure that each has a strong topic sentence. Present in a logical order the details that support this sentence. Use transitional words and phrases to show how these details are related.

When writing the conclusion, you have several choices. These depend upon the type of composition you are writing. You may simply tell the last event in a story. You may restate your main idea in different words and summarize your major points. You may also draw a moral from the material presented in the body. In any case, make sure that your reader is left with the feeling that the composition is over.

Check It Out   Read this first draft. It was written from the pre-writing notes in the last lesson.

> What I'm going to write about is this old general store in town. It's called the Marine and Hardware Store. It's been they're since 1910. That's a long time ago. The store has something for everyone. Seafarers and landlubbers alike.

In the center of it is all kinds of stuff for the kitchen. You can get straw brooms, black cast iron muffin pans, shinny copper molds, and pots and pans.

Along one wall are all kinds of hardware items for do-it-yourself projects. There are hammers, nails, and screwdrivers. Also saws, both regular and power. Plumbing supplies sit on long display shelves. There's even a book section with how-to-do-it manuals for home improvement projects.

In the back of the store is a large section called the Marina. There are many supplies for boaters and people who like to fish. You can get small row boats, electric motors, sail cloth, and bright-orange life preservers. There are also fishing rods, fancy fishing lures, and tackle boxes.

Whatever you want to buy they've got it. From outboard motors to food processors to electric cable, this is the store to find it. It's the most interesting store in town.

- Does this composition have an introduction, a body, and a conclusion? Identify each part. Does each part fulfill its purpose? Explain your answer.

Try Your Skill   Discuss with your classmates the strengths and weaknesses of the composition in **Check It Out**. Talk about some specific ways you could improve the composition.

Keep This in Mind

- Your first draft should have an introduction, a body, and a conclusion.
- Follow your organized pre-writing notes as you write.

Now Write   Using your pre-writing notes as a writing plan, write the first draft of your composition. Follow the guidelines in this lesson. Save your first draft in your folder.

Getting It Right

Revising: Content and Organization

Here's the Idea Good writing is almost always the result of good rewriting. This is why professional journalists, novelists, screenwriters, and playwrights usually revise their work thoroughly. Revising allows them to improve their work.

Revising is no less important when you write compositions. Once you have finished a first draft, look for ways to improve it. Read your composition several times. Pay special attention to the content, the organization, and the language. In this lesson, you will concentrate on the first two: content and organization.

Content refers to the ideas and the details you have used to develop your main idea. Ask yourself these questions about the content of your composition.

1. Is my main idea clearly expressed?
2. Have I included enough details to develop my main idea?
3. Have I chosen the right kinds of details for the type of composition I am writing?
4. Does my composition have unity? That is, do all my details help to support and develop my main idea?

Organization refers to the structure of your composition. Ask these questions to help check the organization of your work.

1. Does my composition have an introduction, a body, and a conclusion?
2. Does each paragraph have an interesting and informative topic sentence? Is this sentence supported by details?
3. Is my composition coherent? That is, are all of my ideas arranged in a clear, logical order?
4. Have I chosen a suitable method of organization?

Check It Out   Look at these paragraphs.

Christopher Columbus *is well known as the discoverer of America.* ~~was a sailor and navigator,~~ He was born in Genoa, *a port city on the northwest coast of Italy.* Altho the date of his birth isnt known, he was probably born sometime between August and October in 1451. ~~Genoa was once a Capital City in Italy.~~ Christopher was the first of five children who were born to Domenico and Susanna Colombo.

Not a lot is known about his youth. He always wanted to go to sea. He didn't go to school much. Most of what he knew he learned himself. He helped his father, a weaver, at the loom. ~~His mother's father had been a weaver.~~

- How has the writer improved these paragraphs?

Try Your Skill   Reread the composition about the Marine and Hardware Store. As a class, revise the content and organization. Add and take out details. Reorganize the details if you wish. Use the questions in this lesson to guide your revision. Save your work so that you can complete it in the next lesson.

Keep This in Mind

- When you revise, try to improve the content and organization of your work.

Now Write   Revise the content and organization of the composition you have been writing. Use the questions in this lesson to guide you. Save your work in your folder.

It's Your Choice

Revising: Word Choice and Proofreading

Here's the Idea   You have learned that it is important to check the content and organization of your writing when you revise. It is equally important to check the language you have used. Choosing the right words can transform dull, flat sentences and paragraphs into lively, interesting ones.

Word choice affects all aspects of your writing. In a description, carefully chosen nouns, adjectives, verbs, and adverbs can help you to suggest **mood. Sensory details** can also benefit from good word choice. The phrase "a lit pumpkin" is a sensory detail. However, the phrase "a pumpkin glowing in soft orange light" is a better expressed sensory detail.

Dialogue can be improved in two ways through careful selection of language. First, choosing the right words will make your characters believable. That is, teenagers will sound like teenagers, frightened children will sound frightened, and so on. Second, you can say more with a **dialogue tag** when the words are right. You can replace "he said" with more expressive tags, such as "he whispered" or "she yelled."

Appropriate **transitional words and phrases** can also improve your writing. They lead your readers from one idea to the next. They show how your ideas are related. They can help you to express chronological and spatial order.

In general, try to replace vague, general language when you revise. Look for specific nouns, adjectives, verbs, and adverbs that say exactly what you mean.

The final step in revising is **proofreading.** When you proofread, you look for and correct any errors you have made in grammar, usage, capitalization, punctuation, and spelling.

Check It Out Notice this further revision.

> *is well known as the*
> *discoverer of America.*
> Christopher Columbus ^~~was~~ a sailor and navigator, He was
> ^ *a port city on the northwest coast of Italy.*
> born in Genoa, Altho the date of his birth isnt known, he was
> probably born sometime between August and October in 1451.
> ~~Genoa was once a Capital City in Italy.~~ Christopher was the
> first of five children who were born to Domenico and Susanna
> Colombo.
>
> Not a lot is known about his youth. He always wanted to go
> to sea. He didn't go to school much. Most of what he knew he
> learned himself. He helped his father, a weaver, at the loom.
> ~~His mother's father had been a weaver.~~

- How have these paragraphs been improved through further revision?

Try Your Skill As a class, continue revising the Marine and Hardware Store composition. Work to improve the word choice. Then, proofread the composition. When you are finished, discuss how you have made the composition better.

Keep This in Mind

- When you revise, replace vague, general words with strong, specific ones.
- Proofread to find and correct errors in grammar, usage, and mechanics.

Now Write Finish revising your composition. Try to improve your word choice. Don't forget to proofread your work. When you are finished, make a final copy of your work. Save your composition in your folder.

What's Its Name?

Choosing a Title

Here's the Idea Whenever you write, you make many decisions. You decide whether to write a narrative, a description, or an explanation. You choose and narrow a topic. You also choose the details you want to include and the method of organization you want to use. Finally, you select the particular words with which to put your ideas down onto paper. Each of these decisions is important to producing interesting, effective writing.

Sometimes you must make yet another important decision. This decision concerns your title. Titles are usually not required for short pieces of writing such as paragraphs. However, longer pieces of writing such as compositions generally do have titles.

The title of a composition is often a simple phrase that suggests what the composition is about. "Learning to Surf" and "My Earliest Memory" are titles of this kind. They serve the purpose of introducing the composition to the reader, but they are not very interesting.

The best titles do more than just suggest the subject. They also capture the attention of the reader. There are many techniques that writers use to do this. Some writers create titles that use puns or clichés. Others use rhyming words or repeated sounds in their titles. Still others try to write titles that express odd or unusual ideas.

The best way to learn how to write titles is to examine the titles that you read in everyday life. When you come across a title that seems particularly good, ask yourself why. Soon, you will learn many of the tricks that writers use when creating titles. Then, when you have to write a title of your own, you will be able to draw upon a model from your own experience.

Check It Out   Read the following titles of stories you may have read.

"The Red-Headed League"	"Jingle Bells"
"By the North Gate"	"The Stone Boy"
"The Circus"	"Evening Flight"
"The Fan Club"	"Happy Birthday"
"See How They Run"	"Strawberry Ice Cream Soda"

- Are these good titles? Why?

Try Your Skill   Choose four of the following possible topics for longer pieces of writing. For each topic, write two titles that might work. Try to express the idea of each topic in simple or surprising titles.

1. a story about a trip you took
2. a description of your neighborhood
3. a report on nutritious breakfast foods
4. an explanation of how to frame a picture
5. an explanation of why space travel is important
6. a story about an imaginary character
7. a report on a famous bridge
8. an explanation of what a hurricane is
9. a description of a beach you like
10. a report on a United States President

Keep This in Mind

- Use a title for longer pieces of writing. A good title should suggest the main idea of your writing. A good title should also attract a reader's interest.

Now Write   Write several titles for the composition you are working on. Each title should be interesting and should suggest the main idea of your composition. Choose the title you like the best. Write it at the top of your revised composition.

Just a Reminder

Guidelines for Writing a Composition

In the next few sections of this book, you will be writing many different kinds of compositions. Whatever type of composition you write, however, the process of writing will remain the same. Below is a list of guidelines to follow when you write a composition. Refer to them often as you write your compositions.

Guidelines for Writing a Composition

Pre-Writing

- Choose a topic that interests you and that you know something about. Narrow the topic so that you can cover it well in the assigned length of your composition.
- Identify your purpose and your audience.
- Gather details to develop your topic.
- Group similar details around two or three main ideas.
- Organize your details into an order that suits the type of composition you are writing.

Writing the First Draft

- Begin your composition with an interesting introductory paragraph that tells your reader what your composition is about.
- After your introduction, write the body of your composition. Use your organized details to develop your topic. Each group of details will become a paragraph in the body of your composition.
- Use transitional words and phrases to lead your readers from one idea to the next.

- Add, take out, and reorganize your ideas if you need to.
- End your first draft with a concluding paragraph that sums up your ideas.
- Add an interesting title to your composition.

Revising

- Be sure your composition has an introduction, a body, and a conclusion.
- Check to see that you have included enough details to develop your topic.
- Organize the paragraphs and the ideas within them logically.
- Be sure the topic sentence of each paragraph presents the main idea of that paragraph.
- Use effective transitional words to make your ideas flow smoothly.
- Make sure you have used vivid language. Use language that suits the audience you are writing for.
- Proofread to find and correct errors in grammar, capitalization, punctuation, and spelling.

Final Copy

- Rewrite your composition neatly in ink on white, lined paper. Or, type your composition, double spaced, on plain white paper.
- Write your name, subject, and the date in the upper right-hand corner of your paper.
- Proofread your final copy one last time. Neatly correct any errors you find.

The Narrative Composition

Start Your Engines

Pre-Writing: Planning a Narrative

Here's the Idea A narrative composition is a story. Stories come in many different forms. However, all share a few elements in common. These elements are the parts of a story— setting, characters, plot, and conflict. To plan a narrative composition, make pre-writing notes on each of these parts.

The **setting** is the background of the story. It tells when and where the action takes place. To plan the setting, choose the time and place of the action. Then, ask questions to fill in the details. Does the story take place in the past, present, or future? Does it take place in the country or the city? Is it set inside or outside? What time of year is it? What time of day?

The **characters** are the people or animals in the story. In a short narrative, the number of characters is small. Ask the following questions when planning characters for a story: What people or animals do I want to write about? Will they be real or imaginary? How will they look, act, and speak? What is important to them? What makes them different from one another?

The **plot** is the series of events in the story. The first events in the story introduce a conflict. The **conflict** is a problem or difficulty faced by the main character. The events that follow show how the main character deals with and finally solves the conflict. When planning the plot of a story, ask these questions: Will the events in the story be real or imaginary? What conflict will my main character face? What events will create this conflict? What events will take place after the conflict is introduced? How will my main character solve this conflict?

Check It Out Read these pre-writing notes.

Setting: Caliphstan, a nation in another world
Characters: Kyril, a young woman; Arius, Kyril's uncle

Plot: Kyril faces an important decision about her future
Conflict: Kyril's desire to please her family versus her need
to be true to herself

- Do these pre-writing notes contain all of the important elements of a narrative?

Try Your Skill   Read this opening for an imaginary narrative.

The letter Kyril held in her trembling hands was brief and to the point.

> Her Eminence, the Exeter of Caliph, is pleased to announce your appointment to the Guardians of Caliphstan. Present yourself to the captain of the Guardians at dawn on the first day of Janius.

Kyril could hardly believe her eyes. An appointment to the Guardians was the dream of every young citizen. The Guardians were the elite defenders of Caliphstan. It was the Guardians who had finally defeated the cruel Voss warriors during the War of the Ages. The Guardians had put down the Illyrian insurrection and freed the Bliss people. Indeed, the Guardians' history was a catalog of the glories of the nation of Caliphstan. And now their history was to become Kyril's history. She felt tears well up in her eyes; not tears of joy or relief, however, but tears of sadness and frustration. Kyril had no real desire to become a Guardian. She wanted a much different life.

How does this opening set the scene? What do you learn about the main character? How is the conflict suggested?

Keep This in Mind

- A narrative has a setting, characters, a plot, and a conflict.

Now Write   Think of a story you would like to tell. It might be something that happened to you or to someone you know. It might be the product of your imagination. Write down story ideas and details as they occur to you. Save your notes.

Know the Course

Pre-Writing: Developing a Plot

Here's the Idea   As you learned in Part 1, every story is about a series of events called the plot. To develop a plot, you must first decide what your central conflict will be.

The conflict may be internal or external. An **internal conflict** takes place in the mind of a character. For instance, a character might have to choose between being wrongly accused and betraying a friend. An **external conflict** takes place between a character and some outside force. This force can be something in nature, another character, or a social custom or rule. For example, a character might be in conflict with a raging forest fire.

After choosing a conflict, you can begin to develop your plot. The pre-writing notes for your plot will be a list of events. First, list the events that suggest the conflict. Then, list the events that take place as the main character deals with the conflict. Finally, decide what event ends the conflict. As you list these events, put them in chronological order.

If you wish to, you may vary the order of your events by inserting a flashback. A **flashback** is a description of something that happened in the past, before the first event in the story. You can use a flashback to explain how certain things in your story came to be. For example, you might use a flashback to explain a young boy's fear of water. You could describe how, years before, the boy almost drowned in a boating accident.

Check It Out   Continue reading this narrative.

> Kyril stared out the window. She remembered how, as a child, her father and mother would tell her stories about the adventures of the Guardians. Kyril and her friends would often play at being Guardians, defending the fields around their homes against invisible Voss warriors and imaginary Illyrian slavemasters. Kyril's uncle, Arius, was a much-decorated

Guardian who had offered Kyril his counsel as she had prepared for the rigorous mental and physical tests that led to becoming a Guardian. Indeed, much of her young life had been influenced by the legends of the Guardians and her parents' strong desire that she should join this elite group.

Kyril remembered another incident from her past. When she was ten star years, her mother had taken her on a voyage to the floating cities of New Caliphstan. Kyril was awestruck as the giant starcruiser approached the first city, gleaming in the reflected light from the sun.

"Whose dream were these places, Mother?" Kyril asked, her face pressed against the cruiser's observation window.

"The Builders have prepared them," her mother replied. "They designed them and built them."

As the cruiser maneuvered for docking, Kyril decided deep in her heart that one day she would help to build the floating cities that her children's children would call home.

Now, Kyril thought, *I must choose my future.* It was a choice Kyril wished she didn't have to make.

- How does the flashback help explain the present conflict?

Try Your Skill   Think about an event from your past that has had an influence on the person you are today. Write a brief narrative paragraph telling about this event.

Keep This in Mind

- In a narrative, the conflict is explained through the plot, a chronological series of events.
- A flashback is an event from the past that explains something about the present.

Now Write   Choose a story to tell. Make some notes about setting, characters, plot, and conflict. Then develop the plot by making a chronological list of the events that will tell your story. Save these pre-writing notes in your folder.

Choosing Your Lane

Pre-Writing: Developing a Point of View

Here's the Idea   Before you write a narrative, you must choose a narrator. A narrator is the person who tells your story. You may choose a narrator who is a character in the story, or one who is not. Your choice will determine the point of view of your story. **Point of view** refers to the eyes and mind through which the story is told.

If you choose a narrator who is a character in the story, you will be using the **first-person point of view.** In stories told from this point of view, the narrator takes part in the events of the story. The narrator tells about these events using the pronouns *I*, *me*, and *we*. The reader learns about only what this one character, the narrator, sees and knows.

If you choose a narrator who is not a character in the story, you will be using the **third-person point of view.** In stories told from this point of view, the narrator is an outsider. The narrator tells about the events of the story using pronouns such as *he*, *she*, *it*, and *they*.

There are two kinds of third-person point of view that you can use. One is called **third-person limited.** In stories told in this way, the narrator reports only what the characters say and do. The other third-person point of view is called **third-person omniscient.** The word *omniscient* means "all knowing." In a story told in this way, the narrator knows everything about the characters. The narrator reports not only what the characters say and do, but also what they think and feel.

Check It Out   Read this passage.

> Kyril's parents were ecstatic when she told them the news. "Imagine, Rana," her father enthused, "our daughter a Guardian."

"She trained hard, Elech," her mother said. "She knew how much this meant to us."

Kyril turned away, feeling sick at heart. How could she possibly turn down the appointment? Her parents' disappointment would be too much to bear. Still, her dream was, as it had always been, to become a Builder. Kyril knew she needed help, and she knew just whom she must seek it from.

"Mother, Father," Kyril said, "I have much to prepare myself for. Do you suppose I might visit Uncle Arius, to gain his counsel?"

"A splendid idea," her father said. "Arius has much to tell you. I shall contact him this evening."

- Is the narrator a character in the story or an outsider?
- What point of view has the writer chosen for this story? Explain how you know.

Try Your Skill   Imagine that you are Kyril, the central character in the narrative you have been reading. Imagine that you are telling your own story. Rewrite the paragraphs in **Check It Out** using the first-person point of view.

Keep This in Mind

- Point of view is the eyes and mind through which a story is told.
- A story can be told from the first-person, third-person limited, or third-person omniscient point of view.

Now Write   Choose a point of view that suits the story you are telling. Add your choice to your pre-writing notes. Save your notes in your folder.

Moving into the Lead

Writing the First Draft

Here's the Idea After choosing a point of view, you are ready to write your first draft. This draft should have three parts: an introduction, a body, and a conclusion. Use your pre-writing notes as you write each part. Feel free to add or change details as they occur to you. However, stick to one point of view and to one central conflict.

Begin with the introductory paragraph. In this paragraph, describe the setting and introduce your characters. The beginning of a narrative should also suggest the conflict.

Next, write the paragraphs of the body. Use the list of events given in your pre-writing notes. Start by developing the conflict. Do not simply *tell* your readers what the conflict is. Instead, *show* your readers the conflict through the actions, speech, and thoughts of your characters. In the rest of the body, describe the events that further develop the conflict. Show how the main character struggles with his or her major problem or difficulty.

In the concluding paragraph, describe the event that settles the conflict. Remember that this event is usually a decision or action on the part of the main character. Do not simply tell your readers how the conflict is settled. Instead, show the conflict being settled by describing what the main character does to end it.

Check It Out Read this paragraph from the body of a narrative.

> During the brief flight to Nutrus, home base of the Guardians, Kyril was beset by doubts. *Perhaps I'm being foolish,* she thought. *Anyone else would give a fortune for an appointment to the Guardians. Besides, if I don't accept the ap-*

pointment, my parents will be furious. They've done so much for me, and seeing me become a Guardian would please them so. Still Kyril could not forget her dream. Remembering the floating cities of New Caliphstan and the vow she made as a young girl seemed to strengthen her resolve. Why shouldn't I become a builder, she reasoned. It's my life, after all. I should be free to pursue my own dreams. Yet, as the shuttle craft eased into the landing bay, Kyril remained undecided. Seeing her uncle in the arrival lounge, dressed in the striking silvers of a Guardian general, only added to her confusion.

- Does this body paragraph further develop the conflict of the narrative? Explain your answer.

Try Your Skill Imagine you are writing a story about a character's struggle for survival after his light plane crashes into a dense rain forest. Write an opening paragraph or two that sets the story in motion by introducing the main character and describing the event that begins his struggles. Compare your opening with those of your classmates.

Keep This in Mind

- In a narrative, the introduction presents the setting and the characters. It also suggests the conflict.
- The body develops the plot and the conflict.
- The conclusion settles the conflict and ends the story.

Now Write Use your pre-writing notes to write the first draft of the introduction to your narrative composition. Be sure your introduction sets the scene, introduces the characters, and suggests a conflict. Save your work in your folder.

Picking up the Pace

The First Draft: Dialogue

Here's the Idea   Many narratives about people include dialogue. Dialogue is simply conversation between characters. Writers use dialogue to communicate important information to their readers.

You can use dialogue to reveal the personalities of your characters. Through dialogue, you can show what your characters think and feel about themselves, about events, and about other characters. You can also use dialogue to tell what events are happening in a story.

When writing dialogue, keep in mind the way people actually speak. Try to make your dialogue as realistic as possible. Use dialogue tags to tell who is speaking and how the words are spoken. A dialogue tag is an expression such as *Laurie replied* or *Carlos whispered*. You can use dialogue tags to show how a character is feeling. For instance, instead of writing *Carlotta said*, you can write *Carlotta shouted*, or *Carlotta whimpered*.

When you give the exact words of a speaker, use quotation marks around them. Begin a new paragraph each time a different character speaks. For more information on writing dialogue correctly, see pages 683–687 in the Handbook.

Check It Out   Read this dialogue.

After dinner on her first night in Nutrus, Kyril explained her problem to Arius.

"What?" Arius exploded. "Not accept your appointment to the Guardians? It's preposterous! Unheard of! An insult to Her Eminence, the Exeter. Have you taken leave of your senses, Kyril?"

"No," Kyril replied softly, "In fact, in some ways I've never been more sure of myself."

"Why did you train so long and hard?" Arius demanded.

"Because I wanted to please Rana and Elech," Kyril answered. "I never thought I'd actually make it."

"Not make it?" Arius sputtered. "You've a brilliant mind, Kyril. A strong body. You were born to be a Guardian."

"I was born to be Kyril," she said simply. "And Kyril's dream is to be a Builder. Have you never pursued a dream, Arius?"

"Of course I have," Arius replied gruffly. "That's why I am a Guardian general today."

"Then help me to have my dream, Arius. Show me the way," Kyril pleaded.

- What does this dialogue reveal about Kyril and Arius?
- Do the dialogue tags explain how each character is feeling? Explain your answer.

Try Your Skill   Write the following dialogue correctly. To check your work, see pages 683–687 in the Handbook.

My tooth hurts so much moaned Joan who was holding her jaw I know how it must ache said Dr. Goldberg gently this won't hurt a bit is that a promise asked Joan Dr. Goldberg reassured her all right said Joan with a sigh let's get on with it.

Keep This in Mind

- Dialogue is conversation between two characters.
- Dialogue can reveal the thoughts and feelings of your characters. It can also advance the action of a story.

Now Write   Continue writing the first draft of the narrative you began in the previous lesson. Add dialogue in appropriate places. Follow the rules for writing dialogue correctly. Save your work in your folder.

One Lap To Go

The First Draft: Transitions

Here's the Idea   As you know, the events in a story should be told in chronological order. If the order of the events is not clear, the reader will become confused. When writing the first draft of a story, keep the order of events clear by using transitions.

In a story, use transitional words and phrases that tell *when* events occur. They are used within paragraphs and between paragraphs. Notice how such words and phrases are used in the following paragraph.

> *While* Felicidad filled the tank with fresh water, I changed the filter. *Soon,* the aquarium was ready for its new occupants. *First*, we poured in the water containing the neon tetras. These were the smallest of our fish. *Then*, we added the angel fish and the pearl gouramis. *Only later* did we realize that the tiny tetras might be in danger of becoming some larger fish's seafood dinner.

You must be particularly careful to use transitions whenever you write flashbacks. A sudden change in time can confuse your readers unless the change is signaled by a transition. Always use transitions, such as *a while before* or *earlier that morning,* to let your readers know what is happening. Then, when you want to return to the present time in your story, use another transition, such as *now* or *at present.*

Check It Out   Read these paragraphs.

> Two days after her dinner with Arius, Kyril left for home. True to his word, Arius had helped Kyril formulate a plan. First she would contact the personal emissary to the Exeter of Cal-

iph. Kyril would thank the Exeter for her kind consideration, express her disappointment at having to decline the appointment, and petition Her Eminence to release her from the Guardians. Next, she would apply for admission to the Builder's Institute. Finally, and this was the part Kyril dreaded, she would inform her parents of her decision. Arius had promised to help with this task.

When the starcruiser was safely in dock, Kyril walked out to meet her waiting parents. She spied them in a corner of the arrival lounge. It was clear from their faces that Arius had already done his work.

"Mother, Father, I am pleased to see you," Kyril said.

"And we to see you," her father said stiffly.

Rana smiled warmly at her daughter.

"Come Kyril, Elech. We have much to talk over," she said.

- Which transitional words and phrases within the first paragraph tell *when?*
- What transitional phrase links the first paragraph with what has come before it? the second paragraph with the first?

Try Your Skill   Look at the list of transitional words and phrases on pages 120–121. See how many words and phrases you can add to this list. Try to add at least ten. Compare your additions with those of your classmates.

Keep This in Mind

- Use transitional words and phrases to show the order of time within and between paragraphs.

Now Write   Finish writing the first draft of your story. Add transitional words and phrases wherever they are needed. Be sure to solve the conflict at the end of your narrative. Save your work in your folder.

The Checkered Flag

Revising Your Narrative Composition

Here's the Idea   You have heard and read many stories. Use this experience to identify strengths and weaknesses when you revise your own narrative composition.

Once you have completed your rough draft, read your story several times. Pretend that you are reading the story in a magazine. If you were just a reader of the story, not its author, would you find the story interesting? Would you like some parts of the story and not like other parts? If so, which parts do you think could be improved? Use the following questions to find ways to make your story better.

1. Does the story have a point? Is that point clear?
2. Does the introduction set the scene and introduce the characters? Does it suggest the conflict?
3. Does the story seem complete? Do more events need to be added to complete the story? Do more details need to be added to keep the reader interested?
4. Are the events arranged in chronological order?
5. If any flashbacks are used, are they effective?
6. Is the conflict clear? Does the body of the story develop the conflict in an interesting way?
7. Does the story use a single point of view throughout?
8. Does the story use dialogue to relate events and to reveal the thoughts and feelings of characters? Does it use dialogue tags to tell who is speaking?
9. Does the story use transitions effectively?
10. Does the conclusion show how the conflict is solved? Is the conclusion effective and interesting?

When you are satisfied with your story, proofread it. Find and correct any errors in grammar, usage, and mechanics.

Check It Out   Notice how this narrative has been revised.

¶ *Back at home,*

∧Kyril and her parents~~talked about~~ *discussed* the future.

"I took the tests∧ to ~~make~~ you∧happy *only* *please* Kyril said." I knew how much it meant to you."

"It did mean a∧~~lot~~ to us" Elech said. *great deal* "But your happiness is more important to us than∧ ~~we are.~~ *our own desires."*

"Kyril"∧ Rana said∧ "the decisions you make∧about your future *now* are very important. You∧ ~~should~~ not∧change your ideals. Be- *must* *compromise* come a Builder∧Kyril∧The best builder you can be. That ~~would~~ *will* make us happy."

- How has this first draft been improved?

Try Your Skill   Here is the ending of the narrative you have been reading. Use your revising skills to improve it.

Kyril lay in bed. She thought about her parents. How wonderful they were. How understanding. She thought about the floating cities. She wanted to take her daughter their one day. She hoped her daughter would say "Mother, whose dream was this place."

"Mine" Kyril would reply softly. "All mine".

Keep This in Mind

- Revise your narrative so that it is the best story you can tell.

Now Write   Use the guidelines in this lesson to revise the first draft of your narrative. Proofread it for errors in grammar, usage, and mechanics. Make a final copy. Save your story.

The Descriptive Composition

A Sensible Approach

Pre-Writing: Using Sensory Details

Here's the Idea A descriptive composition is much like a picture. It presents a portrait of a person, place, or thing. Like a picture, a descriptive composition can communicate both information and feelings about the subject.

When planning a descriptive composition, you should choose a subject that appeals to several senses. A song, for example, would not be a good subject. It appeals only to the sense of hearing. However, a rock concert would be a good subject. It appeals to several senses at once.

Once you have chosen a subject, your next step is to gather sensory details. These are details that tell how your subject looks, sounds, smells, feels, and tastes. Not every subject can be described with all five senses. However, you should try to gather many different sensory details about your subject. Gather these details through observation or by using your memory.

When you have finished gathering your details, look them over carefully. All of the details should be about your subject. For example, suppose you were writing about a concert. All of the details would be about the concert. Some details might be about the crowd. Others might be about the atmosphere, the group that was performing, or the music itself. By grouping like details together, you can create idea groups that will become paragraphs in your composition.

After you organize your details into groups, you must decide in what order to present them. Most descriptive compositions are organized according to spatial order. **Spatial order** shows how details are related to each other in space. If your details do not lend themselves to spatial order, you may want to arrange them in whatever order you want the reader to notice them. To learn more about organizing a description, see pages 126–129.

Check It Out   Read these pre-writing notes.

Topic: Greenleaf Beach

air mattress bobbing on waves
hot dogs, chips, candy, ice cream
concession stand (bright red roof)
little kids splashing each other in shallow water
volleyball game in progress ("slap" of ball)
refreshing lemonade, colas, iced tea
lifeguard rowing yellow patrol boat
water cold but not unbearable
kids building sand sculptures
long lines for snacks

* What senses do these pre-writing notes appeal to?

Try Your Skill   The notes in **Check It Out** can be divided into three idea groups. Decide what those idea groups are. Then, on a piece of paper, write a word or phrase to describe each idea group. Under each word or phrase, list the details from the pre-writing notes that belong in that group. Save these notes.

Keep This in Mind

* Develop a descriptive composition with sensory details.
* Organize like details into idea groups.
* Organize your idea groups and the details within them according to spatial order or in the order that you want the reader to notice them.

Now Write   Choose a topic for a descriptive composition. Make a list of sensory details. Organize like details into idea groups. Arrange the idea groups and the details within them in spatial order or in the order that you want your readers to notice them. Save your organized notes in your folder.

Make the Scene

Writing the First Draft

Here's the Idea   When you write the first draft of your descriptive composition, try to picture your subject clearly in your mind. The clearer this picture is, the more vivid your description will be.

Begin your first draft with an introduction. Try to capture the interest and imagination of your readers. State the specific subject of your description in one sentence of the introduction.

Develop the description of your subject in the body of the composition. Each group of ideas in your pre-writing notes will become a paragraph in the body of your composition.

End your composition with a strong conclusion. This paragraph should sum up the feelings and ideas in the composition.

Don't forget to show the reader where things are in your description by using transitional words and phrases. Examples of words and phrases you can use include *on top of, behind, above, below, to the left, to the right, near,* and *far.*

Try to create a specific mood with your description. Choose nouns, verbs, adjectives, and adverbs that will suggest a certain feeling. To learn more about mood, see pages 130–131.

Check It Out   Read the introduction and body of this descriptive composition.

> Volcanoes have always fascinated me. I have seen color photographs of the Hawaiian volcano Kilauea shooting flames and molten, glowing lava. I have seen other pictures showing the volcanic island Surtsey with dense clouds of dust pouring from the summit. I thought I knew exactly what it would be like to stare into the crater of a volcano. However, my mental image was changed forever by the surprising appearance of Haleakala Crater on the island of Maui in Hawaii.

The towering Haleakala was much bigger than I had expected. The crater itself, which we were allowed to enter, is seven and a half miles long, two and a half miles wide, and more than two thousand feet deep. We could see that the crater formed a bowl-shaped depression dotted with powdery black cones sticking up from its surface. These cones appeared from a distance to be about as tall as a person. As we approached them, though, we realized that they were actually about ten stories tall.

The name *Haleakala* means "House of the Sun," but from its depths, the crater resembled photographs I had seen of the surface of the moon. Everywhere we saw reddish dust and cinders. It was also strangely quiet. The crunching of cinders underfoot was the only sound. The air felt hot and dry, and the gritty dust rose everywhere until I could taste it.

- Does the introduction present the subject?
- Is the body developed with vivid sensory details? What senses do the details appeal to?

Try Your Skill Reread the pre-writing notes you organized in **Try Your Skill** in Part 1. Select one of the three idea groups you developed. Use the notes from this idea group to write a descriptive paragraph. Be sure the paragraph has a strong topic sentence and that the details are well organized. Compare your paragraph with those of your classmates.

Keep This in Mind

- In a descriptive composition, use transitional words and phrases that tell *where* to show the order of your details.

Now Write Begin writing the first draft of your descriptive composition. For now, just write the introduction and the body of your composition. Save your work in your folder.

The End in Sight

The First Draft: Ending a Description

Here's the Idea Suppose that you are listening to your favorite song on the radio. You are really enjoying the music when, suddenly, the disc jockey interrupts the song for a commercial. How would this make you feel? Of course, you would feel cheated. To be completely satisfying, a song must have a conclusion.

A good conclusion is also important in a descriptive composition. The conclusion of a descriptive composition should be a single paragraph. The paragraph should tie together the ideas presented in the rest of the composition. It should also tell the reader how you feel about your subject.

To write the conclusion of a description, think about the ideas and details you have presented. What is the mood created by these details? How can you summarize your feelings about them? What lasting impression about your subject do you want to leave with your readers?

Always make sure that the conclusion follows naturally from what has come before it. For instance, if the composition is light and cheery, the conclusion should not be sad or gloomy. Only if you keep the same mood will the conclusion of your composition make sense.

Check It Out Review the descriptive composition about Haleakala Crater that is shown in the last lesson. Notice how the description is organized. Then read the following conclusion.

> After our return climb up one of the trails within the crater, I thought about my previous images of volcanoes. I thought of the stories I had read about Stromboli and Vesuvius and Krakatoa and their violent eruptions. I realized that quiet, colorful

Haleakala had impressed me because it was so different. In fact, Haleakala Crater was so unexpected that I think I shall never forget it.

- Does the conclusion summarize the ideas presented in the composition?
- How does the writer feel about the subject? How do you know?

Try Your Skill   Imagine you have written the composition about Haleakala. What kind of conclusion would you write? Draft a concluding paragraph for this composition. Sum up the ideas in the composition. Leave the reader with some lasting impression of the subject. Compare your conclusion with those of your classmates.

Keep This in Mind

- In the conclusion, summarize your ideas and show your feelings about the subject.

Now Write   Review the introduction and body of the descriptive composition you have been writing. Then write the conclusion. Summarize your ideas and your feelings in the conclusion. Save your first draft in your folder.

The Final View

Revising Your Descriptive Paragraph

Here's the Idea   The last step in writing a descriptive composition is revising. When you revise, keep in mind that your purpose is to describe your subject as clearly as possible. As you read your first draft, ask yourself whether your composition achieves this goal.

Here are some other questions to ask yourself as you revise your work.

1. Does the introductory paragraph tell the reader what my subject is?

2. Does each paragraph in the body have a good topic sentence?

3. Did I include enough sensory details to develop my description completely?

4. Did I arrange my details in a logical order?

5. Did I use transitional words and phrases to make the order of the details clear?

6. Does the description create a single strong mood or feeling? Did I use specific language to create this mood?

7. Does the conclusion sum up the ideas in my composition? Does it tell the reader how I feel about my subject?

After you have revised the content, organization, and language of your description, proofread the composition carefully. Check for errors in grammar, capitalization, punctuation, and spelling. Correct any errors that you find.

Check It Out   Notice how this introduction to a descriptive composition has been revised.

My Aunt Hattie's house is a nice place wonderful to visit. The house was built over two hundred years ago, and has many unusual features that Its got a lot of things you can't find on houses today. From deep red topped to its ornate Its got towers with iron spikes and leded glass. black wrought-living windows, Aunt Hattie's house is Its like a museum of days gone by.

- How has the topic sentence been improved?
- What kinds of details have been added during revision?
- What errors in grammar and mechanics were corrected?

Try Your Skill Revise the following paragraph from the same composition.

In the basement the floor is made with cobblestone bricks. Their is an old coal cellar. Its really neat inside it. The walls have all been blackened with coal dust. The basement also got a wine cellar. There is metal racks against the wall where wine bottles were. Because the ground has shifted over the years, the floor is very uneven. Its funny how it seems to roll along.

Keep This in Mind

- Revise your descriptive composition so that your subject is described clearly and completely.

Now Write Using the guidelines in this lesson, revise your descriptive composition. Proofread your work. Give your composition a title. Then, make a clean, neat final copy. Proofread this copy one last time and neatly correct any errors you find. Save your composition in your folder.

The Explanatory Composition
Explaining a Process

The Way It's Done

Pre-Writing: Planning an Explanation

Here's the Idea   Everyone has given directions at one time or another. You may have given directions explaining how to make something, such as scrambled eggs or a model rocket. You may have given directions explaining how to do something, such as lift weights or paint with watercolors.

One type of explanatory composition that explains a process includes a set of directions. The directions tell how to do something. Another composition that explains a process might tell how things work or happen. A composition of this type might explain how a car muffler works or how earthquakes happen.

Both types of explanatory compositions explain the steps in a process. When writing such a composition, you must explain each step simply and clearly. You start with the first step and proceed through all the steps in the order in which they happen or should be done.

The first step in writing your explanatory composition is to choose and narrow a topic. The best ideas come from personal experience. For example, if you have played football, you may be able to explain the process of getting prepared for a game. If you have repaired bicycles, you may be able to explain how bicycle gears operate. Always choose a process that you know well so that you can explain it thoroughly.

When you gather details for your pre-writing notes, be sure to include all of the steps in the process you want to explain. If you leave out an important step, your readers may not be able to understand the process. Also be sure to explain the process clearly and directly. List any tools, ingredients, or materials required in the process. Add this list to your pre-writing notes.

Check It Out Read these pre-writing notes.

How To Take Good Photographs

1. Get to know your camera
   no need for expensive camera
   study manual
   learn use of all dials, buttons, and rings
   practice with camera
2. Learn about types of film
   black and white or color
   indoor, outdoor films
3. Take pictures
   subject must be in focus
   hold camera steady
   press shutter-release smoothly

- Do the notes clearly list the steps in a process?

Try Your Skill Do some brainstorming about processes. Make a list of ten processes that would make good topics for an explanatory composition. Save your list.

Keep This in Mind

- When you want to explain a process, write an explanatory composition.
- In your pre-writing notes, include all of the important steps in the process. List any tools, ingredients, or materials that are needed.
- Explain each step in the process simply and clearly.

Now Write Choose a process that you would like to explain. You may want to choose one of the topics you developed in **Try Your Skill.** Narrow your topic. Make a set of pre-writing notes to explain your topic. Be sure to include all of the important steps in the process. List any necessary tools, ingredients, or materials. Save your notes in your folder.

Stepping Ahead

Pre-Writing: Using Step-by-Step Order

Here's the Idea In your pre-writing notes for an explanatory composition, you will have a topic and a list of steps. Before you can begin to write, you must organize these steps logically.

The best way to organize an explanatory composition that explains a process, is to follow **step-by-step order.** This is the order in which the steps in a process happen or are done.

First, organize the details you will use in your introduction. Start with a topic sentence that tells what process you will explain. Follow this sentence with any details that might interest your readers in learning about your topic.

Next, organize the details for the body of your composition. Each paragraph in the body will explain one main step and the smaller steps that are part of this main step. Find the first main step in the process. Group the smaller steps that are part of it around it. Then, find the second main step. Group its smaller steps around it. Continue in this way.

If you wish to do so, you may explain the last step and describe the end result of the process in your conclusion. You may also use the conclusion to summarize or review the process as a whole. Another possibility is to use the conclusion to tell your readers why learning about this process is valuable.

Check It Out Read the body of an explanatory composition about the process of taking good photographs.

> Your first step must be to get to know your camera. You do not need an expensive camera to take good pictures. It is more important to know what your camera can or cannot do. You will probably begin by studying the instruction manual. Then practice with the camera itself. Get to know what every dial, button, and ring on your camera is used for.

A second necessary step is to learn about the different kinds of film available. You may want to ask a clerk at a camera store for help. You may choose black and white film for certain kinds of photographs. You may choose color film, which is more expensive, for other kinds of pictures.

At last, you are ready to take photographs. Through constant use of a camera you will develop your skills. Be sure the subject of your photograph is in focus. Hold the camera steady. Focus on your subject, and press the shutter-release button smoothly.

- What steps are explained in the body of this composition?
- Has the writer used step-by-step order?

Try Your Skill   Here are some jumbled notes that explain a process. Copy the title and list the steps in the correct order.

How To Wax a Car

Apply wax with damp cloth
Wipe off excess, polishing to a bright shine
Remove any old wax with clean, dry cloth
First, wash car
Dry car with chamois or lint-free cloth

Keep This in Mind

- In an explanatory composition that explains a process, use step-by-step order to organize your material.

Now Write   Read the pre-writing notes you made in the previous lesson. Organize the steps according to the guidelines in this lesson. Plan to represent your topic in the introduction. In the body, plan to give a step-by-step explanation of the process. In the conclusion, plan to sum up the process, explain the final step of the process, or tell why the process is important. Save your organized notes in your folder.

First to Last

Writing the First Draft

Here's the Idea   When you write the first draft of your explanatory composition, begin with the introduction. Make sure that this introduction states your topic and captures the interest of your readers. Then, in the body of your composition, present all the steps in the process. Tell about each step in step-by-step order. To make the order of the steps clear, use transitional words and phrases that tell *when*. Here are some examples of these transitions:

first	the next step	when	finally
second	at the same time	before	as soon as
after	after one hour	later	then

Transitions should be used within each paragraph to show the order of each step. Transitions should also be used between paragraphs. They work like bridges to carry the reader from the main idea of one paragraph to the main idea of the next.

Check It Out   Note the transitional words and phrases in the introduction and conclusion of the composition on taking photographs. Review the transitions used in the body of the explanation.

Introduction

What is the best way to recall the most important experience of our lives? Our memories can hold the details of recent experiences with little difficulty. However, most of us need a little help in remembering details about past experiences. The best reminders of special moments are photographs, which capture them forever. With practice, you can take memorable photographs of the special times in your life.

Conclusion

After you shoot a roll of film, it is important to have it developed as soon as possible. Old film will not produce the clearest pictures. When you receive your developed pictures, store the best of them in a photo album or suitable container. Arrange the photographs in a logical order for viewing. As your skill with a camera improves, you will be glad you took the time to take photographs.

- What transitions are used?

Try Your Skill Read the following explanation of the process of repairing walls. The steps are presented in the correct step-by-step order, but the paragraph is missing transitions. Rewrite the paragraph and add transitional words and phrases to make the order clear. Combine steps whenever it makes sense.

Force the spackling mixture into all cracks or holes. Scrape any excess mixture from the surface of the wall. Let the spackling mixture dry. Add more if any spot is not completely filled. Sand the dry spackling mixture. Wipe off dust. Put on one coat of primer. Let it dry. Paint over primer with paint.

Keep This in Mind

- In an explanatory composition that explains a process, use transitional words and phrases to help make step-by-step order clear.

Now Write Write the first draft of an explanatory composition explaining a process. Include a topic sentence in your introduction that states the main idea of your composition. Also, be sure that each paragraph in the body of your composition has a topic sentence. Use transitional words and phrases within and between paragraphs. Explain each step clearly. When you are finished with your first draft, save it.

Clearly the Best

Revising Your Explanation

Here's the Idea Have you ever tried to follow an explanation that has some steps missing, out of order, or poorly explained? This can be very frustrating. To avoid causing your readers the same kind of frustration, you must revise your explanatory composition carefully.

When revising, try to make your explanation as clear and as simple as possible. To do this, pay close attention to step-by-step order. Make sure you have included *all* the steps in the process. Also make sure that each step is explained completely.

Here are some questions to ask yourself as you revise your composition explaining a process.

1. Does my introduction tell what process the composition will explain? Does it capture the interest of the reader?

2. Have I included *all* the steps in the process I am explaining?

3. Are my details presented in step-by-step order?

4. Does each body paragraph contain a main idea and supporting details?

5. Have I used transitional words and phrases that tell *when* within and between paragraphs?

6. Does the conclusion tell the final step in the process, summarize the process, or tell the reader why learning the process is important or valuable?

When you have revised the content, organization, and language of your composition, proofread it carefully. Check for errors in grammar, capitalization, punctuation, and spelling.

Check It Out Notice how the following paragraph from an explanatory composition has been revised.

I want to explain about how to drive a stick shift car *with a manual transmission?* Do you know how A car can have a manual transmission, or an automatic. With a manual, you have to shift gears yourself. It *may* looks complicated, but it's not.

- How has this introduction been improved?
- Has this paragraph been proofread? How do you know?

Try Your Skill   Here is a body paragraph from a composition on driving a car with a manual transmission. Use your revising skills to improve it. Compare your revision with those of your classmates.

> The clutch pedal is the one way on the left. You have to step on it. Shift the lever and put the car in gear. Take your foot off the clutch then you can go. Don't step on the break pedal by mistake. Every time you shift the gears you step on this pedal.

Keep This in Mind

- When revising an explanatory composition, your goal is to make it clear and easy for your readers to understand.

Now Write   Following the guidelines in this lesson, revise your explanatory composition. Make sure you have included *all* the steps in the process you chose to explain. Make sure your explanation is clear and correct. When your revision is complete, proofread your composition. Give your work a title. Then, save your finished composition in your folder.

The Explanatory Composition
Presenting an Opinion

Part 1 **I Believe**
Pre-Writing: Developing an Opinion

Part 2 **The Reasons Why**
Pre-Writing: Organizing an Opinion

Part 3 **Take One**
Writing the First Draft

Part 4 **The End of the Road**
Revising Your Opinion

I Believe

Pre-Writing: Developing an Opinion

Here's the Idea   Your opinions tell who you are. They tell what you like and don't like. They tell what is important to you and what is not. Your opinions make you unique and interesting. In fact, your opinions make you an individual.

At times you may wish to share an opinion with others. One way to do this is to write an explanatory composition that presents an opinion. In a composition of this kind, you state an opinion. You also support or defend it. In other words, you let your readers know why you feel as you do about a subject.

To find a topic for an explanatory composition, think about your life. Think about your neighborhood, your school, your city, your nation. What do you believe in? What do you think should be started or stopped or changed? What do you approve of, dislike, enjoy, or hate? Any opinion that you hold strongly is likely to be a good composition topic.

Once you have chosen a topic, write a sentence clearly stating your opinion. This sentence will be the topic sentence of the introductory paragraph of your composition. The rest of your composition will tell why you hold the opinion you stated in the first paragraph.

To explain your opinion, you must offer logical reasons. Gather specific facts and accurate statistics to support your opinion. You may also use a personal example or an anecdote. There are several possible sources for supporting facts, statistics, and anecdotes. These include personal experiences, books, reference works, and magazine or newspaper articles.

Check It Out   Examine these notes for a student's explanatory composition expressing a personal opinion.

Topic: Professional athletes deserve to be paid well.

Supporting
Details: good reasons for high earnings
1. talented athletes work hard
   men and women train long hours, face tough competition
2. athletes deserve compensation for risks, injuries—head, back, broken bones—which may be a problem for a long time
3. short careers
   athletes perform best when young—family life suffers

- Is an opinion stated clearly and directly?
- What kind of support has the writer gathered to support the opinion?

Try Your Skill Make a list of five subjects about which you have strong opinions. Choose three of your subjects, and for each write a sentence that clearly and directly states how you feel.

Keep This in Mind

- An explanatory composition that presents an opinion should be clear and direct.
- Support an opinion with logical reasons that include specific facts, accurate statistics, or personal examples or anecdotes.

Now Write Think of several opinions that you hold. Choose one opinion that you would like to present in an explanatory composition. Write a sentence that states your opinion clearly and directly. You may want to choose an opinion and sentence that you developed in **Try Your Skill.** Then list the reasons that you will use to support your opinion. Save your notes.

The Reasons Why

Pre-Writing: Organizing an Opinion

Here's the Idea When political candidates debate one another, they do not simply give their opinions. They give reasons, facts, and statistics that support their opinions. They know that to be effective, these ideas must be properly organized.

One way to organize supporting ideas in a composition is by order of importance. Compositions organized in this way start with the weakest supporting idea and end with the strongest. To organize a composition in this way, first study your pre-writing notes. Your notes should contain supporting facts, statistics, and anecdotes. Then, follow these steps:

1. Find two or three major supporting ideas. Write sentences stating each of these ideas. These sentences will serve as topic sentences for paragraphs in the body of your composition.

2. Organize your topic sentences in order of importance, from least important to most important.

3. Find facts, statistics, or anecdotes in your pre-writing notes to support each of your topic sentences. Place these under the topic sentences to which they belong. Then, organize, in order of importance, these supporting ideas for each paragraph.

Check It Out Read the body of a student's composition.

First of all, hundreds of thousands of fans each season are entertained by outstanding athletes. Talented men and women have earned the opportunity to play through continual tough competition with other athletes. Why should spectators begrudge these hardworking athletes their high salaries? Players deserve to be paid well for their performances. In fact, athletes' salaries represent not only their performance in public, but also all their lengthy practice times. Since practice is a professional requirement, athletes should be compensated for it.

More important, athletes need some benefit to compensate for the physical abuse they suffer in certain sports, such as boxing or hockey. Athletes sometimes risk major physical injuries. They may injure their heads or their backs. They may pull tendons, break bones, or lose teeth. As a result of their careers, they may suffer for the rest of their lives. How many people would face such risks without financial reward?

The most important reason athletes should be paid well is based on simple arithmetic. Most athletes are young and have only a short time to perform at their peak. As a result, athletes must spend a great deal of time away from their families in order to work. In addition, when most other people are firmly settled in their careers, athletes may be out of a job. In fact, money earned early may be needed in leaner years ahead.

- Is an opinion supported by specific reasons or facts and figures? Is the evidence given in order of importance, from the least important to the most important?

Try Your Skill   Choose one of the following opinions to support. List at least three supporting reasons or facts and figures. Organize your support according to the order of importance.

1. Everyone should learn basic first aid.
2. A good education is necessary for everyone.
3. Everyone should learn how to cook.
4. Spectators at sports events should be more courteous.

Keep This in Mind

- In an explanatory composition that presents an opinion, organize your supporting evidence according to the order of importance.

Now Write   Review the pre-writing notes you have made for your composition. Organize the support for your opinion in a logical way. Save your notes in your folder.

Take One

Writing the First Draft

Here's the Idea When you write your first draft, do not worry about grammar, usage, and mechanics. Instead, simply write.

Begin your first draft with a one-paragraph introduction that states your opinion and tries to capture your readers' interest. Each paragraph in the body should contain one major idea and its supporting details. Your conclusion should be one paragraph long. It should restate your opinion. It should also summarize your reasons for believing as you do.

As you write, use transitional words and phrases. These will show how your ideas are related and the order of your ideas.

first   the second reason   more importantly   finally

You can also use the following transitions to present reasons and facts.

because   since   if   therefore   as a result

Use transitional words and phrases within and between paragraphs to improve the flow of your ideas.

Check It Out Read this introduction and conclusion.

Introduction

Professional sports is big business. The public must pay for expensive tickets to sporting events. Many of the athletes involved make huge salaries. All of this moneymaking has led some fans to complain that overpaid athletes are the cause of problems in many sports. These angry fans feel that love of the sport should be what motivates athletes. However, I believe that professional athletes deserve to be paid well.

Conclusion

Therefore, the next time someone complains about the extraordinary salaries of athletes, consider the price they pay.

Athletes work long hours and risk serious injuries. They must often give up family life. It is easy to sit in the stands and criticize professional athletes. However, would you be willing to be on the field doing what they do? I believe professional athletes deserve to be paid well for their effort and dedication.

- Does the introduction clearly state an opinion?
- Does the conclusion summarize the argument?
- Which transitions help to state the reasons or facts?

Try Your Skill   Each group of sentences below begins with a topic sentence and is followed by two supporting reasons. Add details that will strengthen the supporting evidence. Then rewrite each group of sentences, adding transitions that state reasons or facts and that show the order of importance.

1. More jobs should be made available to teenagers. Teenagers need to learn how to manage their own money. Teenagers need work experience to prepare themselves for life after graduation.

2. The city is a good place to live. Public transportation is better than it is in the suburbs. There is more to see and do in the city.

Keep This in Mind

- In the introduction, clearly state your opinion.
- In the body, present your supporting evidence.
- In the conclusion, summarize your opinion.
- Use transitional words and phrases to help present supporting evidence in the order of importance and to help state reasons or facts.

Now Write   Write the first draft of your explanatory composition. Use transitional words and phrases to present your opinion and to make the order of your idea clear. Save your first draft.

The End of the Road

Part 4

Revising Your Opinion

Here's the Idea   A movie director may have to shoot a scene ten or twenty times to get it just right. To get your compositions just right, you may have to revise them again and again.

When you revise your explanatory composition, remember that your purpose is to present and support an opinion. Make sure that your evidence is convincing. Also make sure that your reasons, facts, and statistics are in a logical order. You want your audience to be convinced by your evidence. You also want readers to be able to see the logical relationships between your ideas.

When you revise your composition, ask yourself these questions:

1. Did I express my opinion clearly in my introduction?
2. Have I used strong, specific reasons, facts, and statistics to support my opinion?
3. Did I support my main ideas with enough details?
4. Did I use transitional words and phrases both between and within paragraphs?
5. Are my major ideas and the details supporting them arranged logically?
6. Does my conclusion restate my opinion and summarize my reasons for holding it?

Once you have checked your organization and content, proofread your composition. Find and correct all errors in grammar, capitalization, punctuation, and spelling.

Check It Out   Notice how this paragraph from an explanatory paragraph has been revised.

228

The National Parks are important for *too* reasons. They give
americans the chance to see the country *in its natural beauty* as it was. It also serves
to protect many animals and plants *species* that would have died. This
American and foreign *The parks* *become extinct.*
second reason is often forgotten by visitors. We must control
the overcrowding in our Parks. if we want to save our wildlife.

Try Your Skill Here is another paragraph from the composition about the national parks. Use your revising skills to improve it.

In recent years there have been an increase in the number of visitors. This has meant more traffic, and more roads. The air is being polluted. And also many of the timider animals have been scared away from there old, nesting areas. Animals that are not so shy have become a nuisance because people feed them, like bears.

Keep This in Mind

- When revising an explanatory composition that presents on opinion, you want to convince your readers that your opinion is sound and based on good judgment.

Now Write Revise your explanatory composition. Follow the guidelines in this lesson. When you are satisfied that your composition is the best it can be, make a final copy and save it in your folder.

The Explanatory Composition

Stating a Definition

Happiness Is

Pre-Writing: Developing a Definition

Here's the Idea   In an explanatory composition that states a definition, your goal is to define something as clearly and completely as possible. Your topic may be a real object, such as a computer or a subway. It may also be an idea, such as *trust* or *genius.*

After you have chosen a topic for your explanatory composition, write a sentence that defines the term you have chosen. This one-sentence definition should do three things. First, it should tell what term is being defined. Second, it should put the subject into a general class. Third, it should show the particular characteristics of the subject. In other words, it should show how the subject differs from other members of its class. This one-sentence definition can become the topic sentence of your introductory paragraph. Here is an example of a good one-sentence definition. Try to identify the subject being defined, its general class, and its particular characteristics.

> An electric eel is a slender, tube-shaped fish that can give a
> strong electric shock.

To develop your definition, you must gather specific details. If you are defining an object, a dictionary, encyclopedia, or other reference work can supply you with facts and statistics. If you are defining a word that stands for an idea, you may want to use specific examples or anecdotes. These come from research, from interviews, or from your own experience.

As you gather facts, examples, and other details for your pre-writing notes, keep your audience in mind. Your audience may not be familiar with your topic. If so, you will have to keep your explanation simple. On the other hand, your audience may already be very familiar with your topic. In this case, you will be able to provide more detailed or complex information.

Check It Out Read the following pre-writing notes.

Topic: bagels

Introduction: Americans' new interest in food: buying woks, crêpe pans, pasta machines; eating in small, ethnic restaurants but overlooking simple food—bread, especially bagels

Body: bread: most widely eaten food in the world; quick breads—muffins, biscuits, corn bread; flat breads—tortillas, pita bread; yeast breads— white, rye, rolls, bagels

bagels: doughnut-shaped; shiny, crusty outer surface; dense, chewy middle

breakfast food: toasted, warm; good with cream cheese, salmon

Conclusion: bagels are simple, delicious, more popular now

- Do these notes include details or facts and figures that will define the subject clearly?

Try Your Skill Choose three of the following subjects and write a one-sentence definition of each. Be sure the definition presents the subject to be defined, puts the subject in its general class, and shows how the subject differs from others of its class.

catcher   moped   monarchy   patience   nurse

Keep This in Mind

- In an explanatory composition that states a definition, your goal is to define something as clearly and completely as possible.

Now Write Choose and narrow a topic to define in your explanatory composition. Write a one-sentence definition of your subject. Then, gather facts and figures or specific examples to develop your definition. Save your pre-writing notes.

Generally Speaking

Pre-Writing: Organizing a Definition

Here's the Idea Suppose you are writing to a friend in another country. You want to tell your friend about where you live. You start by telling about your city or town. Next, you tell about your neighborhood. Then, you tell about your house or apartment. Finally, you tell about your room and the things in it. If you did this, you would be using **general to specific order.** This is the method of organization that is used for an explanatory composition that states a definition. Such compositions begin with an introductory paragraph. This paragraph gives a general definition of the subject. The introduction is followed by several body paragraphs. The body paragraphs develop the general definition by presenting specific details.

Start by organizing the information for your introduction. Place the one sentence definition of your topic first. Follow this definition with any details you can use to interest your readers.

Next, organize the specific details you will use in the paragraphs of the body. Look at your pre-writing notes. Find two or three main ideas that help to define your topic. Group the rest of your details under these main ideas. Each resulting idea group will become a paragraph in the body of your composition.

Check It Out Read the following paragraph.

A dulcimer is a wooden, stringed instrument that sounds like a cross between a guitar and a banjo. Dulcimers were introduced in Persia nearly five thousand years ago. There are two types of dulcimers. One type is called a *hammered dulcimer*. The hammered dulcimer is a trapezoid-shaped box with two or more strings stretched across it. This type of dulcimer is played by striking the strings with curved wooden hammers. The second type of dulcimer is called the *plucked* or *Appalachian dulcimer.* This dulcimer is shaped like an hourglass with three or four strings stretched across it. It is played by plucking or strumming the strings. Although dulcimers have their origins in antiquity, they remain popular musical instruments today.

- Explain how this definition moves from the general to the specific.

Try Your Skill   Below are some pre-writing notes for an explanatory composition that defines. The subject being defined is *swamp*. Read the notes carefully. Then group the notes around the three most obvious main ideas.

General Definition: A swamp is an area of muddy land, often covered with water, that supports a variety of plant and animal life.

Details: deep-water swamps (fresh water)
bald cypress, juniper, pine trees
bear, deer, swamp birds
snakes, raccoons
mangrove swamps (salt water)
wax myrtles, willows, Spanish moss
alligators, crocodiles, turtles
manatees
orchids, palm trees
shallow-water swamps (fresh water)

Keep This in Mind

- Use general to specific order to organize the details for an explanatory composition that states a definition.

Now Write   Organize the pre-writing notes for your explanatory composition. First identify two or three main ideas that help you to define your topic. Then group your remaining details around these ideas. Save your pre-writing notes.

Famous First Words

Writing the First Draft

Here's the Idea   Like any composition, your explanatory composition should have three parts: an introduction, a body, and a conclusion. Working from your pre-writing notes, write a first draft. Try to write sentences and paragraphs that present your ideas clearly and completely.

Begin with your introduction. The first sentence of this paragraph should present a clear, brief definition of your topic. This will be the topic sentence of your introductory paragraph. Then add some interesting details to capture the interest of your readers.

In the body of your composition, present two or three main ideas that help to define your subject specifically. Present each of these main ideas in a separate paragraph. Use the details from your organized pre-writing notes to develop each main idea.

End your composition with a conclusion. This paragraph should summarize the main ideas of your definition.

Check It Out   Read this introduction and body.

Recently, many Americans have become more interested in favorite foods from other lands. Many busy cooks are buying Chinese woks, French crêpe pans, and Italian pasta machines. Many adventurous diners are seeking out small ethnic restaurants that serve tasty dishes. In their search for specialty foods, however, many people have been overlooking a basic and delicious food—bread. One of the tastiest ethnic varieties of bread is the bagel, a dense, chewy, ring-shaped roll.

In fact, bread is the most widely eaten food in the world. Combinations of flour and water have existed in some form since the beginning of history. There are quick breads which include an enormous variety of muffins and biscuits, as well as corn bread and gingerbread. There are flat breads, including

Mexican *tortillas* and Middle Eastern *pita*. Most common in the United States are yeast breads. Bagels are a kind of yeast bread, unique because they are boiled and then baked.

Bagels are doughnut-shaped, brown, and shiny. Their outer surface looks like smooth, polished wood. Sometimes it is dotted with tangy black onion flakes. The inside of a bagel is dense, heavy, and quite chewy. Bagels are like no other bread, because of their unique texture.

Bagels are usually served for breakfast. They are particularly good when they are served warm or toasted. However, bagels may be eaten any time. They are a perfect companion to cream cheese or smoked salmon.

- Does the introductory paragraph contain a one-sentence definition of the subject?
- Does each body paragraph talk about just one main idea?
- Do the details in each paragraph relate to its main idea?

Try Your Skill   Reread the composition **Check It Out.** Then use the pre-writing notes on page 233 as well as details from your own imagination, to write a conclusion to the composition.

Keep This in Mind

- In an explanatory composition that states a definition, the introduction includes a general, one-sentence definition of the subject.
- The body develops the definition with specific details.
- The conclusion sums up the main ideas of the definition.

Now Write   Write the first draft of your explanatory composition. Follow your organized pre-writing notes as you write. Save your first draft in your folder.

A Definite Improvement

Revising Your Definition

Here's the Idea Revising is a vital step in the process of writing. It is during revision that the careful writer is separated from the careless writer. To make your explanatory composition that states a definition the best it can be, take the time to revise your work thoroughly. Read your composition several times. Make sure that your organization is clear and that your ideas are fully developed.

Here is a list of questions to ask yourself as you revise your composition.

1. Does the topic sentence in my introduction define my subject?
2. Does my one-sentence definition name the subject? Does it place the subject in a general class? Does it name some characteristics that make the subject different from other things in its class?
3. Do the paragraphs of the body develop my definition with enough specific details, facts, statistics, examples, or anecdotes?
4. Does my composition follow general to specific order?
5. Does the conclusion summarize my definition?
6. Is my language interesting, clear, and simple? Will the audience be able to follow my ideas?

After you have checked your ideas, organization, and language, proofread your composition carefully. Correct any errors in grammar, capitalization, punctuation, and spelling.

Check It Out Notice how this conclusion to the composition about bagels has been revised.

First Draft: Bagels are simple food. You can get them frozen in some stores. They might turn up one day on your table. Have a bagel!

Revision: Bagels are a simple but delicious food. They have become so popular that they can now be found in the frozen food sections of many grocery stores. Soon they may turn up on your family's breakfast table. If so, enjoy! Start your day with a bagel.

- Explain why the revised conclusion is better than the first draft.
- Do you see why it is sometimes necessary to rewrite a paragraph in order to improve it?

Try Your Skill   Below are five poorly written general, one-sentence definitions. Each one was taken from the first draft of an introductory paragraph. Decide what is wrong with each definition and then revise it.

1. A *shark* has several rows of sharp teeth.
2. *Pride* is a feeling that you have.
3. An *avocado* is a fruit that is green.
4. *Orchids* can be found in tropical countries.
5. A *quarterback* is a football player.

Keep This in Mind

- Revise your explanatory composition that states a definition to be sure that you have clearly and completely defined your subject.

Now Write   Following the guidelines in this lesson, revise your explanatory paragraph. Make your definition clear and complete. Proofread your composition for errors in grammar and mechanics. When you are finished revising, make a final copy of your composition and save it in your folder.

The Research Paper

To the Source

Developing a Research Paper

Here's the Idea Students in high school are often asked to write a special type of composition called a **research paper.** Research papers, like compositions, are made of several paragraphs that deal with a single topic. However, research papers differ from compositions in one important respect. All the information in a research paper comes from outside sources. These sources may be books, newspapers, or magazines. They may be reference works, such as encyclopedias, atlases, and almanacs. They may even be non-print materials, such as films or interviews.

The first pre-writing step for a research paper is choosing and narrowing a topic. Suppose you are given the subject of careers. This assignment gives you a general subject. You need to find information from which you can select a specific topic.

Begin your research in the library. Look through the card catalog for the subject card *Careers.* Look in the nonfiction section that contains books on careers. Check encyclopedias in the reference section for information on the general subject of careers. Look in the *Readers' Guide to Periodical Literature* for magazine articles relating to careers. Pamphlets found in the vertical file are also good sources.

Another valuable source of information about careers is the guidance counselor or vocational guidance department at your school. Your counselor may have on hand the latest information about careers. He or she will be able to tell you where to look or to write to get that information.

Here is a list of possible sources you might check to find general information about careers.

1. *Occupational Outlook Handbook*, from the U.S. Dept. of Labor

2. "Careers" in *The World Book Encyclopedia*
3. *Encyclopedia of Careers and Vocational Guidance*, 1981 ed.

As you read, you will undoubtedly find several careers that you find appealing. Choose one that you would like to investigate further. Remember you will write your best paper on a career that really interests you.

When you have chosen a particular career to investigate, search again for specific information. Check all the sources already mentioned. If possible, talk to someone in the field of your choice. You can also write to the U.S. Department of Labor, Washington, D.C. Record each source of your information in your notebook. Write the titles of books, encyclopedias, pamphlets, and magazine articles in your notebook. Also write the volume and page number of the encyclopedias you may want to use and the dates of the magazines. This will give you a list of sources that contain information about your topic.

Check It Out   Look at this list of sources for a research paper about a career in the hotel industry.

1. *Occupational Outlook Handbook*, 1985-86, U.S. Dept. of Labor
2. *Hotel Keeping and Catering as a Career* a book by John Fuller
3. *Opportunities in the Hotel and Motel Industry*, a book by Shepard Henkin
4. *Encyclopedia of Careers and Vocational Guidance*, 1981 ed.
5. *Working Woman* magazine, April, 1978, pages 18-19

- How would you have located the second source? the fifth?
- Is this a varied and specific list of sources for a research paper?

Try Your Skill   Choose one of these general career areas to research in the library. Narrow, to a specific career, the career area you have chosen. Then list three different sources where you could find information for a research paper about this career.

manufacturing	health	construction	business
communications	fine arts	public service	recreation

Keep This in Mind

- A research paper is a composition developed with information gathered from outside sources.
- With a general subject in mind, search through books, magazines, and other reference works to find a specific, limited topic for a report.
- With a specific subject chosen, begin research for a report by examining all possible sources. Keep a list of the sources.

Now Write   Choose a career to investigate for a report. Go to the library with a general idea of what you will write about and look for a specific career. Check the reference shelves, the card catalog, the *Readers' Guide,* and the vertical file. Talk to a career counselor and, if possible, to someone working in the career that interests you. Find as many sources of information as you can about your career. Keep a list of these sources in your folder. Note the call numbers, the book titles, the magazine issues, or the vertical file references.

Shortcuts

Taking Notes

Here's the Idea   As you know, the ideas in a research paper are not your own. They come from outside sources. You will have to keep a record of the sources you use. Whenever you take notes from a source, make a **bibliography card.** This card will contain information about the source. You will need the information on your bibliography cards when you list your sources at the end of your paper. Bibliography cards for different kinds of sources contain different types of information, as follows:

Book:	author, title, publisher, date published
Magazine:	author of article (if there is one), title of article, name of magazine, date published, page number of article
Encyclopedia:	name of article, name of encyclopedia, date published
Newspaper:	author of article (if there is one), title of article, name of newspaper, date published, section, page, and column number of article

When you make bibliography cards, number each source. These numbers will be helpful when you write your note cards.

As you read about your topic, write the important information on **note cards.** Follow these guidelines for making note cards.

1. Use a separate 3" × 5" note card for each fact or idea.

2. Write a key phrase at the top of each card that tells the main idea of the note. Keep cards with similar key phrases grouped together. This will help you to organize your notes later.

3. Label each note card with the number given to that source on its bibliography card. Include the exact page reference so you can check out a fact or a specific quotation.

4. Take notes in your own words. Copying another writer's

work is called **plagiarism.** Plagiarism is a serious offense. To avoid plagiarism, jot down information in your own words. To quote a source directly, use quotation marks to show that you have copied a statement. Copy direct quotations exactly as they are. Use direct quotations only for important or unusual ideas.

Check It Out   Look at the sample cards on page 247.

- Which are bibliography cards?
- Which is a note card? What is its source?

Try Your Skill   Read the following information. Make a bibliography card and a note card based on it.

Personal service jobs are as old as civilization. Some jobs fill essential needs. Others provide luxuries. Some personal service workers keep our lives running smoothly. Others help us to feel better about ourselves or our belongings. Jane Thomas is a rehabilitation counselor. John Glover repairs typewriters. John Glover and Jane Thomas have entirely different jobs, but both perform a personal service.

—from *Jobs in Personal Services*, by Beatrice and Calvin Criner, Lothrop, Lee & Shepard Company, New York, 1974, 13.

> **Keep This in Mind**
>
> - Make bibliography cards that contain basic information about all sources for your report.
> - Write note cards. Each card should contain one idea.
> - Take notes in your own words. Avoid plagiarism.

Now Write   Take your list of sources and a stack of 3" × 5" note cards to your library. Make bibliography cards for all suitable sources. Read through those sources and make note cards about the information you find. Save the cards in your folder.

(1)

Henkin, Shepard
Opportunities in the Hotel and
  Motel Industry
Lincolnwood, Illinois, National
Textbook Company, 1978

371.42   public library
H 832 he
rev. ed

(2)

"Hotel Occupations"
Occupational Outlook Handbook,
  1985-86 edition
U.S. Department of Labor
  Bureau of Labor Statistics, 1985

                    guidance counselor

(3)

Hopke, William E.

 "Hotel and Motel Managers,"
The Encyclopedia of Careers and
Vocational Guidance, 1981 ed.

                    school library

(1)

opportunities in hotel work

    "The hotel industry is one of the
few wherein a young person can
secure a position without too much
formal education, and work his
way through the various departments to an executive capacity."

                    page 27

Pileup

Organizing Information

Here's the Idea   Before you can begin to write a research paper, you must organize your information. Start with your note cards. Read your cards and try to find four or five main ideas running through them. The key phrases on your notecards will help you to complete this step. Then separate your cards into piles. Each pile should contain cards dealing with one main idea.

If you were writing about a career in the hotel-motel industry, your information could be organized into four categories: the variety of jobs within this industry, the range of training required, personal traits required, and the benefits of the jobs.

You may find that some cards do not fit into any of your main idea groups. If so, you may decide not to use these ideas in your paper. However, save the cards. They may contain information that you can use in the introduction or conclusion of your paper.

The next step is to write a topic sentence for each of your piles of cards. This topic sentence should state the main idea of the cards in each pile. You will end up with a few topic sentences that you can use when you write the body of your paper.

The last step is to put your notes in order. First, place the piles of cards in the order in which you want to write about them. Then, put the notes in each pile in a sensible order. See pages 96–97 for information on different types of organization. Try several different methods of organization. Find the method or combination of methods that best suits your material.

Check It Out   Read these sentences. They were written to describe the main ideas of the research paper on careers in the hotel-motel industry.

1. The hotel-motel industry consists of a variety of separate operations, those related to the "front of the house" and those related to the "back of the house".

2. Hotel work can be skilled or unskilled so there is a broad range of training required.

3. Certain character traits, such as patience and the ability to get along with people, are also required in this personal service industry.

4. There are many benefits to careers in hotel work.

- Is one main idea stated clearly in each sentence?

Try Your Skill Organize the following careers into five groups. For each group write one sentence that expresses the main idea of the career field represented by the various jobs.

dancer	police officer	railroad engineer
chef	bus driver	licensed practical nurse
actor	X-ray technician	bus boy
firefighter	airline pilot	maitre d'
musician	waiter	medical records clerk

Keep This in Mind

- Organize your note cards. Group together cards with the same main idea. Write one sentence stating the main idea of each group. Arrange the piles and the cards within them into a logical order.

Now Write Read your note cards. Organize them into four or five main groups. Make a list of sentences expressing the main idea of each group. Then arrange the sentences and the cards that go with them into a logical order. Save your work.

The Bare Essentials

Making an Outline

Here's the Idea Once you have listed the main ideas of your research paper, make an **outline**. In an outline, you organize the ideas from your notes in a more detailed way. You decide where each individual note card with its one idea fits into your paper. The outline thus provides you with a plan to follow when you write your rough draft.

To write your outline, use your organized groups of note cards. Each main idea will become a main topic in your outline. The related facts on your note cards will become the subtopics and details of the outline. Each main idea, subtopic, and detail will be stated in a word or phrase.

All outlines follow the same form. You must follow this form whenever you make an outline. An outline begins with a title. Below that, first in importance, are main ideas shown by Roman numerals. Under the main ideas, next in importance, are subtopics, shown by capital letters. Under subtopics, details are shown by Arabic numerals. If more specific details must be shown, small letters are used. You must have no fewer than two main topics or subtopics in an outline.

Each part of an outline is indented from the part above. However, each symbol is in a straight line with the others like it. Each kind of symbol is followed by a period, although the words of the outline are not followed by periods. In a completed outline, the first word and all important words are capitalized in every line, as well as in the title.

Check It Out Examine the outline on the following page. It is based on notes about a career in the hotel-motel industry.

I. Introduction
   A. Function of hotel-motel industry
      1. A personal services industry
      2. Provides sleeping rooms and meals
   B. Range of services offered.
      1. Small inns with few employees
      2. Large complexes with many services

II. Variety of skilled and unskilled occupations
   A. Front of the house
      1. Management
      2. Uniformed service staff
      3. Front office
      4. Accounting and sales
   B. Back of the house
      1. Housekeeping and laundry
      2. Food preparation
      3. Engineering and security

III. Training for a career in hotel industry
   A. Short on-the-job training
      1. Entry-level positions
      2. Part-time work available
   B. Specialty training
      1. Long on-the-job training
      2. Vocational education
      3. Leads to advancement

IV. Personal qualifications
   A. Ability to get along with people
   B. Patience and courtesy
   C. Neatness
   D. Attention to detail

V. Benefits of hotel-motel careers
   A. Flexible schedules, many locations
   B. Promotion, personal growth

- What subtopics and details explain a career in the hotel-motel industry?
- Point out how the form for outlining has been followed correctly.

Try Your Skill   Make an outline of the following paragraph of information taken from *The Guide to Career Education* by Muriel Lederer.

> In order to be a computer technician you need to have good vision because you work with small parts. You also need normal color perception because wires are color coded. Normal hearing is also a requirement because machine breakdowns are sometimes detected by sound. A pleasant manner is an asset, as well as the ability to cope with other people, since you will be dealing with customers. Last, but by no means least, you should be resourceful and able to work independently with little or no supervision.

Keep This in Mind

- Use your notes to write an outline of the ideas and details to be presented in your research paper.
- Follow the correct form for making an outline.

Now Write   Take out your organized note cards. Make an outline, using your list of main ideas and your note cards. Save your work in your folder.

Take the Plunge

Writing the Introduction

Here's the Idea   After you have finished the outline for your paper, most of your next steps will be familiar. Writing the first draft of a research paper is much like writing the first draft of a composition. Both have three parts—an introduction, a body, and a conclusion. The introduction presents your main idea. The body develops the main idea with supporting ideas and details. The conclusion restates the topic and summarizes the important information presented in the body.

However, research papers differ from compositions in one important respect. In some compositions, you can use the first-person point of view. In other words, you can use the pronouns *I, me,* and *my.* You can also include your own opinions. You cannot do these things in a research paper. Research papers are never written using the first-person point of view. They also never include personal observations or opinions. Remember, the ideas in a research paper come from outside sources, not from personal experience.

When you write the introduction to a research paper, be sure to state what the paper will be about. Sometimes you will want to present some of your facts in the introduction. At other times you will want to keep the introduction short and general.

Check It Out   On the following page are the introduction and the first paragraph of the body of the report on a career in hotel work. They are shown as you might have written them after working on a first draft.

- How does this first draft use the information shown in the outline?
- What main idea is presented in the introduction?

¶ Many people choose a career in the field of personal services. That is, they choose jobs in which they attend to the needs of other individuals. One of the largest personal service industries is the hotel-motel business. Basically, The function of this business is to provide sleeping acomodations (sp?) and meals. However, Hotels and motels range from ~~those~~ simple country inns with a few rooms and employees to ~~those~~ elaborate city skyscrapers with more than 1,000 rooms and hundreds of employees. The largest of these businesses offer many additional conveniences for their guests. The services may include gift shops, recreational facilities, and banquet and convention facilities.

To provide this range of services, the hotel industry employs workers in a wide variety of skilled and unskilled occupations. These various occupations can be divided into those related to the "front of the house" and those related to the "back of the house." The "front of the house" is a hotel term for ~~means~~ the operations that deal directly with and are seen by the guests. These operations are those of management, the front office, the uniformed service staff, and the accounting and sales departments. The "back of the house" refers to hotel operations that are seldom ~~not~~ seen by guests. These include housekeeping, food preparation, security, laundry, and engineering.

Try Your Skill   Here is part of an outline for a report on dental assistants. Some of this information would fit nicely into the introduction to such a report. Using the information from the outline, write an introductory paragraph. Compare your introduction with those of your classmates.

I. Nature of the work
   A. Work along with a dentist
      1. Prepare patient for treatment
      2. Hand dentist proper instruments and materials
      3. Keep patient's mouth clear
   B. Work independently
      1. Provide oral health instruction
      2. Make casts of teeth and mouth
      3. Order dental supplies

Keep This in Mind

- Use your outline and note cards to write the first draft of your research paper.
- A research paper, like a composition, has an introduction, a body, and a conclusion.
- In the introduction, state the topic clearly.

Now Write   Take out your outline and note cards. Review them and think about whether to introduce the career you have researched in a general or a detailed way. Decide how you will state the main idea of your information about this career in the introduction.

Using both your outline and your note cards, write the introduction to your paper. Try to present your ideas clearly. However, in this first draft, don't worry about grammar, usage, and mechanics. Save your work in your folder.

Go the Distance

Writing the Body and Conclusion

Here's the Idea   As you write the body of a research paper, follow your outline and your note cards. The topic sentence of each paragraph in the body will correspond to a main topic in your outline. The note cards will supply the details. Use those details, examples, and quotations that will add the most to your report.

Use quotation marks when you use the words of another writer. When you prepare your final copy, you will give that writer credit in the correct way. You will learn how to give proper credit in Part 8. To keep track of information that must be credited, use the source numbers on your note cards. Write the source number in the margin next to any sentence that contains a direct quote or any information that must be credited.

Keep reading and reviewing your work as you write. Are your ideas clearly expressed? Are they organized logically? Is your writing detailed and interesting? Take time to think about how you can best express your information.

A research paper must come to a logical ending. A research paper should have a clear conclusion in which you tie ideas together naturally. You may include additional facts about the topic. Your most important purposes are to restate your main idea and to summarize the information you have presented.

Check It Out   On the next page is the rest of the first draft of the research paper on a career in the hotel industry.

- Compare this first draft with the outline. What details, examples, or quotations are used to develop the body?
- Does the conclusion sum up the information presented in the paper?

Because the hotel industry employs such a broad range of occupations, there is no single type of training necessary. Many entry-level positions require only a short period of on-the-job training. Entry-level jobs are often available on a part-time basis for students, to aquaint [sp?] them with hotel work. These jobs include waiter, maid, clerk, porter, bellhop, and elevator operator. However, longer on-the-job training or vocational education may lead to other, higher-paying positions.[1] For instance, those who have completed programs in cooking, accounting, or maintenance and repair work may eventually become department heads. The hotel industry is one of the few wherein a young person can secure a position without too much formal education, and work his way through the various departments to an executive capacity.[2]

To be successful in any position in the hotel business, several basic personal qualifications are required. A person must be able to deal with all kinds of people in any situation. Courtesy and patience are essential when serving guests. In addition to a neat appearance, a pleasant manner is also important. Finally, constant attention to detail is called for in all aspects of hotel work.

There are many benefits for those who choose a career in the hotel industry. The first, ^advantage^ is a flexible schedule, since hotels and motels operate ~~three shifts a day~~ ^twenty-four hours a day with three shifts.^ Other benefits include ^the^ a choice of part-time, full-time, or seasonal work, and a wide selection of geographic locations. ^At present^ The industry is also looking for capable women and members of minority groups, ^to train as managers^ A career in the hotel industry offers ^many^ opportunities for ~~working and being successful.~~ ^personal and professional growth.^

Try Your Skill

Write a conclusion for a research paper on dental assistants based on information from this outline.

    V. Benefits of the career

        A. Personal growth by helping others

        B. Pleasant work environment

            1. Quiet and relaxed atmosphere

            2. Usually short hours, flexible schedule

Keep This in Mind

- Use the ideas, details, examples, and direct quotations from your outline and note cards to develop the body of a research paper.
- Write a conclusion that summarizes the information presented in the paper.

Now Write

Review your outline and notes, and then write the body and conclusion of your research paper. Use quotation marks if you use another writers' words. Save your first draft.

Better Than Ever

Revising a Research Paper

Here's the Idea Once you have completed your first draft, you can begin to revise your research paper.

Read your work several times. Is it interesting as well as informative? Is there a beginning, a middle, and an end? Are your dates, statistics, and other facts accurate? Are unusual names or words spelled correctly? You will probably need to make some changes. All successful writers spend a great deal of time revising. Here are some questions to help you remember what to look for as you revise your research paper.

1. Does my introduction state what my paper will be about? Is it informative and interesting?

2. Does the paper follow my outline?

3. Are my facts accurate and clearly presented? Are enough facts included to develop my topic thoroughly?

4. Have I used quotation marks when copying a writer's words directly?

5. Does each paragraph deal with one main idea? Do the facts and ideas in each paragraph support the main idea?

6. Have I followed a logical order in presenting my ideas?

7. Did I make sure not to include any personal opinions?

8. Have I used transitions between sentences and paragraphs?

9. Does my conclusion summarize the main ideas?

After checking your organization and content, be sure to proofread your research paper carefully.

Check It Out Notice how this conclusion to a research paper about cameras has been revised.

It is true that the electronic
~~Like I said,~~ new cameras have some advantages over older the less sophisticated
~~ones.~~ manual. The electronic cameras require much to operate, a photo-
~~For one thing, they need alot~~ less skill, ~~And they give you~~ grapher
On the other hand   tend to   more often than manuals.
more freedom. ~~The thing is,~~ they break down a lot. ~~And can't~~
Also, the new cameras are usually plastic.
~~be fixed.~~ ~~Who wants to buy a new camera all the time?~~ For
a — The older manuals were made of brass.
strength, quality and durbility, ~~I say buy a manual camera.~~
it's hard to top a good manual camera.

- Why has the writer taken out all of the references to "I"?
- In what specific ways has the paragraph been improved?

Try Your Skill   Revise this introduction to a research paper about the art of mask making. Be sure the introduction clearly states a main idea. Remember also to proofread the paragraph.

Mask making is an art practiced by people all over the world. Sometimes mask are made for fun, like holloween. Sometimes mask are made for religous reasons like in different tribes in south America, Africa and Asia. I like the masks made by the hopi indians. Called Kachinas. Masks have a long history which I will talk about in my paper.

Keep This in Mind

- When you revise your research paper, try to improve your ideas, organization, and language.
- Check your facts, figures, and dates for accuracy.
- Proofread your paper.

Now Write   Follow the guidelines in this lesson and use the other revising skills you have learned to revise your research paper. Give your paper a good title. Save your revised paper.

Final Details

Footnotes and Bibliography

Here's the Idea   As you know, a research paper is based on information gathered from outside sources. When you prepare your final copy, you must be careful to give these sources credit for their ideas. To credit your sources, you must write footnotes and a bibliography.

A footnote gives credit to a writer whose words, facts, or ideas you have used. A direct quotation requires a footnote. So does a statistic. So do any ideas from a writer that are not common knowledge or that are clearly the writer's personal opinion.

To prepare proper footnotes, follow these steps:

1. Look through your paper for any material that needs to be footnoted. Follow each direct quote, statistic, or idea with a number. The number should be written slightly above the line, like this: [1]. The numbers should run in order, with the first piece of text to be footnoted numbered *1*, the second piece numbered *2*, and so on.

2. On a separate page at the end of your paper, make a list of the sources from which your footnoted material was taken. The order in which the footnotes appear in your paper and the order of the footnotes on the footnote page should be the same.

3. To write your footnotes, look for the source number you wrote after each piece of text you wanted to footnote. If you didn't write these source numbers when you wrote your first draft, look through your note cards for the card that contains the information you are footnoting. That note card should contain the proper source number. Then locate the bibliography card with the same number. This bibliography card, together with the page number from the note card, will give you all of the

information you need to write your footnote.

Each kind of source has its own special footnote form. To find the proper footnote form for the kind of source you are footnoting, see pages 264–265.

Finally, prepare your **bibliography,** which is a complete list of sources you used to prepare your research paper. A bibliography usually appears on a separate, final page. Each entry contains the information from your bibliography cards, except for the source number and library location. The form for a bibliography entry differs slightly for books, magazines, encyclopedias, and other sources. See pages 266–267 for the proper bibliography forms.

Check It Out   Study the form of footnotes and bibliography for a report on a career in the hotel industry.

Footnotes

[1]William E. Hopke, "Hotel and Motel Managers," *The Encyclopedia of Careers and Vocational Guidance*, 1981 ed.

[2]Shepard Henkin, *Opportunities in the Hotel and Motel Industry* (Lincolnwood, Illinois: National Textbook Company, 1978), p. 27.

Bibliography

Henkin, Shepard. *Opportunities in the Hotel and Motel Industry*. Lincolnwood, Illinois: National Textbook Company, 1978.

Hopke, William E. "Hotel and Motel Managers." *The Encyclopedia of Careers and Vocational Guidance*. 1981 ed.

Occupational Outlook Handbook. 1985–86 ed. Washington, D.C.: U.S. Department of Labor, Bureau of Labor Statistics, 1985.

Try Your Skill   Read the following quotation about choosing a career. Notice its source. Write a footnote and a bibliography entry based on this information.

People differ in what they want from a career. Many people desire a high income. Some hope for fame. Others want much leisure time or a life of adventure. Still others want to serve people and help make the world a better place. Before you begin to explore career fields, you should determine (1) your values, or goals in life; (2) your interests; and (3) your abilities. Most people are happiest in occupations that meet their values, interests, and abilities.

from page 172e of an article titled "Careers" by Edwin L. Herr in *The World Book Encyclopedia*, Volume 3 (1979), pages 172d-174

Keep This in Mind

- Use footnotes to give credit to writers whose words or ideas you include in a research paper.
- Prepare a bibliography to show the sources of information you used in writing your research paper.

Now Write Make a final copy of your research paper and include your footnotes and bibliography. First, insert the numbers for your footnotes into the first draft of your research paper. Next, find the information you need for your footnotes on your source cards. Copy it in the correct form on a separate page labeled *Footnotes.*

Then take out your bibliography cards and write a bibliography entry for each source you used in your research paper. Copy the entries in alphabetical order onto a separate page labeled *Bibliography.* Be sure to use the correct form.

Neatly copy your paper in final form.

For help in preparing the final copy of your paper, see Handbook Section 16, **The Correct Form for Writing.**

Also, examine the final copy of the research paper on a career in the hotel industry shown at the end of this section.

Basic Forms for Footnotes

A. A book with an author:

[1]Peter Mansfield, <u>The Arab World</u> (New York: Crowell, 1976), p. 123

B. A book with no author:

[2]<u>Images of South Africa</u> (Cape Town: C. Struik, 1983), p. 21.

C. A book with an editor:

[3]John Lahr, ed., <u>Grove Press Modern Drama</u> (New York: Grove Press, Inc., 1975), pp. 93–101.

D. An encyclopedia article:

[4]"Naval Ships and Crafts," <u>Encyclopedia Britannica</u>, 1981 ed.

E. A magazine article with an author:

[5]Pico Iyer, "Some Reluctant Friends," <u>Time</u>, 16 July 1984, p. 38.

F. A magazine article without an author:

[6]"Sleuthing Is the Fun," <u>Time</u>, 4 July 1983, pp. 52–53.

G. A newspaper article:

[7]Gail Sheehy, "America's Great Awakening," <u>Chicago Tribune</u>, 6 August 1982, Sec. 5, p. 1, cols. 1–3.

H. A report or a pamphlet:

[8]American Medical Association, <u>Medical Relations Under Workmen's Compensation</u> (Chicago: American Medical Association, 1976), p. 3.

If the report is by an individual author rather than by an association or committee, begin with the author's name.

I. A film:

[9]Richard Attenborough, dir., Gandhi, with Ben Kingsley, Columbia Pictures, 1982.

J. A television or radio program:

[10]"A Desert Blooming," writ. Marshall Riggan, Living Wild, dir. Harry L. Gorden, prod. Peter Argentine, PBS, 29 April 1984.

K. An interview:

[11]Personal interview with Robert Hughes, Director, New Playwright's Workshop, University of Washington, Bellingham, Washington, 6 Feb. 1984.

Sources Already Footnoted

To refer to sources already listed in previous complete footnotes, use a shortened form.

A. In most cases, the author's last name, followed by the relevant page numbers, is sufficent.

[12]Robyn Davidson, Tracks (New York: Pantheon Books, 1980), p. 62

[13]Davidson, p. 74.

B. If more than one work by the same author has been referred to, then you should write the author's last name and the title. The title may be in shortened form.

[14]John C. Gardner, Grendel (New York: Alfred A. Knopf, 1971), p. 24.

[15]John C. Gardner, Dragon, Dragon and Other Timeless Tales (New York: Alfred A. Knopf, 1975), p. 6.

[16]Gardner, Dragon, Dragon p. 91.

265

Basic Forms for a Bibliography

The entries in a bibliography are arranged alphabetically according to the author's last name. When there is no author, use the first important word of the entry to determine the correct place in the bibliography for that entry.

A. A book with an author:

> Mansfield, Peter. The Arab World. New
> York: Crowell, 1976.

B. A book with no author:

> Images of South Africa. Cape Town:
> C. Struik, 1983.

C. A book with an editor:

> Lahr, John, ed. Grove Press Modern Drama.
> New York: Grove Press, Inc., 1975.

D. An encyclopedia article:

> "Naval Ships and Crafts." Encyclopedia
> Britannica. 1981 ed.

E. A magazine article with an author:

> Iyer, Pico. "Some Reluctant Friends."
> Time, 16 July 1984, p. 38.

F. A magazine article without an author:

> "Sleuthing Is the Fun." Time, 4 July
> 1983, pp. 52–53.

G. A newspaper article:

> Sheehy, Gail. "America's Great Awaken-
> ing." Chicago Tribune, 6 August
> 1984, Sec. 5, p. 1, cols. 1–3.

H. A report or a pamphlet:

American Medical Association. <u>Medical Relations under Workmen's Compensation</u>. Chicago: American Medical Association, 1976.

If the report is by an individual author rather than by an association or committee, begin with the author's name.

I. A film:

Attenborough, Richard. dir., <u>Gandhi</u>, with Ben Kingsley, Columbia Pictures, 1982.

J. A television or radio program:

"A Desert Blooming." Writ. Marshall Riggan. <u>Living Wild</u>. Dir. Harry L. Gorden. Prod. Peter Argentine. PBS, 29 April 1984.

K. An interview:

Hughes, Robert. Director, New Playwright's Workshop, University of Washington. Personal interview. Bellingham, Washington. 6 Feb. 1984.

Chris Adams

English III

March 8, 1985

Reserve a Future in the Hotel Industry

Many people choose a career in the field of personal
services. That is, they choose jobs in which they attend to the
needs of other individuals. One of the largest personal
service industries is the hotel—motel business. Basically, the
function of this business is to provide sleeping
accommodations and meals. However, hotels and motels range
from simple country inns with a few rooms and employees to
elaborate city skyscrapers with more than 1,000 rooms and
hundreds of employees. The largest of these businesses offer
many additional conveniences for their guests. The services
may include gift shops, recreational facilities, and banquet
and convention facilities.

To provide this range of services, the hotel industry
employs workers in a wide variety of skilled and unskilled
occupations. These various occupations can be divided into
those related to the "front of the house" and those related to
the "back of the house." The "front of the house" is a hotel
term for the operations that deal directly with, and are seen
by, the guests. These operations are those of management, the
front office, the uniformed service staff, and the accounting
and sales departments. The "back of the house" refers to hotel

operations that are seldom seen by guests. These include housekeeping, food preparation, security, laundry, and engineering.

Because the hotel industry employs such a broad range of occupations, no single type of training is necessary. Many entry-level positions require only a short period of on-the-job training. Entry-level jobs are often available on a part-time basis for students, to acquaint them with hotel work. These jobs include waiter, maid, clerk, porter, bellhop, and elevator operator. However, longer on-the-job training or vocational education may lead to other, higher-paying positions.[1] For instance, those who have completed programs in cooking, accounting, or maintenance and repair work may eventually become department heads. "The hotel industry is one of the few wherein a young person can secure a position without too much formal education, and work his way through the various departments to an executive capacity."[2]

To be successful in any position in the hotel business, several basic personal qualifications are required. A person must be able to deal with all kinds of people in any situation. Courtesy and patience are essential when serving guests. In addition to a pleasant manner, a neat appearance is important. Finally, constant attention to detail is called for in all aspects of hotel work.

There are many benefits for those who choose a career in the hotel industry. The first advantage is a flexible schedule, since hotels and motels operate twenty-four hours a day with three shifts. Other benefits include the choice of part—time, full—time, or seasonal work, and a wide selection of geographic locations. At present, the industry is also looking for capable women and members of minority groups to train as managers. A career in the hotel industry offers many opportunities for personal and professional growth.

Footnotes

[1]William E. Hopke, "Hotel and Motel Managers. " The
Encyclopedia of Careers and Vocational Guidance. 1981 ed.

[2]Shepard Henkin, Opportunities in the Hotel and Motel
Industry (Lincolnwood, Illinois: National Textbook Company,
1978), p. 27.

Bibliography

Henkin, Shepard. Opportunities in the Hotel and Motel
    Industry. Lincolnwood, Illinois: National Textbook
    Company, 1978.

Hopke, William E. "Hotel and Motel Managers. " The Encyclopedia
    of Careers and Vocational Guidance. 1981 ed.

Occupational Outlook Handbook. 1985—86 ed. Washington, D.C.:
    U.S. Department of Labor, Bureau of Labor Statistics,
    1985.

Critical Thinking

In Fact

Facts and Opinions

Here's the Idea Critical thinking skills are important tools for learning and presenting new ideas. They can be used in school as you gather information, write papers, and take tests. They can also be used on the job and in making decisions.

Every day you read or hear hundreds of facts and opinions. These come from many sources. Television, books, newspapers, magazines, and other people are just a few of these sources. You must learn to separate facts from opinions. You must also learn how to test facts and opinions to see if they are reliable.

A **fact** is a statement that can be proved true. You can prove a fact in any of the following ways:

1. You can make a personal observation.
2. You can ask an expert.
3. You can check the fact in a reference work (a dictionary, encyclopedia, almanac, or book written by an expert).

The statement "The cheetah is the fastest land animal" is a fact. You can prove it by observing how fast different land animals can run. You can ask an expert on animals. You can also read about the cheetah in an encyclopedia. Whenever you read or hear a statement that is supposed to be a fact, ask yourself whether it can be proved. If it *cannot* be proved, it is *not* a fact.

A statement that cannot be proved is an **opinion.** An example of an opinion is the statement "Michael Jackson is the greatest singer alive." A statement such as this cannot be proved.

Even though opinions cannot be proved, they can be supported. **Sound opinions** are ones that are supported by facts. **Unsound opinions** are ones that are not supported by facts. Whenever you read, hear, or write about an opinion, ask yourself whether it can be supported by facts.

Check It Out Read the following statements.

Many people enjoy science fiction films.
Science fiction films are really entertaining.

- Which of these statements is a fact? Which is an opinion? How do you know?

Try Your Skill Check the following statements of fact. Using the reference works listed in parentheses, tell whether each statement is true or false.

1. Franklin D. Roosevelt was President when World War II began. (textbook or encyclopedia)
2. Chad is the largest country in Africa. (atlas)
3. The word *hippopotamus* comes from two words that mean "river horse." (dictionary)
4. Theodore Roethke is a famous American poet. (textbook or encyclopedia)
5. *Thursday* was named after the Norse god Thor. (dictionary)

Keep This in Mind

- A fact is a statement that can be proved true.
- Facts can be checked by observation, by asking an expert, or by reading in a reference work.
- An opinion is a statement that cannot be proved true.
- Sound opinions can be supported with facts. Be sure to support your opinions whenever you speak or write.

Now Write Write one statement of opinion about each of the following subjects. Then write one statement of fact to support each opinion.

football   music   conservation

It Takes All Kinds

Types of Opinions

Here's the Idea   As you learned in Part 1, an opinion is a statement that cannot be proved. There are three main types of opinions. These are judgments, predictions, and statements of obligation.

A **judgment** is a statement that tells how the speaker or writer feels about a subject. The statement "History class is very interesting" is a judgment because it tells how the speaker feels about history class. This type of opinion often includes judgment words, such as *bad, fine, interesting, lovely,* and *excellent.*

A **prediction** is a statement about the future. It tells about something that has not yet happened. Therefore it cannot be proved. The statement "The Greyhawks will win the regional championship this year" is a prediction.

A **statement of obligation** tells what one should or should not do. Such statements usually include one of the following words or phrases: *should, must,* or *ought to.* The statement "You should exercise every day" is a statement of obligation.

Remember that all opinions must be supported by facts. If an opinion can be supported by facts, it is sound. If it cannot be supported by facts, it is unsound.

Check It Out   Read the following statements.

1. The audience should listen politely when a speaker is talking.
2. By the year 2000, robots will be used in most industries.
3. The novels of Stephen King are terrifying.

- Which of these opinions is a judgment? Which is a prediction? Which is a statement of obligation?

Try Your Skill   Tell whether the following opinions are judgments, predictions, or statements of obligation.

1. Shakespeare was the greatest playwright who ever lived.
2. During the next century, mining will take place on the moon.
3. People who drive should learn a little about automotive repair.
4. Spring is the nicest season of all.
5. Campers ought to be careful not to leave trash at their campsites.
6. The road repairs will be completed by fall.

Keep This in Mind

- A judgment tells how a speaker or writer feels about a subject.
- A prediction is a statement about the future.
- A statement of obligation tells what should or should not be done.

Now Write   Read the following paragraph. Identify the two opinions in this paragraph. Tell what types of opinions they are. Also tell whether these opinions are supported by facts.

In the future we will have to find other sources of energy. There is a limited amount of oil and gas in the ground. These fuels are rapidly being used up. We must begin now to find other methods for creating the energy we need.

Overloaded

Avoiding Loaded Language

Here's the Idea Even though they cannot be proved, opinions are still very important. They express how we feel about things. They tell what we expect of the future. They show what actions we believe are right and wrong. In fact, many of the most important ideas that we have about the world are opinions. You probably have many opinions of your own about which you feel very strongly. Sometimes you may even attempt to convince other people to adopt these opinions. When you do this, you are practicing the art of **persuasion.**

Whenever you present an argument, always support your opinion with facts. By doing this, you give the other person reasons to see things the way you do. Do not make the mistake of simply stating your opinion and expecting someone to accept it. Also avoid using highly emotional, or loaded, language.

Loaded language is language that appeals to a person's emotions. Such language is often used in place of facts to sway the opinions of readers and listeners. There are two types of loaded language: snarl words and purr words. A **snarl word** is one that creates a negative feeling. A **purr word** is one that creates a positive feeling. Read the following examples.

You are a *miser.*
I am *thrifty.*

You are *overbearing.*
I am *forceful.*

The sentences in each pair mean almost the same thing. However, the first sentence in each pair seems negative. This is due to the snarl words *miser* and *overbearing.* The second sentence in each pair seems more positive. This is due to the purr words *thrifty* and *forceful.* Be alert to the use of snarl and purr words when you listen to the ideas of others. Also be careful when you use them yourself. They should never be used in place of facts.

Check It Out   Read the following pairs of statements.

1. Life in the country is simpler and more peaceful than life in the city.
2. Life in the country is more dull and routine than life in the city.

- In what ways are these two statements alike? How do they differ? What snarl words and purr words do they contain?

Try Your Skill   Find the snarl words and purr words in the following sentences.

1. Many actors and actresses are fabulously wealthy.
2. Many actors and actresses are filthy rich.
3. Marietta dresses fashionably.
4. Marietta dresses according to every passing fad.

Keep This in Mind

- Loaded language contains snarl words and purr words.
- Snarl words create negative feelings.
- Purr words create positive feelings.
- When supporting opinions, do not use loaded language in place of facts.

Now Write   Choose a topic about which you feel strongly. Write three statements of opinion on this topic. In the first, use snarl words. In the second, use purr words. In the third, avoid loaded language altogether.

Out on a Limb

Errors in Reasoning

Here's the Idea   Some unsound opinions result from errors in reasoning. A few of these errors have been given names.

Overgeneralization occurs when a person makes a statement about an entire group based on too few examples. Read the following example of an overgeneralization.

> Mr. Gomez was sent to New York on business. The hotel in which he stayed was terrible. When he returned, he told a friend, "Hotels in New York are awful."

This is an overgeneralization because it is based on too few examples. Mr. Gomez would have to stay in many hotels in New York before he could make such a general statement about their quality. Avoid making overgeneralizations yourself. Use **qualifying words** instead of **absolute words**. Here are some examples.

Absolute Words	Qualifying Words
all	most
everyone	many
nobody	few
never	rarely

A **stereotype** is an overgeneralization about an entire group of people. Suppose that you go to a department store and are served by a woman who is extremely rude. If you decide that all female salespeople are rude, you are guilty of stereotyping. Stereotypes are illogical and unreasonable. They are often directed against members of entire racial, ethnic, political, or religious groups. In such cases, stereotypes can be harmful.

Bandwagon is the error of supposing that an action is right simply because a lot of people are doing it. For example, a clothing company may say that you should buy their jeans because everybody is wearing them.

Snob appeal encourages you to take some action because fashionable, or rich people do it. The advertisement "Dine at Des's—where the elite meet" is an example of snob appeal.

Become familiar with these common errors. Learn to recognize them and to avoid them.

Check It Out   Read the following unsound opinions.

> All teenagers are irresponsible.
> That movie must be great; everyone's going to see it.

- What is wrong with these opinions?

Try Your Skill   Each of the following statements contains an error in reasoning. Choose the name of the error from those given in parentheses.

1. You are one of the few who can appreciate the finer things in life. Don't settle for anything less than a Stellar Electronics stereo system. (bandwagon, overgeneralization, snob appeal)

2. All politicians are dishonest. (snob appeal, stereotyping, bandwagon)

3. Don't be the last person on your block to have a Smokey Jones gas barbecue grill! (stereotyping, bandwagon, snob appeal)

Keep This in Mind

- Unsound opinions often result from errors in reasoning.
- Common errors in reasoning include overgeneralization, stereotyping, bandwagon, and snob appeal.

Now Write   Errors in reasoning often appear in advertisements and in television commercials. Using these sources, find an example of each of the four errors in reasoning discussed in this lesson. Describe each error in a paragraph.

Further Out

More Faulty Reasoning

Here's the Idea   People often use reasoning to figure out why something is or why something has happened. Doctors look for the causes of illnesses. Auto mechanics look for the causes of car trouble. All people look for the causes of events in their personal lives. Whenever you reason about causes, you must be careful to avoid two common errors. These errors are called **false-cause reasoning** and **only-cause reasoning.**

When one event happens after another event, people sometimes decide that the first event caused the second one. They may draw this conclusion even though there is no proof that the two events are related. This is an example of **false-cause** reasoning. Many superstitions are based on just such reasoning. For example, suppose a person spills salt and then has bad luck. This person might conclude that spilling salt causes bad luck. However, the two events would actually be unrelated.

Only-cause reasoning is a second type of error. Suppose, for example, that you read the statement "Crime is caused by poverty." This statement is only partly true. Some crime is caused by poverty. However, there are also many other causes that lead to crime, such as greed or anger.

Check It Out   Read the following passages.

> Luis is going to junior college full-time. He also works a full-time job in the evenings. Because of his schedule, he doesn't eat well. Lately, he has been complaining of feeling tired all the time. If he would simply start eating when he is supposed to, he wouldn't feel tired any more.

Last week, a house in our neighborhood burned down. The firefighters couldn't determine the cause of the fire. However, I know that the house must have been hit by lightning. After all, there was a thunderstorm just before the fire.

- Which of these passages contains the false-cause error?
- Which contains the only-cause error?

Try Your Skill   Identify the following statements as examples of false-cause or only-cause reasoning.

1. Jim lost his ring because he broke a mirror two weeks ago.
2. Traffic accidents are caused by carelessness.
3. I won a prize at the carnival because I played the games in booth number seven. Seven is my lucky number.
4. Milk must be good for a cold. I know because I drank two glasses of milk. A few days later, I was better.
5. There has been an increase in violence on TV. There has also been an increase in violent crimes. Therefore, TV violence leads to violent crime.

Keep This in Mind

- *False cause* is the error of mistaking an unrelated event for a cause.
- *Only cause* is the error of assuming that an event has only one cause when it actually has many.
- Avoid these errors whenever you reason about causes and effects.

Now Write   Make up several sentences such as those in **Try Your Skill.** Describe the error in reasoning in each sentence. Then write a more logical statement.

To Sum It All Up

Drawing Conclusions

Here's the Idea   Every day of your life, you will be drawing conclusions. A **conclusion** is a judgment, interpretation, or decision. You reach a conclusion after observing a group of facts.

To draw a conclusion, you must look for relationships between the facts you observe. Imagine that you hear a Senator speaking on television. She says that she supports tougher air pollution laws. Later, you read that she has introduced a bill to control the disposal of waste. In both cases, the Senator has supported anti-pollution measures. You can draw a general conclusion. The Senator is concerned with controlling pollution.

In school and in your personal life, do not simply take in information without thinking about it. Try at all times to look for the connections between things. In this way, you can build on facts to develop new ideas.

Check It Out   Read the following passages.

Every registered voter in our city voted in the last election. Ms. Lupico is a registered voter. She lives in our city. Therefore, she voted in the last election.

House cats, lions, tigers, mountain lions, and cheetahs all have sharp teeth and claws. Therefore, felines must have sharp teeth and claws.

- What facts are presented in these passages?
- What conclusions are drawn from these facts?

Try Your Skill   Study the graph on the next page. Then, answer the questions that follow. Draw conclusions from the facts presented.

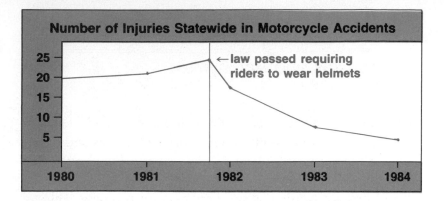

Number of Injuries Statewide in Motorcycle Accidents

←law passed requiring riders to wear helmets

1. What was the trend in motorcycle injuries before the law was passed in November of 1981?

2. What was the trend in injuries after the law was passed?

3. Is it likely that the passage of the law reduced the number of injuries? Why or why not?

Keep This in Mind

- To draw conclusions, you must first observe a group of facts.
- After observing the group of facts, you must determine how the facts are related.
- When you state the relationship between the facts, you have drawn a conclusion.

Now Write Read the following passage from a short story. Notice the facts presented in the passage. Make a list of the conclusions that you can draw about the character described.

When Mark returned the first day, he was tired, more tired than he had ever been. His legs and arms ached unbearably. His skin, now a brilliant red, burned and burned. Perhaps, he thought, I'll get used to it. At least the pay is good. As he settled down in bed, he thought once again of the motorcycle. Three months and he would have it.

Like It or Not

Synonyms and Antonyms

Here's the Idea   One critical thinking skill tested by colleges and employers is the ability to recognize similarities and differences. Studying synonyms and antonyms can help you to develop this skill.

Synonyms are words that are very close in meaning. Pairs of words such as *big* and *large, close* and *near*, and *vague* and *unclear* are examples of synonyms. To tell whether two words are synonyms, use one of the words in a sentence. Then, substitute the other word in the same sentence. If both sentences make sense, and if the meaning of the sentence does not change, the words are synonyms.

Antonyms are words that have opposite meanings. Word pairs such as *tall* and *short, dirty* and *clean*, and *patience* and *impatience* are examples of antonyms. Antonym questions are found on the SAT (Scholastic Aptitude Test). These questions test your vocabulary. They also test your ability to recognize opposites. An antonym question begins by giving you a single word. It then asks you to choose from a list of words the one that is most opposite in meaning. An antonym question looks like this:

ORDINARY: (A) wonderful   (B) funny   (C) unusual
                     (D) common   (E) exciting

To answer an antonym question, use this method:

1. Find the meaning of the given word. Think of how it is used in various sentences.

2. Place the word *not* before the given word. (Example: *not ordinary*)

3. Find the word from the list that means the same as *not* plus the given word. For example, *unusual* is the correct answer to the sample question because it means *not ordinary*.

Check It Out   Read the following pairs of words.

1. hot   cold   3. light   heavy   5. cat   feline
2. sharp   dull   4. test   examination   6. rock   stone

- Which of these pairs of words are antonyms? Which are synonyms?

Try Your Skill   The following questions are like the antonym questions found on the SAT. You are given a word in capital letters. This word is followed by five choices in lower-case letters. Choose the word in lower-case letters that is most nearly opposite the first word.

1. HIT: (A) miss   (B) sit   (C) succeed   (D) mistake
       (E) think
2. LEGALLY: (A) gracefully   (B) suddenly   (C) honestly
             (D) badly   (E) unlawfully
3. INSULT: (A) deny   (B) annoy   (C) compliment
            (D) answer   (E) understand

Keep This in Mind

- The ability to recognize similarities and differences is an important thinking skill.
- Synonyms are words that are similar in meaning.
- Antonyms are words that are opposite in meaning.

Now Write   Choose the correct antonym for each word given in capital letters. Use each antonym in a sentence.

1. COMEDY: (A) story   (B) play   (C) sadness   (D) joke
           (E) tragedy
2. DISGRACE: (A) honor   (B) shame   (C) rumor
             (D) gossip   (E) fame
3. NIMBLE: (A) awkward   (B) clever   (C) quick
            (D) excellent   (E) prompt

Close Relations

Analogies

Here's the Idea   Another important critical thinking skill involves the ability to see relationships. Working with analogies can help you to develop this skill.

An **analogy** is a comparison of two things that are not exactly alike. Read the following example.

> Writing is like getting dressed in the morning. You can keep on changing things until you get them just right.

Writing and getting dressed are very different activities. However, they share at least one quality in common. Therefore, an analogy or comparison can be made between them.

SAT tests have sections on analogies. In an analogy question, you are given two words. You must decide how the two words are related. Then, you must choose a second pair of words that are related in the same way. An analogy question looks like this:

> CAT: KITTEN   (A) bull: cow   (B) ape: chimpanzee (C) tabby: cat   (D) herd: elephant (E) horse: colt

Use the following method to answer analogy questions.

1. Study the first pair of words. Find the relationship between them by using both in a sentence. (A *cat* is an adult *kitten*.)

2. Next, find a second pair of words that you can put in place of the first pair. (A *horse* is an adult *colt*.)

Check It Out   Read the following pairs of words. Also read the sentence next to each one.

1. strike: hammer   A *hammer* is used to *strike* things.
2. virus: cold   A *cold* is caused by a *virus*.
3. bobwhite: bird   A *bobwhite* is a type of *bird*.
4. roof: house   A *roof* is a part of a *house*.

5. soon: now   Soon refers to a time later than *now*.
6. weightlifter: strong   Being *strong* is a characteristic of a
                            weightlifter.

- Do you see how sentences can help you to see how words are related?

Try Your Skill   Complete these analogies. Find the word pair that is related in the same way as the first pair of words.

1. AIRPLANE: PILOT::   (A) ship: anchor   (B) car: chauffeur
   (C) truck: trailer   (D) glider: wood   (E) rocket: space
2. WORD: LETTERS::   (A) night: day   (B) team: players
   (C) judge: sentence   (D) watch: time   (E) forest: trails
3. LENGTH: RULER::   (A) temperature: thermometer
   (B) weight: heavy   (C) scale: pounds   (D) yardstick:
   measure   (E) shadow: sun

Keep This in Mind

- An analogy is a comparison between things that are not exactly alike.
- To answer analogy questions, use the first pair of words in a sentence. Then find another pair that you can substitute for the first pair.

Now Write   Find the pair of words that best completes each analogy. Then choose three pairs of words from your answers. Write three sentences that show how the words are related.

1. EARLY: LATE::   (A) saw: wood   (B) hot: cold   (C) dog:
   master   (D) true: honest   (E) present: gift
2. STUDENT: CLASS::   (A) bull: steer   (B) chemicals:
   chemist   (C) fruit: vegetables   (D) actor: cast
3. SQUIRREL: TREE::   (A) fish: trout   (B) worm: ground
   (C) army: navy   (D) leaf: stem   (E) strawberry: jam
4. BIRD: FEATHERS::   (A) kangaroo: Australia   (B) dogs:
   paws   (C) male: female   (D) cat: fur   (E) winter: cold

The Missing Pieces

Sentence Completion

Here's the Idea   You have practiced recognizing relationships between words. Now you will practice recognizing relationships between words in sentences. This will help you to be aware of less obvious meanings in sentences.

The **sentence completion** questions in SAT tests require you to use this skill. In these questions, you are given a sentence from which one or two words have been removed. You must choose the word or pair of words that best complete the sentence. A typical sentence completion question looks like this:

> The audience seemed not to _____ that the music was loud enough to cause _____ damage to their hearing.
>
> (A) care—funny   (B) wonder—valuable   (C) notice—serious   (D) mention—temporary   (E) hope—fine

To answer sentence completion questions, use this method:

1. Read the incomplete sentence carefully. Note any key words. Look for words that state contrasts (*however, but*). Also look for words that signal similarities (*another, the same as*).

2. Try each choice in the sentence. Do not be misled by answers that have only one word that fits well into the sentence. Answer C is the only choice in which both words make sense in the sample incomplete sentence above.

Check It Out   Read the following incomplete sentences.

1. The fog was too _____ for us to _____ across the lake.

2. The actor threatened to _____ the newspaper for its _____ story about him.

3. Because the ancient Greeks admired athletic _____, they treated champion _____ like heroes.

290

- What words could you use to complete these sentences?

Try Your Skill   Choose the pair of words that best completes the meaning of each of the following sentences.

1. I can vouch for Dan's _____; he always tells the _____.
   (A) honesty—truth   (B) ability—story   (C) hypocrisy—sound   (D) education—tests   (E) happiness—story
2. The _____ child very nearly lost _____ of himself.
   (A) older—pictures   (B) hysterical—control   (C) lazy—comments   (D) uninterested—most   (E) shy—friends
3. In many _____ humans have been _____ by robots.
   (A) actions—seen   (B) books—built   (C) evenings—valued   (D) factories—replaced   (E) ways—lent

Keep This in Mind

- Words in sentences have particular relationships to one another.
- Sentence completion questions require you to recognize relationships between words in sentences.
- When answering sentence completion questions, make sure that both words make sense.

Now Write   Write the pairs of words that best complete the meaning of each of the following sentences.

1. The doctor _____ penicillin for the _____ ear.
   (A) bought—well   (B) left—tiny   (C) prescribed—infected   (D) injected—healed   (E) diagnosed—symptom
2. The accident _____ was knocked _____ by the blow.
   (A) victim—unconscious   (B) report—underground   (C) later—out   (D) simply—everywhere
3. _____ athletes cannot compete in the _____.
   (A) Good—major leagues   (B) Some—contract   (C) Professional—Olympics   (D) Powerful—style

Using
the Library

Part 1 **Shelf by Shelf**
Finding What You Need

Part 2 **On the Track**
Using the Card Catalog

Part 3 **There's One for You**
Using an Encyclopedia

Part 4 **Did You Know That?**
Using Reference Works

Shelf by Shelf

Finding What You Need

Here's the Idea   A library serves the needs of people because of the variety of factual materials and information it has available. You will also find books and magazines that relate unusual imaginary adventures and experiences. To find whatever you need easily, you need to learn how your school or public library is organized.

You will find that all library books are classified into two general groups, fiction and nonfiction. **Fiction** books are arranged alphabetically according to the author's last name. For example, the novel *A Tale of Two Cities*, by Charles Dickens, would be filed under *D*.

Nonfiction books are arranged according to their subjects on a separate section of shelves. Many libraries use a system called the **Dewey Decimal System.** This system groups nonfiction books into ten numbered categories.

000-099	**General Works**	(encyclopedias, almanacs)
100-199	**Philosophy**	(ethics, psychology, occult)
200-299	**Religion**	(the Bible, mythology)
300-399	**Social Science**	(economics, law, education, government)
400-499	**Language**	(languages, grammar, dictionaries)
500-599	**Science**	(mathematics, biology, chemistry)
600-699	**Useful Arts**	(farming, cooking, sewing, television, business)
700-799	**Fine Arts**	(music, photography, dance, sports)
800-899	**Literature**	(poetry, plays)
900-999	**History**	(biography, travel, geography)

Every nonfiction book has a **call number** written on the spine. This call number includes the Dewey Decimal number and other information. A call number identifies a book. Some libraries add the letter *B* to the spine of a biography or the letter *R* to the spine of a reference work, such as an encyclopedia.

Look at this example of a nonfiction book.

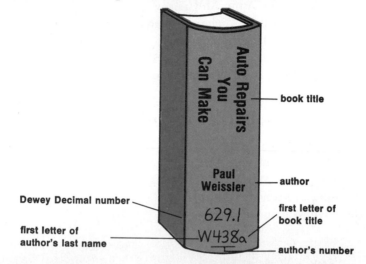

Auto Repairs You Can Make — book title

Paul Weissler — author

Dewey Decimal number — 629.1

first letter of author's last name — W438a

first letter of book title

author's number

Check It Out Examine the spines of the books represented here.

Better Vacations for Your Money — Michael Frome — 917.3 F926b

The Black Pearl — Scott O'Dell

Listening to Jazz — Jerry Coker — 781.57 C669ℓ

Snow Bound — Harry Mazer

Exploring Apprenticeship Careers — Charlotte Lobb — 331.55 LOB

Shape Up for Sports — Ray Slegener — 613.71 SLE

Sounder — William H. Armstrong

All Quiet on the Western Front — Erich Maria Remarque

- Which books are fiction and which are nonfiction?
- What is the general category of each nonfiction book?

Try Your Skill   Write the answers to these questions.

1. Under what letter on the library shelves would you find the following fiction books?

Dragonsinger by Anne McCaffrey
Watership Down by Richard Adams
The Clown by Barbara Corcoran
Incident at Hawk's Hill by Allan W. Eckert
The Good-Luck Bogie Hat by Constance C. Greene

2. In which categories of the Dewey Decimal System would you find information on these subjects?

a play about Thanksgiving
directions for making furniture
a biography of Martin Luther King
teaching pre-school children
the Civil War in the U.S.

Keep This in Mind

- In the library, fiction books are filed alphabetically by the author's last name.
- Nonfiction books may be classified in ten major categories of the Dewey Decimal System. Each nonfiction book has a call number.

Now Write   As your teacher directs, learn how materials are arranged in your school or public library. Find out where fiction and nonfiction books are. Find out where reference books, magazines, and special collections are.

In the library, find at least four fiction books and four nonfiction books that you might enjoy reading. You may want to check one out for your own reading. Write the titles and authors of the books you find. Copy the call number of any special marking written on the spine of any of the books. Label your paper **Shelf by Shelf.** Keep it in your folder.

On the Track

Using the Card Catalog

Here's the Idea In every library there is a file called the card catalog. This file organizes information about all the books in that library. Every book is listed in the catalog at least three times—by its author, by its title, and by its subject.

All three cards—author card, title card, and subject card—contain the same information. This information is arranged under different headings so that you will be able to find a book in several ways. All three cards give the call number of a nonfiction book in the upper left corner. This is the same number that appears on the book.

All three cards list the author, title, publisher, date of publication, and the number of pages in the book. There is a notation if the book has illustrations or maps. There may also be a description of the book or a list of related books.

On an **author card,** the author's name is given at the top, last name first. Author cards are filed alphabetically by the author's last name. If there is more than one author, the card is filed by the name of the author whose name is shown first in the book.

On a **title card,** the title appears on the top line, with only the first word of the title capitalized. Title cards are filed alphabetically by the first word of the title. However, if *A, An,* or *The* appears as the first word in a title, look for the card under the first letter of the second word in the title.

On a **subject card,** the subject appears on the top line. The subject may be written in capital letters or in red. Subject cards are filed alphabetically by the first letter of the subject.

You will find some cards that say *See* or *See also.* These **cross reference cards** refer you to other subject headings that are related to the one that you want.

Using the card catalog is simpler if you check the **guide cards.** These blank cards have tabs on which general subject headings are written. These headings will help you to follow the alphabetical arrangement of the card catalog.

650.14   **Souerwine, Andrew H.**
SOU   Career strategies : planning for
                 personal achievement / Andrew H.
                 Souerwine. — New York : AMACOM,
                 © 1978.
                    xii, 292 p. : ill. ; 24 cm.

                    Includes index.
                    Bibliography: p. 280-284.
                    ISBN 0-8144-5454-2 : $14.75

                                O

650.14   **Career Strategies: Planning for Personal Achievement**
SOU   Career strategies : planning for
                 personal achievement / Andrew H.
                 Souerwine. — New York : AMACOM,
                 © 1978.
                    xii, 292 p. : ill. ; 24 cm.

                    Includes index.
                    Bibliography: p. 280-284.
                    ISBN 0-8144-5454-2 : $14.75

                                O

650.14   **JOB SATISFACTION**
SOU   Career strategies : planning for
                 personal achievement / Andrew H.
                 Souerwine. — New York : AMACOM,
                 © 1978.
                    xii, 292 p. : ill. ; 24 cm.

                    includes index.
                    Bibliography: p. 280-284.
                    ISBN 0-8144-5454-2 : $14.75

                                O

Check It Out   Examine the three sample cards.

- Under what letter would each card be filed? Where would you look to find more books by Andrew H. Souerwine? Where would you look to see if there are other books about job satisfaction?

Try Your Skill   Here are the authors, titles, and call numbers for three books about careers. Choose one of the books. Draw three rectangles to represent cards in the card catalog. Use the information given about the book you choose to make an author card, title card, and subject card. Make up the other necessary details for the cards. Compare your sample cards with those in the card catalog.

1. Ruth Lembeck, *Teenage Jobs,* 371.425 L542t
2. Joseph L. Norton, *On the Job,* 371.425 N824o
3. Sarah Splaver, *Nontraditional Careers for Women,* 331.702 Sp5ln

---

Keep This in Mind

- Every book in a library is listed in the card catalog on at least three different cards—author, title, and subject. Each card shows the author, title, publisher, number of pages, and other useful information. Cards for a nonfiction book also list its call number.

Now Write   Choose a subject that interests you and that you can research at the library. Using the card catalog, find at least three nonfiction books about your subject. Copy the important information from the author, title, and subject cards. Label your paper **On the Track,** and keep it in your folder. Also, select the most interesting book you find, and sign it out of the library. Bring the book to class.

There's One for You

Using an Encyclopedia

Here's the Idea An encyclopedia is a general reference work that contains information on a great many different subjects. The articles are arranged in alphabetical order by subject, from the first volume through the last. On the spine of each volume is either a single letter or a set of guide letters indicating what is included.

A large library will have several sets of encyclopedias. You will find that they have different reading levels. When you want to use an encyclopedia, be sure to choose one that you can read easily. Select an encyclopedia suitable for your work by skimming through several. You may want to ask a librarian for help with your selection.

Suppose you wanted information about education. You might select *The World Book Encyclopedia, Collier's Encyclopedia,* or the *Encyclopaedia Britannica,* for example. Find the appropriate volume and look up "Education." The guide words at the top of the page will help you find the subject quickly.

An encyclopedia article on an important subject, education, for example, is usually presented in several parts with subtitles. The article may include such parts as "Kinds of Education," "Education in the United States," "Education Around the World," "The Educative Process," "History," and "Current Issues in U.S. Education." Depending on your purpose, you may need to read all of the article or only parts of it.

At the end of a major article you will find other helpful information. At the end of an article on education, for example, you may find a list of related articles in the same encyclopedia. These might be about people connected with education, educational institutions, and educational programs and agencies. In addition, you may find an outline of the information in the article, books for further reading on the subject, or a research guide to the subject.

Most encyclopedias also include an index. This is usually the first or last volume of the set. Use the index to find information under related subjects in different articles. Some encyclopedias also publish yearbooks, which contain up-to-date information.

Whenever you research a subject, check more than one source of information. Use several encyclopedias as well as other reference books. If you find different information in different sources, try to use the most recent or most reliable reference.

In addition to the general encyclopedias, there are others that provide information only on a single subject. For example, you may find encyclopedias about sports, music, or careers. These encyclopedias will usually be located in the reference room or area of the library.

Check It Out   Look at the encyclopedias shown below.

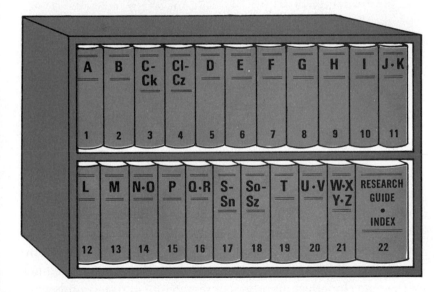

- In what volume, and under what key word, would you find information about canoeing? modern painting? the Panama Canal? William Shakespeare? heredity?

Try Your Skill   As your teacher directs, use an encyclopedia to answer the following questions.

1. Who was the first governor of Virginia?
2. What was the birthplace of Sir Winston Churchill?
3. Name an award won by Jane Addams, who founded Hull House.
4. What languages were spoken by the American Algonquin Indians?
5. What are the principal agricultural exports of Colombia, South America?
6. What is the most famous novel by Louisa May Alcott?
7. What is the difference between a crocodile and an alligator?
8. Name two twentieth-century American architects.
9. In Greek mythology, who was the wife of the god Zeus?
10. What was the importance of D-Day to World War II?

Keep This in Mind

- An encyclopedia is a general reference work that contains information on many different subjects. Articles are arranged alphabetically in numbered volumes. Examine a variety of encyclopedias. Select one that is suitable for your purpose.

Now Write   Write the name of the subject that you researched in the card catalog in the last lesson. Look up that subject in two encyclopedias. List a few of the most interesting facts that you find in each, and compare them. Also, name which encyclopedia you prefer and briefly explain your answer. Be sure to list all important information about your sources: names of the encyclopedias, numbers of the volumes, page numbers of the articles, and titles of other related articles or books on the subject. Label your paper **There's One for You** and put it into your folder.

Did You Know That?

Using Reference Words

Here's the Idea   Usually, a library has an entire room or special section containing reference works. Many of these cannot be taken from the library because they are such useful sources of information for so many people. In addition to such general references as dictionaries and encyclopedias, other references provide information about specific areas of interest.

Atlases are books of maps. Many atlases contain information about population, weather, and places throughout the world. Among the most widely used atlases are the *National Geographic Atlas of the World, The International Atlas from Rand McNally,* and the *Atlas of World History.*

Almanacs and **yearbooks** are published every year. In these references you will find current information about world events, governments, population, and sports. You may want to use the *Guinness Book of World Records,* the *World Almanac and Book of Facts,* the *Information Please Almanac, Atlas, and Yearbook,* or the *Statesman's Yearbook.*

Biographical references contain information about important people. Useful reference books include *The Book of Presidents, Current Biography, Who's Who, Twentieth Century Authors,* and the *Dictionary of American Biography.*

A **vertical file** is the library's collection of pamphlets, handbooks, catalogs, and clippings. Usually kept in a file cabinet, this collection varies from library to library. It often includes special information about local events, travel, and careers.

Magazines are valuable sources of information about a great many subjects. A library may subscribe to any number of the leading magazines published in the United States. In order to find specific information in magazine articles, learn to use the

Readers' Guide to Periodical Literature. The *Readers' Guide* contains the titles of articles, stories, and poems published in more than a hundred leading magazines. One hardcover volume of the *Readers' Guide* covers material published during the entire year. Smaller paperback volumes cover material over shorter time periods. Once you learn to use the abbreviated format, you will find the *Readers' Guide* a useful reference.

Each of these specialized references contains an explanation of how its information is arranged, of the abbreviations that are used, and a sample entry. When you use a reference book for the first time, study these explanations.

Check It Out Examine this portion of a page from the *Readers' Guide to Periodical Literature.*

Earthworms
A reel man's guide to bassin' and wormin'. R. Gerlach. il
Outdoor Life 172:66-7 + O '83
name of magazine

Anecdotes, facetiae, satire, etc.
|All about worms!| E. Zern. il *Field Stream* 88:130 D '83
title of article
Easels
Easy-to-make, easy-to-store easels for young artists. il
Sunset 171:114 + D '83
Easley, Marie B.
In the service. *Work Woman* 8:204 N '83
East, Ben
about
Tribute to Ben East.|V. T. Sparano.|il pors *Outdoor Life*
author
172:110 O '83
East Berlin *See* Berlin (Germany: East)
East Germany |*See* |Germany (East)
cross reference
East Timor *See* Timor
Easter

Greece
Eternal Easter in a Greek village [Olimbos] M. Nic-
olaidis-Karanikolas. il maps *Natl Geogr* |164| 768-77 D
volume number
'83
Easterbrook, Gregg
Examining a media myth. il *Atlantic* 252:10 + O '83
Eastern Air Lines, Inc.
The airline confusion has travel agents flying blind. il
Bus Week p43 O 17 '83
Eastern Air Lines on the brink. S. P. Sherman. il por
Fortune 108:[102-4]+ O 17 '83
page reference
Eastern chief tells employees payroll concessions are vital
[F. Borman] E. H. Kolcum. *Aviat Week Space Technol*
119:30-1|O 3 '83|
date of magazine

304

- Read through one unmarked listing in this sample and explain all the information given. Where is the *Readers' Guide* located in your school or public library? What other kinds of references are in the reference section of your library?

Try Your Skill   Write the name of a reference work in which you would be likely to find an answer to each of the following questions. If magazines would be the best reference, write *Readers' Guide*.

1. Japan consists of how many major islands?
2. What foods might be discussed in a pamphlet called "Eating for Good Health"?
3. What is the present population of California?
4. Name two well-known twentieth-century authors.
5. What baseball team won the 1975 World Series?
6. How was President Franklin Roosevelt related to President Theodore Roosevelt?
7. How many countries are members of the United Nations?
8. What was General Custer's full name?
9. What are some arguments for and against nuclear energy?
10. What is the average yearly rainfall in Michigan?

Keep This in Mind

- There are several kinds of useful specialized references. Learn to use those available in your own library.

Now Write   Choose a well-known person or place that you like. Use several specialized references to find information on your topic. Skim each source and jot down several of the interesting facts. List the titles, call numbers, and volume and page numbers of the sources you find most useful. Label your paper **Did You Know That?** and put it into your folder.

Study and Research Skills

Know It All

Understanding Your Assignments

Here's the Idea   One secret to success in high school is understanding exactly what is expected of you. This involves recording your assignments carefully and following directions.

Recording Your Assignments   Whenever you are given an assignment, listen closely to all the details. Then, write the assignment carefully in an assignment notebook. Record the subject or class, the date the assignment is given, and the date it is due. Write any specific directions for the assignment. Include the page numbers of reading assignments. Also include any materials you will need and the form your final product should take.

Following Directions   If the directions are spoken, listen carefully. Write the directions as you hear them. Note the steps involved in the assignment and the order of these steps. Listen for key words, such as *read, answer,* or *explain,* that tell you what to do. If you have questions about the directions, ask your teacher.

If the directions are written, read them carefully. Divide the assignment into steps. Put these steps in a logical order. Ask your teacher to explain any steps that you don't understand. Before you begin to work, gather any materials you will need to complete the assignment.

Check It Out   Read the following entry from an assignment notebook.

- What does this assignment ask you to do?
- What materials will you need?
- What will the final product be?
- When is the assignment due?

Subject	Assignment	Date Given	Date Due
Health	Write a public-service radio commercial. One minute long. 150 words. Type.	March 21	March 23

Try Your Skill   Read the sample home economics assignment below. Then, answer the questions that follow.

Using a red marker, make seven columns on a sheet of paper. Label these columns for the days of the week. Then, using a black pen, prepare menus for a family of four for one week. Write each menu in the appropriate column. Decide what you would have to buy to make these meals. Write a grocery list on a separate sheet of paper. Then, go to a grocery store. Write the price next to each item on your list. At the bottom of the list, tell how much your meal plan would cost. Turn in your plan and your list on Tuesday.

1. What steps are included in this assignment?
2. What materials will you need?
3. What will the final product be? When is the assignment due?

Keep This in Mind
- Record all assignments in an assignment notebook.
- Listen to or read all directions carefully before you begin an assignment.

Now Write   Begin your own assignment notebook. Divide the notebook into separate sections. Label each section for a different class. Record your assignments in this notebook.

According to Plan

Using SQ3R

Here's the Idea   One plan that you can use to study written materials is the SQ3R study method. The method consists of five steps: **S**urvey, **Q**uestion, **R**ead, **R**ecite, and **R**eview.

Survey the reading assignment.

 1. Look over the material to get a general idea of its content.
 2. Read the titles and subtitles. Notice the illustrations.
 3. Read the introduction and summary.

Question.

 1. List any questions that you should be able to answer after your reading.
 2. Use any study questions provided by your teacher or at the end of the chapter.
 3. Turn titles, topic sentences, and headings into questions.
 4. Make questions based upon any illustrations, maps, tables, charts, or graphs.

Read the selection.

 1. As you read, look for answers to your questions.
 2. Look for main ideas and supporting details.
 3. Pay particular attention to definitions, topic sentences, and chapter headings.

Recite the answers to your questions.

 1. Recite your answers aloud.
 2. Make brief notes to help you remember the answers.
 3. Also make notes on important points from the material.

Review the selection.

 1. Try to answer each of your original questions without looking at your notes.
 2. If necessary, look over the selection to find the answers.
 3. Read your notes again to impress the material on your mind.

Check It Out   Read the questions that can be made from these chapter headings.

Chapter Heading	Questions
Using SQ3R	a. What does "SQ3R" mean?
	b. How is SQ3R used?
Preparing for and Taking	a. How can I prepare for tests?
Tests	b. What should I do when taking a test?

- How can such questions help you to study the material under each heading?

Try Your Skill   Study the following selection. Use the SQ3R study method. Write your questions and answers.

The Edsel: A Car That Had Promise

The 1958–59 Edsel, or "E Car," was introduced by a heavy advertising campaign. The car was intended to be a milestone in automotive history.

Costly Mistakes. Unfortunately, the Edsel was plagued with problems from the beginning. Consumers felt that the car cost too much. In addition, the car had noisy gears, hoods that stuck, hubcaps that fell off, and doors that refused to stay shut. By 1959, Ford had produced 110,000 Edsels. Most of them remained unsold. The name "Edsel" came to mean "a loser."

Keep This in Mind

- The SQ3R study method is made up of five steps: *Survey, Question, Read, Recite,* and *Review.*
- Use the SQ3R method for your reading assignments.

Now Write   Using the SQ3R method, complete a class reading assignment. Write down your questions, answers, and any other notes. Label your paper **Using SQ3R.** Save your work.

The Long and Short

Taking Notes

Here's the Idea It isn't enough just to listen in class or to read your assignments. You must also take notes on what you read and hear. You can then use these notes when you review for tests and quizzes. Taking good notes is a skill that can be learned. The following guidelines will help you.

1. **Keep your notes in a notebook.** Divide your notebook into sections. Label each section for a specific class. Write the date and the name of the class at the top of each page of notes. Make notes on the main ideas presented in class or in your reading. Include any details related to these main ideas.

2. **Take notes as you read.** Include notes on key words, definitions, and main ideas. Also include any questions and answers that you develop while using the SQ3R method.

3. **Take notes as you listen.** Pay particular attention to clues that tell you what information is important. Such clues include phrases like *the result was, the main reason is, most importantly,* and *remember this.* A speaker provides other clues by repeating an idea or pausing to emphasize a point.

4. **Write neatly.** Make sure that you will be able to read your notes several days or weeks later.

5. **Use phrases, abbreviations, and symbols.** Do not write your notes in complete sentences. This will take too much time. Use short phrases and abbreviations, and symbols.

w/ with	info. information
w/o without	→ becomes
+ and	tho. though
* important information	def: definition
M memorize this	= equals
Amer. American	ex: example

6. Record your notes in rough outline form. Write main ideas at the left margin. Begin each idea with a capital letter. Write any examples or details under these main ideas.

Check It Out Read the following notes.

Amer. Lit.
April 12

Robert Frost

Life
— Lived most of life in New England
— Wrote about New England life
— Highly successful poet
— 4 Pulitzer prizes
— Many honorary degrees

- What main idea has the student used when taking these notes?

Try Your Skill Take notes on the selection on the Edsel given in Part 2. Use the guidelines given in this lesson.

Keep This in Mind

- Take notes on material presented in class and in your reading.
- Keep your notes in a notebook.
- Use phrases, abbreviations, and symbols.
- Use a rough outline form.

Now Write Begin a notebook for use in your classes. Divide the notebook into separate sections for each class. Take notes, following the guidelines presented in this lesson.

Speed Zone

Adjusting Your Reading Rate

Here's the Idea   When you page through a magazine in a doctor's office, you read quickly. When you read material that you will be tested on, you read more slowly. You vary your reading speed to suit your purpose.

In-depth reading is used to study material that is new or difficult. Use the SQ3R study method. Survey the selection. Make a list of questions. Then, move your eyes slowly across each line, reading every word. Pay particular attention to definitions, topic sentences, key words, and titles. Look for main ideas and for any details or examples to support them.

Fast reading is used for several different purposes. It is especially useful for surveying or reviewing written material. There are two types of fast reading: skimming and scanning.

Skimming involves moving your eyes quickly over the material. Do not read every word. Glance at titles, subtitles, headings, pictures, and graphic aids. Also look at the first and last sentences of paragraphs. When you are looking at a book, glance at the table of contents. Use skimming to survey material as the first step in the SQ3R study method. Also use it whenever you need to get a general idea of the content of a selection.

Scanning involves moving your eyes quickly across each line or down each page. Use scanning to find specific information. Look for words or phrases that are related to the information that you need. When you spot such a key word or phrase, stop scanning and read more slowly.

Check It Out   Look at the following directions.

> Go to the library. Look through several novels. Find one that interests you. Then, check to see if the author of this novel is listed in *Contemporary Authors*.

- What two reading tasks are called for in this assignment?
- Which task involves skimming? Which involves scanning?

Try Your Skill Would you use skimming, scanning, or in-depth reading for these situations?

1. Reading a textbook chapter to master the material
2. Studying material on a handout in preparation for a test
3. Surveying as part of the SQ3R study method
4. Flipping through a book to see if it contains material about whales
5. Looking through a chapter to find the answer to a study guide question
6. Looking for a definition of "enzyme" in a biology text

Keep This in Mind

- Adjust your reading rate to suit your purpose.
- Read in-depth to study new or difficult material.
- Skim to survey material.
- Scan to look for specific information.

Now Write Scan the following passage for answers to these questions:

1. What method of advertising was used in ancient Rome?
2. What changes took place in advertising in the 17th century?

Write your answers on a piece of paper. Label it **Speed Zone.**

The Early History of Advertising

Printed advertisements have been around for more than three thousand years. In early Rome, circuses and gladiator matches were advertised on posters. In the Middle Ages, handbills and signs advertised items for sale. By the middle of the 17th century, newspaper ads were common.

Between the Lines

Drawing Conclusions from Graphic Aids

Here's the Idea Sometimes information is presented in the form of graphic aids. Graphic aids include diagrams and illustrations. They also include maps, tables, charts, and graphs. When studying a graphic aid, follow these guidelines.

1. Read any titles, captions, legends, or labels given.
2. Ask yourself what facts are presented by the graphic aid.
3. Look for relationships between the facts presented.
4. See if you can draw any conclusions about the facts.

Check It Out Study the following graphs.

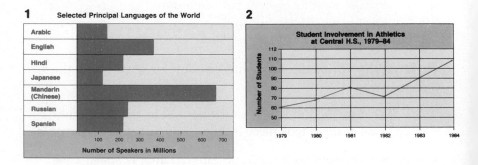

- What is the caption of each graphic aid?
- What two sets of facts does each graphic aid present?
- Which language has the most speakers?

Try Your Skill Study the following graphic aids. Then, answer the questions that follow.

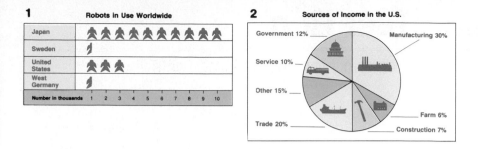

1 Robots in Use Worldwide

	Number in thousands
Japan	🧍🧍🧍🧍🧍🧍🧍🧍🧍
Sweden	🧍
United States	🧍🧍🧍
West Germany	🧍

Number in thousands: 1 2 3 4 5 6 7 8 9 10

2 Sources of Income in the U.S.

Government 12%
Manufacturing 30%
Service 10%
Other 15%
Farm 6%
Trade 20%
Construction 7%

1. What facts are being compared in Graph 1?

2. How does the use of robots in Japan compare to the use of robots in the other three countries?

3. Look at Graph 2. How much income in the United States comes from farming?

4. Manufacturing and trade, taken together, account for what percent of income in the United States?

Keep This in Mind

- Read any titles, captions, legends, or labels given with a graphic aid.
- Decide what facts are presented by the graphic aid. Look for relationships between these facts.
- Draw any conclusions that you can from the facts presented by the graphic aid.

Now Write   List the facts presented by graphic aid 2 in **Check It Out.** (Example: 80 students were involved in athletics at Central High School in 1981.) Then, write at least three conclusions that you can draw based on these facts (Example: Between 1981 and 1982 membership in Central High's athletic teams dropped by about ten students.) Label your paper **Between the Lines.** Save it in your folder.

Test Run

Preparing for and Taking Tests

Here's the Idea Success in high school depends largely upon the ability to do well on tests. You can learn a few simple guidelines that can improve your test scores tremendously.

Preparing for Tests Before a test, always make sure that you know what material the test will cover. If you have any questions about this, ask your teacher. Then, allow yourself enough time to review the materials you will be tested on. Try to review the material several times. Follow these guidelines:

1. **Make a list of study questions.** Include any questions that you wrote while using the SQ3R study method. Also include any study questions given in your textbook or by your teacher.

2. **Review the materials covered by the test.** Skim your notes, textbook chapters, and other reading materials. Write the answers to your study questions.

3. **Find a study coach.** Give your list of study questions to a relative or friend. Ask this person to quiz you. Make a note about each question that you cannot answer correctly.

4. **Review in problem areas.** Go over the questions that you missed when being quizzed by your relative or friend.

5. **Make a list of important names, dates, definitions, events, or formulas.** Quiz yourself on these, or ask someone to quiz you. You may want to use flashcards.

6. **Eat and sleep properly before the test.**

Taking the Test Skim the test to see what types of questions it includes. Read all directions and test questions carefully. Do not answer any question before you understand the directions. After looking at the test questions, decide on the order in which you will answer them. Begin with the easiest questions on the test. Save the most difficult questions for last.

Budget your time carefully. Do not spend too long on any one part of the test. Allow plenty of time to answer any long or complicated questions. When you are finished, read over the test. Make sure you have not left out any answers. Try to answer any questions that you skipped the first time through. Check any answers that you are not certain about.

Check It Out   Read the following passage.

Enrico had to study for a test in his computer class. The test covered the following materials:
1. Chapters 1–3 of his textbook.
2. Material presented in class discussions and lectures during the previous three weeks.

Enrico first made a list of study questions. Some came from his teacher. Some were questions that he wrote in his notes when he first studied the three chapters in his textbook. Enrico skimmed his notes and the three textbook chapters. Then, he wrote answers to his study questions.

- How well did Enrico prepare for his test?
- What else could he have done?

Try Your Skill   Imagine that you are going to be tested on the material given under **Try Your Skill** in Part 5. Make a list of study questions that you could use to prepare for your test.

Keep This in Mind

- Before a test, review your materials carefully.
- When taking the test, read all the directions first. Budget your time, and save time to check answers.

Now Write   Choose a chapter from one of your textbooks. Study it by using the SQ3R method. Make a list of study questions. Also make a list of important names, dates, definitions, events, or formulas. Label these lists **Test Run.** Save them.

Test Types

Answering Test Questions

Here's the Idea In your classes, you take many different types of tests. Sometimes you take **objective tests.** These tests contain true/false, matching, or multiple-choice questions. At other times you take **written tests.** These tests contain completion, short answer, or essay questions. The following rules will help you to answer each of these types of test questions.

True/False Remember that if any part of a statement is false, the entire statement is false. Also remember that words like *all, always, only, never,* and *everyone* often appear in false statements. Words like *some, often, a few, most,* and *usually* often appear in true statements.

Matching First, check the directions. See if each item is used only once. Also check to see if some are not used at all. Read all items in both columns before starting. Match those you know first. Cross out items as you use them.

Multiple choice Read all of the choices before answering. Eliminate any obviously incorrect answers first. Then choose the answer that is most complete or accurate. Pay particular attention to choices such as "all of the above."

Completion, or Fill-in-the-Blank If several words are required, give them all. Write neatly. Use good grammar and punctuation.

Short Answer Use complete sentences. Answer the question completely. Use correct grammar, capitalization, punctuation, and spelling.

Essay Look for action words like *explain* and *compare.* These are words that tell you what to do. Make a list of the details you will need to answer the question. Make a rough outline of your essay on separate paper. Be sure each paragraph contains a topic sentence. Finally, proofread your work.

Check It Out   Read the following test questions.

1. Write a paragraph explaining the differences between skimming and scanning.
2. The "S" in SQ3R stands for _____ .
3. Which of the following is *not* a type of graphic aid?
    a. picture   b. textbook   c. map   d. graph
4. Notes should *not* be written in complete sentences. (true or false) _____
5. Match the following question types with their guidelines.

a. true/false ____   b. essay ____   c. multiple choice ____

1) Make a rough outline.	3) Remember that words
2) Pay particular attention to choices such as *none of the above*.	like *all*, *only*, and *never* often appear in false statements.

• Can you identify each type of test question above?

Try Your Skill   Copy the questions given in **Check It Out** onto your own paper. Then, answer each question.

Keep This in Mind

- Objective tests contain true/false, matching, and multiple choice questions.
- Written tests contain completion, short answer, and essay questions.
- Follow the guidelines in **Here's the Idea** when answering test questions.

Now Write   Review the material in Part 3, **The Long and Short**. Copy the following essay question onto a piece of notebook paper. Circle the key words that tell you what to do. Plan your answer carefully. Then, write and proofread it. Save your work.

ESSAY QUESTION: In your own words, describe how to use a rough outline to take notes. Include a discussion of the use of symbols and abbreviations in note-taking.

Standard Procedure

Preparing for Standardized Tests

Here's the Idea   Many job fields require you to pass a standardized entry test. Tests are also required by many colleges, vocational schools, and apprenticeship programs. A **standardized test** is a type of objective test. Some measure knowledge of a specific subject such as electronics or auto mechanics.

There are two common standardized tests that you will probably take. One is the SAT (Scholastic Aptitude Test). The other is the ACT (American College Testing Program Assessment Test). These tests are required for admission to many colleges. If you wish to attend college, see your guidance counselor. Ask if you must take one of these tests. Your counselor will explain how to sign up for the test and will help you prepare for it.

When you take a standardized test, follow these guidelines:

1. Find out what types of questions will be included on the test. Also find out what material will be covered by the test.

2. Make use of any practice materials supplied by the testing organization. Also make use of the test-taking manuals available in many libraries and bookstores.

3. Study the types of questions included in the test that you plan to take. Learn specific guidelines for answering questions of these types (See Part 9).

4. Rest and eat well before the test.

5. Try not to become nervous before the test. If possible, do some light exercise an hour or so before the test begins. This will clear your mind. It will also relieve tension.

Check It Out   Read the following passage.

Coretta decided to enroll in night classes at a local junior college. According to the college catalog, she had to take the SAT before she could be admitted. Therefore, she went to her guidance counselor. Her counselor signed her up for the PSAT and the SAT. The PSAT is a practice SAT test. It helped Coretta to prepare for the SAT. In addition, Coretta studied the sample questions that were sent to her in the mail by the makers of the SAT test. On the night before the SAT, Coretta ate well and got plenty of sleep.

- What did Coretta do to prepare for her test?
- What else could she have done?

Try Your Skill You are planning to apply for a summer office job. You are told that when you come to the interview, you will have to take a standardized test. The first part of the test will cover grammar, capitalization, punctuation, and spelling. The second part will cover proper form for business letters. The third part will cover basic office procedures. Make a list of the steps that you would take to prepare for this test.

Keep This in Mind

- Many employers, colleges, vocational schools, and other organizations require standardized tests.
- To prepare for standardized tests, make use of the available practice materials.
- Also study the types of questions asked on the test that you plan to take.

Now Write In many states, you must take a standardized test before you can enter any of the following fields.

Radiology	Accounting
Physical therapy	Airplane and power plant mechanics
Stock brokerage	Electronics

Choose one of the above professions. Do some research to find out what sort of test must be taken to enter this field. Write a paragraph explaining how you could prepare for this test.

You've Got the Answer

Answering Standardized Test Questions

Here's the Idea   The SAT and the ACT both contain special types of test questions. Three of these types of questions were discussed in Parts 7–9 of Section 21, **Critical Thinking**. These questions involved antonyms, analogies, and sentence completion. Now, you will learn about two other types of questions.

1. **Sentence Correction.** A sentence correction question tests your ability to find an error in a sentence. If the underlined material in the sentence does not contain an error, mark, "A". "A" repeats the underlined material. If the underlined material does contain an error, choose the answer that corrects the error.

Though Jim has moved, he still <u>be</u> my best friend.

(A) be   (B) are   (C) is   (D) had been

Follow these guidelines when answering sentence corrections:

    a. Find the error, if there is one, before looking at the answers. Look for errors in grammar, usage, and mechanics.
    b. Check your answer by placing it into the sentence.

2. **Reading Comprehension.** Reading comprehension questions measure your understanding of short reading passages. Read the passage carefully. Look for main ideas and supporting details. Look for relationships. Read the question and all the choices before answering. Base your answer on information contained in the passage, not on your own opinion.

    In A.D. 986 Bjarni Herjulfson sailed for Iceland to join his father, Herjulf. On arriving and learning that Herjulf had moved to Greenland, Bjarni and his crew set out to follow them. Sailing west, they missed Greenland. Eventually, they sighted lands no one recognized. These lands are now part of Canada. The Norse sailors turned their boats eastward and finally reached Greenland.

About the year 1000, Leif Ericson set out from Greenland with thirty-five sailors to seek the land Bjarni had described. On finding the land, he called it *Markland.*

The land that Bjarni sighted is now called

(A) Markland   (B) The United States   (C) Norway
(D) Canada

Check It Out   Review the test questions covered in Parts 7–9 of 2, **Critical Thinking.** Then, read the following questions:

1. WORK: (A) job   (B) play   (C) business   (D) labor
2. FOREST: TREE   (A) vacation: travel   (B) musician: guitarist   (C) class: student   (D) afternoon: evening

- What steps would you take to answer these questions?

Try Your Skill   Answer the following questions based on the reading passage given in **Here's the Idea.**

1. The first Europeans to reach the New World were
   (A) English   (B) Portuguese   (C) Norse
2. Bjarni Herjulfson reached the new world
   (A) by accident   (B) by plane   (C) after Leif Ericson

Keep This in Mind

- Before taking a standardized test, study the various types of standardized test questions.
- Questions found on standardized tests include antonyms, analogies, sentence completion, sentence correction, and comprehension questions.

Now Write   Choose a short passage from a textbook. Copy the passage. Then, write five reading comprehension questions dealing with the passage. Exchange your paper with a classmate. Complete each other's questions.

Writing Letters

Keep in Touch

Writing Personal Letters

Here's the Idea   The term **personal letter** includes all letters not written to businesses. Writing personal letters is a way of keeping in touch with absent friends or of expressing your feelings in certain social situations. Personal letters, which are usually handwritten, have five main parts.

The **heading** contains three lines: one line for the writer's street address, one for the city, state, and ZIP code, and one for the date. None of this information should be abbreviated. The heading appears at the top right corner of your letter.

The **salutation** is the greeting. Usually beginning with *Dear*, it is written on the next line below the heading. It starts at the left margin of the page and is followed by a comma.

The **body** of the letter is the main part. There you write what you want to say in a detailed and conversational way. The body begins on the line following the salutation. Each paragraph of the body should be indented.

The **closing** is your way of saying "goodbye." You may say *Love,* or *Your friend,* for instance. The closing is written on the line below the last line of the body and is followed by a comma. The first word of the closing should align with the first words of the heading.

Your **signature** is the last part of a letter. Skip a line after the closing and sign your name in line with the first word of the closing. Usually, only your first name is needed.

Some forms of personal letters are written only for special occasions. These social notes include invitations and thank-you notes. The notes also have five main parts, but the heading may be shortened to the date only.

If you send an **invitation,** include all information about the event. If you receive an invitation, reply at once.

Sometimes you will send **thank-you** notes. One kind of thank-you note is written to thank someone for a gift you have received. Another kind of thank-you thanks someone for his or her hospitality. You would write this kind of note if you stayed overnight as a guest in someone's house.

Check It Out   Read this personal letter.

1315 Albion Drive
St. Paul, Minnesota 55105
April 19, 1985

Dear Susan,
    I am sorry to hear about your broken ankle. I know you're as disappointed as I am that we have to postpone our hiking trip. However, resting for two weeks will give you the perfect chance to catch up on all the reading that you said you had to do — not to mention the letter writing!
    How about rescheduling your visit for the weekend of June 8? You plan whatever will be best for you. I'm looking forward to seeing you soon.

Love,
Chris

- Identify the five parts of this personal letter.
- Is this a well-written letter? Why or why not?

Try Your Skill   Arrange the following information in the correct form for a personal letter. Add any other information or details that you think might be included in the letter. Be sure to add capital letters and correct punctuation wherever necessary.

31 Forest Street, Fairfield, Iowa 52556, October 23, 1984 dear randy Shortly after you left, I discovered your notebook under the stack of newspapers you had been reading. The notebook is in the mail already, so you should get it in time to finish your English assignment next week. Remember, we have plans to watch more football together on Thanksgiving. until then george

Keep This in Mind

- Write personal letters that are conversational, detailed, and neat. Be sure that the heading, salutation, body, closing, and signature follow the correct form.
- Social notes are short forms of personal letters. Write invitations that are specific and thank-you notes that express your appreciation.

Now Write   Write a personal letter to a friend or relative. You may want to write a social note. Use your own address and today's date in the heading. The body of your letter may be based on either real or imaginary events. Make sure that all parts of your letter follow the correct form. Label your paper **Keep in Touch** and put it into your folder. Make a copy of the letter that you could send and save that also.

Special Delivery

Preparing Letters for the Mail

Here's the Idea Once you have written a letter, you must prepare it correctly for mailing. Begin by folding the letter neatly and choosing an envelope that matches the width of the stationery. Insert the folded letter and seal the envelope.

To make sure that your letter reaches its destination without delay, take extra care to address the envelope accurately and neatly. Follow these steps.

1. Address the envelope. Add your return address.
2. Check all numbers to make sure that they are correct.
3. Include the correct ZIP code. To learn the correct use of ZIP codes and state abbreviations, turn to page 333.
4. Put a stamp on the envelope. Be sure that you have used enough postage for the letter or package.

Check It Out Look at the envelope below.

Dee Wendell
162 Exeter Street
Kansas City, MO 64108

Jim Shortelle
2178 Broadway
New Haven, CT 06510

- Who wrote the letter? Who will receive it? What state abbreviations are used? How could you check all the information?

Try Your Skill   Write each of these jumbled addresses as it should appear on an envelope. Also write a return address. Refer to the list of correct state abbreviations on the next page.

1. Mike Ruddy, 31 Sullivan Street, Livingston, New Jersey 07039

2. 580 Rosewood Avenue, Phoenix, Arizona 85002, Maria Cordova

3. Philadelphia, Pennsylvania 19101, 122 Salem Lane, Robert Bernstein

4. 179 Foster Street, Frankfort, Kentucky 40601, Joe Leone

5. Susan Kim, Des Moines, Iowa 50306, 14 Briar Road

6. Enrico Sanchez, 259 Bennett Road, Falls Church, Virginia 22046

7. Christine Sobel, Atlanta, Georgia 30302, 3871 Beacon Boulevard

8. Whitinsville, Maryland 01588, Dr. Jonathan Schmitt, 644 Eastern Parkway

9. 22 Lyndon Terrace, Chapel Hill, North Carolina 27514, Ellie Johannson

10. Ms. Susan Lindahl, 2002 Oceanview Drive, Santa Monica, California 90405

Keep This in Mind

- Prepare letters for the mail carefully. Check all information for accuracy.

Now Write   Find your personal letter labeled **Keep in Touch.** On the other side of the paper, add the title of this lesson **Special Delivery.** Draw a rectangle to represent an envelope. Address it as if you were going to mail it to your friend or relative. Keep this paper in your folder.

Copy your work on a real envelope. Fold the copy of the letter that you can send, and put it into the envelope. Put a stamp on your letter and mail it.

ZIP Codes and State Abbreviations

In order to make sure that your letter reaches its destination, check the address, including the ZIP code. The ZIP code is very important today. It enables the postal department to sort your letter for delivery as rapidly as possible. If you don't know a particular ZIP code, call your local post office. Someone will give you the correct ZIP for any address in the United States.

The United States Postal Service has a list of approved state abbreviations to be used on all envelopes and packages. You must use the ZIP code with these abbreviations.

Abbreviations of State Names

Alabama	AL	Montana	MT
Alaska	AK	Nebraska	NE
Arizona	AZ	Nevada	NV
Arkansas	AR	New Hampshire	NH
American Samoa	AS	New Jersey	NJ
California	CA	New Mexico	NM
Canal Zone	CZ	New York	NY
Colorado	CO	North Carolina	NC
Connecticut	CT	North Dakota	ND
Delaware	DE	Ohio	OH
District of Columbia	DC	Oklahoma	OK
Florida	FL	Oregon	OR
Georgia	GA	Pennsylvania	PA
Guam	GU	Puerto Rico	PR
Hawaii	HI	Rhode Island	RI
Idaho	ID	South Carolina	SC
Illinois	IL	South Dakota	SD
Indiana	IN	Tennessee	TN
Iowa	IA	Trust Territories	TT
Kansas	KS	Texas	TX
Kentucky	KY	Utah	UT
Louisiana	LA	Vermont	VT
Maine	ME	Virgina	VA
Maryland	MD	Virgin Islands	VI
Massachusetts	MA	Washington	WA
Michigan	MI	West Virgina	WV
Minnesota	MN	Wisconsin	WI
Mississippi	MS	Wyoming	WY
Missouri	MO		

The World of Business

Writing Business Letters

Here's the Idea In addition to writing personal letters, you will also be writing **business letters**. Learning to write business letters is a useful, practical skill. There will be times when you need to write to a company regarding its products. There will be times when you will want to write to a school or college. In seeking employment you may need to write letters and résumés and to complete application forms. In all of these situations, you will be likely to meet with more success if you follow the correct form for business letters.

In order to make the best impression, you must make your business letters neat. Plain white paper, 8-1/2 × 11 inches, is considered standard, and typing is considered an advantage. It is not required that you type any of your business letters. However, most businesses type letters and reports.

Any business letter that you write may take one of two forms. One form is the **block** form, which should be used only if you type a letter. In the block form, begin every part of a letter at the left margin. Leave two lines of space between paragraphs and do not indent them. Another form, the **modified block** form, may be used either for handwritten or typewritten letters. In this form, place the heading, closing, and signature at the right side of the page. Indent the paragraphs and do not leave extra space between them.

Every business letter has six parts—the five parts of a personal letter, plus an **inside address.** The inside address is the name and address of the company to which you are writing. If possible, the inside address should include the name of an employee or department within the firm. Place an inside address at the left margin between the heading and the salutation.

More formal language is used in business letters than in personal letters. For the greeting use *Dear Mr., Mrs., Miss*, or *Ms.* before the person's name. Or, use a general greeting, like *Dear Sir or Madam*. Place the salutation two lines below the inside address and use a colon (:) after it.

For the more formal closing, write *Sincerely, Yours truly*, or *Very truly yours*, followed by a comma. If you type a letter, leave four lines of space between the closing and your typed signature. Then, write your signature in the space.

Always make a business letter polite, specific, and neat. Keep a copy of each business letter that you write.

Check It Out   Read this business letter.

```
      317 Grantly Boulevard
      Los Angeles, California   90017
      September 8, 1985


      Power Products, Incorporated
      1105 Moore Street
      Reston, Virginia   22091


      Dear Sir or Madam:


      Recently I bought a PPI amplifier, Model 217,
      at The Sound Store in Los Angeles.  The package
      was factory sealed, but when I opened it I found
      no instructions and no schematic diagrams.  The
      salesperson had assured me that I would find
      both of them inside the package.


      Please send me a copy of each as soon as possible.


      Yours truly,

      Edward McKenna

      Edward McKenna
```

- What is the purpose of this business letter?
- In what form is this letter?

Try Your Skill Write a letter from Gina Hampton, president of Power Products Incorporated, to Edward McKenna. Have Ms. Hampton apologize to Edward for any inconvenience, and have her assure him that the papers he requested are on their way. For the purpose of this exercise, use the block form, even though your letter will be handwritten.

Keep This in Mind

- You may write a business letter to request information, to order a product, to apply to a school, or to seek employment. Whether you write or type a business letter, be polite, specific, and neat. Keep a copy of every business letter.
- Use either the *block* or *modified block* form for a business letter. Either form has six parts, including an inside address.

Now Write Write or type a letter to a real organization regarding a real product. Also, draw an envelope and address it. Label your paper **The World of Business** and put it into your folder.

What Do You Need?

Writing Letters of Request

Here's the Idea   Often you will write a business letter because you would like something from a company or an organization. You may need information for a report. You may want tourist information about a place that you plan to visit. You may want to order a product.

Letters of request are business letters. Therefore, they should contain the six parts of a business letter, and they should follow either the *block* or *modified block* form. However, you must keep two additional points in mind when you write a letter of request.

First, be specific. Provide all the information that the other person needs in order to fill your request. If you want information, state exactly what information you need. If you are placing an order, be sure to state exactly what you want and where it is to be sent. Also include any necessary details about the size, color, cost, or identification number of the product you want. Most businesses and organizations can fill your request promptly if it is precise and complete.

Second, remember that you are asking another person to take time to fill your request. Therefore, be especially sure that your letter is courteous, clear, and to the point.

Check It Out   Read the letter of request on page 338.

- Is this letter of request courteous, specific, and to the point? Which form does this business letter have?

28 Plainview Road
Greenfield, Wisconsin   53220
December 3, 1985

Chamber of Commerce
1122 West Main Street
Petersburg, Virginia   23803

Dear Sir or Madam:

I am a junior in high school, and I am working
on a report on Tiffany stained glass. Through
my research I have discovered that the Blanford
Church in Petersburg has windows designed by
Louis Tiffany. I need to know the year the
windows were installed, the dimensions of the
windows, and their original cost. Could you
provide me with this information or give me the
name of someone in town who can?

I also understand that there are free picture
post cards available through your office that
feature the windows. May I have a copy of such
a post card?

This information, plus any additional facts you
might have about the windows, will be very useful
for my report and will be greatly appreciated.

Yours truly,

Frances Russell

Frances Russell

Try Your Skill   Write a letter to the United States Soccer Federation, 350 Fifth Avenue, New York, New York 10001, asking for information about where regulation soccer balls may be purchased locally. Use your home address and today's date.

Keep This in Mind

- Write a letter of request that is courteous, specific, and to the point. You may use either the *block* or *modified block* form for this business letter.

Now Write   Write to the manufacturer of a product that you would like to know more about. You may write to a mail order company that you have seen advertised, or to the manufacturer of a product that is made in your town. Use the phone book or printed advertisements to help you find the address.

Use the modified block form for your handwritten letter. Be sure that you ask for specific information. Write the title of this lesson, **What Do You Need?** on your paper. Put your work into your folder. You may want to make a copy of your letter of request and send it.

Skills for Your Future

Got Your Interest?

Assessing Your Interests and Skills

Here's the Idea   Before long you will begin to make decisions about your future. Choosing the right college or career is, of course, very important. After all, you are likely to spend much of your adult life at work. If you choose work that is personally satisfying, you are more likely to be happy. This is why you should begin your career search by looking at your interests and skills. The following exercises will help you to learn more about yourself. You can then look for a career or a course of study that is suited to you.

Check It Out   Read the following list of job skills.

Acting	Driving	Proving
Building	Entertaining	Questioning
Calculating	Leading	Reading
Computing	Managing	Remembering
Counseling	Measuring	Repairing
Dancing	Organizing	Speaking
Decorating	Operating	Teaching
Designing	Painting	Typing
Drawing	Persuading	Writing

- Which of these skills have you used in the past? On what occasions did you use them?
- Which of these skills are you particularly good at?

Try Your Skill   The following questions will help you to decide what kinds of jobs are right for you. Answer these questions. Then, study your answers. Tell what they reveal about the kinds of jobs you would prefer.

1. Have you had any special training in job skills, such as typing or automotive repair?
2. Do any of your hobbies or other activities involve job skills? Describe any that do.
3. Do you prefer mental work or physical work?
4. Do you prefer working with words or with numbers?
5. Do you prefer working outdoors or indoors?
6. Do you prefer working with people or with machines?
7. Do you prefer working alone or with other people?
8. Are you willing to take additional training or schooling after high school?
9. In what part of the country do you want to live? Would you prefer living in a city or in a rural area?
10. How much money will you have to make to meet your needs?

Keep This in Mind

- Before making a career choice, identify your interests and skills. This will help you to find work that is suited to you.

Now Write   Choose a career possibility that matches the skills and interests that you identified in **Check It Out** and **Try Your Skill.** Write a paragraph explaining why you chose this particular job.

The World of Work

Exploring Careers

Here's the Idea   Once you understand your own interests and skills, you can begin to search for careers to which you are well suited. Sources of information about careers include the following:

1. Reference works, including encyclopedias and almanacs
2. Counselors, teachers, relatives, and employers
3. Books
    a. *Occupational Outlook Handbook.* This book is published by the U.S. Department of Labor. It is available in many guidance offices and public libraries.
    b. *Dictionary of Occupational Titles.* This book is also published by the Department of Labor and is available in guidance offices and libraries.

These sources can tell you about working conditions, job duties, possible earnings, and training or special skills required. They can also tell you about the many sources of job training, including the following:

1. Technical or trade schools
2. Community and junior colleges
3. Apprenticeships
4. Training programs offered by the armed services
5. Colleges and universities
6. On-the-job training programs

Check It Out   The following is a list of the fifteen major job fields and some particular jobs in each field. Read this list.

1. **Agriculture/Natural Resources** (farmer, gardener, forest ranger, fisherman, miner)
2. **Business and Office** (clerk, secretary, bank teller, real estate salesman, bookkeeper)

3. **Communications and Media** (projectionist, telephone line worker, proofreader, reporter, photographer, disc jockey)

4. **Construction** (carpenter, mason, electrician, heavy equipment operator, drafter, surveyor, plumber, civil engineer)

5. **Environment** (sewage disposal worker, fire warden, park maintenance worker, pest control worker, safety inspector)

6. **Fine Arts/Humanities** (stagehand, interior designer, writer)

7. **Health** (nurse, ambulance driver, medical records clerk)

8. **Home Economics** (dry-cleaning machine operator, food service worker, nursing home or child-care aide, chef)

9. **Hospitality/Recreation** (travel agent, hotel desk clerk, lifeguard, tour guide, railroad ticket clerk, usher)

10. **Manufacturing** (cannery worker, machinist, mill worker)

11. **Marine Science** (hatchery worker, marine biologist, sailor)

12. **Marketing** (cashier, shipping clerk, auctioneer)

13. **Personal Services** (beautician, kennel worker, barber, janitor)

14. **Public Service** (teacher, teacher's aide, police officer, soldier, post office clerk, customs inspector)

15. **Transportation** (truck or bus driver, dispatcher)

- Which of these job fields is most appealing to you? Why?

Try Your Skill   Choose any five of the job fields listed in **Check It Out.** For each job field, list one job title not mentioned.

Keep This in Mind

- There are many sources of information about possible careers.
- Use these sources to identify careers that suit your interests and skills.

Now Write   Choose any occupation that interests you. Do some research. You might check the dictionary of occupational titles. Write a paragraph describing the following:

the job title	training required	chances of employment
job duties	skills required	possible earnings

Experience Counts

Writing a Résumé

Here's the Idea   When the time comes for you to look for a job, you will have to prepare materials to send to possible employers. Usually you apply for a job by sending a brief letter and a résumé. A **résumé** (rez′ • oo • mā′) summarizes your life in relation to work. A résumé contains basic information about you, your education, your work experience, and your special skills.

No two résumés are exactly the same. However, most are one page long and typewritten. All résumés contain brief phrases that summarize information. Use these guidelines:

1. State your name, address, and telephone number, including the area code.

2. State your job objective. What kind of position or general area of work are you seeking?

3. Summarize your education. List your high school, its address, your expected date of graduation, and any special subjects helpful for a particular job. If you have attended more than one school, list the most recent first.

4. Summarize your job experience. State the beginning and ending dates of your employment, the name and address of your employer, the position you held, and your duties. Again, list your most recent jobs first. If you have had any related volunteer experience, also include it here.

5. Mention any meaningful personal achievements. Include special skills such as knowledge of computer language or a foreign language, office skills, or community work. Also include awards, hobbies, special interests, and offices held in societies or clubs.

6. Mention at least two or three references. You may list the names of several adults—teachers or employers, for example—who can give you good character or employment references. It

is also standard practice to say that you will supply references on request. If you decide to list references on your résumé, make sure to contact these people before including their names. Only list those people who have agreed to supply written recommendations for you.

As your life and work change, so should your résumé. Revise your résumé so that it is accurate and up to date.

Check It Out   Examine the résumé on page 348.

- Is this résumé well organized and easy to read? Does it include all the necessary information?

Try Your Skill   Which of the following items should be added to the résumé shown in this lesson? Explain why the information is appropriate for the résumé.

1. broke arm, sophomore year, while ice-skating
2. won school attendance medals for freshman and sophomore years
3. won first-place speed certificate in typing class
4. studied Spanish for two years
5. played role in school play

Keep This in Mind

- A résumé summarizes basic information about your life in relation to work.
- Write a résumé that is well organized, easy to read, and up to date.
- Include all information that shows your special experiences and skills.
- Contact the people whom you wish to list as references before putting their names on your résumé.

Now Write   Write your own résumé. Follow the model given on page 348.

                    Elizabeth Ann O'Brien

                    257 Walker Road
                    Memphis, Tennessee   38104
                    (901) 555-3650

        OBJECTIVE   A summer job as a cashier in
                     a supermarket.

        EDUCATION   Central High School
                     Memphis, Tennessee
                     Member of Junior class graduating in
                     June, 1985, with courses in business
                     math and office skills.

WORK EXPERIENCE   Cashier
        Present   Dan's Market
                     522 Sherman Street
                     Memphis, Tennessee
                     On part-time basis.

   Summer, 1983   Stock clerk, bagger
                     Dan's Market
                     Full time.

        PERSONAL   Able to operate calculator, adding
                     machine, and cash register. Secretary,
                     Junior Chamber of Commerce, 1978-79.
                     Member of glee club and volleyball team.

      REFERENCES   Will be provided upon request.

Classified Information

Discovering Job Opportunities

Here's the Idea   Once you have written a résumé, you are ready to look for a job. The following are some of the sources that you can use to find out what jobs are available:

Counselors.   One source of information about jobs is the counseling department in your school. A guidance counselor can give you advice about what jobs are right for you. He or she may be able to suggest particular job opportunities in your area.

Help-Wanted Ads.   These ads appear in most newspapers. They are arranged alphabetically according to job title. Full-time jobs are usually listed separately from part-time jobs. Help-wanted ads may contain all or part of the following information: job title, job description, skills or experience required, number of hours per week, days or shifts to be worked, salary or wages, and how to contact the employer.

Employment Agencies.   Employers sometimes list job openings with employment agencies. The addresses and telephone numbers of these agencies may be found in your telephone directory.

Telephone Directories.   Looking through the yellow pages of your local telephone directory may suggest some places where you might work. Using such a directory, you can make a list of possible employers. Then you can call them to see if any openings exist.

Personal Contacts.   One excellent source for information on job opportunities is your family and friends. Let these people know that you are looking for a job. They may be able to suggest some places where you can apply.

Check It Out   Read the following help-wanted ads.

**DELIVERY PERSON–Social wel-
fare agency.** Full-time, days.
Delivering meals to elderly and hand-
icapped persons. Must be responsible, punctual. Must have own
transportation and valid driver's license. Call 555-3867 for further info.
Ask for Pat.

**COOK/DISHWASHER–Part-time,
evenings.** Some weekends. Exper.
pref., but will train right person. Minimum wage to start. Apply in person,
Rick's Place, 230 Casablanca Blvd.

- Which of these jobs might be appropriate for a high school student? Why?

Try Your Skill   Reread the want ads in **Check It Out.** For each ad, answer the following questions.

1. Is the job full-time or part-time?
2. What are the job duties?
3. Does the ad specify that experience is required?
4. Is this a daytime or an evening job?

Keep This in Mind

- The following sources can supply information about job openings: counselors, help-wanted ads, employment agencies, telephone directories, and friends.

Now Write   Using a telephone directory, make a list of businesses in your area that may hire teens. Give the name, address, and telephone number of each business. Tell what sorts of jobs each business might offer to teenagers.

On the Job

Writing Letters to Employers

Here's the Idea Once you have found a job for which you would like to apply, you will have to contact the employer. One way to do this is to send the employer a letter, along with your résumé.

When you write a letter seeking employment, you need to be clear and direct. Follow these guidelines:

1. State the title of the job you are seeking.
2. Be specific about the kind of job you are looking for. Indicate whether you are looking for full-time, part-time, or temporary employment.
3. Include a brief statement about yourself. Also include your age and grade level in school.
4. Include a brief statement about your qualifications. Be sure to mention any related work experience or courses taken in school.
5. Be specific about your availability for work. Mention particular days or hours you will be available. Always include a starting date.
6. Include a request for an interview if the job is in your area.

If you are sending your letter to a large company, write to the personnel department. If you are writing to a small company, write to the owner or manager. If you answer a newspaper advertisement, look carefully for information telling you how to reply. Many ads will give you a box number to write to in care of the newspaper. Others may contain an address.

Make sure that your letter follows the correct form for business letters. It should be informative, neat, and polite. Also, be sure to proofread your letter carefully. Your attention to detail may lead to a job offer.

257 Walker Road
Memphis, Tennessee 38104
March 18, 1985

Mr. Ralph Owens, Manager
First Federal Food Stores
31 State Street
Memphis, Tennessee 38104

Dear Mr. Owens:

I am interested in working full time this summer as a cashier
in any of the First Federal Food Stores. I am currently a
junior at Central High School. I have taken several business
courses. Last summer I worked as a stock clerk and bagger at
Dan's Market, 522 Sherman Street. I am working part time on
weekends during this school year at the same job. I have had
experience at checking stock, operating a cash register, and
bagging.

I will be available for full-time work on June 6, although I
can also be available part time before that date for any
training that is required. I will be able to continue until
August 28. I am willing to work any schedule, including
weekends.

I will apply in person next week. I will also be available for
an interview at your convenience.

Yours truly,

Elizabeth O'Brien

Elizabeth O'Brien

- Does this letter include all the necessary information?
- Is it courteous and neat?

Try Your Skill   Imagine that you are interested in one of the following jobs. Write a letter seeking employment. Mention your related experiences, including any job experiences you have had.

1. Wanted: Part-time, year-round help for telephone sales. Good spelling and some typing required. Write Advertising Department, *Suburban Tribune*, 425 Warren Street, Northbrook, Illinois 60062.

2. Wanted: Experienced kitchen help for summer. Write The Summit Inn, Pine Crest Road, Boulder, Colorado 80303.

3. Wanted: Part-time clerks in sales and stock during Christmas season. Write Personnel Manager, Lacy's Department Store, 1890 Grant Avenue, Manchester, Connecticut 06040.

Keep This in Mind

- A letter to an employer should create a good impression.
- The letter should be informative, polite, and neat.
- Include specific information about yourself and the job you want.

Now Write   Write a letter seeking employment at a supermarket, restaurant, department store, or other business in your town. Ask to be considered for a particular job. Be sure to include all necessary information. Revise and proofread your letter carefully.

All in a Day's Work

Preparing for a Job Interview

Here's the Idea   A job interview is a speaking situation. You must be prepared to talk with a prospective employer.

The first step in your preparation is to be sure your résumé is up to date. Sometimes you may want to send it in with a letter seeking employment. At other times, you may want to bring it with you to an interview. In any case, be sure you can talk easily about everything you have included.

It is often helpful to ask yourself some questions about the background information you have included on your résumé. For example, you might practice answering the following questions.

1. What are my strongest assets as an employee?
2. What experience do I have that helps qualify me for this particular job?
3. What personal attributes do I have that will make me valuable to this company?

If your résumé shows a weak area—for example, if you were dismissed from a previous job—be prepared to talk about it. You do not want to stumble if asked a difficult question. Simply explain what happened, emphasizing why you think you will be successful this time.

Before you go to your interview, find out as much as you can about the company and the job you want. Perhaps you can talk to someone who is working there now. If not, try to visit the company. For example, if you want a job as a cashier in a supermarket, shop in the store several times. Watch the cashiers. What seem to be their responsibilities? Of course, you should observe quietly and not talk with employees while they are on the job.

Having done this, you will probably have some questions of your own to ask at the interview. Think about them ahead of time. One or two good questions will show the employer that you are thinking and that you have initiative.

It is also important when you go to an interview to give some thought to your personal appearance. Wear clothes that help you feel good about yourself. It is best to dress neatly and appropriately.

Check It Out   Consider the following situation.

Carrie wanted to apply for a job as an office clerk in a nearby auto-parts store. Her résumé was ready, and when she studied it, she discovered this information:

1. My strongest assets are my typing speed and my ability to keep good records.

2. I have two experiences that help qualify me for this job. I worked last summer as a clerk in City Hall. I am now working at school as Ms. Tandy's assistant.

3. My personal attributes include promptness and an ability to get along well with other employees.

Carrie thought of a weakness that could hurt her chances. She was a poor speller. She decided not to mention this problem unless asked. She also planned to explain, if necessary, that her spelling suffered because of a poor beginning in reading. Carrie knew how to use a dictionary, however, and she could promise an employer that she would be careful about looking up words. Carrie had asked Ms. Tandy for a reference. Ms. Tandy had agreed to write a letter for Carrie to take with her.

On the day of her interview, Carrie dressed in her favorite skirt and blouse. She also wore low-heeled shoes that she had cleaned that morning.

- What preparations did Carrie make for her interview?
- What else could Carrie have done to get ready?

Try Your Skill   Tom wants a job at a service station. He would like to work after school and on weekends. He sent in a

résumé and has been offered an interview. Write out and number the steps that Tom should take in getting ready for his interview.

Keep This in Mind

- Before you go to a job interview, review your résumé.
- Be prepared to talk about yourself.
- Learn as much as you can about the company and about the job. Think of questions that you might like to ask at the interview.
- Dress neatly and appropriately.

Now Write   Select a job that interests you. The company and job may be real or imaginary. Make a list of the skills and experience that qualify you for this job. Also list your strongest personal qualities. Finally make a list of questions you might want to ask at your interview.

At Your Best

Having an Interview

Here's the Idea   A job interview will be much easier for you if you have prepared carefully. Get off to a good start by taking with you everything you might need: several copies of your résumé, a pad of paper, a pen or pencil, and identification that includes your social security number. Allow yourself plenty of time in order to be prompt for the interview.

Once you arrive, you will need to introduce yourself. When you meet your interviewer, stand up. It's best to be informal but polite. Perhaps you will say, "Hello, Mr. Logan. I'm Terry Robbins from Jackson High School." Always shake hands if the interviewer extends a hand to you. Look directly at your interviewer.

Be direct and say your name clearly. You should be sure you catch the name of the interviewer. If you don't hear it, ask the interviewer to repeat it.

If you haven't already sent the interviewer a copy of your résumé, offer it now. While the interviewer reads it, sit quietly. Be thinking about what you are going to say.

Once the interview begins, listen carefully. Try not to be distracted by your unfamiliar surroundings. Keep your mind on the interview so that you can answer questions well.

If the interviewer asks a question that is difficult or surprising, remain calm. It is perfectly all right to say, "Let me think about that for a moment." Don't be afraid to pause while you get your ideas together.

In addition, try to avoid some of the common pitfalls in interviewing. For example, if the interviewer asks you a hard question, don't give a negative, dead-end answer, such as "I don't know." Also, the interview is usually not the time for you to ask about salary or advancement opportunities. If the interviewer offers information on these subjects, you should feel free to discuss them. Otherwise, wait until you get a job offer. Finally, all prospective employers want to see evidence of self-control. Let your hands rest quietly in your lap or on the arms of your chair. Don't smoke or chew gum. Keep your voice at a reasonable pitch and volume.

The interviewer will let you know when the interview is over. Before leaving, show your interest in the job. Ask when you can expect to hear something from the company. As you leave, check to be sure you have all your belongings. Thank the interviewer for his or her time. Then shake hands and leave. Don't linger to look around or to talk to employees.

Check It Out   Consider the following situation.

Adam had an interview scheduled for 10:00 Friday morning at a citrus fruit processing plant. He was applying for a summer job in the canning department.

Adam arrived at 10:05. Traffic had been heavy, and he was nervous about being late.

His interviewer greeted him, "Good morning, Adam. I'm John Clark, the foreman."

They shook hands, and Adam said, "Hello, Mr. Clark. I'm Adam Stern. I'm sorry I'm late. The bus was slow."

Adam's interview went well. Here are some of the interviewer's questions and the answers that Adam gave.

Mr. Clark: I see that you worked during the school year. Did you usually get to work on time?

Adam: Yes, I did. I was late only once, and that was the day we had a fire alarm drill at school.

Mr. Clark: What makes you think you could stand the grind of factory work?

Adam: I have a lot of patience. I sometimes spend hours working on wood carvings. My job last year gave me experience, too. I spent most of the time repairing motors on lawnmowers.

Mr. Clark: Why do you want this job?

Adam: I know the plant is good to its employees. I have several friends who have worked here and liked it. There's also the fact that I need the money. My family expects me to earn my own spending money.

- How well did Adam handle this interview? Give specific reasons and details to explain your answer.

Try Your Skill   Imagine that you work at a summer camp. You have been asked to interview students for jobs as grounds-keepers and crafts teachers. Make a list of questions that you would ask applicants for each job.

Keep This in Mind

- Introduce yourself to your interviewer.
- Answer all questions completely and thoughtfully.
- Let your interviewer see your best assets.

Now Write   Choose a job that you would like to have. Imagine that you are the employer. Make a list of questions that you would ask applicants for this job. Then, write the answers you would give if asked these questions.

A Work Sheet

Completing a Job Application

Here's the Idea Whenever you apply for a job, you will probably be asked to complete a job application. The form of the application will vary from company to company. However, there are certain guidelines you should always follow.

1. Be prepared to answer several standard questions. You will be asked to state your address, telephone number, date of birth, social security number, and your citizenship. You will be asked about your education, special skills, and any past work experience. You will also be asked to name references. In other words, you will be asked to name two or three people not related to you who have known you for some time and who would be willing to discuss your strengths and abilities. A reference may be a former employer, a teacher, or a clergyman, for example.

2. Be neat. Print your answers carefully. You are being judged on your ability to follow directions and to work neatly. Use a good pen with blue or black ink. Because there is never enough space for the information requested, plan your answers before you print them. Read all instructions carefully, especially those in fine print. For example, you may be asked to give your last name first.

3. Complete every item. There may be questions that you cannot answer, such as a question about military service or home ownership. However, you should never leave any space blank on an application. Leaving a blank space only causes confusion. If an item does not apply to you, write "does not apply."

4. Be honest. You will be asked to sign your name to a statement that all information is correct.

Check It Out Examine the completed job application on page 361.

FEDERAL FOOD STORES

APPLICATION FOR EMPLOYMENT

Date _March 25, 198_

Name _O'Brien, Elizabeth Ann_   Tel. No. _555-3650_
     Last   First   Middle

Present Address _257 Walker Road,   Memphis,   Tenn.   38104_
     Street   City   State   Zip

Do you rent? ☐   Own your home? ☐   Live with parents? ☑

Previous Address _____
     Street   City   State   Zip

Soc. Sec. No. _986-77-2166_ Date of Birth _6/15/6_   Are you a citizen? Yes ☑ No ☐

Person to be notified in case of accident or emergency _Francis O'Brien_

Address _same as above_   Phone _same_

Position applied for _cashier_   Date available for work? _June 16, 1981_

RECORD OF EDUCATION

School	Name and Address of School	Years Attended	Circle last year completed
Elementary	Columbus Elementary School Memphis, Tennessee	197 -19	5 6 7 ⑧
High	Central High School Memphis, Tennessee	19 -Present	1 2 ③ 4
College			1 2 3 4

Did you serve in the military? Yes ☐   No ☑   Which branch? _____

Rank _____   Date of discharge _____

RECORD OF EMPLOYMENT   (List your last two employers, starting with the more recent one)

Dates	Name and Address of Employer	Salary	Position	Reason for Leaving
Sept. 198	Dan's Market, 522 Sherman, Memphis	$3.50/hr.	cashier	
Summer 198	Dan's Market, 522 Sherman, Memphis	$3.10/hr.	stockclerk, bagger	

Check the following office operations with which you have had experience

☑ Adding Machine   ☐ Switchboard   ☐ Shorthand   ☐ Addressograph   Other _cash register_
☐ Proof Machine (IBM)   ☐ Dictaphone   ☐ Typewriter   ☐ Bookkeeping Machine

PERSONAL REFERENCES   (Not former employers or relatives)

Name and Occupation	Address	Phone No.
Ruth Watson, M.D.	12 Elm Rd., Memphis, Tenn. 38104	555-8611
Michael Simpson (teacher)	Central High, Memphis, Tenn. 38104	555-3274
Rev. John Bucci	St. Mary's Church, Memphis, Tenn. 38104	555-4337

I hereby affirm that my answers to the foregoing questions are true and correct and that I have not knowingly withheld any information which would, if disclosed, be considered sufficient cause for dismissal.

In the event of my employment, I promise to comply faithfully with all the rules and regulations presently in effect, or which may hereafter become effective, relating to the conduct and performance of the employees of Federal Food Stores.

Applicant's Signature _Elizabeth Ann O'Brien_

- Have all items on the form been completed? How might an employer check that the information is correct?
- Has the application been filled in neatly? Have all of the instructions been followed carefully?

Try Your Skill Suppose that you are applying to First Federal Food Stores for a part-time job as a cashier. You are interested in working after school or on weekends. Refer to the application for employment on page 361. On a separate sheet of paper, list the information as you would write it on the application. Your teacher may give you a copy of the actual application to complete.

Keep This in Mind

- Answer all items on an application form honestly, correctly, and completely.
- Fill in the items on the application by printing neatly, using ink. Work carefully. Read all instructions.

Now Write Complete an actual employment application. Use a form given to you by your teacher or one from a business in your community. Complete the form honestly and neatly, following the guidelines you have learned.

To Your Knowledge

Writing Letters to Schools

Here's the Idea   After high school, you may decide to take additional schooling before starting a career. You can learn a great deal about various schools and colleges from your guidance department and from the school or public library. Usually, these sources have catalogs for you to look through, as well as some scholarship information. You will also find valuable information about our nation's schools, including their addresses, in such references as *Barron's Profiles of American Colleges.*

However, the best way to get specific information about a particular school that interests you is to write to the school itself. A letter to a vocational school or college is a business letter. Address it to the Admissions Office of the school and follow either of the standard business forms described on pages 334–336. Briefly give the school the information it needs in order to supply you with the information you need.

The school that you might attend will want to know about you. Include information about the name of your school, your grade level, and the date of your graduation. State your main area of interest. Also, you want to know about the school. Request information about entrance requirements, special programs offered, the size and location of the school, tuition costs, and scholarships. Also request a copy of the college catalog.

Because the cost of education is often high, you may also be interested in information about student loans and scholarships. If so, write directly to the Office of Financial Aid. Ask about financial assistance available for the year you plan to enter. The school will send you information about its programs and the necessary forms to be completed.

Deciding to continue your education is an important decision. You need to compare several schools in order to make the best choice. Writing letters to schools is a good way to start.

Check It Out   Read the following letter.

---

32 Meyer Road
Galveston, Texas   77550
February 16, 1985

Admissions Office
Texas College of Arts and Industries
Kingsville, Texas   78363

Dear Sir or Madam:

I am a junior and will graduate from Galveston West High
School in the spring of 1986. I am interested in continuing
my education in the field of data processing, and I am
particularly interested in the program you offer. Do you
anticipate many openings in your program for the fall of
1986, or will there be a limited enrollment?

I would also like to know what subjects you advise potential
students to take during their senior year in high school.
Also, is job experience required of applicants? If so, what
type of experience is preferred?

Please send me a copy of your catalog so that I may examine
the tuition costs, entrance requirements, and the specific
courses offered in the data processing program.

Very truly yours,

Jessica Roberts

Jessica Roberts

- What specific information does this business letter include? What specific information does it request?

Try Your Skill Suppose you are a high school senior interested in hospital work. You are considering a career as an emergency medical technician. Write a letter to the Admissions Office of Midwest Vocational Institute, 3527 Western Avenue, Chicago, Illinois 60604. Request a catalog and other important information about the program offered by the school. Include the important information about yourself described in **Here's the Idea.**

Keep This in Mind

- When you write to vocational schools and colleges, use the correct business letter form.
- Include specific information about yourself and request specific information from the school.

Now Write Write a letter to a real vocational school or college that interests you. Use either correct business letter form. Ask about various aspects of a program in the field of your choice. Request a catalog. Be sure to revise and proofread the letter carefully.

Speaking and Listening

Your Public Awaits

Developing Speaking Skills

Here's the Idea   Both in school and in later life, the ability to speak well is a key to success. Good speaking skills are important when you take part in a discussion or give an oral report. These skills are also important when you meet new people or interview for a job. The following guidelines will help you to make a good impression whenever you speak.

1. Appearance. Stand up straight. Try to look confident and relaxed. Make sure that your clothes suit the occasion.

2. Eye Contact. Look directly at your listeners. This will help you to keep their attention. Never stare at your notes or at any one person.

3. Voice. Speak loudly enough for your listeners to hear you without difficulty. Do not speak so loudly that your listeners become uncomfortable. Pronounce your words clearly. Do not rush or speak too slowly. Make sure that your tone of voice fits what you are saying. Vary your volume, tone, pitch, and pace. Pause for emphasis, especially before important points.

4. Gestures and Facial Expressions. Use natural gestures and facial expressions. These will help you to appear relaxed and confident. They will also help your audience to understand how you feel. For example, if you are talking about an important problem, you can show its importance by looking concerned. If you are talking about an exciting event, you can show your feelings by looking excited.

Check It Out   Read the following descriptions. Think about how each speaker presents his or her ideas.

1. Margaret saw a *Help Wanted* sign in a bakery window. She went into the shop and asked for the manager. "I see you need

help," she said in a low voice while looking out the window. "Maybe I could work here."

2. Andy was asked to represent the ski team at the opening day assembly. He was very nervous. His legs shook, and his hands trembled. He stared at his notes and spoke quickly so he could get the speech over with.

- How could the performance of each speaker be improved?

Try Your Skill Read the following sentences aloud. Practice pronouncing each word clearly.

1. A tiny toddler came tumbling down the slope.
2. Arthur, the author, read his guest his best stories.
3. Darlene cleaned these kitchen cabinets, didn't she?
4. My sister Sarah sings sensationally.
5. The clouds now looked like billowy, downy, pillows.

Keep This in Mind

- Whenever you speak in public, stand up straight and look at your audience.
- Speak loudly enough to be heard. Pronounce your words clearly. Vary your volume, pitch, pace, and tone. Pause when necessary.
- Use natural gestures and facial expressions to communicate your feelings.

Now Write Think of a time when you heard a really interesting speaker. This speaker may have been a teacher, another student, or a politician on television. Write a paragraph telling why this speaker's performance was effective. Share your paragraph with your classmates.

Listen to This!

Developing Listening Skills

Here's the Idea Listening is a skill that you use every day. In school you listen to lectures, speeches, and class discussions. Outside of school, you listen to the conversation of people around you. Developing good listening skills will increase your understanding of materials presented in your classes. In addition, these skills will help you to communicate better with others. The following guidelines will help you to develop good listening skills.

Guidelines for Good Listening

1. When someone is speaking, give the speaker your full attention.

2. Try to make the speaker feel comfortable. Let your eyes and expression show that you are interested in what the speaker is saying.

3. Do not make distracting noises or movements. Never speak when someone else is speaking.

4. Think about what the speaker is saying. Listen for main ideas and supporting details. In some situations, you may wish to take notes.

5. Be open-minded. Do not judge the speaker's ideas before you hear how they are supported.

Check It Out Rolanda went to hear a speech by a Senator who was running for President. The audience was very excited.

Several people clapped and cheered throughout the speech. They were so loud that Rolanda couldn't hear a word.

- How could the Senator's audience have been more considerate?

Try Your Skill Read the following descriptions of poor listening. Tell what each listener could do to improve his or her listening skills.

1. Marietta won first place in a speech contest. When she returned home, she ran to tell her brother about it. She found her brother watching television. She told him all about the contest. Her brother said, "That's nice," and continued watching TV.

2. A guest speaker visited Bill's United States history class. Bill listened to the first couple of sentences. Then, he decided that he wasn't interested. For the rest of the class period, Bill did his mathematics homework.

Keep This in Mind

- Always be polite when listening to a speaker. Show your interest. Do not make distracting movements or noises.
- Think about what the speaker is saying. Listen for main ideas and supporting details.

Now Write Think of a time when you had difficulty hearing a speaker. Write a paragraph describing this situation. Label your paper **Listen to This!** Save it in your folder.

Small Talk

Part 3

Preparing an Informal Talk

Here's the Idea On many occasions you will be required to give an informal talk. An informal talk is a short talk used to present information quickly. There are four types of informal talks.

1. **Announcements** tell about an event that has happened or will happen.
2. **Introductions** present people to audiences.
3. **Demonstrations** show how something is done.
4. **Directions** tell how to do something.

To prepare an informal talk, decide what facts you need to present. Then, gather these facts and put them in a logical order. The facts you include depend on the type of talk you want to give.

1. **Announcements** should answer the questions *who? what? when? where?* and *why?* Keep your announcement short and simple. Leave out any unnecessary details.

2. **Introductions** should provide information about the person you are introducing. Make sure that you have something interesting to say about this person. You may have to interview the person beforehand to gather this information. Be enthusiastic and polite.

3. **Demonstrations** should present the activity you wish to demonstrate in separate steps. Perform each step for your audience. Explain each step as you perform it. Suppose you wanted to demonstrate how to prepare a new aquarium. To do so, you would actually set up an aquarium in front of your audience. During each step, you would explain what you are doing and why. If you wish to use props in a demonstration, practice using

372

these props before your talk. When giving the talk, keep your props where your audience can see them.

4. **Directions** should include all necessary or helpful details. Arrange these details in step-by-step order. Make sure that each step is presented in the right order.

Check It Out   Read the following talk.

> To change a tire on a car, loosen the lug nuts. Take off the tire. Then, put on the new tire.

- What type of informal talk is this?
- What is wrong with this talk? How could it be improved?

Try Your Skill   Write an informal talk on one of these topics.

1. A demonstration of a craft or hobby
2. An introduction presenting one of your teachers to a group of parents
3. An announcement telling about a special event at your school (Include details that would make people want to attend.)
4. Directions explaining how to get from your school to a local movie theater

Keep This in Mind

- An informal talk is a short talk used to present information quickly.
- Informal talks include announcements, introductions, demonstrations, and directions.
- To prepare an informal talk, gather all the necessary information. Then, place this information in a logical order.

Now Write   Choose a second topic from the list given in **Try Your Skill.** Write another informal talk. If your teacher directs you to do so, deliver your talk to your class.

In Good Form

Preparing a Formal Speech

Here's the Idea Formal speeches require more preparation than informal talks. A formal speech is longer and presents a subject in detail. Book reports, lectures, sermons, and campaign speeches are all types of formal speeches. When preparing a formal speech, follow these steps:

Pre-Writing

1. **Choose your topic.** Narrow it to fit the time available.
2. **Define your purpose.** Your purpose may be to explain, to persuade, or to entertain.
3. **Identify your audience.** Think about your audience. Make sure that your topic is one that they will enjoy.
4. **Determine your main idea.** Write a sentence stating this idea.
5. **Gather supporting information.** Use sources such as personal experience, other people, and reference works.
6. **Organize your information.** A speech may be organized in any of these ways: spatial order, chronological order, the order of importance, or order of familiarity.

Writing

1. Write an introduction that states your main idea and gains the attention of your audience.
2. Write the body of the speech. Develop your main idea using facts, details, and examples.
3. Write a conclusion that "wraps up" your speech. If your purpose is to entertain, end on a note of amusement or interest. If your purpose is to explain or persuade, end in one of these ways:
   a. Repeat the main idea in different words. Then, summarize the major points made in the speech.
   b. Draw a lesson or moral from the ideas presented.

    c. Make an appeal for some sort of action on the part of your listeners.

Revising

1. See that all the material relates to your main idea.
2. Check your speech for errors in grammar and usage.

Check It Out   Read the following passage.

    Sarah was asked to give a speech in her social studies class. She remembered seeing an old silver certificate in her uncle's coin collection. She began to wonder what other types of money had been used in the past. She thought this would make a good subject for her speech. Her teacher agreed. He said that United States currency has gone through several changes.

- What sources could Sarah check for information?

Try Your Skill   Choose one of the following topics for a five-minute speech. Narrow the topic. Then write an interesting introduction, that states the main idea.

    athletics   the Old West   famous scientists

Keep This in Mind

- When preparing a speech, narrow your topic. Identify your purpose and audience. State your main idea. Organize your information.
- Make sure that your speech has an introduction, a body, and a conclusion.
- Make sure that your ideas are all related to your main idea. Proofread your rough draft.

Now Write   Write the body and conclusion of the speech that you began in **Try Your Skill.** Make sure that your information is organized logically. Revise and proofread your final draft.

Down Pat

Practicing and Presenting a Speech

Here's the Idea What would happen if no one on the U.S. Olympic Team ever practiced? Of course, the team would lose every event. Practice is necessary in order to perfect any skill. Speakers, like athletes, must practice in order to do their best.

Before practicing a speech, decide how much of the speech you wish to memorize. You can memorize the entire speech. You can also memorize just the introduction and conclusion. Notes or an outline can then be used for the body of the speech. If you do decide to use notes or an outline, practice with these beforehand. When giving the speech, try not to look at your notes or outline too often.

Use the following method to memorize all or part of a speech:

1. Read one sentence.
2. Recite the sentence several times without looking at it.
3. Read the next sentence.
4. Recite both sentences without looking.
5. Go through all the material in this manner. When you miss a sentence, start all over again.

When you practice, say your speech aloud several times. If possible, make a tape recording of your presentation. Then, play back this tape to check your voice. Practice before a mirror at least once. Check your posture, facial expressions, and gestures. Ask friends or relatives to listen to your speech. See if they have suggestions for improvements.

When you deliver your speech, keep in mind the guidelines for effective speaking given in Part 1, **Your Public Awaits.** Try to appear relaxed and confident. Look at your audience. Speak loudly enough to be heard. Use natural gestures and facial expressions.

Check It Out Arthur wrote a speech for his science class on how batteries work. He memorized the entire speech. Then, he practiced his speech several times. First, he made a tape recording of the speech. He noticed that he was talking too fast, so he slowed the speech down. Second, he practiced his speech in front of a mirror. He noticed that he wasn't standing up straight, so he corrected this problem, too. Finally, he practiced his speech for two of his friends. They suggested that he use a drawing of a battery as a visual aid. Arthur did this. Then, he practiced the speech again using the drawing.

- How thoroughly did Arthur practice his speech?

Try Your Skill Practice giving one of the informal talks that you wrote for Part 3, **Small Talk.** As you practice, make a list of problems that you notice in your delivery. Then list the improvements that you make as you practice.

Keep This in Mind

- Memorize your entire talk, or memorize just the introduction and the conclusion. If you use notes or an outline, practice with these.
- Practice your talk several times. Use a tape recorder and a mirror, if possible.
- Ask your friends or relatives to listen to your speech. Listen to their suggestions.
- When you deliver your talk, follow the guidelines given in Part 1, **Your Public Awaits.**

Now Write Practice the speech you wrote for Part 4, **In Good Form.** Memorize the introduction and conclusion. Use note cards or an outline for the body. Practice the speech yourself and in front of other people. List any improvements that you make as you practice. Label this list **Down Pat.** Save it.

United We Stand

Organizing a Group Discussion

Here's the Idea You have probably heard the expression "Two heads are better than one." Like many old sayings, this one contains a great deal of truth. Groups can often accomplish much more than one person acting alone. This is why group discussion is so widely used in businesses and schools.

Every group discussion should have a **chairperson.** This person's duty is to keep order and to lead the discussion. In addition, a discussion group may choose a **secretary.** This person takes notes on what is said. The other members of the group act as **participants.** They discuss the topic under the guidance of the chairperson.

The chairperson should begin by stating the topic and purpose. The purpose may be to explore an idea or to exchange information. It may also be to solve a problem or to plan a course of action. The participants then define any key terms that will be used in the discussion. By doing this, members of the group can be certain that they are talking about the same things. A group may also decide to narrow their discussion topic before continuing. Doing this will keep the group from getting off the subject.

During a discussion, members of the group should ask to be recognized by the chairperson. Then, they should offer their ideas and opinions. They may also wish to question other group members. What happens during the discussion will vary, depending on the subject being discussed.

At the end of the discussion, the chairperson or the secretary should summarize what has been said. The summary should include any agreements or decisions arrived at during the discussion.

Check It Out   Read the following description of a discussion.

A group of students at Central High School decided to start a computer club. Six of these students got together one day after school to discuss forming this club. They hoped to receive official approval and support from their school.

The group decided not to choose a chairperson because they wanted everyone to be on an equal footing. Two of the students spent most of the time talking about a new computer game. One of the students told the group about the new computer terminals being purchased by the school. A fourth student said that she thought the club would teach people how to use computers. At the end of an hour, everyone realized that the group had not discussed their initial topic.

- What went wrong in this discussion?

Try Your Skill   Imagine that your state is considering a bill to raise the legal age for obtaining a driver's license. You have been elected chairperson of a group of students who will discuss this question on a local cable television station. Write an introduction to the discussion. In your introduction, state the topic and purpose of the discussion.

Keep This in Mind

- The chairperson, secretary, and participants all have important roles to play in a discussion.
- A discussion should begin with an explanation of the topic and purpose and end with a summary.

Now Write   Think of an interesting or successful discussion in which you have taken part. This may be a discussion from one of your classes. It may also be from a club or team meeting. Write a paragraph describing this discussion. Tell who led the discussion and describe its topic and purpose. Label your paper **United We Stand.** Save it in your folder.

Job Descriptions

Participating in a Discussion

Here's the Idea   Each person in a discussion group has specific duties. If you understand what these duties are, you can help a discussion to flow smoothly.

Duties of a Chairperson

1. Prepare for the discussion by researching the topic.
2. Introduce the topic and purpose of the discussion.
3. Allow time for the introduction, the discussion, and the summary.
4. Keep order in the discussion group.
   a. Allow only one person to speak at a time.
   b. Insist that members of the group ask to be recognized before they speak.
5. Encourage everyone in the group to participate.
6. Ask questions to keep the group interested in the topic.
7. Keep the discussion on the topic.
8. Take notes in order to summarize what has been said.

Each participant can also affect the success of a discussion.

Duties of a Participant

1. Speak only when the chairperson recognizes you.
2. Take part in the discussion.
3. Support your statements with facts. (See Chapter 21, **Critical Thinking.**)
4. Listen carefully, following the guidelines for good listening given in Part 2, **Listen to This!**
5. Be polite, especially when disagreeing with another member of the group. Use phrases such as "You've made a good point, but don't you think that . . . ?"
6. Be open-minded. Try to understand the views of other group members. Ask questions if you do not understand a point.

Check It Out   Read the following selection from a discussion.

CHAIRPERSON: Our topic for today is "Should students be allowed to drive their automobiles to school?" As you know, the school administration is considering . . .

ERICA: (Interrupting) Who cares? I don't drive.

CHAIRPERSON: Excuse me, Erica. Please wait to be recognized. Also, please give me a moment to introduce the topic. Then you will have a chance to voice your opinion.

As you know, the school administration is considering banning student-driven vehicles from school property. Our purpose for meeting today is to decide what recommendation we should make to the school board. Yes, Luis?

LUIS: Don't you think we ought to talk about getting some new basketball uniforms instead?

- Is the chairperson in this group doing his or her job?
- Are the comments of Erica and Luis appropriate?

Try Your Skill   You have been asked to lead a discussion on a short story or poem of your choice. Write a list of five questions that you could ask to keep the discussion going.

Keep This in Mind

- The chairperson should introduce the topic and purpose. This person should also keep order and keep the discussion on the topic.
- A participant in a discussion group should take part in the discussion, listen carefully, and be polite.

Now Speak   If your teacher directs you to.do so, join a small group. Elect a chairperson to lead your group. Also elect a secretary to take notes. Discuss this question.

What new courses should be taught at this school?

Choose someone to report your group's conclusions.

Handbook

A detailed Table of Contents for the Handbook appears in the front of this book.

The Sentence and Its Parts

Clear communication is the purpose of language. Once small children learn a number of words, they start putting them together to express their needs. Soon they are speaking in simple sentences.

Milk. (One word)
More milk. (Two words)
I want more milk. (Sentence)

The sentence is the basic unit of communication. In order to write good sentences, it is helpful to know the parts of the sentence—subjects, verbs, objects, modifiers, and more.

In this section you will learn about the parts of a sentence and how they are put into working order.

Part 1 The Complete Sentence

In everyday speech, you sometimes use only parts of sentences. For example, you might answer a question with one or two words:

Tomorrow.   No.   Maggie's house.

In writing, however, complete sentences are important. With them, your ideas are clear and understandable. **A sentence is a group of words that expresses a complete thought.** A sentence makes sense because it is a whole idea, not just part of one.

These groups of words are sentences:

Paul caught a bass.
Our soccer team won the match.
The car skidded into a snowbank.

Sometimes part of an idea is missing from a sentence. Then the group of words is a sentence fragment. A **sentence fragment** is a group of words that does not express a complete thought. For example, these are sentence fragments:

Caught a bass. (Who caught a bass?)
Our soccer team. (What about the team?)
Into a snowbank. (What happened?)

Exercise A Number your paper from 1 to 10. For each group of words that is a sentence, write *S*. For each group of words that is a sentence fragment, write *F*.

1. Sang a duet.
2. The horses raced around the track.
3. A mysterious stranger.
4. Completed the jigsaw puzzle.
5. Mom drove through the car wash.
6. The smell of cinnamon.
7. Ben waited patiently.

8. Ads in the school newspaper.
9. Eric planted the seeds.
10. Where did Mildred go?

Exercise B Follow the directions for Exercise A.

1. Scratched the paint on the fender.
2. Andrea won the tennis match.
3. The referee called a foul.
4. Drives a brown van.
5. A conference of senior citizens.
6. What made that noise?
7. Exhaust fumes from the cars.
8. Accepted the collect phone call.
9. Lee signed the receipt.
10. The wind whipped the trees.

Part 2 The Subject and the Predicate

Every sentence is made up of two basic parts: the subject and the predicate. The **subject** tells *who* or *what* the sentence is about. The **predicate** tells *what is done* or *what happens*.

Subject (Who or what)	Predicate (What is done or what happens)
A hurricane	hit Miami.
The teller at the desk	sounded the alarm.
Our track team	won the trophy.

Each of these sentences expresses a complete thought.

There is an easy way to remember the parts of a sentence. Think of the sentence as telling who did something or what happened. The subject tells *who* or *what*. The predicate tells *did* or *happened*.

Who or What	Did or Happened
The members of our band	led the parade.
The shortstop	tagged the runner.
That car	conserves gas.

The subject of the sentence tells *who* or *what* did something, or what the sentence is about.

The predicate of the sentence tells what is done or what happens.

Exercise A Head two columns *Subject* and *Predicate*. Write the proper words from each sentence in the columns.

Example: My brother paints houses.

Subject	Predicate
My brother	paints houses.

1. A dozen jets lined the runway.
2. Our coach distributed information about scholarships.
3. Marsha wears a digital watch.
4. Those trucks carry produce to the city.
5. The surf pounded the reef.
6. A lovely garden surrounds the old hotel.
7. Today's newspaper ran a story about the street fair.
8. Canoes glided down the canal.
9. Ned lost his wool mittens.
10. Auditions for the play begin today.

Exercise B Follow the directions for Exercise A.

1. Mindy's kite soared over our heads.
2. The workers poured new sidewalks.
3. Some animals hibernate during the winter.
4. Steve designed the set for our play.
5. That horror film frightens many people.

6. A spring blizzard blanketed the Midwest with snow.
7. The litter of puppies whined all night.
8. Three of my friends joined the volunteer group.
9. The rescue helicopter landed in the jungle.
10. Karen munched popcorn during the movie.

Part 3 Simple Subjects and Verbs

In every sentence, certain words are more important than the others. These words are the basic framework of the sentence. Look at these sentences once again:

Subject	Predicate
A **hurricane**	**hit** Miami.
The **teller** at the desk	**sounded** the alarm.
Our track **team**	**won** the trophy.

All the words in the subject part of the sentence are called the **complete subject.** Within the complete subject is a key word, the **simple subject.** In the last example above, *our track team* is the complete subject. *Team* is the simple subject.

The **complete predicate** is all the words that tell what was done or what happened. The key word within the complete predicate is the **simple predicate.** In the sentence about the track team, the complete predicate is *won the trophy.* The key word is *won.* *Won* is the simple predicate.

The key word in the subject of a sentence is called the simple subject. It is also called the *subject* of the verb.

The key word in the predicate is the simple predicate. The simple predicate is the verb.

Verbs that tell about an action are called **action verbs.** Some verbs tell about an action that can be seen.

The wheel *fell* off.   Jack *painted* my portrait.

Other action verbs tell of an action that cannot be seen.

They *remembered* the answer.   Steven *thought* about the question.

Another kind of verb tells that something *is* or *exists*. These verbs are called **state-of-being verbs**.

The puppy *is* a dalmation.   The water *seemed* warm.

A verb is a word that shows action or state of being.

Finding the Verb and Its Subject

In any sentence, the verb and its subject are the most important words. Other words in the sentence tell more about these key words. To find the key words in any sentence, first find the verb. It tells what was done or what happened. Then ask *who* or *what* before the verb. That answer will give you the subject of the verb.

The pilot of the plane signaled the tower.
   Verb: signaled
   Who signaled? pilot
The subject is *pilot*.
The boat sailed into the harbor.
   Verb: sailed
   What sailed? boat
The subject is *boat*.

Diagraming Subjects and Verbs

A sentence diagram is a drawing of the parts of a sentence. It shows how the parts fit together.

A sentence diagram shows the importance of the subject and the verb. These key parts are placed on a horizontal main line. They are separated by a vertical line that crosses the main line. The subject appears before the verb. Later you will learn how every other word in the sentence has its own place in the diagram, too.

In diagraming, only words capitalized in the sentence are capitalized in the diagram. No punctuation is used.

Eric walked quickly.

Lorraine studied the problem.

Lorraine	studied

Exercise A Label two columns *Verb* and *Subject*. Number your paper from 1 to 10. For each sentence, write the verb and its subject.

1. George sealed the packages.
2. Some dancers practiced all afternoon.
3. Our tour of the museum includes a stop for lunch.
4. The Army nurses worked double shifts.
5. This stew needs onions.
6. Cary's sister plays racquetball twice a week.
7. Bright red spots covered the child's face.
8. A heart specialist performed the surgery.
9. This porch light attracts insects.
10. That ladder collapses easily.

Exercise B Follow the directions for Exercise A.

1. The waiter took our dinner order.
2. Barbara Mandrell sang at the state fair.
3. Severe floods forced residents from their homes.
4. The bells in that tower ring every hour.
5. Two ducks swam across the lake.
6. The attendant at the gas station gave us a road map.
7. This restaurant serves lunch outdoors.
8. The sound of the alarm startled me.
9. Ice on the runway created a hazard.
10. A vendor at the gate sold balloons.

Part 4   The Parts of a Verb

A verb may consist of one word or several words. The verb may be composed of a **main verb** and one or more **helping verbs.**

Helping Verbs	+	Main Verb	=	Verb
shall		leave		shall leave
should		go		should go
is		talking		is talking
could have		found		could have found

To name the verb in any sentence, you must name all the words that make up the verb.

These words are frequently used as helping verbs:

am	are	have	will	may
is	be	do	would	might
was	has	does	can	shall
were	had	did	could	should

Separated Parts of a Verb

At times you will find words inserted between the parts of a verb. These words are not included in the verb. Look at the following sentences. The parts of the verb are in bold print.

> Laura **had** never **flown** before.
> My car **would** not **start** during the blizzard.
> This frame **will** easily **fit** that picture.

Some verbs are joined with other words to make contractions. In naming verbs that appear in contractions, pick out only the verb. The word *not* and its contraction *n't* are adverbs. They are never verb parts.

> Mark **did**n't **attend** the meeting. (*Did attend* is the verb.)
> Ms. Vernon **has**n't **ordered** the costumes yet. (*Has ordered* is the verb.)

Exercise A Number your paper from 1 to 10. List the verbs in the following sentences.

1. Several riders have not practiced their jumps.
2. The program hasn't begun yet.
3. I will never finish this project on time.
4. Sue has often attended council meetings.
5. They shouldn't arrive for at least another hour.
6. Larry will probably go to the concert.
7. This train has never been late.
8. Sara can usually do the algebra homework.
9. Marty can't go to the beach this afternoon.
10. I am still reading *The Scarlet Letter*.

Exercise B Follow the directions for Exercise A.

1. The artist was carefully cleaning her brushes.
2. The baseball season hasn't started yet.
3. Our dog doesn't usually bark at neighbors.
4. We couldn't even see the mountains through the fog.
5. The trailer was safely hitched to the car.
6. Jill could not remember the address.
7. Troops are sometimes stationed at this border.
8. George did not understand the chemistry experiment.
9. That store has never accepted credit cards.
10. Laura didn't really enjoy that movie.

Part 5 Subjects in Unusual Positions

The subject of a sentence usually comes before the verb. In some sentences, however, part or all of the verb comes before the subject.

To find the subject in any sentence, first find the verb. Then ask *who* or *what* before it. The answer will be the subject.

Sentences Beginning with *There*

In sentences beginning with *there,* the verb often comes before the subject.

There is used in two ways. It may be used to tell something about the verb. It tells *where* something is.

> There are my boots. (*Boots* is the subject; *are* is the verb. *There* tells where the boots are.)

> There is the elevator. (*Elevator* is the subject; *is* is the verb. *There* tells where the elevator is.)

Sometimes *there* is used simply as an introductory word to get a sentence started.

> There was an air controllers' strike. (*Strike* is the subject; *was* is the verb.)

> There is an error in this article. (*Error* is the subject; *is* is the verb.)

To diagram sentences beginning with *there,* you must know if *there* tells *where* or is an introductory word. If *there* tells *where,* it belongs on a slanted line below the verb. If *there* is an introductory word, it belongs on a horizontal line above the subject.

There are the dancers.

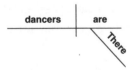

There has been an accident.

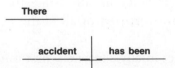

Exercise A Write the subject and the verb in each sentence. Tell whether *there* is used to tell *where* or as an introductory word.

1. There is the stage door.
2. There weren't any messages for you.
3. There is the Sears Tower.
4. There was a freeze in Florida.
5. There are my new roller skates.
6. There was an epidemic of cholera.
7. There is the reptile house.
8. There will be cash prizes.
9. There aren't any napkins left.
10. There will be rain later today.

Exercise B Follow the directions for Exercise A.

1. There was an elephant in the parade.
2. There is the exit.
3. There was a party for my brother.
4. There must have been some mistake.
5. There should have been some mail.
6. There are my tennis shoes.
7. There is the grocery store.
8. There is never enough ice.
9. There was an avalanche near the ski resort.
10. There is the key to the mailbox.

Other Sentences with Unusual Word Order

Sentences beginning with *there* are just one kind of sentence with unusual word order. Here are some others.

1. **Sentences beginning with *here***

   Here comes the sun. (*Sun* is the subject; *comes* is the verb.)

   Here is the bus. (*Bus* is the subject; *is* is the verb.)

The word *here* always tells *where* about the verb. It is not used as an introductory word.

2. Questions

Have you eaten? (*You* is the subject; *have eaten* is the verb.)

Will Mike be waiting for us? (*Mike* is the subject; *will be waiting* is the verb.)

3. Sentences starting with phrases or other words

Up the hill lurched the old car. (*Car* is the subject; *lurched* is the verb.)

Gently flows the river. (*River* is the subject; *flows* is the verb.)

When you are looking for the subject in a sentence with unusual word order, first find the verb. Then ask *who* or *what* before the verb.

Here are the tools.
Verb: are
Who or what are? tools
Subject: tools

Unusual word order in a sentence does not change the sentence diagram. The verb and the subject are still placed on the horizontal main line with the subject first and then the verb.

Around the bend raced the cyclist.

cyclist	raced

Sentences Giving Commands

In sentences that give commands, the subject is usually not stated. Since commands are always given to the person spoken to, the subject is *you*. The word *you* is not stated, but it is *understood*.

Help yourself. (*You* is the subject of *help*.)

Turn right at the corner. (*You* is the subject of *turn*.)

To diagram a sentence giving a command, place the subject *you* in parentheses.

Write soon.

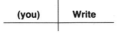

Exercise A Label two columns *Subject* and *Verb*. Number your paper from 1 to 10. Write the subject and verb for each sentence.

1. Here is an extension cord.
2. Open all the windows.
3. Are the roads icy?
4. Here is the paperback book section.
5. Out of the bag tumbled the groceries.
6. Can you hear the crickets?
7. Plant the marigolds near the porch.
8. Here comes Jim on his bicycle.
9. Into the water fell my sunglasses.
10. Try some of this chili.

Exercise B Follow the directions for Exercise A.

1. Look at this gift from my dad.
2. Where is Julia?
3. Out of the sky dropped a parachute.
4. Into the cave walked the explorers.
5. Here is my ticket stub.
6. Don't forget your plane tickets.
7. Have the scissors been found yet?
8. Through the dark tunnel raced the roller coaster.
9. Here is the last piece of the puzzle.
10. May Elizabeth go to the art fair?

Part 6   Objects of Verbs

Some verbs do not need other words to complete their meaning in a sentence. The action they describe is complete.

The team *cheered.*   The car usually *starts.*
Craig *was leaving.*   The storm *will end.*

There are other verbs that do not express a complete action by themselves. These verbs need other words to complete their meaning.

Lisa tossed _____. (Tossed what?)
Mr. Wright mailed _____. (Mailed what?)

Direct Objects

One kind of word that completes the meaning of a verb is the direct object. A **direct object** receives the action of the verb.

Lisa tossed the *salad.*
Mr. Wright mailed the *package.*

In the sentences above, *salad* receives the action of *tossed.* *Package* receives the action of *mailed.*

A direct object can also tell the *result* of an action.

The farmer raised *soybeans.*
Robert Cormier wrote a *book.*

When you are looking for a direct object, first find the verb. Then ask *whom* or *what* after it.

Martha telephoned Amy.
   Verb: telephoned
   Telephoned whom? Amy
   Direct object: Amy

Matt ordered a sandwich.
   Verb: ordered
   Ordered what? sandwich
   Direct object: sandwich

When a verb has a direct object, the verb is a **transitive verb**. When a verb does not have a direct object, the verb is an **intransitive verb**. Notice the difference in these sentences:

> The ice cream melted. (*Melted* is intransitive. It has no direct object.)
>
> Bert discovered the solution. (*Discovered* is transitive. It has a direct object, *solution*.)

Some verbs may be intransitive in one sentence and transitive in another.

> Intransitive: The police officer stopped.
>
> Transitive: The police officer stopped the car.

Transitive or Intransitive?

Look at the following sentences. Are the verbs transitive or intransitive?

> Dick *sang* softly.
>
> Dick *sang* in the variety show.
>
> Dick *sang* a solo.

In the first two examples, the verb *sang* has no direct object. In those sentences, *sang* is intransitive. However, in the third sentence, if you ask *whom* or *what* after the verb, you find that *solo* is the direct object. In that sentence, *sang* is a transitive verb.

> Dick sang a solo.
> *Verb:* sang
> *Sang what?* solo
> *Direct object:* solo

Exercise A   Number your paper from 1 to 10. For each sentence, write the direct object of the verb.

1. A clown walked the tightrope.
2. Mr. Benson donated a turkey for the raffle.

3. Mary Jo has accepted the award for the team.
4. Chris usually brings the volleyball.
5. After dinner, I will finish my project.
6. Play another song on the juke box.
7. Mom appreciated the flowers.
8. I forgot the coupons.
9. Michele answered the question thoughtfully.
10. Jeff studies business in college.

Exercise B Number your paper from 1 to 10. Decide whether the verb in each sentence is *Transitive* or *Intransitive*.

1. Ann can speak Chinese.
2. The auctioneer speaks rapidly.
3. Sam ate early today.
4. Hank ate lunch at noon.
5. The electrician climbed to the top of the tower.
6. Marcy climbed the ladder.
7. The sunbathers roasted in the tropical sun.
8. The boys roasted the corn on the grill.
9. Mike drives a Fiat.
10. Gayle drives carefully.

Indirect Objects

In addition to direct objects, some sentences also have **indirect objects** of the verb. Indirect objects sometimes tell *to whom* or *to what* about the verb. At other times they tell *for whom* or *for what* about the verb.

> Sue gave **Len** the *gift*. (gave *to* Len)
>
> The guide showed **us** the *landmarks*. (showed *to* us)
>
> Linda made **me** a hot fudge *sundae*. (made *for* me)

The words *Len, us,* and *me* are indirect objects. The direct objects are in italics. Indirect objects appear only in sentences with direct objects. Indirect objects are found between the verb and direct object. Never use the words *to* or *for* with an indirect object.

> Mark showed the driver his bus pass. (*Driver* is the indirect object of *showed*.)

> Mark showed his bus pass to the driver. (*Driver* is not an indirect object.)

In a diagram, place a direct object on the main line after the verb. The vertical line between the verb and object does not go below the main line.

> Marilyn wrote a letter.

The indirect object belongs on a horizontal line attached below the verb.

> Marilyn wrote the newspaper a letter.

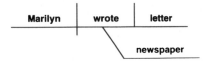

Exercise A   Number your paper from 1 to 10. Label three columns *Verb, Indirect Object,* and *Direct Object.* For each of the following sentences list those parts. Not all sentences will have all three parts.

Example: The waitress brought me the check.

Verb	Indirect Object	Direct Object
brought	me	check

1. The artist drew us a sketch.
2. Joe tossed Jill the Frisbee.

3. Pay the manager the rent on the first of the month.
4. Grace prepared chicken for lunch.
5. Max told us the bad news.
6. Someone handed Rose a free sample of pizza.
7. Send Bob a postcard from Florida.
8. Peggy practiced her serve all afternoon.
9. The nurse gave the patient a shot.
10. The audience gave the speaker a warm round of applause.

Exercise B Follow the directions for Exercise A.

1. The police officer wrote Bill a ticket.
2. Marty left his pole on the boat.
3. Carrie called me from a phone booth.
4. Collin read us the review.
5. Give the plants some water.
6. That bakery makes delicious rye bread.
7. The quarterback passed the football.
8. Bring me the saucepan.
9. The golfer chipped his ball onto the green.
10. Did Mom save me a piece of pie?

Part 7 Linking Verbs and Predicate Words

Not all verbs express action. Some tell of a state of being. These verbs link the subject with a word or group of words in the predicate. Verbs that link the subject with another word are called **linking verbs.**

Luke *is* a tenor.   Charlotte *must be* upset.
We *are* the losers.   The children *were* happy.

The verb *be* is the most commonly used linking verb and has many forms. This list will help you to become familiar with them.

be	been	is	was
being	am	are	were

The verbs *be*, *being*, and *been* can also be used with helping verbs. These are examples:

should be	were being	had been
may be	was being	could have been
will be	is being	might have been

Words that are linked to the subject by linking verbs are called **predicate words.** The three kinds of predicate words are **predicate nouns, predicate pronouns,** and **predicate adjectives.** Predicate words tell something about the subject.

Nancy is a *drummer.* (predicate noun)

That was *she.* (predicate pronoun)

Warren was *calm.* (predicate adjective)

In the above sentences, the subjects and predicate words are linked by the verbs *is* and *was*.

Here are some other common linking verbs.

appear	seem	sound	grow
feel	look	taste	become

Like *be*, these linking verbs have various forms (*grew, looked, tastes*). Linking verbs can also be used with helping verbs (*will become, can seem, might have sounded*).

The record *sounded* scratchy.

The juice *tasted* fresh.

Fran *has become* a fine swimmer.

In a sentence diagram, place a predicate word on the main line after the verb. A slanted line above the main line separates the verb from the predicate word. That line, like the predicate word, points back to the subject.

Dr. Weaver is a surgeon.

That bus looks empty.

Direct Object or Predicate Word?

A verb may be completed in one of two ways. It may have a direct object, or it may have a predicate word. How can you tell the difference between a predicate word and a direct object?

The verb is the key word. Decide whether the verb is an action verb. If it is, the word following the verb that tells *whom* or *what* is a direct object.

> The florist arranged the flowers. (*Arranged* is an action verb. *Flowers* is its direct object.)
>
> The dog chewed my slipper. (*Chewed* is an action verb. *Slipper* is its direct object.)

Is the verb a linking verb? If it is, the word following the verb that tells about the subject is a predicate word.

> Alexander Godunov is a *dancer*. (*Is* is a linking verb. *Dancer* is a predicate word.)
>
> These potatoes seem *dry*. (*Seem* is a linking verb. *Dry* is a predicate word.)

Read the following sentences.

> Ms. Edwards is a lawyer.
>
> Ms. Edwards called a lawyer.

The first sentence contains a linking verb, *is*. The word *lawyer* follows the linking verb and tells about the subject. *Lawyer* is a predicate word. In the second sentence, *called* is an action verb. In this sentence, *lawyer* tells *whom* about the action verb. *Lawyer* is a direct object.

Exercise A   Label three columns *Subject, Linking Verb,* and *Predicate Word.* Find these parts in the following sentences and write them in the proper columns.

1. These boots are warm.
2. The crew looked weary.
3. Parents were the sponsors.
4. Those puzzles were easy.
5. The yogurt tasted tart.
6. The ocean seems rough.
7. Lance must be nervous.
8. The winner is he.
9. Judy will become captain.
10. These old chairs are antiques.

Exercise B   Make four columns. Head the columns *Subject, Verb, Direct Object,* and *Predicate Word.* Find these parts in the following sentences and place them in the proper columns. Remember, no sentence can contain a direct object *and* a predicate word.

1. The Bears are a football team.
2. Their home is Chicago.
3. They were finalists in 1977.
4. They lost the play-off game.
5. The team has had several unsuccessful seasons.
6. However, their fans are loyal.
7. They support the Bears every year.
8. Most games are sellouts.
9. The Bears beat San Diego in overtime in 1981.
10. Someday the Bears will be champions.

Part 8 Compound Parts in a Sentence

Compound means "made up of two or more parts."

Each of the sentence parts described so far in this section can be compound—subjects, verbs, direct objects, indirect objects, and predicate words.

Join the two parts of a compound construction with a conjunction (*and, or, but*). If a compound construction has three or more parts, the conjunction comes between the last two parts.

Compound Subject: Jan, Ramon, and Lisa will arrive soon.
Compound Verb: They will sing and dance for us.
Direct Object: Jan will bring the guitars and castanets.
Indirect Object: Maybe Ramon will show you and me how to use castanets.
Predicate Words: Those three are the best Spanish dancers and singers I've ever seen.

Diagraming Compound Subjects

To diagram compound subjects, split the subject line. Place the conjunction on a dotted line connecting the subjects.

Bottles, cans, and papers littered the park.

Diagraming Compound Verbs

To diagram compound verbs, split the verb line in the same way.

The tourist waved, whistled, and shouted for a taxi.

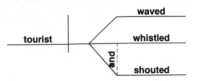

Diagraming Compound Objects

To diagram compound direct objects or indirect objects, split the object line.

Clara bought a watermelon and some peaches. (compound direct object)

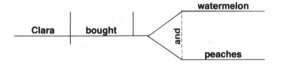

Mr. Maltas gave Chuck and Bob a catalog.

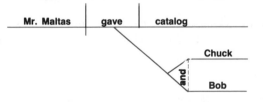

Diagraming Compound Predicate Words

To diagram compound predicate words, split the predicate word line.

The new co-captains are Kirsten and Claudia. (compound predicate word)

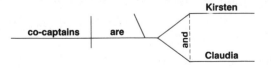

Exercise A As your teacher directs, show the compound parts in the following sentences. Tell whether they are compound subjects, verbs, objects, or predicate words.

1. Boston and Philadelphia were two stops on our trip.
2. Lee cut and raked the lawn.
3. Joshua is the secretary and treasurer of the tennis club.
4. Kelly put raisins and cinnamon into the bread.
5. Mr. Simmons wrote and directed the play.
6. Dad planted maples, elms, and lilacs in the yard.
7. Spring and fall are her favorite seasons.
8. The decorators painted the kitchen, the hallway, and the porch.
9. The carpet was soft and thick.
10. Dancers and musicians from many different countries entertained us.

Exercise B For each of the following sentences, make the part noted in parentheses compound. Write the new sentences.

> Example: The parakeet whistled all afternoon. (*verb*)
> The parakeet whistled and chattered all afternoon.

1. Marilyn wrote several songs for the musical. (*subject*)
2. The cook tasted the stew. (*verb*)
3. Brian bought some new jeans. (*direct object*)
4. The apples were crisp. (*predicate adjective*)
5. The coach congratulated the players. (*subject*)
6. Dave sang in the variety show. (*verb*)
7. The day was chilly. (*predicate word*)
8. Liz brought the badminton set. (*subject*)
9. The fire chief gave the students a talk on fire prevention. (*indirect object*)
10. Nellie toasted the muffins. (*direct object*)

408

Part 9   Kinds of Sentences

There are several different reasons for using sentences. Sometimes you want to state something. Sometimes you want to ask a question. At other times, you want to give a command. There are also times when you want to express strong feeling. In each case, you use a different kind of sentence.

A **declarative sentence** makes a statement. It ends with a period (.).

> The guard patrolled the grounds.
> We saw that movie on TV.

An **interrogative sentence** asks a question. It ends with a question mark (?).

> Have the guests arrived?   When is the test?

An **imperative sentence** gives a command. It usually ends with a period.

> Turn left at the stoplight.   Please pass the pepper.

An **exclamatory sentence** expresses strong emotion. It ends with an exclamation point (!).

> You saved the day!   What a great game that was!

Exercise A   For each of the following sentences, write *Declarative, Interrogative, Imperative,* or *Exclamatory* to show what kind each is. Add the proper punctuation mark.

1. John paints with watercolors
2. What a surprise this is
3. Was the pizza delivered on time
4. Rewind the tape, please
5. Which picture do you prefer
6. Debby finished the crossword puzzle
7. Don't take too long
8. Go out the back way

9. Does Harry play tennis
10. Carol fed the goldfish

Exercise B   Follow the directions for Exercise A.

1. What a ride that was
2. The parrot squawked at the visitors
3. Is that your umbrella
4. The storm damaged the crops
5. Be ready for anything
6. What a team we have
7. When does the bank open
8. Jane filed the documents
9. Roger typed his report
10. Does anyone need a pen

Part 10   Basic Sentence Patterns

Words can be organized into sentences in an endless number of ways. However, most sentences follow certain basic **sentence patterns.** The five patterns that follow are the most common ones.

Study each sentence pattern carefully. Try to think of an example of your own for each pattern.

Pattern One

This is the simplest type of sentence. It has a subject and a verb. The subject is usually a noun or pronoun. In this chart, N stands for the noun (or pronoun) in the complete subject. V stands for the verb in the complete predicate.

N	V
Time	flies.
She	studied hard.
Our neighbor	runs daily.

Pattern Two

In this pattern, the noun (or pronoun) that follows the verb is a direct object.

N	V	N
The detective	solved	the crime.
Laura	lost	her favorite ring.
The tutor	helped	us.

Pattern Three

Two nouns follow the verb in this pattern. The first is an *indirect object*. The second is a *direct object*.

N	V	N	N
Kathy	told	me	a joke.
Nobody	would give	us	information.
The jockey	gave	the horse	an apple.

Pattern Four

The verb in this pattern is a *linking verb* (LV). The noun that follows it is a *predicate noun* (or predicate pronoun).

N	LV	N
That notebook	is	yours.
The play	was	a success.

Pattern Five

In this sentence pattern, a linking verb is followed by a *predicate adjective* (Adj).

N	LV	Adj
Ballet	is	graceful.
The water	was	icy.
The test	will be	complicated.

Exercise A Tell which sentence pattern is used in each sentence.

1. The gardener trimmed the hedge.
2. The Cubs were the winners.
3. Food was plentiful.
4. Sean talks softly.
5. The oysters are raw.
6. Martha waxed her surfboard.
7. Ralph showed us his experiment.
8. The valley flooded.
9. These shoes seem tight.
10. Those flowers are geraniums.

Exercise B Follow the directions for Exercise A.

1. The milk tastes sour.
2. The train left already.
3. Elliott collects toy soldiers.
4. Maggie gave Dirk a souvenir.
5. Japan is an island.
6. Paul gave Andy some advice.
7. These vegetables are fresh.
8. The book was a biography.
9. James left early.
10. Ed signed Mary's cast.

ADDITIONAL EXERCISES

The Sentence and Its Parts

A. Sentences and Fragments Number your paper from 1 to 10. For each group of words that is a sentence, write *S*. For each sentence fragment, write *F*. In class, be ready to add words to change fragments into sentences.

1. Rachel floated on her back.
2. Tossed the mitt into the air.
3. The glass of water is too full.
4. Large, lazy flakes of snow.
5. Derrick took the engine out of the car.
6. Speed is important in soccer.
7. Are the top bleachers full?
8. Are moving to Texas.
9. Several old exercise mats.
10. Stephanie answered.

B. Complete Subjects and Complete Predicates Number your paper from 1 to 10. Label two columns *Complete Subject* and *Complete Predicate.* Write the proper words in each column.

1. One passenger would not move from the doorway.
2. Contact lenses can be a nuisance.
3. Sam's best friends go to a different school.
4. Truckers from all over gathered at Mel's.
5. The Navy was recruiting here.
6. Goats will eat almost anything.
7. The pens without caps dried up.
8. This street is noisy in summer.
9. Those small radios are also popular.
10. Natives of Peru are called Peruvians.

C. Verbs and Simple Subjects Number your paper from 1 to 10. Write the simple subject and the verb in each sentence.

1. The big race is at Indianapolis.
2. The two trainers disagreed.
3. Dirty grease coated the machine.
4. Wet towels belong in the bin by the showers.
5. A red bandana hung from his pocket.
6. Few words begin with x.
7. An inspector from city hall visited the building.
8. The plumber parked her truck in front of the house.
9. A fire in the tunnel delayed the trains.
10. Caroline oiled the chains of her bike.

D. The Parts of a Verb Number your paper from 1 to 10. Write the verb in each sentence. Include helping verbs.

1. Tony had recently sold his car.
2. You may certainly react differently.
3. The disc jockey was reading a list of dedications.
4. Vacation has finally begun.
5. The manager did not return Jeff's call.
6. Someone is standing by the window.
7. Most dentists have used high-speed drills for years.
8. I can't really explain that.
9. The class lists have been printed.
10. Plastic would probably have melted.

E. Subjects and Verbs in Sentences with *There* Number your paper from 1 to 10. Write the subject and verb in each sentence. Tell whether *there* tells *where* or is an introductory word.

1. There will be several new courses.
2. There is no more salad.
3. There are your skates under the bench.
4. There is a good place for the tent.

5. There was a quiz in history this morning.
6. There is a conflict in your schedule.
7. There was not enough time for warm-up exercises.
8. There is the opener.
9. There have been many floods this spring.
10. There goes Jody.

F. Sentences with Unusual Order   Number your paper from 1 to 10. Label two columns *Subject* and *Verb*. Write the subject and verb for each sentence.

1. Here is a secret compartment.
2. Has Amy proved her point?
3. Beside our house sits a tractor.
4. Fry the eggs for five minutes.
5. In the last row sat Heidi.
6. Can you read blueprints?
7. Here are the attendance sheets.
8. Hold your hand out.
9. Finally came the sports announcements.
10. Into the street ran the child.

G. Direct Objects   Number your paper from 1 to 10. If a sentence has a direct object, write the direct object. If a sentence has no direct object, write *Intransitive Verb*.

1. Tamara asked good questions.
2. The coach threw a party after the victory.
3. The clock had stopped.
4. Clean the brushes in soapy water.
5. Aaron dodged.
6. Kenny dodged the ball too late.
7. The Davises have adopted another child.
8. Nina needs some encouragement.
9. Act quickly.
10. The carpenters have finished the new porch.

H. Sentence Parts Label three columns *Verb, Indirect Object,* and *Object.* For each of the following sentences fill in those parts that you find. After each verb write *Transitive* or *Intransitive.*

1. The bank gave Lyle a loan.
2. The teacher handed each student a newspaper.
3. The painters trampled the garden.
4. Bud gave the table a coat of lavender paint.
5. Some drugstores sell food.
6. A door-to-door salesperson sold Al a vacuum.
7. Betsy walks quickly.
8. I wrote the President a letter.
9. He has not answered yet.
10. Julia gave Dave a subscription to that magazine.

I. Direct Object or Predicate Word? Number your paper from 1 to 10. Label four columns *Subject, Verb, Direct Object,* and *Predicate Word.* Fill in the parts that you find for each sentence. You will find either a direct object or a predicate word in each sentence.

1. Your teeth are very straight.
2. This station sounds clear.
3. Rainy days seem long.
4. Jason's pulse felt too fast.
5. Laura is the best bowler on our team.
6. Nancy has perfect pitch.
7. Some gym shoes are washable.
8. Linda hid the rowboat in the reeds.
9. The path looked dangerous.
10. Vince bought an old piano with his first paycheck.

J. Compound Parts As your teacher directs, show the compound parts in the following sentences. Tell whether they are compound subjects, verbs, objects, or predicate words.

1. Their truck makes pick-ups and deliveries.
2. Ice and snow covered the sidewalk.

3. We washed and dried clothes at the laundromat.
4. The horror movie was funny but scary.
5. We had a parade and fireworks on Independence Day.
6. Delia or Joanne will go with you to the nurse's office.
7. That company is small but successful.
8. Jamaica and Dominica are independent countries.
9. The Harts celebrate Christmas and Hanuka.
10. The wind howled, hissed, and whistled all night.

K. Kinds of Sentences Write whether the following sentences are *Declarative, Interrogative, Imperative,* or *Exclamatory.* Add the correct punctuation.

1. What does this code mean
2. Please fill this order
3. What a gossip he is
4. Plumbers charge an hourly rate
5. Move with the music
6. How she has changed
7. How has she changed
8. Does the high school offer business courses
9. Call the emergency room first
10. Ms. Rojac recommended thermal window shades

L. Sentence Patterns Write which sentence pattern is used in each of the following sentences. Each sentence follows one of these patterns: **N V, N V N, N V N N, N LV N, N LV Adj.**

1. Hal photographs sunsets.
2. Allison finally relaxed.
3. Maria wore her uniform.
4. The neighbors were watching.
5. The largest island in the world is Greenland.
6. The work was not easy.
7. Sandra gave Chet her chair.
8. Her shoelaces had rainbows on them.

MIXED REVIEW

The Sentence and Its Parts

A. Finding subjects and predicates and identifying fragments Decide whether the following groups of words are sentences or fragments. Copy each sentence and underline the subject once and the predicate twice. Then write *Declarative, Interrogative, Imperative,* or *Exclamatory* to show what kind of sentence it is. Add the correct punctuation. If a group of words is not a sentence, write *Fragment.*

1. Rolled her sleeves up
2. Roll your sleeves up
3. What a nightmare I had
4. What is the title
5. Clouds hid the mountains
6. A long white scar above his left eyebrow
7. Inflate the soccer ball to twenty-eight inches
8. Faded slowly away
9. Who laughed
10. Where is the tape

B. Finding helping verbs, main verbs, and simple subjects Number your paper from 1 to 10. Label three columns *Helping Verbs, Main Verbs,* and *Simple Subjects.* For each sentence, write the parts in the proper columns.

1. Sandra does know Julie.
2. The plane was flying too low.
3. The band had finally arrived.
4. Across the highway was limping a dog.
5. Maybe he couldn't think clearly.
6. There might be a few problems.
7. Did you check the spark plugs?
8. Will your family watch the game on television?

9. A huge brown spider was building a web.
10. After all, Jerome hasn't often been wrong.

C. Finding sentence parts   Number your paper from 1 to 10. Label five columns on your paper *Subject, Verb, Predicate Word, Indirect Object,* and *Direct Object.* Fill in the parts that you find in each sentence. No sentence will have every part.

1. The ladder was too short.
2. Alison never skips lunch.
3. The company sent Martin a refund.
4. The leaves are yellow now.
5. The usher handed me a program.
6. Marcus Dupree plays football.
7. This instrument is a trumpet.
8. Ms. Hammond found Simon another textbook.
9. I found my cat at the animal shelter.
10. Jeff was slicing onions in the kitchen.

D. Finding compound sentence parts   Number your paper from 1 to 10. Write the compound parts for the following sentences. Write whether each is a compound subject, verb, direct object, indirect object, or predicate word.

1. The ground rumbled and cracked.
2. The mornings and evenings grew darker.
3. Ms. Sands took Mary and Loretta to Williamsburg.
4. You can use an orange or a lemon.
5. The attic was dusty, hot, and dark.
6. The best volleyball servers are Pam and Kristy.
7. Darryl has an atlas, an almanac, an encyclopedia, and a dictionary.
8. The acorns and foliage of the oak are poisonous.
9. Dr. Alvarez will give Franklin or Stacy the job.
10. The skater wobbled but stayed on her feet.

E. Finding sentence patterns Write the pattern for each of the following sentences.

1. A computer broke the code.
2. Winter arrived.
3. The goalie was alert.
4. This car is almost an antique.
5. Some viruses give people colds.
6. The sun bleached the wood.
7. The fever tree has yellow bark.
8. The muffler fell onto the road.
9. She sounded cheerful.
10. The guard spotted the open window.

F. Using sentence patterns Write two original sentences for each of the following sentence patterns.

1. N V
2. N V N
3. N V N N
4. N LV N
5. N LV Adj

USING GRAMMAR IN WRITING
The Sentence and Its Parts

A. Upon returning home from school one day, you are surprised to find a special-delivery letter. The envelope is marked URGENT. You tear the envelope open and find a computer-written letter. Unfortunately, a malfunction of the computer's printer has left gaps in the message. Below are the fragments that were printed. Supply the missing sentence parts.

You have been chosen for _____. _____ that you will accept the mission. We must receive _____. Your country _____. Of course, you _____. _____ the thanks and admiration of your friends.

B. Imagine that you have just set a world record for staying awake. At a press conference, reporters ask you questions about the experience. Complete the following interview. Write an answer to each reporter's question. For each statement, write the question that might have been asked.

Q: How long have you been awake?

A: _____

Q: _____

A: My sense of balance was poor, and I had trouble focusing my eyes.

Q: In what ways did your appetite change?

A: _____

Q: _____

A: I felt colder and colder as time went by.

Q: If your record is broken, will you try again?

A: _____

Using Complete Sentences

Sentences express thoughts and feelings. When they are clear, sentences communicate the speaker's message. When sentences are not clear, the message is lost.

One common problem in writing is omitting part of a sentence. An incomplete sentence is called a **sentence fragment**. Another common problem is writing two or more sentences as one. The result is called a **run-on sentence**.

Sentence fragments and run-on sentences weaken communication. In this section you will learn how to avoid them.

Part 1 What Is a Sentence Fragment?

A group of words that is only part of a sentence is a **sentence fragment**. A sentence fragment does not express a complete thought.

A fragment is confusing because something is missing from the sentence. Sometimes the subject is left out. Then the reader wonders *who* or *what* the sentence is about. At other times the verb is left out. Then the reader wonders *what happened?* or *what about it?*

Fragment: Raced to the finish line. (Who raced? The subject is missing.)

Sentence: The sprinter raced to the finish line.

Fragment: The trombone player in the back. (What happened? The verb is missing.)

Sentence: The trombone player in the back dropped her music.

Fragments Due to Incomplete Thoughts

Sometimes when you write, you are in a hurry. You jot down only bits of ideas. What you write are incomplete thoughts. Your pen doesn't keep up with the flow of your ideas.

Maybe you can understand these pieces of ideas. However, to a reader they will probably seem unclear.

Here is an example of a series of fragments:

Solar energy an alternative. Solar collectors expensive. Will reduce gas and electric bills.

These complete sentences show what the writer meant:

Solar energy is an alternative energy source. The solar collectors are expensive. However, using solar energy will reduce gas and electric bills.

Fragments Due to Incorrect Punctuation

Every sentence ends with a punctuation mark. The mark may be a period, a question mark, or an exclamation point. If you use one of these marks before your idea is complete, a sentence fragment results.

Fragment: Long distance runners. Gathered from all over the country.

Sentence: Long distance runners gathered from all over the country.

Fragment: On a clear, cold day. Skiers dotted the hills.

Sentence: On a clear, cold day skiers dotted the hills.

Fragment: The magician pulled a rabbit. From her hat.

Sentence: The magician pulled a rabbit from her hat.

Exercise A For each group of words that is a sentence, write *S* on your paper. For each sentence fragment, write *F*. Be ready to add words to change the fragments into sentences.

1. The line was busy
2. The juggler in the program
3. Asked for some help
4. Ask Linda for some help
5. Came in second place
6. Landed on an island in the Caribbean
7. Cindy caught up with us
8. The clock on the mantel ticks loudly
9. What was that
10. Fell off the ladder

Exercise B Follow the directions for Exercise A.

1. Betsy mailed the entry form
2. Included three box tops in the envelope

3. The grand prize is a trip to Europe
4. All expenses paid
5. The odds of winning are slim
6. Millions of entrants
7. Second prize is a television set
8. A self-addressed, stamped envelope
9. Winners will be notified
10. Prizes must be claimed by June 1

Part 2   What Is a Run-on Sentence?

A **run-on sentence** is two or more sentences written incorrectly as one.

A run-on confuses the reader. It does not show where the first idea ends and the second one begins. The sentences need a period or other punctuation mark to signal the end of each complete thought. Here are some examples:

Run-on: The pistol shot rang out it signaled the start of the race.

Correct: The pistol shot rang out. It signaled the start of the race.

Run-on: Carl ate spaghetti Jack ate lasagna.

Correct: Carl ate spaghetti. Jack ate lasagna.

Sometimes writers make the mistake of using a comma instead of a period. Again, the result is a run-on.

Run-on: The center tossed the ball from mid-court, she made a basket.

Correct: The center tossed the ball from mid-court. She made a basket.

Run-on: The car is ready, we can leave now.

Correct: The car is ready. We can leave now.

Exercise A Correct the following run-on sentences.

1. The days grew longer, we knew that spring would be here soon.
2. The beagle ran down the steps, it was chasing a rabbit.
3. Jan looked through the catalogs, she selected hiking boots and some books.
4. The scouts are collecting newspapers this week, Dad put out four big bundles.
5. I received a letter from my cousin in Oregon, I hadn't heard from him in months.
6. Air controllers direct air traffic, they use radios.
7. I placed the plant in the window, it can get light.
8. We rode our horses down the trail in the forest preserve, we stopped to eat our lunch by a stream.
9. Storms swept the West Coast, many homes were destroyed in the floods.
10. Put the milk and cheese in the refrigerator, put the canned goods on the shelves.

Exercise B Follow the directions for Exercise A.

1. Steve is very talented, he plays the piano.
2. Microwave ovens are different from conventional ovens, in microwave ovens, no metal pans can be used.
3. Corn has many uses, it can be used for animal feed.
4. I like oranges, they are good for you.
5. Frost can damage a citrus crop, growers use heaters called smudge pots.
6. Some poisonous snakes have triangular-shaped heads, the rattlesnake is poisonous.
7. Drifting snow closed the road, people were stranded.
8. Snakes have jaws that can unhinge, a snake can swallow a mouse whole.
9. The play was about to begin, the lights dimmed.
10. Preheat the oven to 350 degrees, bake for one hour.

ADDITIONAL EXERCISES

Using Complete Sentences

A. Sentences and Fragments Number your paper from 1 to 10. Write *Fragment* or *Sentence* for each of the following groups of words to show what each group is.

1. Rachel repairs cars in her spare time
2. An overturned truck blocked traffic
3. A nationally known cartoonist
4. Steve types at a fast pace
5. Draws sketches with charcoal
6. The cook grilled two hamburgers
7. The apartment on the fourth floor
8. A subway train sped past
9. Led the group in exercises to the music
10. A German neighborhood held a fall festival

B. Sentences and Run-ons Number your paper from 1 to 10. Write *Sentence* or *Run-on* for each of the following groups of words to show what each group is.

1. Ray Charles sometimes uses back-up singers they are usually the Rayettes
2. Tony tried to skate, he ended up with a sprained arm
3. We attended the opening of the football season
4. Larry was trained as a welder, he learned the skills quickly
5. Add some powdered milk to the batter
6. Alligators, crocodiles, and lizards descended from ancient reptiles
7. A pipe burst water flooded the basement
8. Sunlight streamed through the window

9. Six squad cars, an ambulance, and a fire truck sped by
10. The school district sponsors adult classes, many courses are offered

C. Sentences, Fragments, and Run-ons

Number your paper from 1 to 10. Write *Fragment, Sentence,* or *Run-on* for each of the following groups of words to show what each group is.

1. A part-time job at the grocery store
2. A movie with a surprise ending
3. The lights went out everyone lit candles
4. The antique clock on the mantel is a gift from Aunt Helen
5. All the gym students climbed the rope, only Holly got to the ceiling
6. Crews piled sandbags along the river banks
7. The horoscope in the daily newspaper
8. Styles change
9. Rice, tomatoes, onions, green peppers, and spices
10. Sean sang Maureen clapped

MIXED REVIEW

Using Complete Sentences

A.   Identifying sentences, fragments, and run-ons   Write *Fragment, Sentence,* or *Run-on* for each of the following groups of words to show what each one is. Then correct fragments by adding words to make complete sentences. Correct run-ons by using the correct capitalization and punctuation.

1. Tomato sauce, vinegar, and chili powder.
2. The ball dropped through the net, everybody cheered.
3. Balloons and buttons carried the slogan.
4. Kate listened.
5. Finally read the instructions.
6. Finally the wasp landed.
7. Turned the radio off during my favorite song.
8. The wind was brisk Joachim pulled his collar up.
9. The coach shouted and waved a towel.
10. The telephone had no dial, there were pushbuttons on the receiver.

B.   Correcting fragments and run-on   The following paragraph contains fragments and run-on sentences. Rewrite the paragraph, correcting the fragments and run-ons.

The tight space between the seat cushion and the frame of our armchair. Is a little like a personal safe. All kinds of objects are hidden there, push your hand down into the chair and pick out a surprise. Almost anything small can be wedged in our safe, we have found pencils, coins, pocket mirrors, scissors, old birthday cards. And even an overdue library book. There is one big difference between our armchair safe and an ordinary safe the owners of a regular home safe usually know its contents. Our safe gets filled by chance.

USING GRAMMAR IN WRITING
Using Complete Sentences

A. You awaken in the night to find your room flooded with pale green light. You go to the window and find a small object hovering in the air outside your window. You call the police and excitedly deliver this description to the desk sergeant.

> You're going to think I'm crazy I think there's an alien space ship right outside my window. Just hanging in the air. A small thing, about the size of a football. I always thought that an alien ship would be enormous didn't you think it would take a lot of fuel to travel from another solar system? Better get over here fast. 1280 14th Street.

Your call was recorded at the station. A newspaper reporter corrected the run-on sentences and completed the fragments. Write the statement as it appeared in the newspaper.

B. Imagine that you have overslept. You race to get to school. You dash into your first class to find that a surprise quiz is in progress. Here is what you say:

> I'm sorry that I'm late, it really wasn't my fault. You see it all started when the cat knocked the fish tank. Onto the floor, of course. The water spilled onto a lamp cord the next thing we knew all the lights were out Not only was our power off. But every apartment in our building had no power. The power company finally repaired the damage at midnight, by then I was asleep. I never reset my clock, that's why I was late.

Your teacher agrees to give you a make-up quiz if you put your story in writing. Rewrite the explanation, correcting the sentence fragments and run-on sentences.

Using
Nouns

Words are the building blocks of communication. Putting words together correctly to create good, clear sentences is something that you do every day.

The words used in sentences fall into certain groups called the parts of speech. You can talk and write without knowing the names of the parts of speech. However, skilled speakers and writers recognize the different parts of speech and use them properly.

In this section you will learn about one of the eight parts of speech: nouns.

Part 1 What Are Nouns?

You use words to name the people, places, and things around you. Words that name are called **nouns**.

A noun is a word used to name a person, place, or thing.

Nouns name things that you can see, like cities, streets, furniture, and books. They also name things you cannot see, such as feelings, ideas, and beliefs.

Persons: plumber, Sally, Christopher Reeves, singer
Places: Alabama, hospital, Denver, restaurant
Things: towel, brush, spirit, kindness

Exercise   Make three columns on a sheet of paper. Label them *Names of Persons, Names of Places,* and *Names of Things.* Find the nouns in the following paragraph. List each one in the proper column.

> The *Double Eagle V*, a large balloon filled with helium, made a historic flight across the Pacific Ocean. The balloon lifted off in Japan and touched down in California. The trip was almost 6,000 miles. Four men flew in the gondola. One problem during the trip was ice forming on the balloon. Another problem was a storm off the coast of California. Ben Abruzzo, the captain, feels that teamwork carried the *Double Eagle V* to victory.

Proper Nouns and Common Nouns

How do these two italicized nouns differ?

Mary Cassatt, an American *artist*, lived in France.

The word *artist* is a general term. It refers to many people. It is a **common noun**. A common noun is a general name.

The noun *Mary Cassatt*, on the other hand, refers to only one person. It is a **proper noun**. A proper noun is a specific name.

A common noun is the name of a whole class of persons, places, or things. It is a name that is common to the class.

A proper noun is the name of a particular person, place, or thing. Proper nouns are capitalized.

Look at the following examples of common nouns and proper nouns. As you can see, some nouns are made up of more than one word.

Common Nouns	Proper Nouns
movie	*Casablanca*
river	Danube River
columnist	Ann Landers
week	Fire Prevention Week
country	France
state	Ohio
governor	Governor Henderson

Exercise A Make two columns on your paper. Label one column *Common Nouns* and the other *Proper Nouns*. Place each of the following nouns in the correct column. Capitalize all proper nouns.

1. snack bar, mc donald's, restaurant, taco bell
2. al's body shop, gas station, standard oil, garage
3. josé feliciano, guitar, chuck mangione, trumpet, brass
4. nashville, capital, city, frankfort, town
5. park, zoo, san diego zoo, animals, milwaukee zoo
6. mexico, country, border, texas, river
7. chevrolet, ford, chrysler, automobile, car
8. st. francis hospital, clinic, hospital, maryhaven nursing home, nurse
9. store, sears, catalog, j. c. penney, clerk
10. new york mets, baseball, team, manager, sport

Exercise B: Writing Write five sentences of your own, using at least one proper noun in each sentence.

Part 2 How Are Nouns Used?

Nouns Used as Subjects

As you learned in Section 1, the **subject** of a sentence tells who or what is being talked about. Nouns are frequently used as subjects.

> *Fish* stole the bait from my hook. (The noun *fish* is the subject of the verb *stole*.)
>
> My *uncle* from Ohio writes me often. (The noun *uncle* is the subject of the verb *writes*. Notice that in this sentence, the subject is not next to the verb.)

Two or more nouns may form a compound subject.

> *Dennis* and *Joshua* competed for the title. (The nouns *Dennis* and *Joshua* are the subject of the verb *competed*.)
>
> *Diamonds* and *emeralds* adorned the crown. (The nouns *diamonds* and *emeralds* are the subject of the verb *adorned*.)

Exercise A   Number your paper from 1 to 10. Write the nouns used as the subjects of these sentences.

1. Raccoons raided the trash cans.
2. The singer crooned lovely ballads.
3. The girls won the soccer game.
4. That rumor is spreading all over town.
5. Lawyers and accountants provide services.
6. Some secretaries take shorthand.
7. Marge and Kent planned the party.
8. Prices have gone up each year.
9. Mel has been writing a story for the creative writing contest.
10. Many neighborhoods are having block parties to celebrate the holiday.

1. The smell of popcorn filled the theater.
2. Mark painted the neighbor's garage.
3. Many students eat at the snack bar.
4. Travelers shopped for souvenirs at the market.
5. The nurse checked the patient's blood pressure.
6. A flock of geese flew overhead.
7. The magician mystified the audience.
8. Anwar Sadat was an Egyptian leader.
9. Kevin and Fred are good salesmen.
10. Paris is the capital of France.

Nouns Used as Direct Objects

A **direct object** completes the action of a verb. It answers *whom* or *what* about the verb. Nouns are frequently used as direct objects.

> The clown entertained the *children.* (The noun *children* tells *whom* about the verb *entertained.*)
>
> Dean took *slides* during his vacation. (The noun *slides* tells *what* about the verb *took.*)
>
> Beth made a *belt* and a *wallet* from the leather. (Both the nouns *belt* and *wallet* are the compound direct object. They tell *what* about the verb *made.*)

Exercise A As your teacher directs, write the nouns used as direct objects in the following sentences.

1. A player dunked the basketball through the hoop.
2. Colleen has a good attitude.
3. Tennis built Ken's endurance.
4. Children like opera, too.
5. Heather reads her horoscope every day.
6. Those shoes have long laces.
7. John heaped spaghetti onto his plate.

8. Judy cut her own hair.
9. Artists brought their crafts to the fair.
10. Brett plays chess and backgammon.

Exercise B   Follow the directions for Exercise A.

1. Josh rode a bicycle through the park.
2. The lawyer interviewed her client.
3. The doctor hired a receptionist.
4. Most companies have insurance.
5. Lifeguards usually wear whistles.
6. That restaurant serves lunch and dinner.
7. Lee ordered a jacket from the catalog.
8. Mosquitoes bit my wrists and ankles.
9. Max tutored his younger brother.
10. A stream borders the property.

Nouns Used as Indirect Objects

Another use of the noun is as an **indirect object**. The indirect object tells *to whom* or *for whom* or *to what* or *for what* about the verb.

> The guide showed the *tourists* the monument. (The noun *tourists* is the indirect object. It tells *to whom* about the verb *showed*.)
>
> Angela gave the *beagle* and the *terrier* a bath. (The nouns *beagle* and *terrier* are the compound indirect object, telling *to what* about the verb *gave*.)

An indirect object is used only with a direct object. The indirect object appears before the direct object in the sentence.

Subject	Verb	Indirect Object(s)	Direct Object
Jan	gave	the driver	directions.
Mom	fixed	the guests	a snack.
Allen	showed	Curt and Bill	the play.

The words *to* or *for* are never used with an indirect object.

Exercise A Find the nouns used as indirect objects in the following sentences.

1. Tanya gave the waiter our order.
2. Larry paid Mr. Crane the rent.
3. The electrician sent the company a bill.
4. Mr. Jackson gave Toni some advice.
5. J.C. Penney sent the Dawsons a catalog.
6. Dad handed Chuck a dish towel.
7. Rose showed Alex the photo album.
8. Leo gave the walls and the ceiling a fresh coat of paint.
9. Kelly saved Susan a seat.
10. Mickey told Jerry a secret.

Exercise B Follow the directions for Exercise A.

1. The lawyer asked the witness a question.
2. John passed Tracy the hamburgers.
3. Dr. Phillips gave Carol some vitamins.
4. Jackie mixed her friends some lemonade.
5. Kate loaned Kim her navy sweatshirt.
6. Don owes Luke a favor.
7. Loud music gives Casey a headache.
8. Ann made Judy a promise.
9. Bill handed the checker a coupon.
10. The actor gave the magazine an exclusive interview.

Nouns Used as Predicate Words

Sometimes a noun in the complete predicate of a sentence is linked to the subject. That noun is called a **predicate noun**. It always follows a linking verb. The predicate noun usually means the same thing as the subject.

Marilyn is a dental *hygienist.*

The workers were all *volunteers.*

The flowers in the vase are *roses* and *carnations.*

The nouns *hygienist, volunteers, roses,* and *carnations* are predicate nouns.

Exercise A   Find the nouns used as predicate nouns in the following sentences.

1. Al is an excellent golfer.
2. Russia was an ally during World War II.
3. Friday is the day of the history test.
4. The symptoms of the illness are fever and a rash.
5. Mabel's choice for dinner is shrimp.
6. Albany is the capital of New York.
7. Mr. Allen became the assistant principal.
8. Denise's brother is a pilot in the Air Force.
9. The winners of the contest are Mike, Sally, and Kim.
10. The opponents were Jimmy Connors and John McEnroe.

Exercise B   Follow the directions for Exercise A.

1. Some teachers become school administrators.
2. David Letterman is the host of the program.
3. Brooklyn is a borough of New York City.
4. Homework can be a problem for students with part-time jobs.
5. The luncheon specials were chicken and ham.
6. Oak Street Beach is a popular spot for sunbathers.
7. That house is the home of the mayor.
8. Jack Benny was a famous comedian.
9. The President was a former governor.
10. The ducks in the pond are mallards.

Part 3 The Plurals of Nouns

When a noun names one thing, it is singular. When a noun names more than one thing, it is plural.

Here are some rules for forming the plurals of nouns.

1. To form the plural of most nouns, just add -s:

juices   actors   squares   nations

2. When a singular noun ends in s, sh, ch, x, or z, add -es:

dresses   ashes   churches   foxes   buzzes

3. When a singular noun ends in o, add -s:

trios   halos   radios   photos   stereos

For a few words ending in *o*, add *-es*:

heroes   tomatoes   potatoes   echoes   cargoes

4. When a singular noun ends in y with a consonant before it, change the y to i and add -es:

story—stories   lady—ladies   hobby—hobbies

When a vowel (*a, e, i, o, u*) comes before the *y*, do not change the *y* to *i*. Just add *-s*:

toy—toys   bay—bays   monkey—monkeys

5. For some nouns ending in f, add -s to make the plural:

roofs   chiefs   reefs   beliefs

For many nouns ending in *f* or *fe*, change the *f* to *v* and add *-s* or *-es*. Since there is no rule to follow, you will have to memorize such words. Here are some examples:

leaf—leaves   loaf—loaves   calf—calves
shelf—shelves   thief—thieves   knife—knives

6. Some nouns have the same form for both singular and plural. They must be memorized.

deer   sheep   moose   salmon   trout

7. Some nouns form their plurals in special ways. They, too, must be memorized.

man—men	tooth—teeth	ox—oxen
woman—women	mouse—mice	foot—feet
goose—geese	child—children	louse—lice

Dictionaries show the plural of a word if it is formed in an unusual way. Here is a dictionary entry for the noun *knife*. The entry shows the plural, *knives*.

> **knife** (nīf) *n., pl.* **knives** [OE. *cnif:* for IE. base see KNEAD]
> **1.** a cutting or stabbing instrument with a sharp blade, single-edged or double-edged, set in a handle **2.** a cutting blade, as in a machine —*vt.* **knifed, knif′ing 1.** to cut or stab with a knife ☆**2.** [Colloq.] to use underhanded methods in order to hurt, defeat, or betray —☆*vi.* to pass into or through something quickly, like a sharp knife —☆**under the knife** [Colloq.] undergoing surgery —**knife′like′** *adj.*

Use the dictionary if you have a question about plurals.

Exercise A Write the plural of each of these nouns. Then use your dictionary to see if you are correct.

1. life	6. baby	11. hero	16. fly
2. fear	7. leaf	12. goose	17. potato
3. salmon	8. moose	13. ditch	18. door
4. jockey	9. studio	14. hoof	19. dish
5. waitress	10. ax	15. tooth	20. reply

Exercise B Write each sentence. Correct the errors in plural forms of nouns.

1. The womans will meet in these roomes.
2. The churchs planned the Easter services together.
3. The deeres ran across the fieldes.
4. Cut the loafes of bread with these knifes.
5. The babys are both twenty-one inchs long.

6. Each of the studioes has at least two pianoes.
7. The mans discussed their believes.
8. Two kinds of fishes are salmons and tunas.
9. Many countrys sponsor Olympic teames.
10. The climbers heard echos.

Part 4   The Possessives of Nouns

Nouns can indicate possession or ownership.

Dad's camera   a tourist's suitcase   Larry's paper

Nouns can show that something is part of a person.

Jan's personality   Dr. Feldman's smile

The *'s* makes the above nouns show ownership. Words like *Dad's, tourist's,* and *Larry's* are called **possessive nouns.**

Usually, people and animals possess things. Sometimes, however, things are also in the possessive. Some examples are *a week's wages, a day's work,* or *a city's growth.*

Forming Possessives

There are three rules for forming the possessive of nouns.

1. If the noun is singular, add an apostrophe (') and s.

Ralph—Ralph's dog
Emma—Emma's sweater

2. If the noun is plural and ends in s, add just the apostrophe.

bankers—bankers' hours
Russells—Russells' cottage

3. If the noun is plural but does not end in s, add an apostrophe and s.

gentlemen—gentlemen's agreement
people—people's vote

Exercise A Write the possessive form of each of these nouns.

1. senator	6. branch	11. bike	16. general
2. Peg	7. girl	12. James	17. Donny
3. city	8. runner	13. jogger	18. librarian
4. realtor	9. Mary	14. guide	19. secretary
5. yesterday	10. guest	15. boss	20. Carla

Exercise B Follow the directions for Exercise A.

1. pans	6. hosts	11. knives	16. armies
2. people	7. students	12. geese	17. children
3. sisters	8. men	13. players	18. states
4. birds	9. dentists	14. deer	19. deserts
5. engineers	10. lawyers	15. Johnsons	20. ladies

Exercise C Write the possessive form for each italicized word.

1. *Wednesday* meeting is important.
2. *Terry* bike needs a new chain.
3. The *Cardinals* pitcher was injured.
4. The *winners* comments were in the paper.
5. The *golfers* scores were high because of the wind.
6. *Lois* appointment was at five o'clock.
7. That was the space *shuttle* third trip.
8. Dale broke the *men* track record.
9. Coffee spilled on the *nurse* uniform.
10. *Amanda* relatives live in England.

ADDITIONAL EXERCISES

Using Nouns

A. Common and Proper Nouns Label two columns *Common Nouns* and *Proper Nouns*. Decide whether the following nouns are common or proper. Place each in the correct column. Capitalize the proper nouns.

1. basketball, net, celtics, julius erving, referee
2. africa, land, continent, island, philippines
3. students, priscilla, employees, andrew, people
4. newspaper, magazine, *detroit free press, newsweek*
5. pioneer, chisholm trail, wagons, trapper, rocky mountains
6. arctic ocean, red sea, ocean, sea, cape cod
7. movie, play, *annie*, characters, script
8. tammy wynette, music, diana ross, kenny rogers, radio
9. automobile, convertible, jeep, chevy citation, chrysler
10. store, clothes, thompson's hardware store, customer, carson, pirie, scott and co.

B. How Nouns Are Used Decide how each italicized noun is used in the following sentences. Write the word and label it *Subject, Direct Object, Indirect Object,* or *Predicate Noun.*

1. Jody received a *telegram* on her birthday.
2. Bill showed his *friends* the winning lottery *ticket*.
3. *Kara* took movies at the ceremony.
4. The accident was a head-on *collision*.
5. The *Yankees* made four *runs* in the fifth inning.
6. The *hurricane* tore through Cuba and Haiti.
7. After a tour of the lake, the *boat* docked in Milwaukee.
8. Mr. Rodriguez identified the *thief* from a photograph.
9. On Monday, *Lee* polished the *chrome* on her bike.
10. The *police* gave the *firefighters* some *help*.

C. Plurals of Nouns Write the plural of each of these nouns.

1. match	6. story	11. thief	16. woman
2. life	7. trout	12. studio	17. belief
3. class	8. cargo	13. pony	18. potato
4. time	9. victory	14. half	19. key
5. rodeo	10. ax	15. joy	20. dash

D. Possessives of Nouns Write the possessive form in the singular or plural as indicated.

Example: the officer (singular) message
the officer's message

1. Roberta (singular) tour of duty
2. the scientist (plural) reports
3. the pitcher (plural) styles
4. a captain (singular) job
5. Nicholas (singular) answer
6. some driver (plural) licenses
7. the critic (singular) favorable review
8. an actress (singular) career
9. two grandchild (plural) pictures
10. several company (plural) personnel offices
11. March (singular) cold weather
12. the waitress (plural) uniforms
13. the runner (singular) speed
14. the woman (plural) shoe department
15. the Jarvis (plural) house
16. Wes (singular) idea
17. the sky (singular) odd color
18. the fish (singular) gills
19. the brush (plural) handles
20. the deer (plural) habitat

MIXED REVIEW

Using Nouns

A. Identifying nouns and their uses   Copy the nouns from these sentences. After each, write *Subject, Direct Object, Indirect Object,* or *Predicate Noun* to show how it is used.

1. That insect is a cricket.
2. A neighbor takes my grandfather a hot lunch.
3. The motorcycle needs new cylinders.
4. Mary Shelley created Frankenstein.
5. Nolan showed Marvin the blueprints.
6. Rosita was watching the Super Bowl.
7. Your friend is certainly a character.
8. Russell dialed the number again.
9. Her older brother joined the Marines.
10. A dingo is a wild dog.

B. Using plural and possessive forms correctly   Rewrite these sentences, correcting the errors in the plural and possessive forms of nouns. If a sentence is correct, write *Correct.*

1. A thoroughbred horses lungs and nostrils are unusually large.
2. White mouses are often used in laboratories.
3. Bess bookshelves were the best in the carpentry class.
4. The two dogs owners untangled the leashes.
5. Mr. Curtis's car had two flat tires.
6. Patchs of sunlight fell on the living room floor.
7. Ann's four friend have the same hobbies.
8. These photos show the baby's new teeth.
9. The men's watches had alarms.
10. The knives go to the right of the dishes.

USING GRAMMAR IN WRITING
Using Nouns

A. A close friend of yours is going to move to a distant city. The friend has invited you and some other close friends to a goodbye party. The friend has asked you and the other guests to promise to meet again in ten years. At the party, each of you will give to your friend a sealed envelope containing written predictions about what you and the others will be doing ten years from today. Choose several friends and write predictions for them. Where will each be living? What work will each be doing? Will there be a family? Write your predictions in paragraph form. Underline every noun. Underline proper nouns twice.

B. You work as a courier for a famous art museum. Your job is to see that an important and valuable painting reaches London safely. Rumors have been circulating that a gang of international art thieves will try to steal the painting somewhere between the airport and the National Gallery in London. Cautiously, you study the people waiting to board the plane with you.

Choose four of the people to describe. Describe each in a short paragraph. First describe what the person looks like. Then tell what the person is wearing. Finally, describe the person's attitude and actions. When you have finished your descriptions, underline the nouns. Label each one *S* (subject), *DO* (direct object), *IO* (indirect object), or *PN* (predicate noun).

C. Your family will be away from home for two weeks. You have made arrangements for a neighbor to take care of the pets, collect mail, and water the plants. Write a paragraph of instructions for the neighbor. When you refer to the things that the neighbor is to do, use at least three plural nouns (such as *guppies* and *ferns*) and three possessive nouns (such as *cats'* food, *Jean's* letters, and *Rowdy's* leash).

446

Using Pronouns

Nouns name people, places, and things. However, using too many nouns can make a sentence sound awkward and repetitious. Read this example:

Beth wrote Beth's report and then typed the report.

Sentences like this can be improved by using another part of speech, the **pronoun.** A pronoun is a word that takes the place of a noun.

Beth wrote *her* report and then typed *it.*

Her takes the place of the noun *Beth,* and *it* takes the place of the noun *report.*

In this section you will learn to identify and use pronouns correctly.

Part 1   Personal Pronouns

A pronoun is a word used in place of a noun. Pronouns are very helpful words. They may be used in three situations:

1. They may refer to the person speaking.

   I jog.   *We* bought the tickets.

2. They may refer to the person spoken to.

   You plant *your* own garden, don't *you?*

3. They may refer to other people, places, or things.

   He gave *her* a hand.   *They* ate *their* lunch outside.

The examples above show that a pronoun often refers to a person. For that reason, these pronouns are called **personal pronouns.**

There are many forms of personal pronouns. Like nouns, personal pronouns may be singular or plural. In the following chart, see how personal pronouns change from singular to plural.

Singular:	I	me	my, mine
	you	you	your, yours
	he, she, it	him, her, it	his, her, hers, its
Plural:	we	us	our, ours
	you	you	your, yours
	they	them	their, theirs

As the chart shows, most plural pronouns are totally different from their singular forms. Notice these examples:

Singular	Plural
I forgot.	*We* forgot.
Help *him!*	Help *them!*
It broke.	*They* broke.

Exercise A Number your paper from 1 to 10. Write the pronouns used in place of nouns in these sentences. After each pronoun, write the noun or nouns it stands for.

1. Sue looks at magazines while she watches TV.
2. Amy and Jo cleaned their typewriters.
3. The drummers played as they marched.
4. Fred recorded his speech for practice.
5. "We have a surprise for you," announced the twins.
6. The elephant grabbed the tent pole and lifted it.
7. The students displayed their art projects.
8. When the workers arrived, they repaired the roof.
9. Dean, did you feed the dog?
10. The egg broke when it rolled off the counter.

Exercise B Follow the directions for Exercise A.

1. Sam and Hy sold their deli.
2. The scientist wrote her autobiography.
3. Julie planted the tree and watered it.
4. Flo waited for the bus at her corner.
5. Lenny checked the air in his bicycle tires.
6. Some tourists lost their traveler's checks.
7. Brendon and Mike brought flashlights with them.
8. The cashier gave Pat his receipt.
9. "Do you like sunflower seeds?" Doris asked Rob.
10. Jeff bought roses and gave them to his mom.

Part 2 The Forms of Pronouns

Pronouns can be used in all the ways that nouns are used. Personal pronouns can be subjects, objects, predicate words, and possessives.

However, a personal pronoun changes form as its use in a sentence changes. Look at these sentences:

449

She missed. (*She* is the subject.)
Kathy fouled *her*. (*Her* is the direct object.)
Her free throw was good. (*Her* shows possession.)

The three pronouns in these examples all refer to the same person. The forms, though, are different.

The three forms of a personal pronoun are **subject form, object form,** and **possessive form.** Here are the forms for all the personal pronouns:

	Subject	Object	Possessive
Singular:	I	me	my, mine
	you	you	your, yours
	he, she, it	him, her, it	his, her, hers, its
Plural:	we	us	our, ours
	you	you	your, yours
	they	them	their, theirs

Exercise The following sentences use different forms of pronouns correctly. Read each sentence aloud.

1. *We* accepted the package.
2. Did *you* receive *your* paycheck?
3. The guard dog frightened *us*.
4. Mr. Daley and *she* gave *their* permission.
5. This is *he*.
6. The smoke detector warned *me* of the fire.
7. That locker is *his*.
8. *They* visited the Orient.
9. *I* went hiking with Max and *him*.
10. *Our* dog chases *their* cat.
11. The robin flew to *its* nest.
12. Marty buys old cars and rebuilds *them*.
13. This album is *yours*.
14. The doctor gave *him* some medication.
15. The error was *mine*.

The Subject Form of Pronouns

Subject Pronouns

I	we
you	you
he, she, it	they

For the subject of a sentence, the subject form of the personal pronoun is used. The following sentences use the subject form for the subject:

They plotted and planned.   *He* created a monster.
She did the experiment.   *I* called the police.

Using pronouns as subjects usually causes few problems. A more troublesome use, though, is the predicate pronoun. A **predicate pronoun** is a pronoun that is linked with the subject. It follows a linking verb, just as a predicate noun does.

Look at these examples of predicate pronouns:

The winner was *she*. (*She* is a predicate pronoun used after the linking verb *was*.)

That must be *he*. (*He* is a predicate pronoun used after the linking verb *must be*.)

As you see, the subject forms of pronouns are used for predicate pronouns. This may not sound natural at first. If you are in doubt about which form to use, reverse the subject and the predicate pronoun. The sentence should still sound correct.

The coach was *he*.
He was the coach.

Here are more examples of the correct use of the subject form for predicate pronouns:

That was *she* in the car.
Was it *he* on the phone?
The announcer was *she*.

Always use the subject form for subjects and predicate pronouns.

The Object Form of Pronouns

Object Pronouns

me	us
you	you
him, her, it	them

When personal pronouns are used as objects, the object form of the pronoun is used. There are three kinds of objects: direct objects, indirect objects, and objects of prepositions.

In these sentences the object form of the pronoun is used for direct objects.

> Darrell avoided *them.* The puzzle fascinated *me.*
> Carol led *us.* The paramedics revived *her.*

These sentences use the object form for indirect objects:

> Ms. Abbott gave *me* a job. Tracy promised *them* a reward.
> Ned fixed *us* some popcorn. Cole lent *him* a jacket.

The third kind of object is the object of a preposition. Prepositions are short connecting words like *to, for,* and *with.* The pronouns that follow such words are the objects. For more explanation of prepositions, see Handbook Section 7.

These sentences use the object form for objects of prepositions:

> They rehearsed with *us.*
> Vicki made a promise to *her.*
> Craig brought the information to *me.*
> The cashier wrapped the gift for *them.*

The Possessive Form of Pronouns

Possessive Pronouns

my, mine	our, ours
your, yours	your, yours
his, her, hers, its	their, theirs

Possessive pronouns show possession or ownership. Many times, possessive pronouns are used by themselves. Then, like a noun, a possessive pronoun has one of these uses: subject, object, or predicate word. Read these examples:

That bicycle is *his*. (predicate pronoun)
Hers is in the garage. (subject)
Paul and Ron are riding *theirs*. (direct object)
Sean gave *his* a push. (indirect object)
This bike looks like *mine*. (object of preposition)

At other times, possessive pronouns are not used alone. Instead, they are used to tell about nouns. Look at these sentences:

Sally brushed *her* Siamese cat.
Each university has *its* strengths.
The students scheduled *their* field trip.
It is *your* turn now.

Exercise A Choose the correct pronoun from the two given in parentheses. Write it. Read the sentence to yourself.

1. (They, Them) competed in the Olympics.
2. The results astonished (we, us).
3. That taxi splashed mud on (I, me).
4. Was that (she, her)?
5. The usher handed (he, him) the ticket stubs.
6. Most of (we, us) like cheese pizza.
7. The painting is (my mine).
8. Jack received (him, his) invitation today.
9. Nora sent (he, him) a singing telegram.
10. The audience applauded (we, us).

Exercise B Follow the directions for Exercise A.

1. Is that radio (your, yours)?
2. The mosquitoes bothered (we, us).
3. The sitter is (she, her).

4. Usually (I, me) run a mile each day.

5. Soon (we, us) will choose a new uniform.

6. It was (he, him) in the photograph.

7. A heavy fog enveloped (they, them).

8. Dan handed a letter to (I, me).

9. Ken checked (him, his) watch.

10. The music was composed by (she, her).

Exercise C The personal pronouns in the following sentences are in italics. Write each pronoun and label it *Subject Form*, *Object Form*, or *Possessive Form*.

1. *She* arranged the flowers in a vase.

2. Kurt wrestled with *him*.

3. Is it *they?*

4. That comment annoyed *us*.

5. For once *I* finished on time.

6. Jane gave *him* a campaign button.

7. The most original idea was *hers*.

8. Tim was nervous during *his* interview.

9. *We* devoured the tacos.

10. Ms. Valenti showed *me* the blueprints.

Part 3 Pronouns in Compound Constructions

Compound sentence parts, or **compound constructions,** in a sentence have more than one part. The parts are joined by *and, or,* or *nor,* as in *Ned and me.* A pronoun may be one or both of these parts.

You may wonder which pronoun form to use in a compound construction. Here are sentences with pronouns used correctly as compound parts:

Jesse and *I* studied for the exam. (*Jesse* and *I* are both subjects. The subject form *I* is used.)

Mr. Justice gave *him* and *me* the programs. (*Him* and *me* are both indirect objects. The object forms are used.)

This secret is between *you* and *me*. (*You* and *me* are both objects of the preposition *between*. The object forms are used.)

You can avoid problems with compound parts if you think of each part separately. For instance, in the first example above, omit the words *Jesse and*. Should the sentence read *I studied for the exam* or *Me studied for the exam?* The pronoun *I* is correct.

Here is another example:

Scott offered Heather and (I, me) a suggestion.
Scott offered *me* a suggestion.

Exercise A   Choose the right pronoun from the two given.

1. Vera and (he, him) are working this evening.
2. Mr. Olivera gave (we, us) the test results.
3. Cancel the orders for Judd and (I, me).
4. The performance was given by Erin and (they, them).
5. The argument was between Chris and (I, me).
6. Kate's partners were Ralph and (her, she).
7. The manager fired Susan and (he, him).
8. Todd and (he, him) share a locker.
9. Just between you and (I, me), I'm worried.
10. The refreshments were provided by (she, her) and (I, me).

Exercise B   Follow the directions for Exercise A.

1. Save seats for Jenny and (he, him).
2. The directors are Louis and (she, her).
3. Meg and (I, me) prefer math to science.

4. Heidi reminded Gayle and (she, her).
5. Mark and (he, him) played cards.
6. The dog barked at Terry and (I, me).
7. The nurse gave Lon and (I, me) ice packs.
8. Marsha waved at Gary and (he, him).
9. Carl waited for (they, them) and (we, us).
10. The McMahons and (we, us) planted a vegetable garden.

Part 4 Pronouns and Antecedents

A pronoun is a word used in place of a noun. The noun that the pronoun replaces is called the **antecedent.** A pronoun refers to its antecedent.

> Joan reviewed *her* notes.
> (*Her* takes the place of the noun *Joan. Joan* is the antecedent.)
> The silver lost *its* shine.
> (*Its* refers to the noun *silver. Silver* is the antecedent.)

The antecedent usually appears before the pronoun. The antecedent may appear in the same sentence or in the preceding sentence, as in this example:

> The space shuttle landed this morning. *It* had made another successful trip.
> (*It* stands for the antecedent *shuttle.*)

Pronouns may be the antecedents of other pronouns:

> You forgot *your* newspaper.
> (*You* is the antecedent of *your*).

A pronoun must be like its antecedent in one important way. A pronoun must have the same number as its antecedent. If the antecedent is singular, the pronoun must be singular. If the antecedent is plural, then the pronoun must be plural.

A pronoun must agree with its antecedent in number.

The swimmers grabbed *their* towels.
(*Swimmers* is plural; *their* is plural.)

The actress read *her* script.
(*Actress* is singular; *her* is singular.)

The children have *their* own playroom.
(*Children* is plural; *their* is plural.)

Exercise A   Write each personal pronoun that is italicized. Then write its antecedent.

1. Ms. Landen waxed *her* car.
2. Tom finished the puzzle and glued *it* together.
3. Ann and I discussed *our* plans.
4. The conductor gave the violinists *their* music.
5. Lois dropped the coins into *her* pocket.
6. DePaul lost *its* chance to win the championship.
7. The boys put *their* sleeping bags into the trunk.
8. Sally set the record in the broad jump and then broke *it*.
9. Marty forgot *his* lines.
10. Water the plants when *they* get dry.

Exercise B   Follow the directions for Exercise A.

1. The hawk flew from *its* perch.
2. Some people invest *their* money in gold.
3. The spy decoded *her* instructions.
4. I have outlined *my* project.
5. The carpenter measured the wood and cut *it*.
6. Those trees have Spanish moss on *them*.
7. Janet practiced *her* serve.
8. Rhonda and I placed the game between *us*.
9. Can you remember *your* way home?
10. Did Eric check the stores near *him*?

Part 5 Compound Personal Pronouns

A **compound personal pronoun** is a pronoun with *-self* or *-selves* added.

myself	ourselves
yourself	yourselves
himself, herself, itself	themselves

Notice how compound personal pronouns are used for emphasis:

> The President *himself* presented the award.
> Tina *herself* wallpapered the room.
> I mowed the lawn *myself*.
> They moved the piano *themselves*.

Exercise A   Number your paper from 1 to 10. Beside each number write the correct compound personal pronoun for each of the following sentences. After it, write its antecedent.

> Example: Our dog Bob thinks of (pronoun) as a person.
>   himself, dog

1. Donna and I cleaned the fish by (pronoun).
2. The students (pronoun) supervise the study hall at our school.
3. Kathy (pronoun) prepared the report.
4. The mayor (pronoun) led the parade.
5. I wrote this story by (pronoun).
6. The children (pronoun) planned the trip.
7. We yelled (pronoun) hoarse at the game.
8. The workers (pronoun) were not allowed to vote on the new hours.
9. We made (pronoun) a snack.
10. Help (pronoun) to some lunch, Gordon.

Exercise B   Follow the directions for Exercise A.

1. Carole King (pronoun) appeared at the rally.
2. Ed and Adam helped (pronoun) to the strawberries.
3. The dentist (pronoun) cleaned my teeth.
4. Bridget studied (pronoun) in the mirror.
5. Give (pronoun) credit, Luke.
6. Mario programed the computer by (pronoun).
7. Fran (pronoun) flew the plane.
8. The brush fire burned (pronoun) out.
9. The problem (pronoun) remains unsolved.
10. Pam and I warmed (pronoun) by the fire.

Part 6   Demonstrative Pronouns

The pronouns *this, that, these,* and *those* point out people or things. They are called **demonstrative pronouns**.

This and *these* point to people or things that are near in space or time. *That* and *those* point to people or things that are farther away in space or time.

> *This* makes a good shelter.   *These* are fake furs.
> *That* was a compliment.   *Those* were funny cartoons.

Exercise   Number your paper from 1 to 10. Write the correct demonstrative pronoun for the blank space in each sentence.

1. _____ are better than those.
2. _____ was a close golf match yesterday.
3. _____ are your snapshots, not these.
4. _____ are valuable gems in that necklace.
5. _____ is my sister beside me.
6. _____ must be our moving van over there.
7. _____ is my dog chasing the ducks.
8. _____ is a wonderful view here.
9. _____ is the ocean out there.
10. _____ are the old dishes in that box.

Part 7 Interrogative Pronouns

Certain pronouns are used to ask questions. They are called **interrogative pronouns**. The interrogative pronouns are *who, whom, whose, which,* and *what.*

> *Who* parked a car in the alley?   *Which* is the best buy?
> *Whom* did Bonny ask?   *What* cured your cold?
> *Whose* is this suitcase?

Exercise   Number your paper from 1 to 10. Write all the pronouns in these sentences. After each pronoun, write *Demonstrative* or *Interrogative* to show what kind it is.

> Example: Who brought the apple pie?
> *Who*—Interrogative

1. That is confusing.
2. Who has seen Jason?
3. Which is the more expensive?
4. These are unusual doorknobs.
5. Is that Betty's signature?
6. Whom does Mr. Price tutor?
7. These are the overdue books.
8. Are those the party decorations?
9. Whose are those?
10. What makes this chili so spicy?

Part 8 Indefinite Pronouns

Some pronouns do not refer to a definite person or thing. Such pronouns are called **indefinite pronouns**.

The following are indefinite pronouns. They are singular. Because they are singular, these pronouns are used with the singular possessive pronouns *his, her,* and *its.*

another	each	everything	one
anybody	either	neither	somebody
anyone	everybody	nobody	someone
anything	everyone	no one	

Each of the apartments has *its* own fireplace.
Nobody ate *his* dinner.
Nobody ate *his* or *her* dinner.

The last example uses the phrase *his or her* instead of simply *his*. That phrase shows that the indefinite pronoun may refer to a male or female. Many people prefer such a phrase.

Although most indefinite pronouns are singular, some are plural. They refer to more than one person or thing. The following indefinite pronouns are plural. They are used with the plural possessive *their*. Study these examples.

both   many   few   several

Several of the dancers practiced *their* routines.
Few of the tenants knew *their* neighbors.
Many of my friends sew *their* own clothes.
Both of the dogs broke *their* leashes.

A few indefinite pronouns can be either singular or plural, depending on their meaning in a sentence. Read these examples:

all   none   some

All of the drinking water has flouride in *it*.
All of the ribs have barbeque sauce on *them*.
None of the music had life in *it*.
None of the politicians wrote *their* own speeches.
Some of the ice cream has strawberries in *it*.
Some of the dancers changed *their* costumes.

Exercise A Number your paper from 1 to 10 For each sentence write the indefinite pronoun.

1. No one brought a can opener.
2. Where is everyone going?

3. None of us missed the bus.
4. Did anyone write down the address?
5. Karen found all the Easter eggs.
6. Many of the tourists photographed the view.
7. Tim walked both of the dogs.
8. Why is everybody upset?
9. Several of the bulbs were broken.
10. Only one of the trees died.

Exercise B   Choose the correct pronoun from the two given.

1. Some of the musicians forgot (his or her, their) music.
2. Neither of the men brought (his, their) briefcase.
3. If anyone arrives early, have (him, them) wait for me.
4. Everybody introduced (his or her, their) guests.
5. Somebody left (his or her, their) picnic basket.
6. All of the rookies have completed (his or her, their) training program.
7. One of the eagles spread (its, their) wings.
8. Did somebody forget (his or her, their) newspaper?
9. All of the drivers adjusted (his or her, their) face masks.
10. Each of these Indian tribes has (its, their) own special customs.

Exercise C   Number your paper from 1 to 10. For each of the following sentences write the indefinite pronoun and the correct verb from the two in parentheses.

1. Everyone (take, takes) chances.
2. Nobody (confuse, confuses) me with my sister.
3. All of these melons (is, are) ripe.
4. Neither of the towns (has, have) a daily newspaper.
5. One of my cats (has, have) an infection.
6. Many of the magazines (is, are) printed here.
7. Some of the shows (is, are) reruns.

8. Many of the athletes (is, are) becoming celebrities.
9. Each of the mechanics (use, uses) his or her own tools.
10. Some of the butter (is, are) salt-free.

Part 9 Special Problems with Pronouns

Contractions and Possessive Pronouns

Certain contractions are sometimes confused with possessive pronouns.

Contractions are formed by joining two words and omitting one or more letters. An apostrophe shows where letters are left out.

it's = it + is   they're = they + are
you're = you + are   who's = who + is

The above contractions are sometimes confused with the possessive pronouns *its, your, their,* and *whose.* The words sound alike but are spelled differently.

Incorrect: Who's turn is it?
Correct: Whose turn is it?

If you can't decide which word is correct, substitute the words the contraction stands for. If the sentence sounds right, then the contraction is correct.

Exercise A Choose the right word from the two in parentheses.

1. (Whose, Who's) pen is this?
2. (Your, You're) new here, aren't you?
3. The divers left (their, they're) gear in the boat.
4. (Their, They're) lost in the crowd of people.
5. (Its, It's) time for the kickoff.
6. (Whose, Who's) the anchor for the news on channel 5?

7. (Your, You're) name was in the paper.
8. That cat has lost (its, it's) collar.
9. Is that (your, you're) wallet?
10. (Whose, Who's) the gentleman on the stage?

Exercise B Write the words each contraction below stands for.

1. Who's going to the concert in the park?
2. They've volunteered for the clean-up committee.
3. She's shoveling the snow on the sidewalk.
4. You're the first guest to arrive.
5. We'll organize the meeting.
6. I'd like a glass of water.
7. They're waiting for us at the theater.
8. What's on the menu?
9. I'm allergic to milk.
10. We'd better leave early.

Who and *Whom*

Many people have problems with the pronouns *who* and *whom*.

Who sounds natural in most questions. Use *who* as the subject of a sentence.

> *Who* wound the clock?   *Who* is that?

Whom is harder to get used to. *Whom* is used as an object.

> *Whom* did you invite?
>> (direct object of the verb *did invite*)
> To *whom* are the applications given?
>> (object of the preposition *to*)

Exercise A Choose the right pronoun from the two in parentheses.

1. (Who, Whom) can reach that shelf?
2. (Who, Whom) won the game?

3. (Who, Whom) did you videotape?
4. (Who, Whom) were you helping?
5. (Who, Whom) is the newspaper reporter?
6. (Who, Whom) fixed your TV?
7. (Who, Whom) directed that movie?
8. With (who, whom) will you meet?
9. (Who, Whom) did the committee select?
10. (Who, Whom) do you support?

Exercise B Follow the directions for Exercise A.

1. (Who, Whom) programs the computer?
2. (Who, Whom) did the lawyer question?
3. To (who, whom) were the flowers sent?
4. (Who, Whom) were they expecting?
5. (Who, Whom) did the voters elect?
6. (Who, Whom) rehearsed last night?
7. To (who, whom) was the building dedicated?
8. (Who, Whom) cultivated the field?
9. With (who, whom) did you meet?
10. (Who, Whom) needs a daily vitamin?

We and *Us* with Nouns

The pronouns *we* and *us* are often used with nouns, as in the phrases *we girls* or *us players*. Such phrases can cause problems.

To decide whether to use *we* or *us*, omit the noun. Say the sentence with *we* and then with *us*. You will then probably be able to choose the correct pronoun.

Problem: (We, Us) divers practice daily.
Correct: We practice daily.
Correct: We divers practice daily.

Problem: Low grain prices hurt (we, us) farmers.
Correct: Low grain prices hurt us.
Correct: Low grain prices hurt us farmers.

465

Them and *Those*

Them and *those* are sometimes confused. To use the words correctly, remember that *them* is always a pronoun. It takes the place of a noun.

> The state trooper helped *them.* (In this sentence, *them* is used as the direct object.)

Them is never used to tell about or describe a noun. *Those* should be used.

> Incorrect: Lorraine baked them muffins.
>
> Correct: Lorraine baked those muffins.

Exercise A Choose the correct pronoun from the two given in parentheses.

1. The mayor thanked (we, us) volunteers.
2. Did you find (them, those) pliers?
3. (Them, Those) foods are nutritious.
4. Exchange (them, those) gloves for the right size.
5. (We, Us) bowlers formed a summer league.
6. (Them, Those) plants look healthy.
7. The coach congratulated (we, us) winners.
8. (We, Us) campers enjoy peace and quiet.
9. Bill bought one of (them, those) radios.
10. The monkey made faces at (we, us) tourists.

Exercise B Follow the directions for Exercise A.

1. (We, Us) girls organized the picnic.
2. Are (them, those) ski vests warm?
3. (Them, Those) peppers are hot.
4. The photographer snapped a picture of (we, us) graduates.
5. I prefer (them, those) boots.

6. Do you like (them, those) alfalfa sprouts in your sand-wich?
7. (We, Us) bookworms should start a book exchange.
8. Should (them, those) pants be dry-cleaned?
9. The power failure in the store gave (we, us) shoppers a fright.
10. Today (we, us) gymnasts face our toughest rivals.

Exercise C In the sentences that follow, there are some errors in the use of pronouns. If a sentence is incorrect, correct it. If it is correct, write *Correct*.

1. She will lend the book to we girls when she is through with it.
2. Bring them pictures of the team with you.
3. Us cyclists are hoping to win the race next Thursday.
4. Did Henry bring them peaches, or did Marla?
5. We students are going to visit Taos Pueblo this summer.
6. André saw them skaters in his home town.
7. Those shoes were left here by mistake.
8. Us three split the cost of the album.
9. Will you play Monopoly with us if it rains?
10. Who talked to them strangers?

ADDITIONAL EXERCISES

Using Pronouns

A. Nouns and Pronouns   Number your paper from 1 to 10. Write the pronouns you find in each of the following sentences. After each pronoun, write the noun or nouns it stands for.

1. The zipper had gone off its track.
2. Ian took his time.
3. The Oak Ridge Boys sang their most recent hit.
4. Are you in training, Amy?
5. Turtles never leave their shells.
6. Ms. Neff rewired her stereo.
7. "My guitar needs tuning," said Judi.
8. "Here we are!" shouted the children.
9. Wendy was the first to call Mark on his new phone.
10. Tamara and Chuck were reading from their scripts.

B. The Use of Pronouns   Choose the correct pronoun from the two given in parentheses. Be ready to explain how it is used in the sentence.

1. (They, Them) put new shingles on the roof.
2. Does (she, her) work in a lab?
3. The alderman asked (she, her) for help.
4. Jackson tossed the ball to (she, her) for the third out.
5. A chunk of plaster landed on (him, his) head.
6. The tenants discussed (they, their) requests with the landlord.
7. The newest recruit was (he, him).
8. The chef for the evening is (I, me).
9. The class sent (she, her) a get-well card.
10. Maybe (we, us) should hold a block party.

C. Pronouns in Compound Constructions Choose the correct pronoun from the two given in parentheses.

1. Julia and (he, him) work in a sporting goods shop.
2. Alec took Nancy and (I, me) to a roller derby.
3. Todd and (I, me) dug holes for the fence posts.
4. The trail was too rough for Matthew and (she, her).
5. The McCoys and (they, them) take vacations together.
6. Chandra and (we, us) designed the mural.
7. Don't give Sam and (he, him) all the credit.
8. The farmer hired Billie and (we, us) to harvest the hay.
9. Just between you and (I, me), I should have won that race.
10. The vice-principals are Mr. Guiterrez and (she, her).

D. Pronouns and Antecedents Write the antecedent for each italicized pronoun.

1. Betsy put *her* lunchbag into the backpack.
2. Tony bought the groceries and had *them* delivered.
3. Fran found some change under the cushions and pocketed *it*.
4. May I give *my* report first, Mr. Byers?
5. You seem angry about *your* mistake.
6. Gina realigned the drainpipe and fastened *it*.
7. Ronnie has a habit of rubbing *his* forehead.
8. James photographed the does and *their* fawns.
9. The shop has burglar bars on *its* windows.
10. We strapped suitcases and boxes onto *our* luggage rack.

E. Compound Personal Pronouns Number your paper from 1 to 10. Beside each number write a correct compound personal pronoun for each of the following sentences. After it, write the noun or pronoun to which it refers.

1. Don't hurt (pronoun) with that blade, Mike.

2. Some men shave (pronoun) without using a mirror.
3. Rachel treated (pronoun) to a pizza.
4. Andy is too young to cross the street by (pronoun).
5. We serve (pronoun) at the salad bar.
6. The alarm turns (pronoun) off too soon.
7. The tourists found (pronoun) stranded in a strange town.
8. I (pronoun) prefer swimming in a pool.
9. Please grade (pronoun), students.
10. He soon found (pronoun) friendless.

F. Different Kinds of Pronouns   Number your paper from 1 to 10. Write all the pronouns in each sentence. After each pronoun, write *Indefinite, Demostrative,* or *Interrogative* to show what kind it is.

1. That is Mt. Rainier off in the distance.
2. Everything went smoothly until the last act.
3. What is bothering Jonathan?
4. This has been a long day.
5. Has anybody ever tried that before?
6. Whom are those for?
7. Which are the left-handed scissors?
8. Please give each of the patients one of these.
9. Who is playing the saxophone upstairs?
10. Neither of the suspects admitted anything.

G. Indefinite Pronouns   Number your paper from 1 to 10. For each sentence write the indefinite pronoun. Then, write the word that agrees with the indefinite pronoun.

1. Has anyone ever had (his or her, their) fortune told?
2. Some of the gymnasts have (her, their) own warm-up exercises.
3. Each of the parking lots has (its, their) own rates.
4. Few of the players had signed (his, their) contracts yet.

5. Both of the runners broke (her, their) own records.
6. Nobody (knows, know) the cause of the crash.
7. Neither of them (works, work) at the gas station.
8. One of these medicine bottles is missing (its, their) label.
9. Everything (depends, depend) on the weather.
10. None of the food had salt in (it, them).

H. Special Pronoun Problems Choose the correct word from the two given in parentheses.

1. The bikers loaded (their, they're) backpacks with food for the trip.
2. Does (your, you're) car use unleaded fuel?
3. (Who, Whom) did she sign a contract with?
4. (Who, Whom) brought the FM radio?
5. (We, Us) city dwellers are used to noise.
6. Have you tried one of (them, those) egg rolls?
7. (It's, Its) rude to call at dinner time.
8. That mountain is not for (we, us) amateur climbers.
9. The computer terminal prints (it's, its) message on this screen.
10. (Whose, Who's) using the gym on Thursday night?

MIXED REVIEW

Using Pronouns

A. Using personal pronouns Write the correct pronoun for each of the following sentences. After each one, write its antecedent.

1. An arctic fox changes (its, their) color in winter.
2. "Is the backpack (your, yours)?" Elam asked Rich.
3. Judy said, "The person in charge is (I, me)."
4. Polish the shoes and then buff (it, them, they).
5. Natalie, have (you, your) seen Kelly?
6. Mark pointed to Carl and said, "The boss asked (he, him)."
7. Shirley forgot (her, hers, she) pen.
8. Both coaches praised (his, their, they) teams.
9. Melissa and Tony saw the accident. (Them, They) will testify.
10. Ms. Chen smiled at Lisa and gave (her, she) the card.

B. Using compound pronouns and pronouns in compound parts correctly Some of the following sentences use pronouns incorrectly. Rewrite correctly any sentences that do. If a sentence is correct, write *Correct.*

1. The players themself insist on proper equipment.
2. Angela and you will solve the problem by yourself.
3. I was waving to Ginger and him.
4. The Wilsons and them have Thanksgiving dinner with us.
5. Sara and me talked ourselves out of the idea.
6. A fire can burn themselves out.
7. The thunder scared Junior and she.
8. The principal handed Martha and he their science fair ribbons.

9. Just between you and I, Ron and he made the same mistake themselves.
10. The high scorers in the game between Eastern and us were Jo and she.

C. Using the correct form of pronouns Write the correct pronoun from those given in parentheses.

1. (This, That) must be Paula on the other side of the gym.
2. Nobody forgot (his or her, their) coat today.
3. (Who, Whose) is at the door?
4. (This, That) is the shallow end right here.
5. Neither of the dogs has had (its, their) rabies shot.
6. (Who, Whose) are the black skates?
7. Everyone wore (her, their) corsage to the dance.
8. Each of the students has (his or her, their) own locker.
9. Few of the students have (his or her, their) own computers.
10. None of the soldiers remembered (his or her, their) orders.

D. Using pronouns correctly Write the correct pronoun from those given in parentheses.

1. The taxicab had one of (them, those) glass partitions.
2. (Who, Whom) is running with the ball?
3. (Us, We) people in wheelchairs can't get into that building.
4. I checked the wires; (their, they're) fine.
5. (Who's, Whose) wearing a beeper?
6. The gusts of wind were losing (their, they're) force.
7. (Who, Whom) have you told?
8. Maybe (their, they're) invisible.
9. Did the cashier put the change on (your, you're) tray?
10. The bird builds (it's, its) nest by instinct.

USING GRAMMAR IN WRITING
Using Pronouns

The following poem has been rewritten incorrectly with few pronouns. Correct the poem by replacing the underlined words with pronouns. You may choose *he, she,* or *it,* but be consistent throughout the poem.

The Fox and the Grapes
A Moral Tale for Those Who Fail

One summer's day a Fox was passing through
An orchard; faint <u>the Fox</u> was and hungry, too.
When suddenly <u>the Fox's</u> keen eye chanced to fall
Upon a bunch of grapes above the wall.
"Ha! Just the thing!" <u>the Fox</u> said. "Who could resist
   <u>the bunch of grapes!</u>"
<u>The Fox</u> eyed the purple cluster—jumped—and missed
   <u>the purple cluster.</u>
"Ahem!" <u>the Fox</u> coughed. "I'll take more careful aim,"
And sprang again. Results were much the same,
Although <u>the Fox's</u> leaps were desperate and high.
At length <u>the Fox</u> paused to wipe a tearful eye,
And shrug a shoulder. "I am not so dry,
And lunch is bound to come within the hour . . .
Besides," <u>the Fox</u> said, "I'm sure those grapes are
   sour."

THE MORAL is: We somehow want the peach
That always dangles just beyond our reach;
Until we learn never to be upset
With what we find too difficult to get.

—JOSEPH LAUREN

Using Verbs

You already know something about the verb. It is the most important part of a sentence. A verb tells of an action or a state of being.

The verb is another one of the parts of speech. In this section you will find out more about verbs and how they are used.

Part 1   What Is a Verb?

A verb tells of an action or a state of being.

Action Verbs

One kind of verb indicates action, even if the action is unseen.

Ella *frowned*.   Mary *organized* her thoughts.
The train *stopped*.   Craig *has* a cold.

An **action verb** tells that something is happening, has happened, or will happen.

Linking Verbs

Some verbs simply tell that something exists. Such verbs express a state of being rather than action.

The assembly *is* tomorrow.   Lee *was* anxious.
Lynn *seems* upset.   The paint *feels* tacky.

These verbs are called **linking verbs**. They link the subject with some other word or words in the sentence.

Here are the most common linking verbs:

be (am, are, is, was,   look   smell   seem
    were, been, being)   appear   taste   sound
become   feel   grow

Some linking verbs can also be used as action verbs.

Linking Verbs   **Action Verbs**
The bread *tasted* dry.   Kate *tasted* the chili.
The children *grew* sleepy.   Larry *grew* vegetables.

When you look at the verb in a sentence, see how it is used. Decide whether it expresses action or simply links the subject with a word in the predicate.

Transitive and Intransitive Verbs

In many sentences an action verb expresses an idea by itself. In other sentences a direct object completes the action of the verb. The direct object, as you have learned, answers *whom* or *what* about the verb.

Verbs that have direct objects are **transitive verbs**.

> Myra *examined* the envelope.
> (The direct object *envelope* completes the meaning of the verb *examined*.)

> The car *towed* a trailer.
> (The direct object *trailer* completes the meaning of the verb *towed*.)

Verbs that do not have direct objects are another kind of verb. They are called **intransitive verbs**.

> The audience *rose*.
> (The verb *rose* has no direct object.)

> Warren *swam* in the stream.
> (The verb *swam* has no direct object.)

Some action verbs are always transitive or always intransitive. Other verbs change. The same verb may be transitive in one sentence and intransitive in another. Compare these examples.

Transitive Verbs	Intransitive Verbs
The chorus *sang* a medley.	The chorus *sang* at the assembly.
The fans *shouted* a cheer.	The fans *shouted*.
Pam *parked* the car.	Pam *parked* near the library.

Exercise A   Write the verb in each sentence. After each verb write *Action* or *Linking* to show what kind it is.

1. The general issued a statement.
2. Iowa farm land is fertile.
3. The judge called for order in the courtroom.

4. That jingle is catchy.
5. The critic praised the performance.
6. A resort was down in the valley.
7. The banker seemed confident.
8. Joe daydreamed about his vacation.
9. Gasoline became scarce during the oil embargo.
10. We saw a three-ring circus.

Exercise B   Follow the directions for Exercise A.

1. A tornado destroyed the town.
2. The WPA created jobs during the Depression.
3. The turtles basked in the sun.
4. The Bedouins are nomads.
5. This collar feels stiff.
6. Can you leave a message for the doctor?
7. The DC–10 is a jumbo jet.
8. Milton Friedman won a Nobel Prize in economics.
9. Wreckers demolished the building.
10. The faces of the firefighters were grim.

Exercise C   Write the action verb in each sentence. After it write *Transitive* or *Intransitive* to show what kind it is.

1. The hound howled at the moon.
2. Every year new fads appear.
3. That radio station only plays rock music.
4. The scientist checked the test tubes.
5. Paramedics arrived on the scene.
6. Our houseguests finally left.
7. Clare rarely drinks milk.
8. During the winter the pool closes.
9. Lou made bacon and eggs.
10. Some cars have diesel engines.

Part 2 The Parts of a Verb

Many verbs are made up of a **main verb** plus one or more **helping verbs**.

The most common helping verbs are forms of *be, have,* and *do*. They may also be used as main verbs. Here are their forms:

be—am, is, are, was, were, be, being, been
have—has, have, had
do—does, do, did

Used as Main Verb	Used as Helping Verb
I *was* happy.	I *was baking* a pizza.
Nick *has* a headache.	Nick *has ordered* the tickets.
We *did* the laundry.	We *did receive* invitations.

Here are other frequently used helping verbs:

can	will	shall	may	must
could	would	should	might	

Helping verbs combine with the main verb to become part of the verb.

Helping Verb(s) +	Main Verb =	Verb
will	play	will play
had	played	had played
should have	played	should have played
must	walk	must walk
has	walked	has walked

Sometimes the parts of the verb are separated. The words that come between them are not part of the verb. Study these examples.

Baseball *has* always *been* a popular sport.
The kite *was* barely *staying* aloft.
When *will* the senator *give* her speech?
Did the catalog order *arrive?*
Our puppy *will* not *eat* dog food.

Exercise A Make two columns. Label them *Helping Verb* and *Main Verb*. Find the parts of the verb in each sentence. Write them in the proper columns.

1. The pool was overflowing.
2. The neighborhood grocery has closed.
3. The burglars could not hear the silent alarm.
4. The chef will dice the vegetables.
5. Has the test been postponed?
6. The piano should be tuned occasionally.
7. Did you win a prize in the raffle?
8. Kelly had never met my sister.
9. Newspaper reporters must often work odd hours.
10. A bulletproof vest would have protected the police officer.

Exercise B Follow the directions for Exercise A

1. The ambulance had been called by a bystander.
2. Dee is rehearsing her lines.
3. David has read that story before.
4. Will Mr. Langan consider our offer?
5. Molly should have taken the make-up test.
6. Can Ginny find the map?
7. The river has nearly reached flood level.
8. Have you ever camped in the desert?
9. Your cousin will certainly call you from the airport.
10. This floor must be waxed regularly.

Part 3 Verb Tenses

Verbs indicate time. They tell when an action or state of being occurs. Verbs can indicate past time, present time, or future time by changing form.

These changes in form to show time are called **tenses**. The changes are usually made in these ways:

1. Change in spelling

   sit —→ sat   cry —→ cried   walk —→ walked

2. Use of helping verbs

   had shown   will compete   has taken

This list shows examples of the six main tenses for the verbs *listen* and *skate*.

Present Tense	I listen.	She skates.
Past Tense	I listened.	She skated.
Future Tense	I will listen.	She will skate.
Present Perfect Tense	I have listened.	She has skated.
Past Perfect Tense	I had listened.	She had skated.
Future Perfect Tense	I will have listened.	She will have skated.

Simple Tenses

The **present tense** shows time in the present. The present tense form is usually the same as the name of the verb. For verbs used with most singular subjects, an -*s* is added to the verb.

I swim.   David swims.   My brother swims.

The **past tense** shows past time. Most verbs form the past tense by adding -*d* or -*ed*.

Ron cooked.   Sue phoned.   He chuckled.

Some verbs form the past tense in different ways.

They swam.   Marge went to the movies.   Eve thought.

The **future tense** shows time in the future. In this tense, use *shall* or *will* with the verb.

Ed will finish.   I shall continue.   Annette will try.

The three tenses just described are called the **simple tenses**.

Perfect Tenses

The **perfect tenses** are used when you speak of two different times, one earlier than the other. The perfect tenses are formed by using the helping verbs *has, have,* and *had.*

The **present perfect tense** tells of an action or state of being in some indefinite time before the present. The helping verb *has* or *have* is used.

> Louis has skied often. Joan has won.
> They have finished Terry and Bill have left already.
> their work.

The **past perfect tense** tells of a time *before* another time in the past. The helping verb *had* is used.

> Mother *had* not *been* nervous before she *went* for the test.
> Wayne *had filled* the tire with air, but it *leaked.*
> We *had* just *arrived* at the airport when the plane *landed.*

The **future perfect tense** tells of a time in the future *before* some other time in the future.

> By midnight tonight, you *will have missed* the deadline.
> When the class is over, we *will have read* ten books.

Exercise A Find the verbs in the following sentences. Tell the tense of each.

1. Jesse aimed the bow and arrow.
2. Two schools in this district have closed.
3. The team has won the play-off game.
4. Andrea plays the clarinet.
5. Your speech will conclude the program.
6. The nurses will change shifts at eleven.
7. Most colas contain caffeine.
8. By July the temperature will have risen.
9. The exterminators sprayed the apartment.
10. The bloodhounds had almost lost the trail.

Exercise B: Writing Write a sentence for each of the verbs below. Use the tense indicated.

1. plant (past)
2. copy (present)
3. walk (present perfect)
4. fly (future)
5. wait (past perfect)
6. sing (present)
7. borrow (past)
8. cook (present perfect)
9. repair (future)
10. run (future perfect)

Part 4 The Principal Parts of a Verb

The **principal parts** of a verb are its basic forms. By combining these forms with helping verbs, you can make all tenses.

The principal parts of a verb are the **present tense**, the **past tense**, and the **past participle**. They are usually written in that order.

Most verbs form the past tense and past participle by adding -*d* or -*ed* to the present form. These verbs are called **regular verbs**. They are called regular verbs because they form the past tense and past participle in regular ways.

Present	Past	Past Participle
work	worked	(have) worked
talk	talked	(have) talked
march	marched	(have) marched
repeat	repeated	(have) repeated

Some regular verbs change their spelling when the -*d* or -*ed* is added. Study the examples on the next page.

Present	Past	Past Participle
cry	cried	(have) cried
blot	blotted	(have) blotted
drop	dropped	(have) dropped
plan	planned	(have) planned

The past participle is used for perfect tenses. It must have a helping verb.

They have worked.	Mimi has written to us.
Tony must have eaten.	They have planned it.

Exercise   Make three columns on your paper. Label them *Present, Past,* and *Past Participle.* List the principle parts of these verbs in the proper columns.

1. wash
2. carry
3. close
4. own
5. push

6. reply
7. occur
8. rip
9. juggle
10. tug

Part 5 Irregular Verbs

You have learned the principal parts for regular verbs. Many verbs, though, do not follow the regular pattern. They do not add -*d* or -*ed* to form the past tense and past participle. They are called irregular verbs. Here are some examples:

Present	Past	Past Participle
break	broke	(have) broken
bring	brought	(have) brought
ring	rang	(have) rung
see	saw	(have) seen
put	put	(have) put

You will notice that some of the verbs have one or two different forms. Others have three different forms.

If you do not know the principal parts of a verb, look up the verb in a dictionary. If no parts are listed, the verb is regular. If the verb is irregular, the dictionary will list the irregular forms. It will give two forms if both the past and past participle are the same, as in *catch, caught,* for example. It will give three forms if all principal parts are different, as in *ring, rang, rung,* for example.

Using Irregular Verbs

There are two ways to be sure of the forms of irregular verbs. One way is to look up the verbs in the dictionary. The other way is to learn the principal parts of commonly used irregular verbs.

Once you know the principal parts, keep these rules in mind: Use the past participle with *have* and *be* helping verbs. The past participle is used for present perfect and past perfect tenses. The past form is not used with helping verbs.

The principal parts of irregular verbs can be confusing. They may seem simpler if you learn the following five patterns.

Group 1 Some irregular verbs keep the same form for all three principal parts. These are easy to remember.

Present	Past	Past Participle
burst	burst	(have) burst
cost	cost	(have) cost
cut	cut	(have) cut
let	let	(have) let
put	put	(have) put
read	read	(have) read
set	set	(have) set

Here are some sentences using verbs from this group:

Carl's mother *lets* him use the car. (present)
Martin *set* the table. (past)
That mistake *has cost* us time. (past participle)

Group 2 Another group of irregular verbs changes form only once. The past and the past participle are the same.

Present	Past	Past Participle
bring	brought	(have) brought
catch	caught	(have) caught
lead	led	(have) led
lend	lent	(have) lent
lose	lost	(have) lost
say	said	(have) said
sit	sat	(have) sat

These sentences use irregular verbs from Group 2:

Tim usually *catches* with his right hand. (present)
Marla *lost* her purse. (past)
The scouts *have brought* a compass. (past participle)

Exercise A   Choose the correct form of the verb.

1. The hen (sat, sitted) on the eggs.
2. Tina (said, sayed) her name softly.
3. Greg has (lost, losed) his keys.
4. Mark has (lent, lended) me his tent.
5. Lewis and Clark (leaded, led) the expedition.
6. Myra has (catched, caught) the flu.
7. The campers (brought, brang) a lantern.
8. The floodwaters (burst, bursted) the dam.
9. The auto repairs (costed, cost) Al $700.53.
10. The barber (cut, cutted) my hair.

Exercise B   Follow the directions for Exercise A.

1. Mom has (let, letted) Dad choose the wallpaper.
2. Fido (put, putted) my slippers in his doghouse.
3. Tom and Jim have (set, setted) the timer for twenty minutes.
4. Mandy has (brung, brought) her pictures from the trip.

5. Detective Thorpe (catched, caught) the mugger.
6. Megan has (lost, losed) her place in line.
7. The runners have (setted, set) a new record.
8. The guide (leaded, led) the climbers to the peak.
9. Carol has (put, putted) her savings in the bank.
10. That toy helicopter (costed, cost) $2.98.

Group 3 Verbs in this group add -*n* or -*en* to the past tense to form the past participle.

Present	Past	Past Participle
break	broke	(have) broken
choose	chose	(have) chosen
freeze	froze	(have) frozen
speak	spoke	(have) spoken
steal	stole	(have) stolen
tear	tore	(have) torn
wear	wore	(have) worn

Here are three sentences using Group 3 verbs:

Break the eggs into a bowl. (present)
The UN delegates *spoke* different languages. (past)
Thieves *have stolen* the jewels. (past participle)

Exercise A   Choose the correct form of the verb from those given.

1. Matt (chose, chosen) the blue stone for his class ring.
2. Carrie has (broke, broken) the school high jump record.
3. Much of the orange crop (froze, frozen) last winter.
4. Someone has (stole, stolen) my wallet!
5. Liz has (wore, worn) contact lenses for years.
6. The principal (spoke, spoken) to the students at the assembly.
7. Tom has (chose, chosen) a topic for his term paper.
8. The milk has (froze, frozen) on the back porch.
9. The football team (wore, worn) new jerseys.
10. The fish (stole, stolen) the bait from my hook.

Exercise B Follow the directions for Exercise A.

1. Julie (broke, broken) the candy bar in half.
2. The witnesses have (spoke, spoken) to the detective.
3. Chris had been (chose, chosen) by the class.
4. A tornado (tore, torn) through the countryside.
5. Spies have (stole, stolen) the secret documents.
6. Mom has (froze, frozen) the extra spaghetti sauce.
7. Craig (wore, worn) a tuxedo to the dance.
8. Melissa has (tore, torn) the article from the newspaper.
9. Ken (chose, chosen) a blue plaid shirt.
10. Mr. Ross has (wore, worn) a neck brace since the accident.

Group 4 The irregular verbs in this group change their final vowels. The vowel changes from *i* in the present tense to *a* in the past tense and *u* in the past participle.

Present	Past	Past Participle
begin	began	(have) begun
drink	drank	(have) drunk
ring	rang	(have) rung
sing	sang	(have) sung
swim	swam	(have) swum

Here are examples of irregular verbs from Group 4:

I *drink* root beer. (present)
The mother *sang* softly. (past)
Gary *has swum* in the new pool. (past participle)

Exercise A Choose the correct verb form.

1. Someone must have (rang, rung) our doorbell by mistake.
2. Class (began, begun) at nine o'clock.
3. Mark Spitz (swam, swum) in the Olympics.
4. The school choir has (sang, sung) at many civic events.
5. Ms. Silva (drank, drunk) her coffee black.

6. The baby must have (drank, drunk) his bottle.
7. Our school has (began, begun) a new admission policy.
8. The phone (rang, rung) ten times.
9. Cindy has already (swam, swum) fifty laps.
10. Diana Ross (sang, sung) a medley of her hits.

Exercise B Follow the directions for Exercise A.

1. Carl (drank, drunk) three glasses of lemonade.
2. Mr. Evans has (rang, rung) the church bells for years.
3. Laura (swam, swum) in the water ballet.
4. Local farmers have (began, begun) the harvest.
5. Martha (sang, sung) a solo in the musical.
6. The hospital patient (rang, rung) for the nurse.
7. That child has (swam, swum) four lengths of the pool.
8. The kittens have (drank, drunk) all of the milk.
9. Dad has (sang, sung) with a barbershop quartet.
10. Nora (began, begun) her driving lessons today.

Group 5 For some irregular verbs the past participle is formed from the present tense. The past participle looks more like the present tense than the past tense.

Present	Past	Past Participle
come	came	(have) come
do	did	(have) done
eat	ate	(have) eaten
fall	fell	(have) fallen
give	gave	(have) given
go	went	(have) gone
grow	grew	(have) grown
know	knew	(have) known
ride	rode	(have) ridden
run	ran	(have) run
see	saw	(have) seen
take	took	(have) taken
throw	threw	(have) thrown
write	wrote	(have) written

Here are sentences using Group 5 verbs:

I *know* the address. (present)
Marty *gave* a speech. (past)
The leaves *have fallen*. (past participle)

Exercise A   Choose the correct verb form from the two given.

1. Crowds of people (came, come) to the grand opening of the new department store.
2. Michele has (did, done) the assignment thoroughly and is prepared for the test.
3. Mr. Price (gave, given) the class a quiz.
4. Jean (knew, known) the algebra equation.
5. We (rode, ridden) the subway downtown.
6. The nest has (fell, fallen) from the tree.
7. That horse has (ran, run) its last race.
8. Terry has (went, gone) on vacation.
9. Bob and Jim have (saw, seen) all of the *Star Wars* movies four times.
10. Clara has never (ate, eaten) Mexican food.

Exercise B   Follow the directions for Exercise A.

1. We (saw, seen) Vicky at the carnival.
2. My brother has (grew, grown) a beard.
3. John (ran, run) to the finish line.
4. The pitcher has (threw, thrown) a curve ball.
5. Jan has (rode, ridden) in horse shows.
6. The police have (come, came) to the same conclusion.
7. Our class (took, taken) the exam yesterday.
8. Bonny has already (wrote, written) a letter to the travel agency.
9. My ring (fell, fallen) down the drain.
10. Pat (did, done) her homework at the library before she came home.

Part 6 Active and Passive Verbs

You have seen how the tenses of verbs indicate time. There is another way that verbs help you say exactly what you mean.

Suppose that a package was delivered. If you knew who delivered it, you could say:

> Beth delivered the package today.

However, if you don't know who delivered the package, you might say:

> The package was delivered today.

In the first sentence, the subject, *Beth*, tells who performed the action. If the subject performs the action, the verb is **active**.

In the second sentence, the subject, *package*, tells what received the action. If the subject names the receiver or the result of the action, the verb is **passive**. The word **passive** means "acted upon."

Forming the Passive

The passive form of the verb is made with the past participle. A form of *be* is the helping verb.

Active	Passive
That store *sells* furniture.	Furniture *is sold* by that store.
Luke *has built* the model.	The model *has been built* by Luke.
The janitor *will paint* the hallway.	The hallway *will be painted* by the janitor.
Gayle *baked* the pie.	The pie *was baked* by Gayle.

Read the direct objects in the sentences in the first column above. You can see that the direct objects have become the subjects of the sentences in the second column. Only verbs that have objects (transitive verbs) can be changed from active to passive.

A verb is active when its subject performs the action stated by the verb.

A verb is passive when its subject names the receiver or result of the action stated by the verb.

Exercise A Write the verb in each sentence. After each, write *Active* or *Passive* to tell what kind it is.

1. Secret talks were arranged by the Secretary of State.
2. The electrician repaired the wiring.
3. The patient was referred to a specialist.
4. A survey had been taken by the student council.
5. Judge Blackwell gave the jury instructions.
6. The Garden Club sponsored a plant sale.
7. The walk-a-thon was organized by our school.
8. Paul fed the stray kitten.
9. Jason compared the two novels in his term paper.
10. Prizes for the raffle were provided by local merchants.

Exercise B Change the verbs in the following sentences from passive to active. Rewrite the sentences.

1. The barn was demolished by the tornado.
2. Larry was given a sedative by the doctor.
3. No information on the case has been released by the police.
4. The door was answered by Mr. Scott.
5. The invitation was written by Lisa.
6. Ten thousand dollars was given by an anonymous donor.
7. Thunderstorms were predicted by the weather reporter.
8. The letters were filed by the secretary.
9. An interview had been arranged by the personnel manager.
10. Refreshments will be provided by a catering service.

ADDITIONAL EXERCISES

Using Verbs

A. Action and Linking Verbs Make three columns on your paper. Label them *Action—Transitive, Action—Intransitive,* and *Linking*. Find the verb in each sentence. Write the verb in the correct column.

1. We climbed into the rowboat.
2. The Navy plane patrolled the North Pacific.
3. The rapids were dangerous.
4. The helicopter landed in a field.
5. Are mouthpieces optional in football?
6. One dancer lost the beat.
7. Eric accompanied the radio with his bongo drums.
8. Ken studied for the history quiz.
9. The clouds seemed motionless.
10. Polly looked at each picture for a long time.

B. Parts of the Verb Find the parts of the verb in each sentence. Write them in two columns labeled *Helping Verbs* and *Main Verbs*.

1. The pilot should have radioed the tower.
2. Nancy must be rehearsing for the play.
3. The countdown will soon begin.
4. Poisonous gases had leaked into the air.
5. By tomorrow the fog will have cleared.
6. The flight to Miami was canceled.
7. Residents have often been told about the danger.
8. A penalty was called on that play.
9. Stan will certainly be removed from the game by the end of the quarter.
10. The divers have thoroughly searched the river and parts of the lake.

C. Verb Tenses Write each verb and its tense.

1. Yolanda now belongs to several of the school clubs.
2. The physical fitness tests will start early tomorrow morning.
3. We will have graduated by then.
4. The carton of milk dripped.
5. Jerome has no locker.
6. Satchel Paige had earned his place in sports history as a great baseball pitcher.
7. Ms. Deer has complained to the Better Business Bureau.
8. He laughed for no apparent reason.
9. I shall see you then.
10. Has Frances ever used a mimeograph machine or an overhead projector before?

D. Principal Parts of the Verb Write the italicized verbs in the form stated in parentheses. If the sentence is already in the form stated in parentheses, write *Correct*.

Example: I *like* those styles. (past)
I liked those styles.

1. Sam had *mist* the plants with a sprayer. (past participle)
2. Jessica *brand* the calf. (past)
3. Ronnie has *apply* for officer's training school. (past participle)
4. Most drivers *obey* the crossing guard. (present)
5. Mud *splatter* over our boots. (past)
6. Aaron should have *block* that pass. (past participle)
7. The hikers had *blaze* a trail. (past participle)
8. Slush can *harden* into ice. (present)
9. Surgeons *work* quickly and carefully. (present)
10. Should Lee have *enter* the contest sooner? (past participle)

E. Irregular Verbs: Groups 1 and 2 Number your paper from 1 to 10. Write the correct verb.

1. Jon had (put, putted) the maps in the car.
2. Medical care has never (cost, costed) more.
3. The raft (brang, brought) us to safety.
4. The Lakers (lost, losed) by one point.
5. The Eskimo (cutted, cut) a circle in the ice.
6. The dentist finally (set, setted) her drill down.
7. Karen (lended, lent) me her radio.
8. Without a glove, Robin (catched, caught) the ball.
9. You have (sayed, said, saided) too much already.
10. We (sat, sitted) in the front row and craned our necks.

F. Irregular Verbs: Group 3 Number your paper from 1 to 10. Write the correct verb.

1. Dad and I (torn, tore) down the old wallpaper.
2. Has anyone (spoke, spoken) to the career counselor?
3. Stephanie has (broke, broken) her glasses.
4. Somebody had (stole, stolen) the portable television.
5. Amanda (chose, choosed, chosen) bright yellow paint.
6. The windows had all (froze, frozen) shut.
7. Should the bandage be (tore, torn) off quickly?
8. Grover (stealed, stole) a look at the price tag.
9. The children (speaked, spoke, spoken) Polish at home.
10. Luke had never (wore, worn) a tuxedo before.

G. Irregular Verbs: Group 4 Number your paper from 1 to 10. Write the correct verb.

1. The actress had (began, begun) with only bit parts.
2. The hikers (drank, drunk) from their canteens.
3. Smokey Robinson (sang, sung) the first song.
4. The camp chef (rang, rung) the dinner bell.
5. A snapping turtle (swam, swum) right past my foot.

6. Nobody had (rang, rung) the fire alarm.
7. Christina had (swam, swum) to the island.
8. I (began, begun) the work in a cheerful mood.
9. Everyone with stomach pains had (drank, drunk) the eggnog.
10. She could have (sang, sung) that song in her sleep.

H. Irregular Verbs: Group 5   Number your paper from 1 to 10. Write the correct verb.

1. That bakery has (went, gone) out of business.
2. Eliza (saw, seen) the filming of a movie.
3. Tom's contact lens had (fell, fallen) into the snow.
4. Melissa Mathison (wrote, written) the script for *E. T.*
5. The roses (grew, grown) near the back porch.
6. Benita has (took, taken) the civil service exam.
7. A path (ran, run) across the cornfield.
8. I hadn't (knew, known) about the law against jaywalking.
9. Earl (did, done) better last season.
10. The coach has (gave, given) Celeste an ice pack.

I. Passive and Active Verbs   Change the verbs in the following sentences from passive to active. Rewrite the sentences.

1. Night crawlers are sold by the Rod and Reel Shop.
2. The home run was made by Gussie.
3. Spanish is spoken by the hospital admissions clerk.
4. A refugee family has been sponsored by our church.
5. "Diamonds and Rust" was written by Joan Baez.
6. A soccer stadium was built by Indiana University.
7. Static had been picked up by the computer.
8. The fire department was called by Ms. Slawek.
9. The holes in this sweater were made by moths.
10. The sense of hearing can be damaged by noise.

MIXED REVIEW

Using Verbs

A. Finding action verbs and linking verbs Write the verbs from each sentence. Next, write whether they are *Action* or *Linking Verbs*. If a verb is an action verb, write whether it is *Transitive* or *Intransitive*.

1. The cow licked the salt block.
2. Rosemary has some good ideas.
3. The sky looks mean.
4. Mr. Vargo looked at the engine.
5. This old sweatshirt feels comfortable.
6. The firefighter carefully felt the hot wall.
7. The vet lifted the dog from the table.
8. Jake is in your science class.
9. Nancy is a good sport.
10. After a few minutes, Joachim and his friends left the movie theater.

B. Helping verbs and main verbs Label two columns on your paper *Helping Verbs* and *Main Verbs*. Fill in the parts from each of the following sentences.

1. That restaurant has been closed all month.
2. The marathon has already started.
3. I might see the movie tomorrow.
4. Did you miss your bus?
5. Have you been working on weekends?
6. Aunt Ruth is still looking for a better job.
7. Craig might yet change his mind.
8. Stacey will probably never change.
9. Should I use cold water?
10. Somebody must have been using this cabin recently.

C. Using verb forms correctly Write each of the following sentences, using the verb and the verb form given in parentheses.

> Example: The spoon (*fall*, past perfect) into the soup.
> The spoon had fallen into the soup.

1. Gene (*swim*, past) underwater.
2. Molly (*ride*, present perfect) a dirt bike.
3. Who (*let*, past) the cat out?
4. The players (*put*, past) their mouthpieces in before the game.
5. The bus driver (*say*, past) nothing to the passengers.
6. Martin (*sing*, past perfect) despite his sore throat.
7. The car (*turn*, past) into the alley.
8. I (*do*, future perfect) most of the research by Monday.
9. The ducks (*go*, future) south in a few weeks.
10. My cousin never (*write*, past) back.

D. Recognizing active and passive verbs Write the verb in each sentence. Write *Active* or *Passive* to tell what kind it is. Then rewrite each sentence. Change each passive verb to an active verb. Change each active verb to a passive verb.

1. The basement was flooded by the rain.
2. The emergency brake was used by the driver.
3. Several video games were played by Terry.
4. The weather changed our plans.
5. A small plane carried the mail.
6. Cold water soothes a burn.
7. That role was played by James Earl Jones.
8. This generator supplies our electricity.
9. The Coast Guard patrols the lake.
10. The test was completed by everyone.

USING GRAMMAR IN WRITING
Using Verbs

A. Verbs power sentences. A strong sentence usually has a strong verb; a weak sentence usually has a weak verb. Pay special attention to verbs as you complete the following writing assignment.

Last weekend, you attended a concert. In the middle of the concert, all electrical power in the building failed. What happened next? Did an emergency lighting system come on automatically? Did the performers help calm the audience? What did you do? How did the other people in the audience react? How did people make their way to the exits? How did you get home? Write a paragraph about the experience. Use vivid verbs that capture the tension and describe people's actions. Circle each verb.

B. You are applying for a very special scholarship. This scholarship allows a student to follow any course of study whatsoever. It can be used for flying lessons, college, art school, clown school, computer programing courses, or any other kind of training. As part of the application, you must write three paragraphs about yourself. These paragraphs should help explain your interest in the field you will choose.

First, write a paragraph about yourself as you were five years ago. Use past tenses for the verbs in this paragraph.

Next, write a paragraph about yourself as you are now. Use present tenses for the verbs in this paragraph.

Finally, write a paragraph about yourself as you hope to be in five years. Use future tenses for the verbs in this paragraph.

Using Modifiers

When you try to describe someone or something, you have to use specific words. Then your listeners will be able to picture in their minds exactly what you are describing.

Look at these sentences:

The cafeteria served chicken.
The cafeteria served *crispy, fried* chicken.

The second sentence is more specific. It uses **modifiers. Modifiers are words that modify, or change, other words.**

In the example above, the modifiers describe a noun. Modifiers can also be used with verbs. Look at these sentences:

Hikers climb this path.
Hikers *usually* climb this path *quickly*.

Modifiers help make your writing more lively and interesting. There are two kinds of modifiers—adjectives and adverbs. Both of them are parts of speech. In this section you will learn to identify and use modifiers.

Part 1 Using Adjectives

One kind of modifier is an **adjective**.

An adjective is a word that modifies a noun or pronoun.

Adjectives can tell three different kinds of things about nouns or pronouns.

Which one or ones?

this cup, *that* hat, *these* gloves, *those* papers

What kind?

black sand, *muddy* shoes, *sad* news, *brilliant* light

How many or how much?

five days, *much* love, *several* opinions, *few* comments

Proper Adjectives

One special kind of adjective is the **proper adjective**.

A proper adjective is formed from a proper noun. Therefore, it refers to a specific person, place, or thing. This kind of adjective is always capitalized. Here are some examples:

Swiss cheese   a Ford car
the French language   a Mediterranean port

Predicate Adjectives

Most adjectives come before the words they modify:

Mom handed me a *cool, refreshing* drink.
(*Cool* and *refreshing* modify *drink*.)

A **predicate adjective**, though, comes after the word it modifies. A predicate adjective follows a linking verb and modifies the subject of the sentence.

Albert seemed *confused.*
(*Confused* modifies the subject, *Albert.*)

The instructions were *clear.*
(*Clear* modifies the subject, *instructions.*)

As you can see, here *confused* and *clear* are predicate adjectives. They follow linking verbs, *seemed* and *were.* Each one also modifies the subject of the sentence.

Articles

The adjectives *a, an,* and *the* are called **articles.**
The is the **definite article.** It points out a specific person, place, or thing.

Guard *the* secret carefully. (a particular secret)

A and *an* are **indefinite articles.**

Do you know *a* secret? (any secret)
I would like *an* egg. (any egg)

Notice that *a* is used before a consonant sound (*a* rock, *a* book, *a* meal). *An* is used before a vowel sound (*an* ear, *an* orange, *an* urn).

Pay attention to the sound, not the spelling. You would say *a* hero, but *an* honor.

Diagraming Adjectives

In a sentence diagram, an adjective appears below the word it modifies. It is placed on a slanted line.

This car has a rebuilt engine.

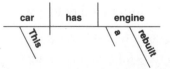

Predicate adjectives are diagramed differently. Like predicate nouns and pronouns, they are placed on the main line. A slanted line goes between the verb and the predicate adjective.

These tires are bald.

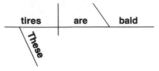

A compound predicate adjective appears on a split line.

The upholstery is old and worn.

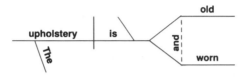

Exercise A Number your paper from 1 to 10. Write the adjectives in each sentence. After each adjective, write the word it modifies. Do not include articles.

1. The bridal bouquet contained white roses, pink carnations, and blue cornflowers.
2. Several mysterious footprints were found in the soft mud by the old shack.
3. Georgina painted green stripes on that old wagon.
4. Mr. Marks wears a rumpled raincoat and a plaid cap.
5. Several political figures attended the public meeting.
6. The physicians disagreed on the proper treatment.
7. Two kites were caught in the old elm tree.
8. Some employees at that bank speak foreign languages.
9. Frank sprinkled a little salt on the tasteless meatloaf.
10. The chilly rain pelted the new flowers in the garden.

Exercise B Number your paper from 1 to 10. Write the predicate adjectives in these sentences.

1. The tennis court is free.
2. The wound looks serious.

3. Power steering is helpful for parking.
4. The vicinity of the trash dump smelled foul.
5. Reservations are necessary.
6. The team felt certain of victory.
7. Interest rates are high now.
8. Angie felt proud of herself.
9. That chair is old and uncomfortable.
10. These houses are expensive.

Part 2   Adjectives in Comparisons

You often learn about new things by making comparisons. You compare new things with things you already know. You might describe a movie, for example, as *"more spectacular* than *Star Wars."* Or you might explain that the grapes were *fresher* than the melons.

Adjectives help you to make such comparisons.

The Comparative

Adjectives have special forms for making comparisons. When you compare one person or thing with another, you use the **comparative** form of an adjective. Here are some examples:

> Melissa is *younger* than Meg.
> This is a *funnier* movie than that one.
> Bill is *more studious* than I am.

The comparative is made in two ways:

1. Add *-er* to short adjectives like *tall* and *great.*

> soft + -er = softer   old + -er = older
> pretty + -er = prettier   small + -er = smaller

Notice that the spelling of some adjectives changes in the comparative form.

2. Use *more* for longer adjectives like *popular*.

more confident   more curious

Most adjectives ending in *-ful* or *-ous* form the comparative with *more*.

more careful   more dangerous

The Superlative

When you compare a person or thing with all others in its class, you use the **superlative** form of the adjective. In addition, use the superlative when you compare a person or thing with two or more others.

Here are some examples:

Mark ate the *largest* piece of pie.
That is the *craziest* idea I've heard yet.
Judy is the *most powerful* swimmer on the team.

The superlative form of an adjective is made by adding *-est* or by using *most*. If an adjective adds *-er* for the comparative, it adds *-est* for the superlative. If an adjective uses *more* for the comparative, it uses *most* for the superlative.

Adjective	Comparative	Superlative
rough	rougher	roughest
light	lighter	lightest
forceful	more forceful	most forceful
terrible	more terrible	most terrible
expensive	more expensive	most expensive

Remember these three points about using adjectives in comparison:

1. To compare two people or things, use the comparative. To compare more than two, use the superlative.

This engine is *more powerful* than that one.
Mel's Market sells the *thickest* steaks in town.

2. Use the word *other* when you compare something with everything else of its kind.

Incorrect: Jeff is smarter than any student.
(This sentence says that Jeff is not a student.)

Correct: Jeff is smarter than any *other* student.

Incorrect: This statue is *more delicate* than any of the porcelain figures.
(This sentence says that the statue is not a piece of porcelain.)

Correct: This statue is *more delicate* than any of the *other* porcelain figures.

3. Do not use *-er* with *more,* or *-est* with *most.*

Incorrect: Chris is much more smaller than his brother.
Correct: Chris is much *smaller* than his brother.
Incorrect: This is the most ugliest Halloween mask here.
Correct: This is the *ugliest* Halloween mask here.

Irregular Comparisons

Some comparatives and superlatives are formed in unusual ways:

Adjective	Comparative	Superlative
good	better	best
well	better	best
bad	worse	worst
little	less or lesser	least
much	more	most
many	more	most
far	farther	farthest

Exercise A Two of the following comparisons are correct. If a sentence is correct, write *Correct.* If it is incorrect, write it correctly.

1. Saudi Arabia contains the world's most largest sand desert, the Rub al-Khali.
2. Riyadh is the largest city in Saudi Arabia.

3. Food is more expensiver in Saudi Arabia than in the United States.
4. Gasoline is the bestest bargain in Saudi Arabia.
5. Of all the O.P.E.C. countries, Saudi Arabia has the friendliest relations with the United States.
6. Today the Saudis have a more better standard of living.
7. Saudi Arabia exports more oil than any nation.
8. The geography in Saudi Arabia is among the most harshest on earth.
9. Of the two kings, King Faisal was the most progressive.
10. In recent years, oil production has become more importanter to the Saudis.

Exercise B Follow the directions for Exercise A.

1. Pink coral grows in more deeper water than black coral.
2. Of all divers, coral divers are the more courageous.
3. Of all coral, shallow water varieties are the most porous.
4. Of black and gold coral, gold is the most valuable.
5. The state of Hawaii is more stricter about managing coral harvests than it used to be.
6. Bamboo coral is more expensive than black coral.
7. Of the two types, black coral is more plentiful.
8. Is gold coral more harder than ivory?
9. When considering safety and profits, divers' safety should be the greatest concern.
10. Pink coral has a more slower growth rate than black coral.

Part 3 Using Adverbs

An **adverb** is another kind of modifier. Adverbs help you to express yourself clearly and vividly. They tell *how, when, where,* or *to what extent* about something.

Adverbs are words that modify verbs, adjectives, and other adverbs.

Using Adverbs with Verbs

Adverbs frequently modify verbs. Adverbs tell *how, when, where,* or *to what extent* something happened.

Adverbs are used with verbs to tell *how:*

Dan *graciously* accepted the award.

The witness answered *completely*.

Adverbs also tell *when* about verbs:

That outdoor cafe opened *recently*.

The dance committee meets *today*.

Adverbs can tell *where* about verbs:

Our car is parked *nearby*.

We eat *here* in the cafeteria.

In addition, adverbs can tell *to what extent:*

Brian *almost* dropped the football.

Study the following list of adverbs.

How?	When?	Where?	To What Extent?
slowly	soon	there	often
happily	then	here	never
speedily	later	nearby	not
carefully	finally	above	seldom

Using Adverbs with Adjectives and Other Adverbs

Besides modifying verbs, adverbs also modify adjectives and other adverbs. Look at these sentences:

Some people are *extremely* nearsighted.
(*Extremely* tells to what extent. It is an adverb modifying the adjective *nearsighted.*)

The pastor spoke *very* softly.

(*Very* tells to what extent. It is an adverb modifying the adverb *softly*.)

Here are other adverbs that often modify adjectives or other adverbs:

too	quite	rather	most	more	extremely
just	nearly	so	really	truly	somewhat

These adverbs tell *to what extent* something is true.

Forming Adverbs

Many adverbs are formed by adding *-ly* to an adjective.

dim + -ly = dimly   perfect + -ly = perfectly
cautious + -ly = cautiously   rapid + -ly = rapidly

At times, the addition of *-ly* causes a spelling change in the adjective.

probable + -ly = probably
dainty + -ly = daintily
full + -ly = fully

Some adverbs are not formed from adjectives. *Quite, so, rather,* and *somewhat* are examples.

The post office had never been *so* crowded before.

John is *quite* capable of this work.

Some words can be either adverbs or adjectives. *Late* and *high* are examples of such words.

The warning came too *late*.
(*Late* is an adverb, modifying the verb *came*.)

Chris watched the *late* movie on TV.
(*Late* is an adjective, modifying the noun *movie*.)

The kite flew *high* above the park.
(*High* is an adverb, modifying the verb *flew*.)

Shoppers hate these *high* prices.
(*High* is an adjective, modifying the noun *prices*.)

Diagraming Adverbs

Adverbs are diagramed like adjectives. An adverb is placed on a slanted line attached to the word it modifies. This diagram shows an adverb modifying a verb:

The paramedics worked quickly.

Adverbs that modify adjectives or other adverbs are diagramed like this:

Too few people eat really well.

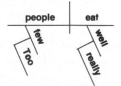

Exercise A   Write the adverbs in these sentences. Then write the word each modifies.

Example: A new movie opened here today.
       today modifies *opened* (tells *when*)
      here modifies *opened* (tells *where*)

1. The wind blew fiercely.
2. Bernadette cautiously stepped back from the door.

3. Helen left yesterday for San Francisco.
4. The dog slept peacefully in the sun.
5. Gloria finally answered the phone.
6. The clerk was quite patient with me.
7. We often take the bus home.
8. Mr. Edwards spoke too quickly.
9. Ink is much neater.
10. The audience was unusually quiet.

Exercise B Follow the directions for Exercise A.

1. We recently went to the ocean.
2. The water seemed very rough.
3. The pool looked especially inviting.
4. The tide was exceptionally high.
5. Swimmers found the water too cold.
6. Pelicans swooped down gracefully.
7. Bathers very often find unusual shells.
8. Sandpipers still hop quickly along the shore.
9. Vendors usually charge very high prices for suntan oil.
10. Tourists frequently come here for vacations.

Exercise C Change the following adjectives into adverbs by adding -ly. Check your spelling in a dictionary.

fearless	stiff	partial	neat	steady
near	painful	lazy	usual	obvious
happy	recent	extreme	formal	nervous

Part 4   Adverbs in Comparisons

You can use adverbs to compare actions. For example, you might say, "This team wins often, but that team wins *more often*." Or you might say, "Of all the players, Erica practices *hardest*." Such comparisons help you to convey ideas clearly. Like adjectives, adverbs have special forms for making comparisons.

The Comparative

The **comparative** form of an adverb compares one action with another. Look at this example:

> Your team plays *rougher* than ours.

The comparative is made in two ways:

1. Add *-er* to short adverbs like *hard* and *fast*.

    Kevin works *harder* than his cousin.

2. Use *more* with most adverbs ending in *-ly*.

    Some people write *more neatly* than others.

The Superlative

The **superlative** form of an adverb compares one action with two or more others. Notice these examples:

> The night security guard works *latest* of all.
> Of all the witnesses, Mr. Lee answered the questions *most completely*.

To form the superlative, either add *-est* or use *most*. If an adverb adds *-er* for the comparative, it adds *-est* for the superlative. If an adverb uses *more* for the comparative, it uses *most* for the superlative.

Adverb	Comparative	Superlative
long	longer	longest
quickly	more quickly	most quickly

Remember these points about adverbs in comparisons:

1. To compare two actions, use the comparative. To compare more than two actions, use the superlative.

> Driving will take *longer* than flying.
> Biking will take *longest* of all.

2. Use the word *other* when you compare an action with every other action of the same kind.

Incorrect: Mr. Russell tips more generously than any customer.

Correct: Mr. Russell tips more generously than any *other* customer.

3. Do not use -*er* with *more*, or -*est* with *most*.

Incorrect: Some athletes try more harder than others.

Correct: Some athletes try *harder* than others.

Irregular Comparisons

Some adverbs change completely in the comparative and superlative forms. These are examples:

Adverb	Comparative	Superlative
well	better	best
much	more	most
far	farther	farthest

This car goes *far* on a gallon of gas.
That car goes *farther*.
A motorcycle goes *farthest* of all.

Exercise A Write the comparative and superlative forms.

1. calmly
2. steadily
3. fast
4. rapidly
5. late
5. neatly
7. often
8. accurately

Exercise B If a sentence is correct, write *Correct*. If there is an error in the comparison of adverbs, write the sentence correctly.

1. The students exited quicklier during the fire drill.
2. Televised games take more long.
3. Most people sleep better at night.

4. Carpenters worked more steadily last year.
5. We shop here oftenest of all.
6. Of all the cars, this one runs more smoothly.
7. Cheetahs run fastest than gazelles.
8. Ms. Bell dresses more formally than the students.
9. Barbecued chicken tastes bestest of all.
10. Of all the dance students, Tanya practices more often.

Part 5   Adjective or Adverb?

Read these sentences. Which one sounds right to you?

> Sirens screamed *noisy*.
> Sirens screamed *noisily*.

If you said the second sentence, you are correct. An adverb (*noisily*), not an adjective (*noisy*), is needed to modify the verb *screamed*.

Sometimes you may have trouble deciding whether to use an adjective or an adverb. To decide, ask yourself:

1. What kind of words does the modifier tell about? If your answer is an action verb, adjective, or adverb, use the adverb. If your answer is a noun or pronoun, use the adjective.

2. What does the modifier tell about the word it goes with? If it tells *how, when, where,* or *to what extent*, use the adverb. If it tells *which one, what kind,* or *how many*, use the adjective.

An adjective tells	An adverb tells
Which one	How
What kind	When
How many	Where
	To what extent
About a noun or pronoun	About a verb, adjective, or adverb

Exercise A List each adjective and adverb, together with the word it modifies. Do not list articles.

1. The four hawks circled overhead.
2. The black ants slowly carried the crumbs away.
3. Copy those numbers very carefully.
4. Lions attack their prey ferociously.
5. Too few movies are comedies.
6. Two great comedians were Jack Benny and Buster Keaton.
7. The golfer hit precisely onto the green.
8. Several birds had somewhat similar markings.
9. That typewriter requires an expensive ribbon.
10. The program moved rather slowly.

Exercise B Choose the correct modifier from the two in parentheses. Tell whether it is an adjective or an adverb.

1. Francie added the figures (accurate, accurately).
2. Dad looked (furious, furiously) at the dented fender.
3. It was (terrible, terribly) dark inside the cave.
4. The dirt bikes raced (quick, quickly) over the hill.
5. Lucy walked (slow, slowly) through the art gallery.
6. These hamburgers taste (terrible, terribly) greasy.
7. The lawyer seemed (confident, confidently) in the courtroom.
8. Kent was (awful, awfully) confused about the computer.
9. (Heavy, Heavily) rains damaged the crops.
10. Nights in the desert are (extreme, extremely) cold.

Adverb or Predicate Adjective?

You have learned that a predicate adjective follows a linking verb and modifies the subject. Besides forms of *be*, other linking verbs are *become, seem, appear, look, sound, feel, taste, smell,* and *grow*.

Mr. Andrews looks angry. (*Angry* modifes *Mr. Andrews.*)

The paint feels tacky. (*Tacky* modifies *paint.*)

The tea tastes bitter. (*Bitter* modifies *tea.*)

The verbs *looks, feels,* and *tastes* can also be action verbs. So can *sound, appear, smells,* and *grew.* When these verbs are action verbs, they are followed by adverbs instead of predicate adjectives. Adverbs tell *how, when, where,* or *to what extent* about the action verbs.

Here are sentences using the same words as linking verbs and as action verbs.

Linking Verbs with Adjectives	Action Verbs with Adverbs
The sky *looked* clear.	Carol *looked* carefully.
The pilot *appeared* calm.	A train *appeared* suddenly.
The soup *smells* delicious.	A retriever *smells* keenly.
The traffic *sounds* hectic.	The chime *sounds* often.

If you can't decide whether to use an adverb or an adjective in a certain sentence, ask these questions:

1. Can you substitute *is* or *was* for the verb? If so, the modifier is probably an adjective.

2. Does the modifier tell *how, when, where,* or *to what extent*? If so, the modifier is probably an adverb.

Exercise Choose the right modifier for the following sentences.

1. The speaker (nervous, nervously) approached the stage.
2. The huge diamond looked (flawless, flawlessly).
3. The robbery suspect appeared (calm, calmly).
4. Detective Burke looked (careful, carefully) for clues.
5. During the show the children grew (quiet, quietly).

6. Mandy did her chores (quick, quickly).
7. That man looks (suspicious, suspiciously).
8. Aunt Jane looked (sad, sadly) at the broken vase.
9. Sandpaper feels (rough, roughly) to the touch.
10. The soldiers retreated (slow, slowly) into the jungle.

Part 6 Troublesome Modifiers

Certain modifiers are frequently used incorrectly.

Them and Those

Those can be used as an adjective.

Who has the combinations for *those* locks?

Them is never an adjective. It cannot substitute for *those*.

Incorrect: We took them snapshots.
Correct: We took *those* snapshots.
Correct: We took *them*.

Here and There

Sometimes people incorrectly say "this here jacket" or "that there room." "This here" and "that there" repeat ideas. The word *this* includes the idea of *here*. The word *that* includes the idea of *there*. Avoid "this here" and "that there."

Kind and Sort

Kind and *sort* are singular. *Kinds* and *sorts* are plural. No matter what words follow, use *this* or *that* with *kind* and *sort*. Use *these* and *those* with *kinds* and *sorts*.

This *kind* of ink is erasable. (singular)
Those sorts of colas contain caffeine. (plural)

Good and Well

Good and *well* have similar meanings, but the words are not the same. You cannot always substitute one word for the other. Look at the differences in these sentences:

That is a *good* car for you. (The adjective *good* modifies the noun *car.*)

You dance *well.* (The adverb *well* modifies the verb *dance.*)

Good is always an adjective modifying nouns and pronouns. It is never used to describe an action.

Well can be either an adjective or an adverb. In the sentence above, *well* is used as an adverb modifying an action verb. *Well* can also be used after a linking verb to mean "in good health."

Brad doesn't look *well.*
(*Well* is a predicate adjective modifying *Brad.*)

Stacy sings *well.*
(*Well* is an adverb modifying the action verb *sings.*)

If you are describing an action, use *well.*

The Double Negative

The use of two negative words when only one is necessary is called a **double negative**. Avoid using double negatives.

Incorrect: I didn't take no breaks.

Correct: I did*n't* take *any* breaks.

Incorrect: The twins never want no advice.

Correct: The twins *never* want *any* advice.

Incorrect: Richard couldn't do nothing all day.

Correct: Richard could*n't* do *anything* all day.

Contractions like *couldn't* contain a shortened form of the negative *not.* Do not use other negative words after them.

Some common negative words are *no, none, not, nothing,* and *never.* Instead of these words, use *any, anything,* or *ever* after negative contractions.

> Jim Thompson has*n't ever* lost an election.
> Jeff could*n't* understand *any* French.
> The storm did*n't* damage *anything.*

Other negative words are *hardly* and *barely.* Don't use them with negative contractions like *hasn't* and *didn't.*

> Incorrect: Anne couldn't barely speak.
> Correct: Anne *could barely* speak.

> Incorrect: The speaker hadn't scarcely begun.
> Correct: The speaker *had scarcely* begun.

> Incorrect: The police hardly never patrol the park.
> Correct: The police *hardly ever* patrol the park.

Exercise A Choose the correct word from the two in parentheses.

1. Have (them, those) apples been washed?
2. I prefer (this, these) kind of lotion.
3. How do you cook (them, those) crabs?
4. (That, That there) letter is for Peggy.
5. Evan collects (this, these) kinds of shells.
6. Which store sells (them, those) orange golf balls?
7. Mike drew (that, that there) picture.
8. (This, These) sorts of plants are hardy.
9. The critics raved about (this, this here) movie.
10. Is (this, these) sort of camera easy to use?

Exercise B Follow the directions for Exercise A.

1. The cook at camp feeds us (good, well).
2. This magazine prints many (good, well) short stories.
3. Mr. Nabor ran very (good, well) in the marathon.

4. Most athletes stay in (good, well) health.
5. Tom gave a (good, well) performance at the piano recital.
6. This taco salad tastes (good, well).
7. The horse took the jumps (good, well).
8. Have you read any (good, well) books lately?
9. Bess and I work (good, well) together.
10. Does Joe write (good, well) enough to enter the essay contest?

Exercise C Number your paper from 1 to 10. Correct the double negatives in the following sentences. If a sentence does not contain a double negative, write *Correct*.

1. Our team hasn't played no games lately.
2. Haven't you never been to Chinatown?
3. Dan couldn't barely read the tiny print.
4. The trapped miners could hardly breathe.
5. Matt didn't want nothing on his hamburger.
6. These fries don't have no salt on them.
7. Janet hardly keeps nothing in her purse.
8. Because of the blizzard, we haven't scarcely gone out of the house.
9. Nancy hasn't given any time to her studies lately.
10. Bob doesn't have hardly any camping equipment.

ADDITIONAL EXERCISES

Using Modifiers

A. Adjectives Write the adjectives you find in each sentence. Then write the word each modifies. Do not include *a, an,* or *the*.

1. This film was made on a low budget.
2. Does anyone know the true story?
3. That Italian sports car has a deluxe interior.
4. Dense, black smoke poured out of the tailpipe.
5. One candidate received a special award.
6. Two mysterious strangers appeared at the meeting.
7. No newspaper can print every bit of news.
8. Everyone likes these new wider sidewalks.
9. Some Indian food is cooked in a clay oven.
10. Reggae music is from the tropical island of Jamaica.

B. Predicate Adjectives Write the predicate adjective in each sentence. After each adjective, write the word it modifies.

1. Rebecca seems unusually quiet.
2. That dead tree is hollow.
3. The track team is strong this year.
4. The California sun is intense.
5. That African nation has just become independent.
6. The heat in a sauna is dry.
7. Most puppies are clumsy.
8. Baseball fans can be very rude.
9. The brass doorknob felt sticky.
10. The night buses are almost empty.

C. Adjectives in Comparisons Choose the correct adjective.

1. Have you ever tasted (more spicier, spicier) chili?
2. Who was the (younger, youngest) of all the Presidents?

3. This year the business was (more profitable, most profitable) than last year.
4. Jennifer looks (happier, happiest) than her friend.
5. Of all the paperbacks, this one is the (more enjoyable, most enjoyable).
6. Nardi is the (better, best) of the two trainers.
7. That was the (worse, worst) mistake you ever made.
8. Mr. Katoka had the (most, mostest) customers.
9. Which is the (lesser, least) of the two evils?
10. The top shelf is (dustier, more dustier) than the bottom shelf.

D. Adverbs and Words They Modify Number your paper from 1 to 10. Write the adverbs in the following sentences. After each adverb, write the word it modifies.

1. Cindy Nicholas swam the English Channel twice.
2. My grandparents arrived yesterday.
3. A trapdoor slowly opened.
4. Two helicopters hovered overhead.
5. Carrie is too busy.
6. The union members very reluctantly signed a contract.
7. The skaters practice here quite frequently.
8. Furious, Seth stomped out.
9. Congress is seriously considering other budget cuts.
10. That painter usually throws paint wildly at the canvas.

E. Adverbs in Comparisons Choose the correct adverb.

1. The hurricane hit (hardest, most hard) in the tropics.
2. Randy can repair appliances (more skillfully, most skillfully) than his brother.
3. Amanda parked (closer, closest) to the curb than I did.
4. Washington played (badder, worse, worst) than usual.
5. The flood waters receded (quicklier, more quickly) than expected.

6. The brakes work (gooder, better, more well) now.
7. Cynthia dances (better, more better) barefoot.
8. Blue-collar workers were hurt (most hardest, hardest).
9. Nina answered the (more, most) thoughtfully of all four candidates.
10. Ty stood (farther, farthest) from the basket than Bo did.

F. Adjectives and Adverbs   Choose the correct modifier.

1. The veterans talked (honest, honestly) about their problems.
2. The ice-cold watermelon tasted (sweet, sweetly).
3. Nicole looked (eager, eagerly) at the swimming pool.
4. The lizard's tiny ribs moved (rapid, rapidly) in and out.
5. He had (careless, carelessly) set the tea on the floor.
6. One player felt (real, really) bad about being traded.
7. Vicky felt (sad, sadly) about the loss.
8. The outcome is by no means (certain, certainly).
9. The clean mirrors looked (bright, brightly).
10. You are (certain, certainly) punctual today.

G. Special Problems with Modifiers   If there is an error, write the sentence correctly. If it is correct, write *Correct*.

1. The health department inspects restaurants good.
2. These kinds of motor bikes use hardly no gasoline.
3. The security guard didn't see nobody on her rounds.
4. Sherry brought two bags of laundry and left them here.
5. He hadn't ever seen them insects before.
6. "Magic" Johnson didn't hardly touch the basketball.
7. That there hockey stick was autographed by Phil Esposito.
8. These sort of shirts don't look good with jeans.
9. This bread isn't no more nutritious than that.
10. The engine runs well, and the body shows hardly any rust.

MIXED REVIEW

Using Modifiers

A. Finding adjectives and adverbs   Copy the following sentences. Underline each adjective once and each adverb twice. Then draw an arrow from each modifier to the word it modifies. Do not include articles.

1. The American audience barely understood the Japanese movie.
2. That breakfast was too hearty for me.
3. Those small, simple cars can actually be very expensive.
4. Four new students enrolled today.
5. Many old songs are still popular.
6. The hockey fans were certainly angry about the unfair penalty.
7. Natalie is too patient sometimes.
8. The rough, bumpy oysters most often produce the pearls.
9. The bland rice went well with the spicy chili.
10. The tall woman in the blue dress made the Olympic team.

B. Using modifiers correctly   All of these sentences contain errors in the use of modifiers. Rewrite each sentence correctly.

1. China has a more bigger population than India.
2. The singer sounded even worser than the band.
3. A dog will usually wander more farther from home than a cat.
4. Nathan is the obedientest child on our block.
5. Is a piranha viciouser than a shark?

6. The first chapter is easier than any part of the math textbook.
7. Sheila performed the bestest of the four gymnasts.
8. The paramedics arrived more faster than the firefighters.
9. Chad smiles oftener than Trisha.
10. Of the two boxers, Liston fought roughest.

C. Choosing the correct modifier Write the correct word from the two in parentheses.

1. Becky felt (nervous, nervously) about the interview.
2. Ellis looked (nervous, nervously) over his shoulder.
3. (That, That there) mirror makes me look thinner.
4. Night falls (sudden, suddenly) in Africa.
5. Those (kind, kinds) of comments are not helpful.
6. For a beginner, Gus works (good, well).
7. Are you (real, really) certain about your plans?
8. I don't want (no, any) lettuce on my sandwich.
9. (Them, Those) valves are clogged again.
10. The bran muffins tasted very (good, well).

USING GRAMMAR IN WRITING
Using Modifiers

A. You are in charge of publicity for a fund-raising event. All the members of a club contributed items for a yard sale. Following are some of the items.

camera	radio	books
desk	table	tray
pen	game	pitcher

The local paper will give your group a free classified ad, but you may use no more than twenty-five words to describe all of the items. Write the classified ad, describing the items as well as you can within the limit of twenty-five words.

A local radio station has agreed to describe the items to listeners. The people at the station will let you write as much about each item as you wish. Expand the descriptions that you wrote for the classified ad. Use vivid modifiers to help the listeners picture each item.

B. Think of two rides that give a person very different feelings. Write a paragraph about each ride. Use many strong modifiers to make the contrast clear. Use details from your experience, or use your imagination to invent details. You might contrast a merry-go-round and a roller coaster, a rowboat and a sailboard, or a hot-air-balloon ride and a ski lift.

C. Writers of science fiction and fantasy create settings, objects, plants, and creatures that no one has ever seen. To bring their creations to life for a reader, they must describe them especially vividly. They must paint a word picture for the reader. Imagine a setting, plant, or creature for a fantasy that you might write. Describe your imaginary thing vividly enough so that a reader can picture it. Underline each modifier.

Using Prepositions and Conjunctions

The purpose of language is to express ideas. With nouns and verbs you can express simple ideas:

> Robert walked.
> The bird eats oranges.

When you add adjectives and adverbs, the sentences become more specific.

> Robert walked briskly.
> The pesky mynah bird eats oranges.

When you want to express relationships, you use words that connect other words. One type of connecting word is a preposition. This sentence shows where Robert walked by using a prepositional phrase.

> Robert walked briskly through the deserted streets.

Another type of connecting word is a conjunction. By using a conjunction, this sentence shows other things the bird eats.

The pesky mynah bird eats oranges and apples.

Prepositions and **conjunctions** are parts of speech. In this section you will learn to identify these parts of speech and to use them properly.

Part 1 What Are Prepositions?

Words that join other words or word groups are called **connectives**. One important kind of connective is the **preposition**. Prepositions show relationships. Look at the relationships expressed in the following sentences:

Mary walked *up* the stairs.
Mary walked *down* the stairs.
Mary walked *around* the stairs.

The prepositions *up, down,* and *around* show the relationship between the noun *stairs* and the verb *walked.* In each of the above sentences, *stairs* is the **object of the preposition.** Like all prepositions, *up, down,* and *around* connect their objects to another part of the sentence.

Prepositions do not show relationships all by themselves. They begin a *phrase,* a group of words that does not have a subject or verb. The **prepositional phrase** makes the relationship clear. In the above sentences, *up the stairs, down the stairs,* and *around the stairs* are prepositional phrases. Here are some other sentences with prepositional phrases:

The poster glowed *in the dark.*
During the summer, Ned went *to camp.*
The stack *of napkins* blew *off the table.*

A preposition is a word used with a noun or pronoun, called its *object,* **to show the relationship between the noun or pronoun and some other word in the sentence.**

A prepositional phrase consists of a preposition, its object, and any modifiers of the object.

The list below shows words often used as prepositions. Many of them, like *above*, *over*, *in*, and *beside*, show location. Others, like *until*, *after*, and *before*, show time. Still others show other kinds of relationships. Look at these prepositions and see if you can tell the relationship each one suggests.

Words Often Used as Prepositions

about	behind	during	off	to
above	below	except	on	toward
across	beneath	for	onto	under
after	beside	from	out	until
against	between	in	outside	up
along	beyond	inside	over	upon
among	but (*except*)	into	past	with
around	by	like	since	within
at	concerning	near	through	without
before	down	of	throughout	

Exercise A Number your paper from 1 to 10. Find the prepositional phrases in the following sentences.

> Example: Sean leaves for school at seven o'clock.
> for school, at seven o'clock

1. The train raced through the tunnel.
2. No one worked during the strike.
3. Brian walked toward the ballpark after school.
4. Linda tripped clumsily over the rug.
5. Ask Dad for the keys to the boat.
6. The doorman stands inside the lobby during winter.
7. Have you looked for your umbrella in the closet?

8. The signature on the check is a forgery.
9. David drove past the driveway.
10. Without a doubt, this is the best restaurant in town.

Exercise B Follow the directions for Exercise A.

1. The safe is behind the painting on this wall.
2. A flock of geese landed beyond the ridge.
3. An assortment of wildflowers grew in the meadow.
4. You sound like Helen on the phone.
5. A horseshoe was nailed over the door.
6. We parked in the lot near the bank.
7. Without a doubt, Natalie will arrive before us.
8. Cassie has not been in town since last month.
9. Throughout the day, newscasters broke into the regular programs with special bulletins.
10. June sat on a bench against the wall.

Preposition or Adverb?

Many words used as prepositions can also be used as adverbs. How can you tell the difference?

A preposition is never used alone. It is always followed by a noun or pronoun as part of a phrase. If the word is in a phrase, it is probably a preposition. If the word has no object, it is probably an adverb.

> The commuters walked *across* the bridge. (preposition)
> The commuters walked *across*. (adverb)
> Jim went *inside* the garage. (preposition)
> Jim went *inside*. (adverb)

Exercise A Decide whether the italicized words in these sentences are adverbs or prepositions. Write *Adverb* or *Preposition* for each sentence.

1. Please turn *off* the stereo.

2. The shoe box fell *off* the shelf.
3. Turn the lights *on*.
4. The trophies were *on* the mantle.
5. Fred sang *along*.
6. Jean planted flowers *along* the fence.
7. The laundry fell *down* the chute.
8. The power lines blew *down*.
9. Mr. Drew dropped the letters *into* the mailbox.
10. The ballerina spun *around* dizzily.

Exercise B Follow the directions for Exercise A.

1. Mario Andretti put his helmet *on*.
2. You'll find the map *in* the glove compartment.
3. *Without* a sound, the mouse scurried across the room.
4. Dick got *on* the wrong bus.
5. Is Jason going to tag *along* again?
6. Katherine walked *along* the shore.
7. Mom put some carrots *into* the stew.
8. The jeep drove *through* the snowdrift.
9. I tried to drive *through*, but I got stuck.
10. Has Lauren been *around* lately?

Part 2 Prepositional Phrases as Modifiers

Single words are often used as modifiers. However, groups of words can also be modifiers. Prepositional phrases can modify different parts of a sentence. They work in the same way that single adjectives or adverbs do.

An adjective phrase is a prepositional phrase that modifies a noun or pronoun. The phrase always includes the preposition, its object, and any modifiers of the object.

John has a car *with a sun roof.*
(*With a sun roof* is an adjective phrase, modifying the noun
car. It tells *what kind* of car.)

The key *on the hook* unlocks the garage.
(*On the hook* is an adjective phrase, modifying the noun *key.*
It tells *which one.*)

Some *of the runners* are doing warm-up exercises.
(*Of the runners* is an adjective phrase that modifies the
pronoun *some.* It tells *what kind.*)

As you can see, adjective phrases, like adjectives, tell *which
one* or *what kind.*

Adverbs tell *how, when, where,* and *to what extent* about
verbs. Adverb phrases modify verbs in the same way.

Adverb phrases are prepositional phrases that modify verbs.

The coupons are sent *by mail.*
(*By mail* is an adverb phrase telling *how.* It modifies the verb
are sent.)

The play will start *at eight o'clock.*
(*At eight o'clock* is an adverb phrase. It tells *when* about the
verb *will start.*)

The dog snoozed *by the fireplace.*
(*By the fireplace* is an adverb phrase. It tells *where* about the
verb *snoozed.*)

Sometimes one prepositional phrase follows another. Frequently, the second phrase is an adjective phrase modifying the
object in the first phrase.

Paula went *to the market on Fifth Street.*
(*To the market* is an adverb phrase modifying the verb *went.*
On Fifth Street is an adjective phrase modifying the noun
market.)

Hansel marked the trail *with crumbs of bread.*
(The adverb phrase *with crumbs* tells *how* about the verb
marked. Of bread is an adjective phrase describing the
noun *crumbs.*)

532

Diagraming Prepositional Phrases

To diagram a prepositional phrase, place it under the word it modifies.

The students at the rally cheered for their team.

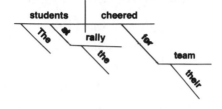

At times a preposition may have two or more nouns or pronouns as objects in the prepositional phrase.

On Saturday Marla shopped for shoes and a purse.

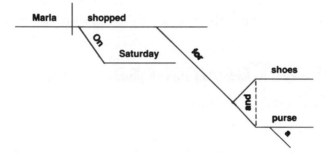

Exercise A Copy these sentences. Circle each prepositional phrase. Draw an arrow from the phrase to the word it modifies. Tell whether the phrase is an adjective phrase or an adverb phrase.

1. Jerry has a Ford with a stick shift.
2. Carol searched through the stack of photographs.
3. Do you study on weekends?
4. The two schools have been rivals for dozens of years.
5. Orange juice is a good source of vitamin C.
6. We waved to the driver of the truck.
7. The pool is closed after 9:00 P.M.

8. Did you lock your keys in the car?
9. We played tennis during the day and danced at night.
10. With a little luck, one of the Jets recovered the football.

Exercise B   Follow the directions for Exercise A.

1. Connie is studying in the library.
2. The cafe in the park sells pink lemonade.
3. A neon sign flashed over the door.
4. The truck parked near the garage in the alley.
5. Nobody except Angie wants the notes for that lecture.
6. The car behind the shop belongs to Darrell.
7. We sailed past the canal and into the open sea.
8. The trainer put a muzzle on the dog in the pen.
9. The woman with the tennis racket is my mom.
10. Betsy returned the books on the table to the library.

Part 3   Conjunctions

A conjunction is another kind of word that shows relationships.

A conjunction is a word that connects words or groups of words.

Look at the conjunctions in the following sentences:

Doug *and* Tom will trim the hedges.
The weather reporter predicted *either* rain *or* snow.
JoAnne designed *and* made the costumes.
That jacket is warm *but* stylish.
Tickets are on sale *both* at the office *and* in the lounge.

Like prepositions, conjunctions show a relationship between the words they connect. Conjunctions differ from prepositions, however, in two ways. Conjunctions link similar kinds of words, like two nouns or two phrases. Also, conjunctions do not have objects.

Coordinating Conjunctions

Coordinating conjunctions are used to join single words or groups of words of the same kind. *And, but,* and *or* are the most common coordinating conjunctions.

The words joined by coordinating conjunctions are compound constructions. Compound constructions include compound subjects, compound direct objects, and compound verbs, for example.

> Students *and* teachers share the same cafeteria.
> (*And* links *students* and *teachers*, making them a compound subject of the verb *share*.)
> The children ran *and* jumped.
> (*And* connects *ran*, and *jumped*, forming a compound verb.)
> Ann wanted that dress *but* couldn't afford it.
> (*But* connects the two predicates.)
> The iced tea looked cool *and* refreshing.
> (*And* connects two predicate adjectives.)
> The thieves worked quickly *and* quietly.
> (*And* connects two adverbs.)
> Bob ordered mushrooms, onions, *and* sausage on his pizza.
> (*And* connects the three parts of the compound direct object.)
> Give Marcy *or* Joe your dues.
> (*Or* connects the compound indirect object.)
> Kirsten can babysit on Friday *or* Saturday.
> (*Or* connects the compound object of a preposition.)

Correlative Conjunctions

Some conjunctions are used in pairs. They are called **correlative conjunctions**. These are correlative conjunctions:

both . . . and	not only . . . but (also)
either . . . or	whether . . . or
neither . . . nor	

Both Don *and* Sam are on the team.

You may have *either* a sandwich *or* a bowl of soup.

Neither ducklings *nor* baby chicks make good pets.

Dad is grilling *not only* hamburgers, *but also* bratwurst.

The class voted on *whether* Chuck *or* Kim should be the
president.

Exercise A Find the conjunctions in the following sentences. Tell
what words or word groups are connected by the conjunction. Give
the part of speech of the connected words.

> Example: The 747 banked and turned.
> The verbs *banked* and *turned* are connected by
> the conjunction *and.*

1. Either Chuck or Marge will introduce us.
2. Mr. Morton spoke to the children softly but firmly.
3. The locker room was hot and humid.
4. Sean fell and broke his arm.
5. Should I wear a sweater or a coat?
6. Kangaroos and koala bears are natives of Australia.
7. Gene spends his money on movies and records.
8. Ann not only designs but also builds furniture.
9. Mr. Anderson enjoys both classical music and jazz.
10. The stowaway on the ship had neither a ticket nor the
    money for one.

Exercise B Write the kind of compound construction in each
sentence. Write the construction with its conjunction.

1. The farmer plowed and fertilized the field.
2. The detective knew the identity of the thief but
   couldn't prove it.
3. Zucchini and tomatoes grow in the garden.
4. The pendulum swung back and forth.
5. The letters from the attic were old, brittle, and dusty.
6. Take either a taxi or a limousine to the airport.

7. Gary cleaned not only the basement but also the attic.
8. Is Marilyn disappointed or relieved?
9. Both the walls and the cabinets in the kitchen need painting.
10. Passengers bought snacks, magazines, and newspapers on the train.

Exercise C: Writing Write two sentences using *and*, two sentences using *but*, and two sentences using *or*. After each sentence, write the words or groups of words that are joined by the conjunctions.

Exercise D: Writing Write one sentence for each of the following pairs of correlative conjunctions:

both . . . and   either . . . or   neither . . .nor

ADDITIONAL EXERCISES

Using Prepositions and Conjunctions

A. Prepositions and Their Objects Number your paper from 1 to 10. Write the prepositions in the following sentences. Also, write the object of each preposition.

1. Both Sonny Rollins and Miles Davis have played at that club.
2. Mary searched for the envelope with the address on it.
3. I enjoy games like Monopoly.
4. Jane woke at dawn to the sound of birds outside her window.
5. The cables ran along the roof.
6. Since yesterday I have changed my mind about my plans.
7. The plane passed through the cluster of clouds.
8. Have you looked under the chair for your shoes?
9. Electric cars might be the autos of the future.
10. Julie left her bike by the tree near the corner.

B. Adverbs and Prepositions Decide whether the italicized words in these sentences are adverbs or prepositions. Write *Adverb* or *Preposition* for each sentence.

1. The papers blew *off* the table.
2. Eddie ran *toward* the airplane terminal.
3. A scar ran *down* his cheek.
4. Stand *by*, please.
5. There is a pay phone *by* the subway entrance.
6. The news is *out*.
7. Marilyn grabbed the vine and swung *across* the creek.
8. Has the search party given *up*?
9. The patient looked *around* the room.
10. The trial is not *over* yet.

C. Prepositional Phrases as Modifiers Copy these sentences. Circle each prepositional phrase. Draw an arrow from the phrase to the word it modifies. Label each phrase *Adjective* or *Adverb* to tell how it is used.

1. Pat threw the line into the river.
2. Are Volkswagens made in the United States now?
3. A movie about a baseball player is playing here.
4. Bert hung his hat carefully on the hook.
5. These gloves are lined with fur.
6. The woman with the briefcase is Dr. Sanchez.
7. A crowd of people swarmed the stage.
8. The young man in the green jacket is Jake Houston.
9. The ball landed in the bleachers.
10. Nobody but Rachel understood the question.

D. Conjunctions Find the conjunctions in the following sentences. Write the words connected by each conjunction.

1. The Pirates and the Steelers are Pittsburgh teams.
2. Father Hidalgo of Mexico was both a priest and a political leader.
3. Gilda Radner talked and joked with the audience.
4. The speaker's voice was quiet but firm.
5. Andrew was not only hungry but also thirsty.
6. Can you tell whether a computer or a person made the mistake?
7. Somebody called for you but left no message.
8. In gym class, we'll play either volleyball or softball.
9. Rugs, drapes, and furniture muffle the noises in a room.
10. Neither Kelley nor Rivera caught the grounder to left field.

MIXED REVIEW

Using Prepositions and Conjunctions

A. Recognizing prepositional phrases Copy these sentences. Circle the prepositional phrases. Draw arrows from each prepositional phrase to the word it modifies.

1. Angelo struggled against the dusty wind.
2. For two years Kyle lived in Florida.
3. Everybody at the party moved toward the table of food.
4. The actors in the movie were amateurs.
5. Don't stand under a tree during a storm.
6. Nobody except you could have hit that ball.
7. We drove past a pond with an alligator in it.
8. From the top of the mountain he could see the ocean.
9. I cannot speak for anyone but myself.
10. The coach kept Evans on the bench during the entire game.

B. Recognizing adverbs, prepositions, and conjunctions Write the italicized words in the following sentences. After each, write *Adverb, Preposition,* or *Conjunction* to show how it is used in the sentence.

1. The package was delivered *by* UPS.
2. Jonathan stood *by*.
3. Are you shivering *or* trembling?
4. Everybody *but* Emily went on the field trip.
5. The road curved *but* then suddenly straightened.
6. Talk the situation *over* with Brenda.
7. Melissa put a sheet *over* the chair.
8. *Either* Atlanta *or* Miami is their destination.
9. *Outside* the house, the air felt warmer.
10. *Both* Samuel *and* Nancy answered at the same time.

USING GRAMMAR IN WRITING
Using Prepositions and Conjunctions

A. Imagine that you are attending an air show as a reporter for a news magazine. The show will feature acrobatic stunt planes, sky diving, the newest ultralight aircraft, and balloon flights. Write a paragraph describing some of the things that you see. Use prepositional phrases in your paragraph to tell where and when things happen. Underline the prepositional phrases and circle the prepositions. You may want to include the following phrases.

above the crowd	into the air	with the wind
into a small circle	on the ground	
under a brilliant yellow parachute		

B. The following notes are instructions for assembling a cookbook stand. You are to write the instructions from these notes and add some ideas of your own about how useful the cookbook stand is. Notice how choppy the notes are. Conjunctions can be used to connect related ideas and make a piece of writing flow more smoothly. Use each of the following conjunctions at least once: *and, or, but, either . . . or, both . . . and.*

Unpack the base. Unpack the rear support. Unpack the bookrest. Slide the bookrest into the slot in the middle of the base. Secure it with two screws. Do not tighten the screws fully. Slide the rear support into the slot at the back of the bookrest. Be sure that it meets the base on the center line. Secure the rear support with one screw through the bookrest. Also secure it with another screw through the base. Tighten all screws. The cookbook stand is now ready.

Review of Parts of Speech

Part 1 The Parts of Speech

You have studied seven **parts of speech** so far—nouns, pronouns, verbs, adjectives, adverbs, prepositions, and conjunctions. There is one more part of speech. It is called the **interjection**.

A word is labeled a particular part of speech depending on how it is used in a sentence. One word may be used as different parts of speech.

You will review all the parts of speech in this section.

What Is an Interjection?

An interjection is a word or group of words used to express strong feeling.

An interjection may be either a phrase or a word. In either case, the interjection shows strong feeling. These feelings might be joy, anger, terror, surprise, disgust, or sadness. Because it conveys strong emotions, an interjection is followed by an exclamation point.

Notice the interjections in the following sentences.

Wow! I like this.
Oh! What a scary mask!
Ugh! There's a dead mouse.

Now you have studied all eight parts of speech:

The Parts of Speech			
nouns	verbs	adverbs	conjunctions
pronouns	adjectives	prepositions	interjections

Exercise A   Write each italicized word. Next to it, write what part of speech it is.

1. The swimmer *grasped* the life preserver.
2. *Wonderful!* I'm glad you'll be there.
3. Did *anyone* find my locket?
4. Doris rode *around* the track.
5. Dan *or* Greg will introduce the speaker.
6. We *seldom* attend baseball games.
7. That parking lot is always *full.*
8. Susan gave me a *silly* grin.
9. Country-western *songs* tell stories.
10. The Supreme Court *reversed* the decision.

Exercise B   Follow the directions for Exercise A.

1. Swenson's serves a variety of soups *and* salads.

2. Jason hiked and *fished* in the Canadian Rockies.
3. Please be home *by* seven.
4. Shoppers swarmed through *Macy's.*
5. *Hurrah!* Superman saved the day!
6. Jennifer sat next to *him* in the assembly.
7. Millie danced the tango *clumsily.*
8. Many airlines serve *light* snacks as well as full meals.
9. Samuel Clemens' pen name *was* Mark Twain.
10. Collectors shop for *antiques* at farm sales.

Part 2 Using Words as Different Parts of Speech

Very often the same word can be used as different parts of speech. For example, a word might be a noun in one sentence and an adjective in another.

There is only one way to tell what part of speech any word is. You must see how that word is used in a sentence.

Here are some examples of one word used as two different parts of speech:

Mr. Hayakawa pruned the *plant.*
(*Plant* is used as a noun, the direct object of the verb *pruned.*)
Jessica bought a book on *plant* care.
(*Plant* is used as an adjective, modifying *care.*)
Time is the most valuable asset we have.
(*Time* is used as a noun, the subject of the sentence.)
Ms. Ricardo will *time* the test.
(*Time* is used as the main verb.)
Is the bookstore on the *lower* level?
(*Lower* is used as an adjective, modifying the noun *level.*)
The temperature fell *lower.*
(*Lower* is used as an adverb, modifying the verb *fell.*)
What is that noise?
(*What* is used as a pronoun, the subject of the sentence.)

What movies are playing in town?

    (*What* is used as an adjective, modifying the noun *movies*.)

Mr. and Mrs. Lewis went *out*.

    (*Out* is used as an adverb, modifying the verb *went*.)

The canary flew *out* the door.

    (*Out* is used as a preposition.)

Great! I love spaghetti!

    (*Great* is used as an interjection.)

Joy had a *great* idea.

    (*Great* is used as an adjective, modifying the noun *idea*.)

Exercise A   Write each italicized word. Next to it, write what part of speech it is in that sentence.

1. Wally visited the *wax* museum.
2. Crayons are made with *wax*.
3. Tim will *wax* the car today.
4. *Pass* the mustard, please.
5. The mountain *pass* was closed during the blizzard.
6. *Ouch!* The stove is still hot.
7. Those sandwiches were *really* good.
8. *That* is our new car.
9. Where did you buy *that* jacket?
10. There is a *fire* in the basement!

Exercise B   Follow the directions for Exercise A.

1. The electrician turned the power *off*.
2. The ping-pong ball bounced *off* the table.
3. That costume doesn't *fool* me.
4. He was a *fool* for endangering our safety.
5. Bring a *light* sweater.
6. Turn on the *light*, please.
7. *Light* the campfire first.
8. Put the silverware in *this* drawer.
9. *This* is my cousin Josh.
10. Martha *cut* the pie into six pieces.

ADDITIONAL EXERCISES

Review of Parts of Speech

The Parts of Speech Copy the italicized word in each sentence. Write what part of speech the word is in that sentence.

1. It rained every day *for* a week.
2. That man looks exactly *like* Louis Gossett, Jr.
3. Did the reporter quote *you* accurately?
4. *Ouch!* That really stings.
5. We planned a *visit* to the space center.
6. Jim talks too fast *and* too much.
7. Laura *dances* to any kind of music.
8. The police officer examined the skid *marks.*
9. *This* is Randy's birthday.
10. Do you feel better *now?*
11. *Americans* drink more than one-third of the world's coffee.
12. Ghana and Zaire are *African* countries.
13. The President tossed out the *game* ball.
14. Mr. Spence *signs* his papers with a flourish.
15. Ben *starches* his collars.
16. *That* shop specializes in repairs for motorcycles.
17. Pueblo Indian *architecture* is very energy-efficient.
18. The emergency room is *always* crowded.
19. Did *anyone* pour cool water on the burn?
20. Here winter begins *early* and ends late.
21. The *leaves* of ginkgo trees look like small fans.
22. The art class designed and *sold* calendars.
23. Robert takes his *youngest* sister to the day-care center every morning.
24. The California Angels *won* their first pennant in 1979.
25. *Phew!* We got here just in time.

MIXED REVIEW

Review of Parts of Speech

Recognizing the parts of speech   Copy the italicized words from these sentences. Write what part of speech each is used as.

1. *Well!* What can possibly happen next?
2. Frogs got into the farmer's *well*.
3. My pen isn't working *well*.
4. Ginny used a circular *saw* for that wood.
5. The hawk *saw* a field mouse in the weeds.
6. Without any *thought* of the long way back, the hiker continued.
7. He *thought* of a snappy comeback a little too late.
8. *This* is the entrance.
9. *This* entrance will take us to the shoe department.
10. *By* the way, Connie called you.
11. The weekend flew *by*.
12. Tom couldn't keep *up* with the other joggers.
13. An *American* tourist interpreted for me.
14. In many countries, an *American* is often the tallest person around.
15. Jackie *and* Tonya always have lunch together.
16. He walked *past* her house.
17. In the *past*, fresh fruits were available only in summer.
18. Twigs and leaves drifted *past*.
19. This *past* season was not the Lakers' best.
20. Elephants were hunted for their *ivory* tusks.
21. *Ivory* was quite valuable.
22. These *lines* are parallel.
23. The class *lines* up during fire drills.
24. The team plays *better* with an audience.
25. I am *better* now.

USING GRAMMAR IN WRITING
Review of Parts of Speech

A. You are on a hike with a small group of your friends. One of your friends has brought a dog along. The dog is especially frisky, and it enjoys running off into the woods to chase birds, chipmunks, and toads. Suddenly, the dog begins digging furiously at a spot just off the trail. All of you gather around the spot, and soon you see that the dog is uncovering a metal box. You lift the box out of the hole. It is locked. What happens next? Write about the events that follow the discovery. You may want to include some dialogue. Use all eight parts of speech. Label each one the first time you use it. Be sure to use strong verbs, vivid modifiers, and prepositional phrases to make your story lively.

B. Each word below can be used as at least two different parts of speech. Write two brief stories, each using all of the words. Use each word as a different part of speech in each story.

Example: light

The light of the candle threw strange shadows. (noun)
We ate a light breakfast. (adjective)
I'm using light blue yarn for the sweater. (adverb)
Wait here while I light the lamp. (verb)

1. shop
2. cut
3. park
4. present
5. reverse
6. turn

Using Verbals

In addition to the eight parts of speech, there are three other kinds of words. They are **gerunds, participles,** and **infinitives.** These three kinds of words are made from verbs. They are called **verbals.** Although verbals look like verbs, they are used as other parts of speech.

This section will explain how to identify verbals and how to use them.

Part 1 Gerunds

A gerund is a verb form that is used as a noun. A gerund ends in *-ing*. It may be used in any way that a noun is used.

Like a noun, a gerund may be used as a subject.

> *Swimming* is good exercise.
> (*Swimming* is a gerund, the subject of the verb *is*.)

Like a noun, a gerund may be used as a direct object.

> Ron enjoys *skating*.
> (*Skating* is a gerund, the object of the verb *enjoys*.)

Like a noun, a gerund may be used as an object of a preposition.

> Kate relaxes by *reading*.
> (*Reading* is a gerund, the object of the preposition *by*.)

The Gerund Phrase

A gerund is not always used alone. Often a gerund has a modifier or an object or both. Together, they form a **gerund phrase.** The entire gerund phrase is used as a noun.

Because a gerund is formed from a verb, it can have an object.

> Dirk earns extra money by *mowing lawns*.
> (*Mowing* is a gerund; *lawns* is the object of *mowing*. The phrase *mowing lawns* is the object of the preposition *by*.)

Because a gerund is formed from a verb, it can be modified by adverbs.

> The crew began *working again*.
> (*Working* is a gerund; *again* is an adverb modifying *working*. The phrase *working again* is the object of the verb *began*.)

Because a gerund is used as a noun, it can be modified by adjectives.

Careful planning was our main advantage.
(*Planning* is a gerund; *careful* is an adjective modifying *planning*. The phrase *careful planning* is the subject of the verb *was*.)

Gerunds can also be modified by prepositional phrases.

Standing in line is tiresome.
(*Standing* is a gerund; *in line* is a prepositional phrase modifying *standing*. The entire gerund phrase is the subject of *is*.)

In these examples you can see that gerunds are used as nouns, even though they look like verbs. *Swimming, skating, reading, mowing, working, planning,* and *standing* all look like verbs but are not used as verbs. Because they are used as nouns, they are gerunds. Modifiers and objects that are used with them form gerund phrases.

Diagraming Gerunds

A gerund or gerund phrase used as a subject or direct object is diagramed on a line above the main line. The gerund belongs on a line drawn as a step. Its modifiers are placed on slanted lines below it. Its object is shown on the horizontal line following the gerund.

Fixing old cars is Jay's hobby.

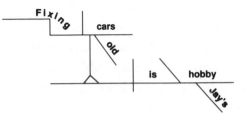

The project includes giving an oral report.

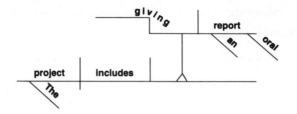

A gerund or gerund phrase used as the object of a preposition is diagramed below the main line. The preposition belongs on a slanted line going down from the word modified. Again, the gerund appears on a stepped line.

We were exhausted from cross-country skiing.

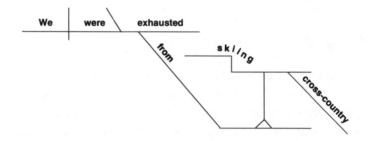

Exercise A Find the gerunds or gerund phrases in these sentences. As your teacher directs, show how each is used.

1. Jack started using gasohol in his car.
2. Working in the coal mines is dangerous.
3. Sewing costumes is Jean's job.
4. We were hoarse from cheering so much.
5. Shoplifting is a crime.
6. Use this container for watering the plants.
7. Everyone appreciates good cooking.
8. Following the suspect was difficult.

9. Playing chess requires concentration.

10. Outlining can be the key to a successful paper.

Exercise B Follow the directions for Exercise A.

1. Jan increased her speed by running daily.
2. Stamp collecting is Randy's hobby.
3. Will replacing the furnace be expensive?
4. Mountain climbing can be dangerous.
5. The children were filthy from playing in the mud.
6. Scaring away evil spirits is the witch doctor's job.
7. Matching that shade of green will be impossible.
8. The Scotts considered moving to Alaska.
9. An hour of swimming burns about five hundred calories.
10. David earns extra money by shoveling snow.

Part 2   Participles

A participle is a verb form that is used as an adjective.

You learned about the **past participle** as one of the principal parts of a verb. It is formed by adding *-d* or *-ed* to the present tense, as in *wave—waved* or *pass—passed*. The past participles of irregular verbs are formed differently and must be learned separately: *ring—rung, wear—worn.*

There is another kind of participle besides the past participle. It is called the **present participle.** The present participle is always formed by adding *-ing* to the present tense: *wave—waving, pass—passing, ring—ringing, wear—wearing.*

Here are more examples of participles:

Verb	Past Participle	Present Participle
pack	packed	packing
sing	sung	singing
try	tried	trying

As verbals, participles are always used as adjectives. A participle modifies either a noun or a pronoun.

> *Refreshed*, Mr. Jordan challenged me to another game of tennis.
> (*Refreshed* is a past participle modifying the noun *Mr. Jordan*.)
> *Running*, she arrived just in time.
> (*Running* is a present participle modifying the pronoun *she*.)
> The *sunken* treasure has never been found.
> (*Sunken* is a past participle modifying the noun *treasure*.)
> The *traveling* circus came to our town.
> (*Traveling* is a present participle modifying the noun *circus*.)

The Participial Phrase

A participle is not always used alone. Often a participle has a modifier or an object or both. Together, they form a **participial phrase.** The entire participial phrase is used as an adjective.

Because a participle is formed from a verb, it may have an object.

> The girl *selling tickets* is Ben's sister.
> (*Selling tickets* is a participial phrase modifying *girl*. *Tickets* is the object of the participle *selling*.)

Because a participle comes from a verb, it may be modified by adverbs.

> *Laughing hysterically*, Mary Jo tried to tell us the joke.
> (*Laughing hysterically* is a participial phrase modifying *Mary Jo. Hysterically* is an adverb modifying the participle *laughing*.)
> Children played in the water *spurting from the fire hydrant*.
> (*Spurting from the fire hydrant* is a participial phrase modifying *water. From the fire hydrant* is a prepositional phrase modifying the participle *spurting*.)

In all of these examples you can see that participles are used as adjectives, even though they look like verbs. *Refreshed, running, sunken, traveling, selling, laughing,* and *spurting* all look like verbs but are not used as verbs. Because they are used as adjectives, they are called participles. Modifiers and objects used with them form participial phrases.

Diagraming Participles

To diagram a participle, place it below the noun or pronoun it modifies. Place the participle on an angled line. Put modifiers of the participle on lines slanted down from it. An object follows the participle on the horizontal line.

Listening carefully, Meg took notes.

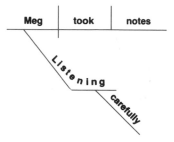

Exercise A Write the participles or participial phrases in these sentences. Show which word the participle or phrase modifies.

Example: Raising her eyebrows, Regina stared at the conductor.
Raising her eyebrows (participial phrase, modifying *Regina*)

1. Running water is a luxury in many countries.
2. Breathing hard, the jogger slowed his pace.
3. The bank returned the canceled checks.
4. Ken stirred the bubbling casserole.
5. Confused, Vinnie checked the instruction sheet.

6. Adam showed us the refinished furniture.
7. The woman playing the violin is a member of several orchestras.
8. The birds nesting in the garage are swallows.
9. Still proclaiming his innocence, the suspect was led to jail.
10. The house with the lilac bushes surrounding it is my grandmother's.

Exercise B   Follow the directions for Exercise A.

1. Twirling a baton, the majorette led the parade.
2. That is a fully grown German shepherd.
3. What is behind the locked door?
4. Turning the key in the lock, Nancy Drew quickly looked around.
5. Many retired senior citizens move to warmer climates.
6. Packages of dried fruit are sold at most grocery stores.
7. A broken mirror means seven years bad luck.
8. Walking fearlessly into the cage, the lion tamer cracked the whip.
9. Baying at the moon, the dog woke up half the neighborhood.
10. Cory, grinning from ear to ear, told us about her raise.

Gerund or Participle?

The two kinds of verbals you have studied, gerunds and participles, often look the same. Gerunds and present participles are both formed by adding -*ing* to the present tense of verbs. How can you avoid confusing them?

To tell whether a word is a gerund or a present participle, look at how it is used. If it is used as a modifier, it is a participle. If it is used as a noun, it is a gerund.

Read the following sentences.

Fishing in a mountain stream is Paul's idea of a vacation. (The gerund phrase *fishing in a mountain stream* is the subject of the verb *is*.)

Fishing in a mountain stream, Paul enjoyed his vacation. (The participial phrase *fishing in a mountain stream* modifies the noun *Paul*.)

Exercise For each sentence, write the gerund or participle and say which each is. Be prepared to explain your answer.

1. Swimming against the current, Dave was getting tired.
2. Swimming against the current is hard work.
3. Painting the house will improve its appearance.
4. Painting the house, Dan stood on the ladder.
5. Eating a taco, Sherry spilled the filling on her blouse.
6. Eating a taco can be messy.
7. Trimming the bushes is Steve's job.
8. Shoveling snow, Dad strained his back.
9. Ellen won the contest by spelling *conscience* correctly.
10. The official checking the luggage is a customs agent.

Part 3   Infinitives

The third kind of verbal is the **infinitive. An infinitive is a verbal form that usually begins with the word *to*.** *To* is called the **sign of the infinitive.**

to print	to whisper	to win	to remember
to speak	to choose	to quit	to help

Note: You have learned that the word *to* is used as a preposition. *To* is a preposition when it is followed by a noun or pronoun as its object. However, when *to* is followed by a verb, it is the sign of the infinitive. Compare these examples:

Prepositional Phrases	Infinitives
Cathy ran to the door.	The team wanted to win.
Mark wrote to Alex.	The prisoner tried to escape.

The Infinitive Phrase

Like gerunds and participles, infinitives are not always used alone.

An infinitive can have modifiers and objects. The infinitive with its modifiers and objects forms an **infinitive phrase.**

Because an infinitive is formed from a verb, it is like a verb in some ways. Like a verb, an infinitive can have an object.

> Karen decided *to attend the concert.*
> (*Concert* is the direct object of the infinitive *to attend.*)
>
> Ms. Abbott wanted *to give us some help.*
> (*Us* is the indirect object and *help* is the direct object of the infinitive *to give.*)

Because an infinitive is formed from a verb, it can be modified by adverbs.

> Marlene wanted *to ride along.*
> (*Along* is an adverb modifying the infinitive *to ride.*)
>
> The committee decided *to meet again tomorrow.*
> (*Again* and *tomorrow* are adverbs modifying the infinitive *to meet.*)

Infinitives may also be modified by prepositional phrases.

> The magician appeared *to pull the scarves from his hat.*
> (*From his hat* is a prepositional phrase modifying the infinitive *to pull.*)
>
> Couples began *to dance to the music.*
> (*To the music* is a prepositional phrase modifying the infinitive *to dance.*)

Uses of the Infinitive Phrase

Unlike gerunds and participles, infinitives can be used as more than one part of speech. An infinitive or infinitive phrase can be used as one of the following: a noun, an adjective, or an adverb.

Infinitives and infinitive phrases can be used in ways that nouns are used. As you know, nouns may be subjects or direct objects.

Subject: *To play professional football* is his goal.
(*To play professional football* is the subject.)

Direct Object: Len remembered *to lock the door.*
(*To lock the door* is the direct object.)

Infinitives and infinitive phrases can also be used as adjectives or adverbs. The infinitive or infinitive phrase is used as an adjective if it modifies a noun or pronoun. It is used as an adverb if it modifies a verb, adjective, or adverb.

Adjective: These are the facts *to remember.*
(*To remember* modifies the noun *facts.*)

Adjective: Craig wants the list of books *to read.*
(*To read* modifies the noun *books.*)

Adverb: The voters came *to cast their ballots.*
(*To cast their ballots* modifies the verb *came.*)

Adverb: The chili is too hot *to eat.*
(*To eat* modifies the adjective *hot.*)

Adverb: The disease spread too quickly *to save the tree.*
(*To save the tree* modifies the adverb *quickly.*)

From all of the examples, you can see that infinitives look like verbs, but are not used as verbs. Infinitives and their phrases are used as nouns, adjectives, and adverbs.

The Split Infinitive

Sometimes a modifier is placed between the word *to* and the verb of an infinitive. A modifier in that position is said to split the infinitive. Usually, a split infinitive sounds awkward and should be avoided.

Awkward: Clay wanted to *immediately* leave.
Better: Clay wanted to leave *immediately.*

Diagraming Infinitives

To diagram an infinitive or infinitive phrase used as a noun, place it on a bridge above the main line. *To,* the sign of the infinitive, belongs on a slanted line. The infinitive is shown on a horizontal line. Modifiers appear on lines slanted down from the infinitive. An object is shown on a horizontal line following the infinitive.

Sean wanted to finish his chores quickly.

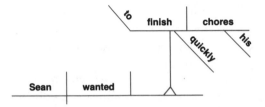

To diagram an infinitive or infinitive phrase used as a modifier, place it below the word modified. Modifiers and objects of the infinitive appear as explained above.

Insulation helps to cut energy costs.

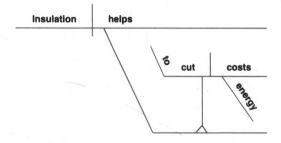

Exercise A Write each infinitive or infinitive phrase. Be prepared to tell how it is used in the sentence.

> Example: Caroline wants to take pictures of us.
> *to take pictures of us* (infinitive phrase, used as direct object)

1. Mr. Johnson forgot to pay his electric bill.

2. The pizza was too large to finish.
3. Arthur is afraid to enter the talent contest.
4. Craig had planned to visit Pike's Peak.
5. To find a new world was the explorers' goal.
6. Does Jason intend to stay late?
7. Alice went to mail the invitations.
8. Has anyone tried to climb that tree?
9. Does Lisa intend to do all that housework herself?
10. To landscape the building is the architect's responsibility.

Exercise B Follow the directions for Exercise A.

1. Doug bought tools to repair the plumbing.
2. Celia is the person to represent our class.
3. Do you want to take a picnic lunch?
4. Mr. Drake told us to write a letter to the company president.
5. To lose a game in overtime is heartbreaking.
6. The Indians fought to protect their hunting grounds.
7. An omelet is easy to make.
8. To fly to San Diego for the reunion is their plan.
9. Roger always tries to complete his homework assignments.
10. The union asked its members to take a cut in pay.

A Review of Verbals

Although verbals are verb forms, they are never used as verbs. They are used as other parts of speech.

The three kinds of verbals are gerunds, participles, and infinitives. All three kinds of verbals may be used alone. At times, though, they are used in phrases. These phrases are called gerund phrases, participial phrases, and infinitive phrases. Because they are like verbs, all three kinds of verbals can have objects or modifiers.

Gerunds are the verb forms used as nouns. Gerunds, which end in *-ing*, may be used in all the ways nouns are used.

> *Jogging* is a popular sport. (subject)
> Dick started *jogging* last year. (direct object)
> Dr. Ellis suggested *jogging* to his patient.
>   (direct object)
> Kris keeps in shape by *jogging*. (object of preposition)

Participles are verb forms used as adjectives. Like adjectives, participles modify nouns and pronouns. Present participles end in *-ing*. Past participles of regular verbs end in *-d* or *-ed*.

> *Drying the dishes*, Kate dropped a plate.
> The woman *drying her hair* is Ms. Bell.
> Nancy arranges *dried* flowers.
> *Dried in the sun*, apricots keep well.

Infinitives are the verbals that begin with the word *to*. Infinitives may be used as three different parts of speech. They may be *nouns*, *adjectives*, or *adverbs*.

> *To make the team* was Ed's goal. (noun, subject)
> Lucy asked the girls *to make their own costumes*. (noun, direct object)
> Dr. Matthews has a few comments *to make*. (adjective)
> Everyone moved over *to make room*. (adverb)
> This bread is not difficult *to make*. (adverb)

Exercise A   Find the verbal in each sentence. Write the verbal or verbal phrase. Tell whether the verbal is a gerund, a participle, or an infinitive.

1. The vice-principal's job is to handle discipline problems.
2. You will find canned chili in the prepared foods section.
3. Sweet corn sold at roadside stands is really fresh.
4. Who taught you to play the harmonica?
5. Absorbed in the novel, Judy lost track of time.

6. Keeping quiet is difficult for small children.
7. Emptying the wastebaskets is Brenda's job.
8. Have you ever seen a falling star?
9. Mr. Stiles is in charge of organizing the car pool this semester.
10. The witness is unable to identify the criminal.

Exercise B Follow the directions for Exercise A.

1. The retired admiral lives in Florida.
2. Arrange to meet me at the airport.
3. Studying hard is easy for Susan.
4. Looking out the window, Eric daydreamed about his vacation.
5. The suitcase was stuffed with wrinkled clothes.
6. Connecting the Atlantic Ocean and the Pacific Ocean, the Panama Canal saves ships time.
7. Using dental floss helps prevent cavities.
8. Peggy has collected enough leaves to make a display for the science fair.
9. Knocking on the door, the realtor waited for the owner of the house.
10. Believing in yourself is the key to success.

ADDITIONAL EXERCISES

Using Verbals

A. Gerunds and Gerund Phrases Write the gerunds and gerund phrases in these sentences.

1. Rabbits survive by running away.
2. Washing those clothes in hot water might shrink or fade them.
3. Gluing the pieces together took several hours.
4. There is an observation deck for viewing the city.
5. Nora suggested returning the carton of sour milk.
6. Tony practiced parallel parking.
7. Stu couldn't keep from arguing with the coach.
8. Stop giggling, Fred.
9. Jeremy has often talked about learning a trade.
10. Sky diving can be a dangerous sport.

B. Participles and Participial Phrases Write the participles and participial phrases in these sentences.

1. Watch out for hidden rocks.
2. Discouraged, the team retreated to the locker room at half-time.
3. Adjusting the wheels, Lee discovered a new problem.
4. The wildflowers growing in the park are goldenrod.
5. Thrusting itself up out of the water, the dolphin sailed through the hoop.
6. Does anybody want this burnt bratwurst?
7. Tapping her white cane, the woman found the curb.
8. Even used clothing has become expensive.
9. The driver's voice wakened the dozing passengers.
10. Occasionally jotting notes, Domenica listened closely.

C. Gerunds and Participles Write the gerund or participle from each sentence. Label it *Gerund* or *Participle*.

1. This coat has reinforced pockets.
2. Reinforced with steel, the door was almost unbreakable.
3. Her hair, parted in the middle, hung straight to her shoulders.
4. Recognizing nobody at the party, Jacob left early.
5. Check the suspect's alibi by interviewing her friends.
6. Getting the ball past Ron wasn't easy.
7. I have never enjoyed riding Ferris wheels.
8. Using a loudspeaker, the state trooper ordered the driver to the side of the road.
9. Using an electric drill would save time.
10. On summer nights, the chirping of crickets fills the air.

D. Infinitives and Infinitive Phrases Find the infinitives and infinitive phrases in these sentences.

1. Julie is training to work as a tour guide.
2. I expect to see Mel this afternoon.
3. The government attempts to warn us of health hazards.
4. Did you try to talk to Lena first?
5. This copy is too faint to read.
6. Tricia wants to skate to school.
7. Native Americans used certain plants to cure many illnesses.
8. To keep the wallet seems wrong to me.
9. My grandfather thought of a way to feed the baby bird.
10. Molly absolutely refuses to join us for tennis.

E. The Kinds of Verbals Write the verbal or verbal phrase in each sentence. Label it *Gerund, Participle,* or *Infinitive.*

1. Moving West solved many problems in earlier times.

2. We had almost persuaded Sandy to stay.
3. Forced out of their native country, the refugees sought protection in the United States.
4. Is tap-dancing still popular?
5. The crowd waiting for the bus grew impatient.
6. Trucks take longer to brake than cars.
7. Tyler is nervous about speaking in public.
8. Chameleons will eat only living prey.
9. Getting away from it all is quite impossible.
10. Is it too late to order some flowers?
11. Whistling bravely, Ilana walked into the principal's office.
12. My father wanted to leave at noon, but nobody was ready then.
13. It was hard to hear the telephone from outside.
14. The twins tried to move the couch and chairs closer to the fireplace.
15. Doing a double somersault, the gymnast flipped off the balance beam.
16. The bottle cap was labeled *easy to open.*
17. The fans, booing loudly, did not agree with the umpire.
18. Cooking can be both a hobby and a profession.
19. The label on the sweater said to wash it by hand.
20. Cindy always draws smiling faces next to her signature.

MIXED REVIEW

Using Verbals

A. Recognizing verbals Write the verbals and verbal phrases from the following sentences. Then write whether the verbal or verbal phrase is a *Gerund, Participle,* or an *Infinitive*. A sentence may contain more than one verbal.

1. Bragging annoys almost everybody.
2. Some football coaches forbid practicing on hot days.
3. Put the camping gear in the sun to dry.
4. The flashing lights warned us of a train approaching.
5. Thursday morning we took a standardized test.
6. Ingrid wants to get Michael Jackson's autograph.
7. Holiday shoppers crowding the store barely listened to the carols.
8. Mr. Vallina plans to saw the decayed branch off.
9. Mr. Calvey makes delicious barbecued ribs.
10. Rose told the children not to turn on the hydrant.

B. Identifying verbals and their uses Write the verbals and verbal phrases from the following sentences. If a verbal is used as a noun, write whether it is a *Subject,* an *Object,* or a *Predicate Word*. If it is used as a modifier, write whether it is an *Adjective* or *Adverb*.

1. Don't put the rug in the washing machine.
2. Washing the dog is Jim's responsibility.
3. I tried to explain to Maggie.
4. That is no way to treat a friend.
5. Buying a new clutch for the old car is foolish.
6. Checking her pay stub, June found a mistake.
7. Celia has improved her timing.
8. To get to Monterey from here takes two hours.
9. It isn't comfortable to sleep on the floor.
10. Without knowing it, Ann had hit the wrong button.

USING GRAMMAR IN WRITING
Using Verbals

A. You are writing a celebrity exercise book, such as those put out by Hollywood stars and sports figures. Each chapter will focus on one fitness activity. Gerunds and gerund phrases are especially useful for naming activities. Think about the activities that a person might do to keep fit. Write an opening sentence for each of ten chapters. In each opening sentence, tell how one activity helps a person stay fit. Use a gerund or a gerund phrase in each sentence. You might want to use the following gerund phrases in your sentences.

> walking around the block in the morning or evening
> playing tennis with a friend on weekends
> swimming at a municipal pool

B. Participial phrases are modifiers, but they also give a sense of action. Imagine, or recall, a chase scene in an adventure movie. Describe part of the scene in a paragraph of at least five sentences. Try to include a participial phrase in each sentence. You might want to use some of the following.

> racing through downtown San Francisco
> dashing through the crowds on the sidewalk
> ducking into a highrise office building
> running up the stairs two at a time

C. Imagine a scene from a horror story. The narrator is alone, or is supposed to be alone, in an empty house at night. A storm is beginning. Write a paragraph describing the scene. Include at least five infinitive phrases. Begin your paragraph with the sentence *The wind began to howl.* You might want to include some of the following.

> decided to telephone   afraid to look
> caused me to shiver   tried not to worry

CUMULATIVE REVIEW

The Parts of Speech

Identifying parts of speech   There are twenty underlined words in the following paragraph. Decide what part of speech each word is used as. Number your paper from 1 to 20. Write *Noun, Verb, Pronoun, Adjective, Adverb, Preposition,* or *Conjunction* for each word. Be sure to check *how* the word is used in the sentence.

Many athletes <u>are going</u> "bananas" <u>these</u> days. The
₁   ₂

banana is the most popular fruit in the United States.

Americans <u>consume</u> about 12 billion bananas <u>annually</u>.

        3   4

<u>They</u> are particularly <u>popular</u> with athletes who need a

5   6

great deal <u>of</u> <u>endurance</u>—cyclists, triathletes, mar-

          7   8

athoners, and long-distance swimmers. Why are

bananas so valuable? They <u>are</u> an <u>extremely</u> healthy

              9   10

food. Bananas have no cholesterol <u>and</u> almost no fat. In

                               11

addition, they contain more potassium than any other

fruit <u>except</u> avocados. Potassium is important for ath-

     12

letes <u>because</u> it controls <u>the</u> amount of water in the

    13   14

body tissues. It also helps the <u>muscle</u> cells perform

      15   16

well. <u>Eating</u> a banana also provides an athlete with a

17   18

supply of sucrose, which supplies <u>energy</u>. Not only are

                                 19

bananas good for <u>you</u>, but, best of all, they taste

           20

good, too!

Making Subjects and Verbs Agree

The subject and the verb of a sentence must be alike in certain ways. When they are alike, they are said to agree. For example, if the subject of a sentence is plural, the verb must also be plural. Then they agree. In this section you will learn how to make subjects and verbs agree.

Part 1 Making Subjects and Verbs Agree in Number

The **number** of a word refers to whether the word is singular or plural. A word is **singular** when it refers to one thing. A word is **plural** when it refers to more than one thing. If a subject and verb are the same in number, they agree.

A verb must agree in number with its subject.

If a subject is singular, its verb must be singular. If a subject is plural, then its verb must be plural.

Singular	Plural
He *sings*.	They *sing*.
It *falls*.	They *fall*.
She *reads*.	They *read*.

You can see that in the examples, the singular of each verb ends in *s*. In each plural verb, there is no *s*.

Subject and verb agreement usually seems natural. Problems arise, though, when you are not sure which word is the subject of the sentence. Remember that to find the subject, first find the verb. Then ask *who?* or *what?* before it.

> The pictures in this album are recent.
> *Verb*: are
> *What are?* pictures
> The subject is *pictures*.

The subject of the verb is never found in a prepositional phrase.

When you are trying to make subjects and verbs agree, watch out for phrases. Often a phrase appears between the subject and the verb.

> The *apples* in the refrigerator *are* cold.
> That *bunch* of bananas *is* green.
> The *books* by that author *are* thrillers.
> *One* of the pieces *is* missing.

Phrases beginning with the words *with, together with, including, as well as,* and *in addition to* are not part of the subject.

> *Aunt Agnes*, in addition to Aunt Rita, *is* here.
> Hard *work*, as well as ambition, *is* necessary.
> The *class*, including our teacher, *takes* a field trip in the spring.

Exercise A Choose the verb that agrees with the subject.

1. Those reports, including the one by Len, (is, are) on the bulletin board.
2. The table, as well as the chairs, (needs, need) polishing.
3. The box of pins (is, are) on the shelf.
4. The strength of chimpanzees (is, are) amazing.
5. Two of the pages from this book (is, are) missing.
6. The quilt on the bed (was, were) made by my great-grandmother.
7. New players for the marching band (is, are) needed.
8. The jockey in the yellow silks (ride, rides) the horse Suncat.
9. The cups, as well as the teapot, (has, have) been washed.
10. Even the worst times (get, gets) better.

Exercise B Follow the directions for Exercise A.

1. That girl with the braids (walk, walks) to school.
2. Fay, as well as the other swimmers, (practice, practices) after school.
3. All of the options on this car (cost, costs) a fortune.
4. A car with weak brakes (is, are) dangerous.
5. The stops on the bus tour (include, includes) Chinatown.
6. The hinges on that trunk (is, are) rusty.
7. Two reporters on the paper (cover, covers) city news.

8. The tickets at this booth (cost, costs) half price.
9. All the players on the team (work, works) together.
10. The house, together with the garage, (is, are) freshly painted.

Part 2 Compound Subjects

A compound subject is two or more subjects used with the same verb.

A compound subject joined by *and* is plural. Therefore, it requires a plural verb.

> The store *manager* and the *clerks* **are preparing** for the sale.
> *Laurie* and *Jim* **sing** in the choir.

When the parts of a compound subject are joined by *or* or *nor*, the verb should agree with the subject nearer to the verb.

> Neither Liz nor her brothers *take* the bus.
> Either sandwiches or a salad *is* a good lunch.

Exercise A Choose the verb that agrees with the subject.

1. Mark and Scott (is, are) planning a fishing trip.
2. The oven and the refrigerator (need, needs) cleaning.
3. Egypt and Tunisia (is, are) in Africa.
4. Both the bread and the muffins (seem, seems) to be fresh.
5. Neither dessert nor the beverages (has, have) been included in the price.
6. Neither the beverages nor dessert (has, have) been included in the price.
7. Either Mom or Dad (cook, cooks) dinner.
8. Either the dog or the cats (is, are) in the garage.
9. Both Joan and Kirsten (live, lives) on that block.
10. Neither Dan nor Greg (shop, shops) at that store.

Exercise B   Follow the directions for Exercise A.

1. Either Sharon or Kim (work, works) tonight.
2. Neither the movie nor the TV show (is, are) as good as the book.
3. Either a diet or medication (is, are) prescribed for diabetes.
4. Neither snow nor icy roads (stop, stops) this little jeep.
5. Suntan oil and sun visors (is, are) sold at the beach.
6. Both the detergent and the bleach (work, works) better in soft water.
7. Ghost stories and monster movies (upset, upsets) me.
8. Neither the sales clerk nor her manager (was, were) very helpful.
9. Hot dogs and baked beans (was, were) on the menu for Tuesday.
10. Either the radio or the TV (get, gets) turned off.

Part 3   Indefinite Pronouns

To make a verb agree with an indefinite pronoun used as the subject, you must know if the pronoun is singular or plural. As you have learned, some indefinite pronouns are singular, and some are plural. Others may be either singular or plural.

The following indefinite pronouns are **singular:**

another	each	everything	one
anybody	either	neither	somebody
anyone	everybody	nobody	someone
anything	everyone	no one	

Nobody there *wants* to go.
Somebody plans the activities.
Each of the students *has* a locker.

The following indefinite pronouns are **plural:**

both   few   many   several

Many of the voters *support* that candidate.
Several of the children *have* chicken pox.

The following indefinite pronouns are **singular** if they refer to one thing. They are **plural** if they refer to several things.

all   any   most   none   some

All of the sugar *is* in the tin.
All of the tools *are* in the garage.

None of the paint *is* red.
None of the pears *are* ripe.

Some of the music *is* Lauren's.
Some of the horses *are* in the barn.

Exercise A   Choose the verb that agrees with the subject.

1. Most of the jackets (is, are) waterproof.
2. (Is, Are) all of the tickets sold?
3. Few of the secretaries (take, takes) shorthand.
4. Each of the boats (has, have) two sails.
5. No one here (has, have) played rugby before.
6. Someone on the elevator (want, wants) to get off.
7. Some of the glue (is, are) stuck on the table.
8. Everything in the kitchen (is, are) unbreakable.
9. Most of those rumors (is, are) not true.
10. Some of the rolls (was, were) burned.

Exercise B   Follow the directions for Exercise A.

1. Some of the hats (has, have) brims.
2. Most of the paint (is, are) peeling.
3. Neither of the dogs (has, have) a collar.
4. Someone (prepare, prepares) the newsletter each month.
5. None of the potato salad (was, were) eaten.
6. Most of the flowers (has, have) been planted.
7. Many of the tomatoes (is, are) ripe.

8. One of the cars (is, are) low on gas.
9. Everyone on vacation (want, wants) pleasant weather.
10. Each of the welders (wear, wears) safety glasses.

Part 4 Other Problems of Agreement

Doesn't and Don't

The verb *doesn't* is singular. *Doesn't* is used with the subjects *she*, *he*, and *it*. All other personal pronouns are used with *don't*.

It *doesn't* please me.   They *don't* work nights.
He *doesn't* work nearby.   I *don't* play an instrument.
She *doesn't* like squash.   We *don't* grow asparagus.

Sentences Beginning with There

When sentences begin with *there*, *here*, or *where*, the subject comes after the verb. You must look ahead to find the subject of the sentence. Then you must use the verb that agrees with that subject.

There *are* several good *songs* on that album.
Here *are* the *plums*.
Where *is* my other *shoe?*

Exercise A Choose the verb that agrees with the subject.

1. Elliot (doesn't, don't) play soccer.
2. It (doesn't, don't) take that long.
3. He (doesn't, don't) enjoy that program.
4. Where (is, are) the ambulance?
5. These shoes (doesn't, don't) fit well.
6. (Doesn't, Don't) Flo play chess?
7. (Doesn't, Don't) egg rolls contain cabbage?

8. There (is, are) some napkins in the pantry.
9. There (goes, go) the ducklings.
10. There (was, were) a snake in the garden.

Exercise B Follow the directions for Exercise A.

1. Mary Beth (doesn't, don't) eat red meat.
2. Here (is, are) a vegetarian dinner.
3. (Isn't, Aren't) there any meat in this casserole?
4. Where (is, are) the cheese?
5. Sheila (doesn't, don't) enjoy fried foods.
6. Where (is, are) the hard-boiled eggs?
7. Hamburgers (doesn't, don't) taste good without onions.
8. Mr. Fraser (doesn't, don't) agree with me.
9. Here (is, are) the dill pickles.
10. There (is, are) two jars of garlic salt.

ADDITIONAL EXERCISES

Making Subjects and Verbs Agree

A. Verbs and Their Subjects Write the verb that agrees with the subject.

1. Two pieces of pizza (is, are) left.
2. Several people, including Marion, (has, have) a key to that door.
3. Vic, as well as his co-workers, (attends, attend) staff meetings.
4. Noises from the street (drifts, drift) up to my room.
5. Our chances of winning (is, are) better than theirs.
6. The slices of bread in this loaf (isn't, aren't) moldy.
7. Two rooms, in addition to this one, (is, are) not in use.
8. The barn, together with the stables, (is, are) by the dirt road.
9. Rats in a building (endangers, endanger) health.
10. The mood in those classrooms (is, are) peaceful.

B. Verbs and Compound Subjects Write the verb that agrees with the subject.

1. Privacy and free time (is, are) not always easy to find.
2. The suitcase and the totebag (is, are) both stuffed with clothes.
3. As children, both Thomas Edison and Albert Einstein (was, were) thought to be rather stupid.
4. Farming and ranching (has, have) replaced buffalo hunting for many Plains Indians.
5. Mirrors and water (reflects, reflect) print backwards.
6. Neither white rice nor white bread (provides, provide) as much nutrition as brown rice or whole-grain bread.
7. Both rice and bread (contains, contain) carbohydrates.

8. Neither Katy nor her sister (looks, look) pleased.
9. Either the manager or one of her assistants (handles, handle) complaints.
10. Masking tape or staples (is, are) used to fasten those envelopes.

C. Verbs and Indefinite Pronouns Write the verb that agrees with the subject.

1. Each of the bikes (has, have) been customized.
2. Both of the books (contains, contain) information on the Olympics.
3. Some of the injured players (insists, insist) on returning to the field.
4. Some of the fudge (is, are) for the bake sale.
5. Another of those old war movies (is, are) on tonight.
6. Only one of the hotels (faces, face) the ocean.
7. Few of the factories (hires, hire) summer help.
8. Everybody in the bleachers (was, were) standing.
9. Everything certainly (seems, seem) under control.
10. (Was, Were) all of the money refunded?

D. Problems of Agreement Write the verb that agrees with the subject.

1. He really (doesn't, don't) seem to feel at home.
2. Here (is, are) the rules.
3. There (is, are) several thin sheets of wood in plywood.
4. (Doesn't, Don't) Carol and Ruth have their ticket stubs?
5. Where (was, were) the junior prom held last year?
6. It (don't, doesn't) bother me much.
7. There (is, are) no easy answer to that question.
8. Where (has, have) the flood victims been housed?
9. Those sandwiches in the vending machine (don't, doesn't) look fresh.
10. There (is, are) pedalboats for rent at the lagoon.

MIXED REVIEW

Making Subjects and Verbs Agree

A. Choosing the correct verb In each of the following sentences, write the verb that agrees with the subject.

1. Neither his socks nor his gloves (matches, match).
2. Neither gossip nor rumors (belongs, belong) in a news story.
3. Neither the window nor the door (is, are) locked.
4. The jokes in her speech (was, were) funny.
5. One of the doves (coos, coo) every morning.
6. Counties near Chicago (includes, include) Kane and Lake.
7. The greens, as well as the chicken, (needs, need) salt.
8. Both the greens and the chicken (needs, need) some pepper.
9. Eve, together with her friends, (sits, sit) on the porch.
10. Mr. Bensdorf and Mr. Fletcher (works, work) at the same post office.

B. Using the correct verb Some of the following sentences contain errors in subject-verb agreement. If a sentence contains an error, rewrite it correctly. If a sentence is correct, write *Correct*.

1. Neither of those hobbies require much money.
2. Both of those albums is available as cassettes.
3. Everyone depends on Vincent.
4. Where is the vending machines?
5. Sandra don't have last year's yearbook.
6. Don't parakeets sing?
7. There was two notes taped on the classroom door.
8. It do bother me sometimes.
9. None of the waiters get sick leave.
10. None of the garden gets enough sun.

USING GRAMMAR IN WRITING
Making Subjects and Verbs Agree

A. Suppose that you have been given a chance to write an editorial for a local paper. What do you want to say? You might point out a situation that you think is unfair. You might praise someone. You might suggest a way to solve a community problem. Choose a topic that interests you, and then write your editorial. Begin the opening sentence with *There*. This sentence should state the problem or identify the person or situation you are writing about. Also use at least four of the following indefinite pronouns in your editorial. Be certain that all verbs agree with their subjects.

anyone	everyone	nobody	someone	something
each	many	several	none	all

B. You have been asked to take a poll for the school newspaper, magazine, or radio station. What questions will you ask students in your school? You might ask their opinions about political candidates. You might ask about school policies. Assume that you have asked your questions and collected the answers. Write a paragraph summarizing the results. Use the following as subjects for your sentences. Be certain that the verbs you use agree with their subjects.

a handful of students	half of the student population
most	nearly every student
few	students who walk to school
many students and the principal	each of the students

CUMULATIVE REVIEW

Usage

Using words correctly   Twenty words are underlined in the following paragraph. Ten of the underlined words contain errors in the use of verbs, nouns, pronouns, adverbs, and adjectives. Ten of the words are correct. Proofread the paragraph. Rewrite it, correcting the errors.

       "Let's go ice-skating," said my friend Brenda. Before I knew it, my feet were laced into skates, and I was being led toward the ice. "What kind of a torture is this?" I asked myself. As I got to the edge of the rink, I decided to approach this sport fearless. I boldly slid into the rink. Then I prompt made a three-point landing. Between chuckles Brenda said, "You won't never make the Olympics that way!" As I struggled to my feet, I requested that Brenda learn me a few basic skills. She mustn't of heard me, because she skated off without me. I decided to learn by watching. "Them skaters seem to be good," I said to myself as I took tiny step across the ice toward a group of three skaters. Each of them was doing their own favorite thing. The nearer skater was doing figure eights, and the farthest skater was skating backwards. Since I needed to learn how to go forward, they weren't much help! Gradually, I slipped and slid my way back to the warming house. "Next time I'll plan our activities!" I told Brenda as I removed the skates.

Using Compound and Complex Sentences

There are four kinds of sentences—simple sentences, compound sentences, complex sentences, and compound-complex sentences. You have already studied the simple sentence, and you know how the parts of a sentence work together. In this section you will learn about the other three types of sentences.

Part 1 Review of the Sentence

The sentence is composed of two basic parts. These key parts are the subject and the predicate.

Subject	Predicate
Birds	sang.
Birds	sang early this morning.
Birds in the trees	sang early this morning.
Several bluebirds in the tree	sang very loudly this morning.

The **subject** tells who or what the sentence is about. The predicate tells what the subject did, what the subject is, or what happens.

The **simple predicate** is called the verb. The simple subject is called the **subject of the verb**.

Within the subject of the sentence are the simple subject and its modifiers. In the predicate of the sentence are the verb, objects, predicate words, and their modifiers.

Compound Parts in a Sentence

You have learned that all parts of the sentence may be **compound**.

Compound subject:	Fresh lemons and limes filled the basket.
Compound verb:	The clown tripped, stumbled, and fell.
Compound predicate:	We went to the pet store and bought a parakeet.
Compound object:	Jenny painted the lawn furniture and the porch swing.
Compound object of the preposition:	During May and June, we plant our garden.
Compound predicate word:	The down comforter is soft and fluffy.

The Simple Sentence

Even though sentences may have compound parts, they still express only one main idea. Such sentences, like all of those you have been studying, are called **simple sentences**.

A simple sentence is a sentence with only one subject and one predicate. The subject and the predicate, along with any part of the subject or predicate, may be compound.

Now you are ready to distinguish simple sentences from other types of sentences.

Exercise A Copy each of the following simple sentences. Then draw a line between the subject and the predicate.

1. Marcy and Joe work for their dad.
2. The IRS and the FTC are government agencies.
3. Noreen put her scarf and her gloves into her locker.
4. The Bee Gees and Men at Work are both from Australia.
5. Iowa and Indiana border Illinois.
6. The houses on that block are old and run-down.
7. Margaret looked up the phone number and then dialed it.
8. The sales clerk was both helpful and courteous.
9. Judy forgot the volleyball and the net.
10. Mr. Kendall ordered a belt and a sweater through the catalog.

Exercise B Write the compound subjects, verbs, predicates, and objects you find in these simple sentences.

1. Dr. Imhof cleaned and examined my teeth.
2. Tracy Austin and Andrea Jaeger are both tennis pros.
3. Stamp and then mail the letter.
4. Tables for the reception were set up in the dining room and living room.

5. The band played either country-western music or gospel songs.
6. Meg, Jo, Beth, and Amy are the sisters in *Little Women*.
7. The farmer planted corn, soybeans, and wheat.
8. Dave washed, waxed, and buffed the tile hallway.
9. Kate and Anna made a spaghetti dinner and then cleaned up the kitchen.
10. Did you and Jim borrow the staple gun and the glue?

Part 2 The Compound Sentence

Sometimes two simple sentences express related ideas, and they are joined to form one sentence. The resulting sentence has more than one subject and more than one predicate. It is called a **compound sentence**.

A compound sentence consists of two or more simple sentences joined together. The parts of the compound sentence may be joined by a coordinating conjunction (*and, or, but*) or by a semicolon (;). Look at the following examples.

> The sun is out, **and** the temperature is in the 80's.
> Our dog sounds ferocious, **but** he is really very friendly.
> Pay your dues, **or** you will be dropped from the club.
> We visited a college in Wisconsin; my sister wants to attend school there.

Why are compound sentences used? Why don't writers use only simple sentences? This passage will help you to see why.

> Many people think that a career in the theater is glamorous. It is really a lot of hard work. You have to be prepared to rehearse at any time of the day or night. You have to memorize moves. You must remember your lines. It is also important that you work well with people. You must be prepared to take instruction from your director.

The series of simple sentences one after another becomes dull and tiresome. Notice how much better the same paragraph sounds with compound sentences.

> Many people think that a career in the theater is glamorous, but it is really a lot of hard work. You have to be prepared to rehearse at any time of the day or night. You have to memorize moves, and you must remember your lines. It is also important that you work well with people, and you must be prepared to take instruction from your director.

Diagraming Compound Sentences

If you can diagram simple sentences, you can diagram compound ones. The diagram simply shows that a compound sentence is two or more simple sentences joined together. The simple sentences are diagramed one under the other. Then the two sentences are connected with a dotted line. The coordinating conjunction sits on a "step" in the line.

> The controller gave the pilot instructions, and the plane taxied down the runway.

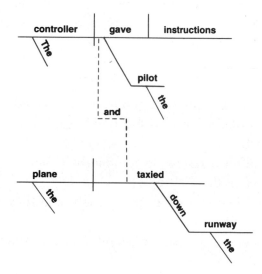

Exercise A Number your paper from 1 to 10. Label three columns *Subject/Verb, Conjunction,* and *Subject/Verb.* For each sentence, fill in the columns.

> Example: Craig plays backgammon, but Jim and Al prefer chess.

Subject/Verb	Conjunction	Subject/Verb
Craig/plays	but	Jim, Al/prefer

1. The performer sang, and the pianist accompanied her.
2. The examination was long, but it was easy.
3. Uncle Jim built a fire in the fireplace, and then we roasted chestnuts.
4. Alligators were on the endangered species list, but now their number is growing.
5. We can ride our bikes, or we can walk.
6. The drama group won the local contest, and now it will compete at the state level.
7. The movie was terrible, but the theater was packed.
8. Should I call a plumber, or can you fix the leak?
9. The United States Post Office has a package delivery service, but many people use private delivery firms.
10. The tourist checked his map, and then he drove onto the interstate highway.

Exercise B Follow the directions for Exercise A.

1. Dad sanded the windowsills, and I stained them.
2. The tornado damaged the buildings, but no one was hurt.
3. The letter carrier rang the doorbell, but no one answered.
4. Mom planted roses in the garden, and they bloomed until October.
5. Hokkaido is a Japanese island, and the Ainu people live there.

6. Would you like some water, or should I make tea?
7. Dandelions and clover covered the lawn, and crabgrass grew in the flower bed.
8. Mark and Pam will telephone the members, or nobody will remember the meeting.
9. Acrylic sweaters look like wool, but wool sweaters are warmer.
10. My grandmother made slipcovers for the chairs, and she ordered new drapes for the windows.

Compound Sentence or Compound Predicate?

A **compound predicate** is two verbs within one predicate. The parts of a compound predicate, like the parts of a compound sentence, are joined by a coordinating conjunction.

> Kristi *memorized the poem* and *recited it for me*.
> (This compound predicate is joined by *and*.)

How can you tell whether a sentence is compound or whether it has a compound predicate? If each verb has its own subject, then the sentence is compound. If the verbs share the same subject, then only the predicate is compound.

> **s.**   **v.**   **v.**
> *Lance walked* to the podium and *gave* his speech.
> (This simple sentence has a compound predicate. Both verbs, *walked* and *gave*, have the same subject, *Lance*.)

> **s.**   **v.**   **s.** **v.**
> *Lance walked* to the podium, and *he gave* his speech.
> (This is a compound sentence. The verb *walked* has its own subject, *Lance*. The verb *gave* has its own subject, *he*.)

> **s.**   **v.**   **v.**
> The *receptionist answers* phones and *types* letters.
> (The conjunction *and* joins the compound predicate of this simple sentence. Both verbs, *answers* and *types*, have the same subject, *receptionist*.)

The *receptionist answers* phones, and the *secretary types* letters.

(This compound sentence is actually two simple sentences joined by the conjunction *and.*)

Exercise A   Number your paper from 1 to 10. Decide whether the following sentences are compound sentences or simple sentences with compound predicates. Write *Compound Sentence* or *Compound Predicate.*

1. Alice does warm-up exercises and then jogs before breakfast.
2. Keith measured the board and sawed it.
3. The Indianapolis 500 time trials are this week, and the unofficial track record is 203.7 mph.
4. Barbra Streisand is the female vocalist, and Andy Gibb is the male vocalist.
5. The lifeguards are on duty, but the beach is not yet open.
6. The children waded in the water and built sand castles.
7. Is that the prince, or is that his cousin?
8. I usually work on Saturdays, but I worked on Sunday this week.
9. Is this plant sick, or did you forget to water it?
10. Has Mike found an apartment, or does he still live at home?

Exercise B   Follow the directions for Exercise A.

1. Adam overhauled the engine and then sold the car.
2. Sara looked at the price of a new car and decided to buy a used one instead.
3. Vince was a member of the team, but he sat on the bench all season.
4. Kelly was absent on the day of the test but was given a make-up exam the next day.

5. Amy Koopman made the Olympic gymnastic team, but the team didn't compete in the 1980 Olympics.
6. We get several FM stations, but the reception isn't very good.
7. Did Marla bake the cake or order it from a bakery?
8. Nancy put on her bathing cap and adjusted her swim goggles; then she dove into the pool.
9. Do you want to bring a picnic, or would you rather buy hot dogs there?
10. Phil, Greg, and Henry may go to the rock concert, but they have to be home by ten.

Punctuating Compound Sentences

One of two punctuation marks is used in a compound sentence. Either a **comma** before a coordinating conjunction or a **semicolon** is needed to separate the two parts of a compound sentence. The punctuation keeps the two parts separate. It also shows where to pause in reading the sentence.

In a compound sentence, a comma is used before a coordinating conjunction. Notice how the comma is used in these compound sentences:

      s.   **v.**   **s.**   **v.**

The theater was already full, **and** the line stretched around the block.

      s.   **v.**   **s.**

The plane was scheduled for a noon departure, **but** the flight
v.
was delayed.

Instead of a comma and a conjunction, a semicolon may be used in a compound sentence.

      s.   **v.**   **s. v.**

New Orleans is an important city; it is one of the largest ports in the United States.

    s.   **v.**   **s.**   **v.**

Scott ordered a turkey sandwich; Lee ordered tuna salad.

A semicolon may also be used with a **conjunctive adverb**. A conjunctive adverb is an adverb like *therefore, however, moreover, consequently,* or *otherwise.* It helps to join the two parts of a compound sentence. It also shows the relationship between them.

s.   v.   s.   v.

Clay parked the car; **however**, he forgot to turn off the lights.

s.   v.   s.   v.

The Dolphins won their last two games; *therefore,* they have a chance for the play-offs.

As you can see, a conjunctive adverb is used after a semicolon. A conjunctive adverb is followed by a comma.

The parts of a compound sentence are separated by either a comma or a semicolon. However, no punctuation is used between the two parts of a compound predicate. Note the following examples:

s.   v.   v.

Nectarines look like peaches but taste different.

s.   v.   v.

The batter swung at the ball and missed it.

In addition, commas are not necessary in very short compound sentences.

> Snow flew and the wind howled.
> They won and we lost.

Exercise A Commas and semicolons have been omitted between the parts of the following compound sentences. For each sentence, write the two words between which punctuation belongs. Put in the comma or semicolon. If a sentence needs no punctuation, write *Correct.*

1. The volcano erupted a cloud of smoke and ash filled the air.
2. The orange crop was damaged by the frost therefore the cost of orange juice increased.

3. Dr. Robert Koch isolated the TB bacillus in 1882 however, a drug therapy was not found until 1944.
4. Dr. Shore is the dentist Ms. Rizzo is the hygienist.
5. Carl went to the art fair and he bought a watercolor painting.
6. Mr. Jackson hooked a marlin on the deep-sea fishing trip but it got away.
7. The secretary composed the letter she typed it on the word processor.
8. The Kentucky Derby is the first race in the Triple Crown and the Preakness is the second.
9. Mark left a message on the answering machine but no one returned his call.
10. Either you go or I will.

Exercise B   Follow the directions for Exercise A.

1. The police questioned a suspect however, they had to let him go.
2. Lightning cracked and thunder roared.
3. Sylvia likes cats but she is allergic to them.
4. Violet parked in a no-parking zone and she got a ticket.
5. Mr. Elliott does the bookkeeping for the company Mr. Fernandes handles the correspondence.
6. Lakes usually contain fresh water nevertheless there are some saltwater lakes.
7. Lake Pontchartrain is in New Orleans Salt Lake is in Salt Lake City.
8. Mudslides are common in California however, people continue to build houses on hills.
9. The elm tree looks healthy but it might have Dutch elm disease.
10. You can take a walking tour of the city or you can take a bus tour.

Part 3   The Complex Sentence

You have learned about simple sentences and compound sentences. Another kind of sentence, the **complex sentence,** can also help you to express your thoughts.

Before you can understand the structure of a complex sentence, you must know what a clause is.

A clause is a group of words containing a verb and its subject.

With this definition, you could say that a simple sentence is a clause. It contains a verb and its subject.

>   **s.**   **v.**
> The lawyer signed the contract.

>   **s.**   **v.**
> Some police officers wear service revolvers.

Your study of sentence structures will be easier, however, if you think of a clause as *part of a sentence*. A clause is *a group of words within a sentence*, containing a subject and verb.

Compound sentences also contain clauses. Compound sentences have two or more groups of words containing a subject and verb. Notice these examples.

>   **s.**   **v.**   **s.** **v.**
> The tour stopped in San Francisco, and we visited Fisherman's Wharf.

>   **s.**   **v.**   **s.**   **v.**
> The air controllers went on strike, but the airlines continued to operate.

Clause or Phrase?

Clauses differ from phrases. Like a clause, a phrase is part of a sentence. However, a clause has a subject and a verb. A phrase does not.

> Phrases: after the dance
>   before breakfast

Clauses: after the music stopped
$\overset{\text{s.}}{}\quad\overset{\text{v.}}{}$

$\overset{\text{s.}}{}\quad\overset{\text{v.}}{}$
before she leaves

Subordinate Clauses

The clauses of a compound sentence are actually two separate sentences. Each one can stand alone. Each is a **main clause.** A main clause, or **independent clause,** is a clause that can stand by itself as a sentence.

Subordinate clauses, or **dependent clauses,** cannot stand alone. A subordinate clause is not a complete sentence.

$\overset{\text{s.}}{}\quad\overset{\text{v.}}{}$
If you enjoyed the play

$\overset{\text{s.}}{}\quad\overset{\text{v.}}{}$
Unless you start immediately

Both of these subordinate clauses contain subjects and verbs, but neither of them expresses a complete thought. Both leave you wondering *then what?*

The words that begin subordinate clauses have an important function. Words like *if* and *unless* are called **subordinating conjunctions.** They make the clause *dependent* on the main clause to complete its meaning. Many, though not all, subordinate clauses begin with subordinating conjunctions.

Study the following chart.

Words Often Used as Subordinating Conjunctions			
after	because	so that	when
although	before	than	whenever
as	if	though	where
as if	in order that	till	wherever
as long as	provided	unless	while
as though	since	until	

Note: the words in the chart on page 595 are subordinating conjunctions only when they begin clauses. Many of them can be used in other ways.

Furthermore, not all subordinate clauses begin with subordinating conjunctions. Some clauses begin with words like these:

that	who, whom, whose
what, whatever	whoever, whomever
which	why
how	

Exercise   Using *if, because, when, after,* and *since,* make subordinate clauses out of these sentences.

1. My ride is early.
2. The towel is damp.
3. Darren enjoys tennis.
4. There is a slow leak in the tire.
5. The boutique sold only handmade items.
6. Fruit is a healthy snack.
7. The seals were sunning on the rocks.
8. Those seats are taken.
9. Peaches are on sale.
10. Estelle shopped at J.C. Penney.

Definition of the Complex Sentence

Now that you know the difference between main clauses and subordinate clauses, you can understand the complex sentence.

A complex sentence is a sentence that contains one main clause and one or more subordinate clauses.

Main Clause	Subordinate Clause
The Lakers will lose	unless Jabbar sinks this basket.
The clambake starts	when the sun goes down.
A pediatrician is a doctor	that specializes in caring for children.

Exercise A Find the subordinate clause in these complex sentences. Copy it, underlining the subject once and the verb twice.

1. It rained while we were in the theater.
2. Phyllis asked if I liked artichoke hearts.
3. Rob read the program before the show began.
4. Peggy visits the museum whenever she gets a chance.
5. Donna refuses to attend unless we go.
6. Let's hurry before the store closes.
7. The family posed while Mr. Valenti focused the camera.
8. The Mortons are moving because Mr. Morton has been transferred.
9. Although Joan prefers classical music, she enjoyed the bluegrass band.
10. Unless it rains, the picnic will be held at Heritage Park tomorrow.

Exercise B Follow the directions for Exercise A.

1. Before he fixed the flat tire, Frank set up the emergency flares.
2. Claudia got a summer job so that she could earn money for college.
3. Larry forgot where he had put the keys.
4. When the subway doors opened, people swarmed out onto the platform.
5. Clara can't remember where we're supposed to meet.
6. Wherever you see a Red Cross flag, there is a first aid station.
7. Mr. Rogers explained how a thermostat works.
8. As the whistle blew, the factory workers left the building.
9. Maria feels better now than she did before lunch.
10. No one knows why the bridge collapsed.

Part 4   Adverb Clauses

Subordinate clauses may be one of three kinds. One type is the **adverb clause.** It has the same function as an adverb.

An **adverb** modifies a verb, an adjective, or another adverb. It tells *how, when, where,* or *to what extent.*

    Adverb: Michael studied *diligently.*

An **adverb phrase** is a prepositional phrase used as an adverb.

    Adverb phrase: Michael studied *in the library.*

An adverb clause is a subordinate clause used as an adverb.

    Adverb clause: Michael studied *after he had finished his chores.*

                When the guests arrived, Mr. Lyons greeted them.

Adverb clauses tell *how, when, where,* and *to what extent.* They modify verbs, adjectives, and adverbs.

Remember that a clause has a subject and a verb.

Diagraming Adverb Clauses

To diagram an adverb clause, place it on a separate horizontal line below the main line. A dotted line connects the adverb clause to the word it modifies in the main clause. The subordinating conjunction is shown on the dotted line.

When the alarm rang, the police responded to the call.

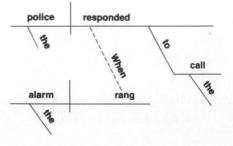

Exercise A Copy the adverb clause from each sentence.

1. We drove until we reached Kansas City.
2. If Marge wins the poster contest, she will get a fifty dollar savings bond.
3. Although the shot hurt, Nancy did not complain.
4. The bridge was raised as the tall ship sailed out of the harbor.
5. Candy's dog always barks when the telephone rings.
6. We haven't heard from Erin since she moved.
7. The waiter prepared the flaming dessert while we watched.
8. The ground shook as the cement mixers roared by.
9. I couldn't get that book because the library was closed yesterday.
10. Martin said goodbye to us before he left.

Exercise B Follow the directions for Exercise A.

1. Ms. Paley will substitute for Mr. Johnson until he returns from jury duty.
2. The carpenter measured the wood before he cut it.
3. When the Irish came to America, they were fleeing the potato famine.
4. Eric makes friends wherever he goes.
5. Although the theater opens at noon, the movie does not begin until 12:30.
6. Laura replaced the battery in her car because the old one was dead.
7. If Joe calls, please take a message.
8. Whenever Martha gives a speech, she gets nervous.
9. Because the program started late, the audience grew restless.
10. Since Ned is interested in computers, he is going to a computer camp.

Part 5 Adjective Clauses

A second type of subordinate clause is the **adjective clause.** An adjective clause has the same function as an adjective.

An **adjective** modifies a noun or pronoun.

> Adjective: The magician wore a *tall black* hat.

An **adjective phrase** is a prepositional phrase that modifies a noun or pronoun.

> Adjective phrase: Olivia read the list *of movies.*

An adjective clause is a subordinate clause used as an adjective to modify a noun or pronoun.

> Adjective clause: A thesaurus is a book *that lists synonyms for words.*
>
> Anyone *who wants a job* should read the want ads.

Adjective clauses, like adjectives and adjective phrases, tell *what kind* or *which one.* An adjective clause comes directly after the word it modifies. Unlike adjective phrases, adjective clauses have subjects and verbs.

There are several words used to introduce adjective clauses. Two of them are *where* and *when.*

> This is the university *where my brother studies.*
>
> June is the time *when schools close for the summer.*

Relative Pronouns

Besides *when* and *where,* the words *who, whom,* and *whose* are also used to begin adjective clauses. *Who, whom,* and *whose* are called **relative pronouns.** They relate a clause, called a **relative clause,** to a noun or pronoun in the sentence. Sometimes *that* and *which* are relative pronouns.

Here are the words used as relative pronouns:

who   whom   whose   that   which

Relative pronouns are special because they have three functions:

1. They introduce adjective clauses.
2. They link the clause to a word in the main clause.
3. They have a function within the clause. They act as subject, object, or predicate pronoun of the verb within the adjective clause. They may also be the object of a preposition in the clause. *Whose* functions as an adjective.

> Doctors *who treat eye diseases* are opthamologists.
> (*Who* is the subject of *treat*.)

> Mexican restaurants serve food *that is spicy*.
> (*That* is the subject of is.)

> The coach *whom we like best* is Mr. Kraus.
> (*Whom* is the direct object of *like*.)

> The partner *with whom I danced* was clumsy.
> (*Whom* is the object of the preposition *with*.)

> Parents *whose children attend that school* are protesting its closing.
> (*Whose* modifies *children*, the subject of the clause.)

Sometimes you may be confused about whether *who* or *whom* is the correct relative pronoun. To decide, see how the pronoun is used within the clause. Keep in mind that *who* is the subject form. *Whom* is the object form.

Diagraming Adjective Clauses

To diagram an adjective clause, use a separate line beneath the main line. A dotted line runs from the relative pronoun to the word in the main clause that the adjective clause modifies.

The manufacturer who makes that part is in Japan.

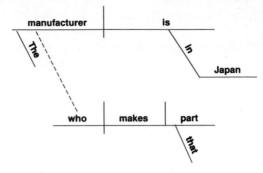

The delivery boy on whom we rely quit yesterday.

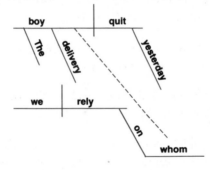

Exercise A Copy the adjective clause from each sentence. Underline the subject once and the verb twice. Before the clause, write the word it modifies.

Example: He is the author who wrote that novel.

author—who wrote that novel

1. It was the cutest kitten that I had ever ever seen.
2. The necklace that I am wearing is an antique.
3. Kirsten is the girl who mows our lawn.
4. One writer whom I enjoy is Agatha Christie.
5. We bought only the food that was necessary for the trip.

6. Workers who earn a monthly salary do not get paid for overtime.
7. The personnel manager is the person to whom your application should be sent.
8. The furniture, which belonged to my grandparents, is made of white oak.
9. The house that Mr. Lee bought was built by my dad.
10. This is the brand of jeans that I like best.

Exercise B   Follow the directions for Exercise A.

1. One of the prizes that Elaine won was a quartz watch.
2. The waiter who took our order has disappeared.
3. Brad is a shopper who cannot resist a sale.
4. The Oldsmobile *Cutlass,* which is a mid-size car, holds six people comfortably.
5. The room in which we met was cold.
6. Barbie made her own greeting cards, which were silk-screen prints.
7. The teacher read a list of students whose assignments were late.
8. The driver whose car hit the wall escaped without any serious injury.
9. Friday night is the night when we eat out.
10. The price, which included tax and tip, was $25.50.

Part 6   Noun Clauses

The noun clause is the third type of subordinate clause.

A noun clause is a clause used as a noun in a sentence. Like a noun, a noun clause can be used as a subject, an object of the verb, a predicate word, or an object of a preposition. It can be used in any of the ways that nouns are used. Unlike adverb and adjective clauses, noun clauses do not modify other words in the sentence.

Uses of Noun Clauses

Subject:	*Whoever sent these flowers* forgot to sign the card.
	What concerns the voters is unemployment.
Direct object:	Dan knows *when the game starts.*
	Kris told us *that she needed help.*
Object of preposition:	The child was frightened by *whatever she saw.*
	You can walk to *where we parked the car.*
Predicate noun:	History is *what Jack usually reads.*
	The message was *that I should call Marnie.*

As you can see from these examples, many noun clauses begin with the words *that* or *what*. The words *whatever, who, whoever,* and *whomever* can also introduce noun clauses. *Where, when, how,* and *why* are used, too.

Diagraming Noun Clauses

To diagram a noun clause, extend a bridge from the place where the clause is used in the sentence. The word that introduces the clause belongs on a line over the clause.

1. Noun clause used as subject

What I really want is a new bike.

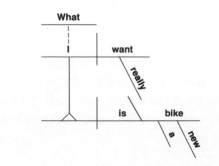

2. Noun clause used as object of the verb

The doctor said that I am in perfect health.

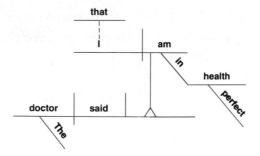

3. Noun clause used as object of a preposition

Mr. Brown will work for whoever will hire him.

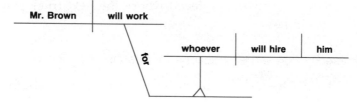

4. Noun clause used as a predicate noun

One problem is that I don't have any money.

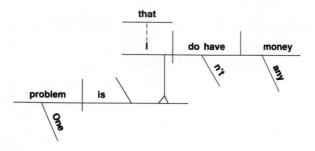

Exercise A Copy the noun clauses in these sentences. Underline the subject once and the verb twice. Tell whether the clause is a direct object, subject, predicate noun, or object of a preposition.

1. Lill explained how the Wankel engine works.
2. Jackson Square in New Orleans is where the Louisiana Purchase was signed.
3. Do you know why John isn't going to the party?
4. The reason is that he dislikes crowds.
5. We'll make soup with whatever leftovers we have.
6. These books will give you whatever information you need.
7. That politician gives favors to whomever he likes.
8. Whoever planned the science fair was very well organized.
9. What I forgot was the map.
10. The truck driver wondered where the next truck stop could be.

Exercise B Follow the directions for Exercise A.

1. Ms. Fischer asked why we were ten minutes late for class.
2. Lois explained that the assembly ran late.
3. My idea is that we organize a household help service for senior citizens.
4. How my parents met is a funny story.
5. I wonder what the big secret is.
6. The date chosen for the junior prom is the committee's decision.
7. Todd thinks that the test on the Constitution was difficult.
8. Freddie said that he is allergic to milk.
9. I will lend the album to whoever wants it.
10. What you have done in the past always affects your future.

Part 7 A Review of Subordinate Clauses

You have learned about the three kinds of subordinate clauses. They are the adverb clause, the adjective clause, and the noun clause.

The only way to identify the kind of clause is to look at its use in the sentence. A clause used as a noun is a noun clause. A clause used as a modifier is an adverb or adjective clause, depending on the word modified.

Exercise A Write the subordinate clause in each sentence. If the clause is used as a noun clause, tell whether it is the subject, direct object, or object of a preposition. If the clause is used as an adjective or adverb clause, tell what it modifies.

1. Sean discovered where Mom had hidden the presents.
2. When the street musicians started playing, a crowd gathered.
3. San Francisco is one city where I would like to live.
4. Robert forgot what he was saying.
5. Harold Washington, who is the mayor of Chicago, led the St. Patrick's Day parade.
6. Emily recognized who was behind the big sunglasses.
7. Mr. Bradstreet waited for whoever needed a ride.
8. The jewels that were stolen in the robbery were recovered.
9. Chris watches old movies whenever they are on TV.
10. Employees who wear uniforms to work save money on clothing.

Exercise B Follow the directions for Exercise A.

1. Go to the information booth if you need directions.
2. The vase, which had been a gift from my aunt, fell and broke.

3. Cars that use diesel fuel are becoming more common.
4. Who wins the car is determined by a contest.
5. The usher who showed us our seats handed us our programs.
6. Liz could not remember why she had tied a string around her finger.
7. Ed listens to cassette tapes while he is jogging.
8. While Amy was practicing her gymnastics routine, she fell off the balance beam.
9. The garden is the place where Dad spends his free time.
10. Before Jacqueline writes a paper, she does a lot of thinking.

Part 8 Clauses as Sentence Fragments

You have studied about sentence fragments. You learned about fragments that do not have subjects and verbs.

The cat on the balcony.   Crowded into the bus.

The subordinate clause is a sentence fragment, too, even though it does have a subject and a verb. It still does not express a complete thought. For that reason, a subordinate clause is a sentence fragment. It is only part of a sentence. It is not meant to stand alone.

Notice the difference between these word groups:

The comedian cracked a few jokes.
While the comedian cracked a few jokes.

The first word group is a sentence. The subordinating conjunction *while*, however, makes the second word group a sentence fragment. A subordinate clause is only part of a sentence.

A subordinate clause must not be written as a complete sentence. It must always be joined to a main clause.

Fragment:	When the snow melts.
Sentence:	When the snow melts, the basement floods.
Fragment:	What Mr. Allen did for a living.
Sentence:	No one knew what Mr. Allen did for a living.
Fragment:	Where we go.
Sentence:	Where we go depends on how much time we have.

Exercise A Number your paper from 1 to 10. Decide whether the groups of words below are sentences or fragments. Write *S* for *Sentence* and *F* for *Fragment*. Add words to make each fragment a complete sentence. Punctuate and capitalize where necessary.

1. What the messenger brought
2. What does Martha want
3. When is the algebra test
4. After the senior class luncheon
5. After lunch everyone went home
6. That jingle is catchy
7. The dress that you wanted
8. Before the speaker began
9. Why the audience is cheering
10. Why is Emily laughing

Exercise B Follow the directions for Exercise A.

1. Why the restaurant is successful
2. Since we were too late
3. Whose shoes are these
4. When French Club meets in the library
5. Before breakfast was served
6. Before dinner Alex studies
7. That is the landmark
8. Where is the nearest mailbox
9. If the dog stays in the kennel
10. Because Margaret works part time

Part 9 Compound-Complex Sentences

You have already been introduced to simple, compound, and complex sentences. The fourth and final kind of sentence is the **compound-complex sentence.**

A compound-complex sentence consists of two or more main clauses and one or more subordinate clauses.

It may help you to think of a compound-complex sentence as a compound sentence plus a subordinate clause. Actually, the compound-complex sentence joins two sentences, at least one of which has a subordinate clause. The clause may be an adjective, adverb, or noun clause. The main clauses are joined by either a coordinating conjunction or a semicolon.

These are examples of compound-complex sentences:

Main Clause　　　　　　　　　**Main Clause**

Doug searched for an hour, but he couldn't find the book

Subordinate Clause

that he wanted.

Subordinate Clause　　　　　**Main Clause**　　　**Main Clause**

When the pioneers traveled, they needed salt; it was the only
　　preservative for their food.

Exercise Identify the two main clauses and the subordinate clause in these compound-complex sentences.

1. Dad liked the golf shirt that I gave him, but it didn't fit.
2. Colonial Virginia needed no port cities; plantations were built on rivers that led to the sea.
3. Ms. Brookman showed us how the potter's wheel works, and then we tried it ourselves.
4. The guard dogs are caged during the day, but they are turned loose in the store after it closes.

5. Sacajawea was a sixteen-year-old Shoshone Indian girl; moreover, she was the guide who led the Lewis and Clark Expedition.
6. The tulips that we planted last fall came up beautifully in the spring; this year we'll plant even more.
7. Tracy liked the scarf that I had knitted, so I made one for her, too.
8. Craig realized that he had forgotten his wallet; consequently, he went back for it.
9. Swimming, which has been called the perfect exercise, requires endurance, but it doesn't put stress on the body joints.
10. The child confided to the babysitter that he could not sleep; therefore, the sitter read him a story.

Part 10 A Review of Sentences

There are four basic kinds of sentences.

A **simple sentence** contains one subject and one predicate. Parts of the simple sentence, however, may be a compound. A simple sentence tells one idea.

> s.   v.
> The airline cancelled the flight.

> s.   v.   v.
> Rod stood in line and bought the tickets.

A **compound sentence** is made up of two simple sentences. These simple sentences are connected by a comma and coordinating conjunction or by a semicolon. Sometimes a conjunctive adverb follows the semicolon. A compound sentence expresses two related ideas.

> s.   v.   s.   v.
> The airline cancelled the flight; the ticket agent notified the passengers.

> s.   v.   s.   v.
> Rod stood in line, and he bought the tickets.

A **complex sentence** contains one main clause and one or more subordinate clauses. The subordinate clauses may be used as adverbs, adjectives, or nouns. A complex sentence expresses one main idea and one or more dependent ideas.

s.　　v.　　　　　s.　　v.
Because the runway was icy, the airline cancelled the flight.

s.　　v.　　　s.　v.
Although the line was long, Rod got the tickets.

A **compound-complex sentence** contains two main clauses and one or more subordinate clauses. The subordinate clauses may be adverb, adjective, or noun clauses. A compound-complex sentence expresses two main ideas, as well as one dependent idea.

s.　　v.　　　　　　　　s.　　v.
The airline cancelled the flight; the ticket agent notified the

s.　　v.
passengers *that they would be delayed*.

s.　v.　　　s.　v.　　　　s.　v.
Although the line was long, Rod stood in it, and he got the tickets.

Exercise A　Number your paper from 1 to 10. For each sentence, write *Simple, Compound, Complex,* or *Compound-Complex* to show what kind it is.

1. Why did Mr. Lawrence go to New Hampshire?
2. Mr. Kramer not only designed the house but also built it.
3. The picnic basket contained fried chicken, potato salad, and fresh strawberries.
4. Phil asked why the train was late, and the conductor explained.
5. What a glorious day this is!
6. When Ms. Flaherty went on vacation, she forgot her travelers' checks but remembered her credit cards.

7. George thinks that he did well on the exam.
8. Since time was running short, we took a cab to the concert hall.
9. Anna put some of the sprouts that she had grown from alfalfa seeds into the tomato and avocado salad.
10. Out in the yard sat an old pick-up truck that hadn't run for years.

Exercise B   Follow the directions for Exercise A.

1. Mom reads the newspaper while she rides the train to work.
2. Before Bill dove into the pond, he checked its depth.
3. The secretary answered the phone as soon as he could, but the caller had already hung up.
4. The waiter brought us water and menus, and then he took our order.
5. After skating, we went home and made hot chocolate.
6. Did you paint the house, or did you put up aluminum siding?
7. Who said that love is blind?
8. We stacked the wood that we had chopped into a neat pile next to the garage.
9. If it is a nice day, we can go to the zoo, or if it rains, we can go to the museum.
10. Mr. Beach, the geography teacher, knew that the students needed a chapter review; therefore, he made a study guide.

ADDITIONAL EXERCISES

Using Compound and Complex Sentences

A. Simple Sentences Label four columns *Subject, Verb, Direct Object,* and *Predicate Word.* Place the parts of the sentence in the appropriate columns. Some parts may be compound.

1. During the winter Jan shoveled snow for her neighbors.
2. The hubcap fell off and clattered down the highway.
3. The emergency room is always open and always full.
4. The Orioles and the Angels have solid pitching staffs.
5. Superman and Batman have amazed children for years.
6. We bought corn and peaches at a roadside stand.
7. The thermos smelled musty and sour.
8. Do you play ice hockey or field hockey?
9. Move your wrists but not your elbows.
10. Gil and Les found spare parts and repaired the bicycle.

B. Simple and Compound Sentences Copy these sentences. Underline each subject once and each verb twice. After each sentence write *Simple* or *Compound* to show what kind it is.

1. Some Islamic women wear veils, but others do not.
2. The fare increased, but the service was no better.
3. Rafael is shy but has a good sense of humor.
4. Debra applied for a job at IBM and got it.
5. The snow has melted, and soon the trees will bud.
6. Dawn set the fishbowl down too hard and cracked it.
7. Dawn set the fishbowl down too hard, and it cracked.
8. Mel pulled himself up and stood, but again lost his balance.
9. Ms. Canchola lengthened the coat, lined it, and replaced the buttons.
10. Some vegetarians will not eat eggs or drink milk.

C. Punctuation of Compound Sentences Number your paper from 1 to 10. Write the last word of the *first* part of each compound sentence. Next write the proper punctuation mark. Then write the first word of the *second* part of the compound sentence.

1. A marshmallow is a spongy candy but a marsh mallow is a flowering plant.
2. Many players dislike artificial turf nevertheless, they must play on it.
3. The beanbag chair had a small rip in its cover and the filling was leaking out.
4. We must catch that train it's the last one today.
5. Barb added some garlic to the sauce and the flavor improved.
6. Will you pick an album or shall I choose one?
7. Ernie will use the bonus for a vacation or maybe he will save it.
8. The truck weighs three tons it cannot stop very fast.
9. After the explosion the plant was closed moreover, the area around it was evacuated.
10. The map is old but it will serve as a general guide.

D. Adverb Clauses Copy the adverb clause in each sentence. Underline the subject once and the verb twice. Draw a circle around the subordinating conjunction.

1. Because Ed works after school, he values his free time.
2. The African Emperor Taharga led his armies into battle when he was sixteen.
3. Since Ian had been benched, Cal got a chance to play.
4. After the other guests had left, Danny stayed and helped with the dishwashing.
5. After her defeat, Natalie trained harder than she ever had before.
6. Since the night before, Tracy had studied as hard as she could.

7. Call me if you get a chance.
8. If you will clean the grill, I'll barbecue the ribs.
9. After the elm trees died, the street never looked as pretty.
10. It looks as though the snow won't stop before morning.

E. Adjective Clauses Copy the adjective clause from each sentence. Underline the subject once and the verb twice. After each clause, write the word it modifies.

1. Ms. Simmons and Mr. Moore are the only choir members who can do justice to that spiritual.
2. The cabinet where the supplies are kept is in here.
3. Where did Karen put the card that I brought?
4. The priest comforted the people whose relatives had been injured.
5. After the wrestling match, we looked for a restaurant that was still open.
6. Red and green are colors that are opposite each other on a color wheel.
7. The American chameleon, which is really an anole, can grow a new tail.
8. Which are the months when hurricanes most often occur?
9. The woman for whom Ty worked gave him a good reference.
10. The odds that we will see you at the festival are quite good.

F. Noun Clauses Copy the noun clause in each sentence. Tell how the clause is used.

1. Rosa said that she would be here before dinner.
2. Alice knew who would get the credit.
3. In the fog, Liz could hardly see what was ahead.
4. How do you know what happened?
5. Nicole explained how an electric car operates.

6. Why traffic laws are necessary is obvious.
7. Clyde's worst fault is that he's always apologizing.
8. Write about whatever you know best.
9. Give the piano to whoever will haul it away.
10. Who do you think will win the pennant?

G. Subordinate Clauses Write the subordinate clause in each sentence. Tell whether it is an *Adverb, Adjective,* or *Noun Clause.*

1. That was the cheese that I had saved for the pizza.
2. Many people dream that they can fly.
3. Sabrina has dreams in which she can fly.
4. Weekends are when the family has breakfast together.
5. There were times when we wanted to turn back.
6. Althea practiced only when she felt like it.
7. Stay in the storm cellar until the tornado siren stops.
8. Who knows where these pipes lead?
9. After that, the cab driver helped passengers who seemed confused.
10. Why doesn't he look at people when they talk to him?

H. Sentence Fragments Decide whether the groups of words below are sentences or fragments. Write *S* for *Sentence* and *F* for *Fragment.*

1. The rainbow that the spacecraft left at the end of *E.T.*
2. When the awards assembly is
3. When is the awards assembly
4. After the ice storm the highway was closed
5. After Julia had checked the lost and found department
6. While the fields are being plowed
7. While washing the dishes, Will listens to the radio
8. That does not surprise me at all
9. That I was right about the address
10. Who knows the answer

I. Compound-Complex Sentences Make three columns. Label them (1) *Verb, First Main Clause;* (2) *Verb, Second Main Clause;* and (3) *Verb, Subordinate Clause.* Put the verbs from each sentence into the correct column.

1. Our morale fell when Joey was injured, and we played poorly after that.
2. The fireball that struck Siberia in 1908 exploded with as much force as an H-bomb, but the impact left no crater.
3. Hilary explained how to tie a square knot, and Don muttered that a picture was worth a thousand words.
4. The car was old, but June liked the fact that the mileage was low.
5. Anthony recognized the customer who was wearing dark glasses, and he waited on her with extra courtesy.
6. Do you want to look through the books before I give them away, or have you already seen them?
7. Check the guarantee if the watch doesn't work; maybe the manufacturer will repair it.
8. Because the princess was born at the end of a drought, her original name meant "Little White Cloud"; only later did she become Pocahantas.
9. One of the world's plant or animal species becomes extinct every day, and conservationists worry that a million species may be gone by the year 2000.
10. While Kim was in Atlanta, she rode a roller coaster called the Mindbender; it offered full-circle loops, dark tunnels, and horrifying drops.

J. Kinds of Sentences For each sentence, write *Simple, Compound, Complex,* or *Compound-Complex.*

1. Pauline and Laura gathered the pages together, and Matt stapled them.

2. Until midnight Jerome rehearsed his speech.
3. Jane steered the jeep down the muddy road to the river, and then she discovered that the bridge had collapsed.
4. The callouses on Martina's hands are not from work; they are from climbing the rope in gym.
5. Long ago, soldiers bit on bullets while they were having surgery.
6. Why didn't Art applaud after the play?
7. Tina asked why Midsummer's Eve comes in June.
8. The witness who testified was brave.
9. Who wants to look around the shopping mall for a while?
10. The tide came in and our raft returned.

MIXED REVIEW

Using Compound and Complex Sentences

A.   Identifying sentences and fragments   Decide whether the following groups of words are sentences or fragments. If a group is a sentence, write *S*. If a group is a fragment, write *F*. Then write whether the fragment is a *phrase* or a *clause*.

1. If there are living creatures on Mars, Venus, and Pluto
2. If I fall, catch me
3. Since her birthday party last January
4. Since Julia is next in line
5. Mike has been running daily since he joined the team
6. Which switch will turn the computer off
7. Which the previous owner did not mention
8. Until yesterday afternoon
9. Because my name is not on the list
10. Until then Roy had worked

B.   Identifying kinds of sentences   For each of the following sentences write *Simple, Compound, Complex,* or *Compound-Complex* to tell what kind it is.

1. The team that wins today will play in the Rose Bowl.
2. The door was open, and I got up to shut it.
3. Quentin and Gil were joking and laughing.
4. Hannibal, who was a general, used elephants in battle.
5. That is hardly the point.
6. After the long hike, Jody slept deeply and did not wake up until the next morning.
7. When there is a disaster, the Red Cross and other relief agencies often work together.
8. When will the pizza that you ordered arrive?
9. When does the popcorn counter in the lobby close?
10. That the driver was a beginner became clear.

C. Recognizing subordinate clauses Copy the subordinate clause. Underline its subject once and its verb twice. Then write *Adverb, Adjective,* or *Noun* to show what kind of clause it is.

1. A helicopter can fly much lower than a plane does.
2. Since the highway was built, the signs have rusted.
3. I wonder what Cheryl wanted.
4. Who is the woman who is ringing the doorbell?
5. The sweatpants that Frank was wearing were gray.
6. Before long, I sensed that the undertow was strong.
7. Al asked because he was curious.
8. The reporter asked where he could find a telephone.
9. Why did you swim where there are sea urchins?
10. Put the plant on a windowsill where it will get sun.

D. Using subordinate clauses correctly Copy the subordinate clause from each of the following sentences. Write *Noun, Adjective,* or *Adverb* to show what kind it is. If the clause is used as a noun, write *Subject, Direct Object, Object of Preposition,* or *Predicate Noun* to show what part of the sentence it is. If the clause is used as an adjective or adverb, write the word it modifies.

1. A driver who makes a right turn on red must give pedestrians the right of way.
2. Bob Marley was the singer for whom a monument was put up.
3. Egypt is not the only country where there are pyramids.
4. Where did you say that you were going?
5. Whoever signs the equipment out must return it.
6. Anybody who shops here must pay cash.
7. Who could study while that noise was going on?
8. As I have said before, I prefer wearing jeans.
9. A pound of lead is no heavier than a pound of feathers is.
10. Al told us that he planned to surprise Ed.

USING GRAMMAR IN WRITING
Using Compound and Complex Sentences

A. Compound sentences joined by *and* are useful for showing that two things are similar. Compound sentences joined by *but* show a contrast. The conjunction *or* in a compound sentence shows a choice. Use these kinds of compound sentences to write a prediction of ways that everyday life will change in the future. For example, you might write:

> Most people will live longer, *but* more of them will need expensive medical care.

At least one compound sentence should show that two of your predictions are similar. Another should show a contrast. A third should show a choice.

B. You will find complex sentences useful for stating opinions. The subordinate clause can give a reason for the opinion or show the result of an action. Study the following examples.

> People should use automobile seat belts because belts reduce the number of serious injuries in accidents.

> If more people ate meals standing up, the furniture industry would collapse.

Write five complex sentences stating reasons why something should be or would be so. Use one clause to state the thing that should or would be. Use the other to give a reason for it. Your sentences may be serious or humorous.

CUMULATIVE REVIEW

The Sentence

A. Identifying kinds of sentences Copy the following sentences. Insert the correct punctuation. After each sentence, write *D* for declarative, *INT* for interrogative, *IMP* for imperative, or *E* for exclamatory. Underline each subject once and each verb twice.

1. Put the tractor in the barn
2. Playing cards were first used in China
3. Are those boots waterproof
4. What a magnificent view this is
5. Louis XIV was called the Sun King

B. Understanding agreement in sentences Write the correct word from the two given in parentheses.

1. Either flowers or a plant (make, makes) a nice gift.
2. Some of the job applicants (seem, seems) prepared.
3. Most of the files (is, are) incomplete.
4. One of these diamond bracelets (is, are) a fake.
5. Where (was, were) those old fishing poles?
6. Evie (don't, doesn't) understand that poem.
7. Here (is, are) the shampoo and a towel.
8. Everyone made (his or her, their) own sundae.
9. That box of recipes (is, are) from my grandmother.
10. Where (was, were) the snow shovel?

C. Correcting fragments and run-on sentences The following paragraph contains fragments and run-on sentences. Rewrite the paragraph. Use capitalization and punctuation to correct the fragments and run-ons. Do not add or change any words.

The bald eagle, our national emblem. Was chosen by our founding fathers in 1782. Not all Americans wanted the bald eagle for a symbol some wanted the golden eagle. Since the golden eagle was also found on other continents. It was rejected for the national emblem. Although the bald eagle is a distinctive looking bird. Benjamin Franklin wanted the wild turkey as the national emblem he thought the bald eagle was not a noble bird. And it is cowardly it preys on smaller and weaker osprey. Which are a kind of hawk. The bald eagle. Is truly a controversial bird. It has been killed by Alaskan fishermen. Who thought it was destroying the salmon. It has been killed by hunters. For sport. DDT has harmed the population growth of bald eagles land development has ruined many nesting and wintering areas. By the 1940's. The bald eagle was in danger. Of extinction. Now, with the Endangered Species Act. The bald eagle is a protected species. The bald eagle will stay a part of the American wilderness.

D. Writing good sentences Rewrite each of the following sentences. Follow the directions in the parentheses.

1. Ingrid sent the graduation gift by mail. (Add the prepositional phrase *for her cousin.*)
2. Eric is taking karate lessons. Eve is taking them, too. (Combine these two sentences into one with a compound subject.)
3. The mechanic charged the battery. The car still wouldn't start. (Combine these two simple sentences into one compound sentence using **, but.**)
4. Gerald Ford spoke at the museum's fund-raising dinner. He was the 38th president of the United States. (Combine these two simple sentences into one complex sentence using *who.*)
5. Allison has a good voice. She didn't try out for the school musical. (Combine these two simple sentences into one complex sentence using *although.*)
6. Aretha baked for the party. (Change this NV sentence to one with a NVN pattern.)

The Right Word

There are certain words in the English language that are often used incorrectly. It is important to know how to use these words correctly in order to write clear standard English.

Standard English is the language of educated people. It is the language that would be judged correct by people in most situations. **Non-standard English** is not generally considered correct in all situations.

In this section, you will learn to use certain troublesome words correctly. By learning to use these words correctly, you can improve your use of standard English.

Part 1 Words Often Confused

The words listed in this section are often misused. The pairs of words may look alike or have similar meanings. However, they are not the same. One word cannot be used in place of the other. Study the lists of words often confused. Try to use the right word at the right time.

capital means "most important." It also names the city or town that is the official center of government for a state or country.

capitol refers to the building where a state legislature meets.

the Capitol is the building in Washington, D.C., where the United States Congress meets.

> The *capital* of California is Sacramento.
> Have you ever toured the state *capitol* building in Springfield?
> The newscaster reported the story from the *Capitol* in Washington.

des′ ert means "a dry, barren region."

de sert′ means "to abandon."

des sert′ (note the difference in spelling) is "a sweet food at the end of a meal."

> Camels are called ships of the *desert*.
> Did the mother bird *desert* the babies?
> Kathy made apple crisp for *dessert*.

hear means "to listen to or to receive sound by the ear."

here refers to this place.

> You could *hear* the siren for miles.
> The meeting will be *here* in the library.

its is a possessive, meaning "belonging to *it*."

it's is the contraction for *it is* or *it has*.

> Put the typewriter into *its* case.
> *It's* time to go.

loose means either "not tight" or "free and untied."

lose means "to be unable to find or keep." It is also the opposite of *win*.

> The doorknob is *loose*.
> I *lose* my sense of direction in a strange place.
> Did you *lose* the race?

principal means "leading, chief, or highest in importance." It also refers to the head of an elementary or high school.

principle refers to a basic truth, rule, or law.

> Ed spoke to the *principal* about his problem.
> San Francisco is one of the *principal* cities of California.
> The *principle* I value most is honesty.

stationary means "not moving, fixed."

stationery refers to writing materials like paper and envelopes.

> The room dividers are *stationary*.
> Clair wrote on yellow *stationery*.

their shows possession by *them*.

there means "in that place."

they're is the contraction for *they are*.

> The twins have *their* own room.
> Put your boots *there* in the hallway.
> *They're* leaving for Dallas tomorrow.

to means "toward or as far as."

too means "also or extremely."

two is the number 2.

> Kelly wrote a letter *to* Gloria.
> The oven is *too* hot.
> *Two* of the meeting rooms are free.

weather refers to the condition of the atmosphere, such as its heat, cold, wetness, or dryness.

whether indicates a choice between two things.

> Did you listen to the *weather* forecast?
> Dan can't decide *whether* or not to quit his job.

who's is the contraction for *who is* or *who has*.

whose is the possessive form of *who*.

> *Who's* playing the piano?
> *Whose* lunch is this?

your shows possession by *you*.

you're is the contraction for *you are* or *you were*.

> Here are *your* gloves.
> *You're* the winner.

Exercise A Choose the right word from the words given.

1. The soldier (deserted, desserted) his unit.
2. Cactus plants grow in the (desert, dessert).
3. The Arabs wear (loose, lose) robes.
4. Will they (loose, lose) the game if Payton doesn't play?
5. (Its, It's) snowing in the Rocky Mountains.
6. Put the canary back in (its, it's) cage.
7. The (capital, Capitol, capitol) of Kentucky is Frankfort.
8. The track is (stationary, stationery); the light fixtures are moveable.
9. The country fought for its (principals, principles).
10. Jenny will meet us (hear, here) at noon.

Exercise B Follow the directions for Exercise A.

1. The water in Lake Michigan was (to, too, two) cold for swimming.
2. The customer complained (to, too, two) the manager.
3. Polly and Sue researched (their, there, they're) topics.
4. When (their, there, they're) through practicing, they will rehearse with Ms. Carlson.

5. The tape recorder is over (their, there, they're).
6. Michele considered (weather, whether) or not to join Pep Club.
7. (Who's, Whose) turn is it?
8. (Who's, Whose) making dinner tonight?
9. (Your, You're) prize is a $25.00 gift certificate.
10. (Your, You're) not feeling well, are you?

Part 2   Troublesome Verbs

These pairs of verbs are often confused. Notice how they differ.

Bring and *Take*

Bring refers to movement toward the person speaking. Example: The pipeline *brings* water here to the desert.

Take refers to motion away from the speaker. Example: Did you *take* those books back to the library?

Here are the principal parts of these verbs:

bring, brought, brought

Present:	*Bring* your camera along.
Past:	They *brought* too much luggage.
Past Participle:	Linda *has brought* the new album.

take, took, taken

Present:	*Take* this message to Mr. Gray.
Past:	He *took* his brother to the park.
Past Participle:	Sara *has taken* my bicycle.

Learn and *Teach*

Learn means "to gain knowledge or skill." Example: When did you *learn* how to cook?

Teach means "to help someone learn." Example: Will you *teach* me that dive?

Here are the principal parts of these verbs:

learn, learned, learned

Present: *Learn* the song by next week.

Past: The children *learned* the multiplication tables.

Past Participle: We *have learned* two magic tricks.

teach, taught, taught

Present: Ms. Stein *teaches* swimming.

Past: Lucy *taught* me about gardening.

Past Participle: This book *has taught* me a lot about the Civil War.

Let and Leave

Let means "to allow or permit." Example: *Let* her go.

Leave means "to go away from" or "to allow something to remain." Example: *Leave* your coats here.

The principal parts of these verbs are as follows:

let, let, let

Present: *Let* the phone ring.

Past: Sylvia *let* her hair grow long.

Past Participle: The mayor *will let* us interview her.

leave, left, left

Present: *Leave* the door open.

Past: Mark *left* on Tuesday.

Past Participle: The taxi *had left* in a hurry.

Lie and Lay

Lie means "to rest in a flat position" or "to be in a certain place." Example: *Lie* still.

Lay means "to place." Example: *Lay* the wreath here.

The principal parts of these verbs are on the next page.

lie, lay, lain

Present: *Lie* down on your bed.

Past: Harry *lay* in the hammock all afternoon.

Past Participle: The dog *has lain* by the fire all night.

lay, laid, laid

Present: *Lay* the books on the desk.

Past: The hen *laid* an egg.

Past Participle: Dad *has laid* the carpeting.

May and Can

May refers to permission. *May* also refers to something that is possible. *Might* is another form of the word.

May we go to the concert?   I *might be* a little late.

Can refers to ability. *Can* means being physically or mentally able to do something. *Could* is another form.

Can you play the piano?   We *could* walk to the beach.

May and *might* and *can* and *could* have no principal parts. They are used as helping verbs.

Rise and Raise

Rise means "to go upward." Example: The sun *rises*.

Raise means "to lift or to make something go up." It also means "to grow." Example: *Raise* your right hand.

The principal parts of these verbs are as follows:

rise, rose, risen

Present: Did you see the moon *rise?*

Past: Dale *rose* from his chair.

Past Participle: The temperature *has risen* to 80°.

raise, raised, raised

Present: Please *raise* the flag.

Past: Lynn *raised* these tomatoes.

Past Participle: The school *has raised* its tuition.

Sit and Set

Sit means "to occupy a seat." Example: *Sit* on this bench.
Set means "to place." Example: *Set* the tools there.
The principal parts of these verbs are as follows:

sit, sat, sat
Present: *Sit* at the head of the table.
Past: They *sat* around the pool.
Past Participle: The candidates *have sat* in the first row.

set, set, set
Present: *Set* the bottles on the back porch.
Past: Lois *set* the box on the floor.
Past Participle: They *have set* the albums on the shelf.

Exercise A   Choose the right verb from the two given.

1. The puppy (lay, laid) in the chair.
2. The price has (raised, risen) to $14.95.
3. We (sat, set) the baby in the stroller.
4. Nat will (bring, take) Karen back here by noon.
5. (May, Can) I ride with you?
6. Carl (sat, set) on Dad's hat.
7. Who (let, left) the ice cream on the counter?
8. The pep club has (raised, risen) money for new uniforms.
9. Pat (learned, taught) us a new dance step.
10. Nancy (let, left) the water out of the tub.

Exercise B   Follow the directions for Exercise A.

1. (Bring, Take) the shovel here, please.
2. Many children (may not, cannot) swim.
3. Who (learned, taught) you about soil conservation?
4. Sherry has (laid, lain) by the pool all afternoon.
5. Who (may, can) lift those boxes?
6. (Let, Leave) the chairs on the patio.

7. The reporters (raised, rose) when the President entered the room.
8. Marnie (lay, laid) the groceries on the counter.
9. Ms. Harris said I (may, can) leave early.
10. Did you (let, leave) Dan borrow your skates?

Part 3 Usage Problems

The words in this section are often used incorrectly. Notice the standard usages for these problem words.

accept means "to agree to something or to receive something willingly."

except means "to leave out." *Except* also means "not including."

> "I will *accept* the call," said Joe to the operator.
> "We will *except* you from the requirement," said the clerk.
> Everyone *except* Todd was there.

agree on means "to come to an understanding." You and others agree *on* a plan.

agree to means "to consent to." You agree *to* do something.

agree with means "to have the same opinion as someone else." You agree *with* somebody. *Agree with* may also refer to something being suitable, as when certain foods don't *agree with* you.

> The committee members *agreed on* a date for the meeting.
> We *agreed to* meet again.
> Laura never *agrees with* Jean.
> The tuna salad didn't *agree with* Bill.

all right is the correct spelling. *Alright* is nonstandard. There are two words.

> *All right*, I'll do the dishes.
> John felt *all right* after the accident.

among refers to a group of more than two people or things.

between refers to two people or things.

> We split up the work *among* the six of us.
> The conversation *between* the two of them ended abruptly.

anywhere, nowhere, somewhere, and **anyway** are standard usages. The words *anywheres, nowheres, somewheres,* and *anyways* are nonstandard. The final *s* should be dropped.

> Nonstandard: Cary was nowheres to be found.
>
> Standard: Cary was *nowhere* to be found.
>
> Nonstandard: That note is here somewheres.
>
> Standard: That note is here *somewhere.*

between each, followed by a singular noun, is incorrect. *Between* should not be used with a singular noun.

> Nonstandard: Between each speech there was a five-minute break.
>
> Standard: *Between speeches,* there was a five-minute break.
>
> Nonstandard: Carol practiced her dives between every meet.
>
> Standard: Carol practiced her dives *between meets.*

borrow means "to receive something on loan." Don't confuse it with *lend,* meaning "to give out temporarily."

> Nonstandard: Will you borrow me your car?
>
> Standard: Will you lend me your car?
>
> Standard: May I borrow your car?

Exercise A Look for sentences with nonstandard usage. Rewrite those sentences, using the right words. If a sentence is correct, write *Correct* after that number.

1. Bob excepted the award.
2. The key is somewhere in my purse.

3. There are file cabinets between each desk.
4. Kent will borrow you his notes.
5. Did you agree with Lois about what happened?
6. We divided the cookies between the three of us.
7. Put the box down anywhere.
8. Toni accepted the award with pleasure.
9. The college basketball coaches agreed to the schedule.
10. Everyone accept Helen had dessert.

Exercise B Follow the directions for Exercise A.

1. Allison had to choose among the two magazines.
2. The farmer walked between each row of beans.
3. Alright, who has my lunch?
4. Mike and Gayle agreed to the best candidate for mayor.
5. Ben will borrow me his flashlight.
6. I like all vegetables accept peas.
7. Anyways, I'm busy Saturday night.
8. Jessica agrees with me about what to wear.
9. The restaurant did not except personal checks.
10. Betty and Ellen split the reward between them.

fewer refers to numbers or things that can be counted.

less refers to amount or quantity.

> Curt's bike has *fewer* gears than Al's.
> It takes *less* time to take the short cut.

in means "inside something."

into tells of motion from the outside to the inside of something.

| Nonstandard: | The security guard went in the bank. |
| Standard: | The security guard went *into* the bank. |

| Nonstandard: | Sam put a dime in the parking meter. |
| Standard: | Sam put a dime *into* the parking meter. |

kind of a and **sort of a** are nonstandard. The *a* is not necessary.

> Nonstandard: What kind of a car is that?
>
> Standard: What *kind of* car is that?

> Nonstandard: There is some sort of a form to fill out.
>
> Standard: There is some *sort of* form to fill out.

like is a preposition. Using *like* as a conjunction before a clause is not fully accepted. Especially in writing, it is better to use *as* or *as if*.

> Nonstandard: Like the almanac predicted, it rained today.
>
> Standard: *As* the almanac predicted, it rained today.

> Nonstandard: Jake walked like he knew the way there.
>
> Standard: Jake walked *as if* he knew the way there.

of is sometimes incorrectly used in phrases like *could of*, *shouldn't of*, and *must of*. The correct word is *have* or its contraction: *could have*, *could've*, *shouldn't have*, *must have*, *might have*, *might've*.

> Nonstandard: Sally should of left earlier.
>
> Standard: Sally *should have* left earlier.

ways does not refer to distance. *Way* is correct.

> Nonstandard: It is a short ways to the pool.
>
> Standard: It is a short *way* to the pool.

Exercise A Correct the sentences with nonstandard usage. If a sentence is correct, write *Correct*.

1. Irma poured the orange juice in the glasses.
2. The grain elevator is a ways down the highway.
3. That kind of a jacket is waterproof.
4. Ginger could of driven you.
5. There are less summer jobs available this year.
6. Like the coach said, we have to practice every day.

7. Marge put her boots in her locker.
8. There are fewer Spanish Club members this year.
9. This cola has less calories.
10. Betsy acted like she had lost her best friend.

Exercise B Follow the directions for Exercise A.

1. We should of done our homework first.
2. What ingredients did you put into this barbeque sauce?
3. Kelly looks as if she is tired.
4. Less people drive downtown.
5. The barn is quite a ways from the house.
6. Fewer sales clerks are hired after the holidays are over.
7. Jack put his check in his savings account.
8. Pete and Al got along like they were old friends.
9. Abby chose this kind of a bike.
10. Jeff looked like he had seen a ghost.

ADDITIONAL EXERCISES

The Right Word

A. Words Often Confused Choose the correct word from those given in parentheses.

1. Have you claimed (your, you're) prize yet?
2. Did you (loose, lose) your ticket stub?
3. (Who's, Whose) the passenger in the sidecar?
4. (It's, Its) almost time to leave.
5. The fish had jumped out of (it's, its) bowl.
6. I always keep the Turners' mail for them when (there, they're, their) on vacation.
7. Saudi Arabia is a kingdom in the (desert, dessert).
8. (Their, There, They're) is a whistle that only a dog can (hear, here).
9. Erin doesn't go (to, too, two) the youth center (to, too, two) often.
10. The lifeguards put on (their, there, they're) jackets if the (weather, whether) turns chilly.

B. Troublesome Verbs Choose the correct verb from those given in parentheses.

1. Please (bring, take) me a glass of water.
2. (May, Can) we make a U-turn on this street, officer?
3. The trainer has (learned, taught) the boxer proper footwork.
4. A huge crane (raised, rose) steel beams to the upper stories.
5. The tug-of-war ends when one team (lets, leaves) go of the rope.
6. The test pilot (sat, set) at the controls.
7. Meredith (lay, laid) awake and couldn't sleep.

8. The oil has (raised, risen) to the surface of the sea.
9. Jude (lay, laid) cloth over the picnic table.
10. Don't (sit, set) the plastic bowl on the hot stove.

C. Usage Problems Choose the correct word or phrase from the two given in parentheses.

1. Will you (borrow, lend) me some warmer gloves?
2. (All right, Alright), operator, we'll (accept, except) the charges.
3. Our family divides the work (among, between) the five of us.
4. Trisha ran (in, into) the room (as if, like) she was terribly excited.
5. There is some (sort of, sort of a) curb (between the, between each) parking spaces.
6. I should (have, of) eaten (fewer, less) pretzels and drunk (fewer, less) 7-Up.
7. (Anyway, Anyways), Rick has (nowhere, nowheres) else to go.
8. Has Mr. Roman (agreed on, agreed to, agreed with) let you take Saturday off?
9. The players in the huddle quickly (agreed on, agreed to, agreed with) a strategy.
10. Everyone (accept, except) Bev had biked a long (way, ways).

MIXED REVIEW

The Right Word

A. Using the right word Correct any errors in spelling or usage. If there is no error, write *Correct*.

1. What kind of book is that?
2. He sometimes acts like he can't hear well.
3. I should not of driven into the desert with so little gas.
4. Your clothes will feel loose after you loose weight.
5. Pour less batter in the pan for all the pancake except Vi's.
6. The chairs are stationary; the tables are to heavy to move.
7. Let's have fewer arguments; we're getting nowheres.
8. I agree with your idea of borrowing Ms. Barber's shovel and dividing the work among the three of us.
9. Between each act their was an intermission.
10. It's a long ways from here to the Capitol, and I don't know whether Congress is still in session.

B. Using troublesome verbs correctly The verbs in these sentences are used incorrectly. Rewrite each sentence correctly.

1. The cat laid on laundry that I had set on the table.
2. Can you rise your injured arm?
3. Can I please lie down for a few minutes?
4. Jan brought the television set to that shop.
5. Please learn that dog not to lie on the bed.
6. May I take some tea to you while you sit here?
7. The children in class learned to set and listen.
8. Nick's voice raised as he asked the boss to raise his salary.
9. Leave Amanda set the chess pieces on the board.
10. The paramedics laid the stretcher down and left the victim laying there.

USING GRAMMAR IN WRITING
The Right Word

A. Imagine that you work on the staff of a local newspaper. You have the job of correcting errors in letters to the editor. Of course, you may not change any of the ideas in a letter. However, you may correct errors of grammar and usage. Following is one of the letters that you must correct. Read the letter to learn what the writer's ideas are. Then rewrite the letter, using standard English.

The city shouldn't of cancelled the summer music program. Hundreds of people came to here the concerts last summer. Did the city council ask they're opinion about cancelling the concerts? No. I think the city should of left the concerts go on for at least another year. If their to expensive, why not charge some kind of a fee? Anyone who went to the concerts would say they liked them. Let's see the city give the music program one more chance.

B. Rewrite the following passage in standard English.

My first day on my first job was almost my last. I thought it would be so fun. Then I missed my bus I got there 5 minutes late and my boss goes "you gotta do better then that." So he gives me a uniform that was to large and I'm holding it up with one hand and trying to hear what hes learning me. And then my friends come in and order hamburgers and I forget the fries. It sure wasn't my best day, no way.

Capitalization

Capital letters are signals. They make the reader aware of certain important words and of the first words in sentences.

This section will show you the specific rules for capitalizing words. You should refer to this section at any time if you are in doubt about whether or not to capitalize a word.

Proper Nouns and Adjectives

Capitalize proper nouns and proper adjectives.

A **proper noun** is the name of a particular person, place, or thing. In contrast, a **common noun** is the name of a whole class of people, places, or things. A **proper adjective** is an adjective formed from a proper noun.

Common Noun	Proper Noun	Proper Adjective
king	Edward	Edwardian
country	Spain	Spanish
government	Congress	Congressional

There are many kinds of proper nouns. The following rules will help you decide whether or not a noun is a proper noun.

Names of People

Capitalize people's names. Also capitalize the initials or abbreviations that stand for names.

J.F. Kennedy	John Fitzgerald Kennedy
Louis C. Tiffany	Louis Comfort Tiffany

Capitalize the titles used with people's names. Also capitalize the initials or abreviations that stand for those titles.

The titles *Miss, Ms., Mrs.,* and *Mr.* are always capitalized.

Gov. James Thompson	Major Margaret Houlihan
Ms. Marianne Rizzo	Dr. Carlos Rodriguez
Judge Sandra Day O'Connor	Rev. J.L. Bluett

Do not capitalize a title that is used without a name. It is a common noun.

Who is the governor of Missouri?
Richard Posner is a federal judge.

Capitalize titles of very high importance, even when they are used without names.

> the President of the United States
> the Chief Justice of the Supreme Court
> the Prime Minister of Canada
> a Congresswoman
> the Pope

Family Relationships

Capitalize such words as *mother, father, aunt,* **and** *uncle* **when they are used as names.** If the noun is preceded by a possessive word or by *a* or *the,* it is not capitalized.

> My mom will give you a ride home.
> Was Dad a good student, Grandpa?
> My aunt and uncle have confusing names, Uncle Gene and
> Aunt Jean.
> Do you need any help, Mom?

The Pronoun *I*

Capitalize the pronoun *I.*

> She and I played video games.   I study after dinner.

The Supreme Being and Sacred Writings

Capitalize all words referring to God, to the Holy Family, and to religious scriptures.

the Almighty	the Bible	the Son of God
the Lord	the Talmud	the New Testament
the Blessed Virgin	Allah	the Book of Job

Capitalize personal pronouns referring to God.

> They thanked the Lord for His bounty.

Exercise A   Copy the following sentences. Change small letters to capital letters wherever necessary.

1. The car broke down while mom and i were out shopping.
2. The reading at the funeral was from the book of psalms.
3. My father enjoys the short stories of o. henry.
4. My brother introduced rev. smyth to dr. shores.
5. Did the name on the envelope say major jean reilly or mayor jean reilly?
6. The prime minister of England is margaret thatcher.
7. My aunt, michele elaine levine, is a curator.
8. Did senator adlai stevenson resign his position to run for governor?
9. The soldier thanked the lord for sparing his life.
10. Professor friedman shook hands with professor samuelson before the debate.

Exercise B   Follow the directions for Exercise A.

1. Will len accompany uncle robert to St. Louis?
2. My sister reads from the bible every day.
3. The president met with the pope during his last visit to Europe.
4. Did florence write a thank-you note to her grandmother?
5. Mr. miller wrote a letter to sen. charles percy.
6. The reverend arthur dimmesdale is a character in a novel.
7. The book of genesis in the bible tells the story of creation.
8. Has mom met dr. johnson yet?
9. The novelist bill granger also writes under the name of william griffin.
10. Our neighbor, mr. j.b. masters, met the president at a fund-raising dinner.

Geographical Names

In a geographical name, capitalize the first letter of each word except articles and prepositions.

If the article *the* appears before a place name, it is not part of the name and is therefore not capitalized.

Continents:	Australia, Africa, South America, Asia
Bodies of Water:	the Indian Ocean, the Sangamon River, the Gulf of Mexico, the Mediterranean Sea, Tampa Bay, the Suez Canal, Lake Erie
Landforms:	Mount Rushmore, the Hawaiian Islands, the Rocky Mountains, the Sahara Desert, Cape Horn, the Grand Canyon
Political Units:	Colorado, Orlando, the Province of Quebec, the Republic of Chad, United Mexican States, Tenth Congressional District
Public Areas:	Yellowstone National Park, Fort Pulaski, the Statue of Liberty, Blackhawk State Park, Arlington House, Custer Battlefield
Roads and Highways:	Route 47, Interstate Highway 75, Glenview Road, Michigan Avenue, Market Street

Directions and Sections

Capitalize names of sections of the country.

The Midwest includes Wisconsin and Minnesota.
Many people retire to the South.
The climate in the Northwest is very different from that in the Southwest.

Capitalize proper adjectives that come from names of sections of the country.

a Midwestern farm   a Western resort
Southern hospitality   a West Coast fad

Do not capitalize directions of the compass.

San Diego is south of Los Angeles.
The airport is west of the city.

Do not capitalize adjectives that come from words showing direction.

The drug store is on the west side of the street.
The kitchen window has a southern exposure.

Exercise A Number your paper from 1 to 10. Find the words in the following sentences that should be capitalized. Write the words after the proper number, using the necessary capital letters.

1. They backpacked in glacier national park.
2. We traveled from washington into british columbia.
3. The business center of the south is atlanta, georgia.
4. The mojave desert is in california.
5. The panama canal connects the atlantic ocean with the pacific ocean.
6. The caspian sea is really a lake bordered by the soviet union and iran.
7. Is interstate 55 the same road as route 66?
8. The southeast has a hot, humid climate, and the southwest has a hot, dry climate.
9. The west met the east with the completion of the transcontinental railroad at promontory point, utah.
10. In hong kong many people live on boats.

Exercise B Follow the directions for Exercise A.

1. Sherry lives south of cleveland, ohio.
2. Don met me on the northeast corner of park drive and morse avenue.

3. We visited redwood national park on the west coast.
4. Do you sell southern fried chicken and hush-puppies?
5. Craig reported on the indians of the southwest.
6. The steamboat churned down the mississippi river.
7. Many people vacation in the south to escape harsh mid-western winters.
8. A southern drawl differs from a western twang.
9. The hoover dam spans the colorado river in nevada.
10. The bering sea is on the western coast of alaska.

Names of Organizations and Institutions

Capitalize the names of organizations and institutions, including political parties, governmental bodies or agencies, schools, colleges, churches, hospitals, clubs, businesses, and abbreviations of these names.

Democratic Party   Massachusetts General Hospital
Federal Communications   American Dental Association
    Commission   United Nations
Villa Grove High School   A.M.A.
St. Raymond's Church

Do not capitalize such words as *school, company, church,* and *hospital* when they are not used as parts of names.

That school is between a hospital and a church.

Names of Events, Documents, and Periods of Time

Capitalize the names of historical events, documents, and periods of time.

Battle of Wounded Knee   Webster-Ashburton Treaty
Korean War   the Dark Ages
Bill of Rights   the Industrial Revolution

Months, Days, and Holidays

Capitalize names of months, days, and holidays, but not the names of seasons.

June	Tuesday	fall
Easter	Christmas	spring

Races, Languages, Nationalities, and Religions

Capitalize the names of races, languages, nationalities, and religions. Also capitalize any adjectives that come from these names.

Dutch	Japanese	Catholicism	Protestant
Irish	Buddhism	Cuban	Jewish

School Subjects

Do not capitalize the names of school subjects, except course titles followed by a number.

math	History of Civilization I
home economics	Biology 100

Remember that the names of languages are always capitalized.

French	Spanish	German	English

Ships, Trains, Airplanes, and Automobiles

Capitalize the names of ships, trains, airplanes, and automobiles.

U.S.S. Constitution	Boeing 747	Oldsmobile Cutlass

B.C., A.D.

Capitalize the abbreviations *B.C.* and *A.D.*

The Chou dynasty in China lasted from 770 to 256 B.C.
William of Normandy conquered England in A.D. 1066.

Exercise A Write the words in each sentence that should be capitalized. Use the necessary capital letters.

1. In may, st. francis hospital holds a fund-raising dance.
2. The american economic association convention will be in december.
3. Is there a hospital near glenbrook south high school?
4. Many polish people live in chicago.
5. The jewish new year is called rosh hashana.
6. The flowering of the arts during the late middle ages, a.d. 1300–1600, is called the renaissance.
7. Charles Lindbergh left new york on may 20, 1927, in his plane, the spirit of st. louis.
8. The battle of gettysburg was fought in july of 1863.
9. A phonetic alphabet was developed in phoenicia before 1600 b.c.
10. A chevrolet *chevette* is about the size of a volkswagen *rabbit*.

Exercise B Follow the directions for Exercise A.

1. The fourth thursday in november is celebrated as thanksgiving day.
2. Kevin has advanced art I after his gym class.
3. Both the french and the italians participated in the conference.
4. The fund-raiser for the republican party is on june 24.
5. The illinois education association is part of the national education association.
6. We read about the battle of little big horn in history.
7. Both english and gaelic are spoken in ireland.
8. Many new yorkers escape to the seashore on summer weekends.
9. Dad ordered a new pontiac *firebird.*
10. A graduate of stanford university, susan has worked for the federal reserve bank and also for bank of america.

First Words

Sentences and Poetry

Capitalize the first word of every sentence and the first word of most lines of poetry.

> The quarterback was sacked. He lost five yards on the play.
> Listen my children, and you shall hear
> Of the midnight ride of Paul Revere, . . .
> —from "Paul Revere's Ride," HENRY WADSWORTH LONGFELLOW

Sometimes, especially in modern poetry, the lines of a poem do not begin with capital letters.

Quotations

Capitalize the first word of a direct quotation.

A **direct quotation** tells the exact words of a speaker or writer.

> Wordsworth said, "The child is father of the man."

In a **divided quotation,** a direct quotation is broken into two parts by words like *he said* or *she explained.* Do not capitalize the first word of the second part unless it starts a new sentence.

> "I insist," Mr. Jackson said, "that you join me for dinner."
> "I insist," Mr. Jackson said. "Join me for dinner."

Letter Parts

Capitalize the first word in the greeting of a letter. Also capitalize the name of the person addressed, or words like *Sir* and *Madam* that stand for names.

> Dear Ms. Takamoto,   Dear Mr. Conn,   Dear Sir or Madam:

In the complimentary close, capitalize only the first word.

> Very truly yours,   Sincerely yours,

Outlines

Capitalize the first word of each item in an outline. Also capitalize the letters before each line.

I. Endangered species
   A. Mammals
      1. Florida panther
      2. Utah prairie dog
   B. Reptiles

Titles

Capitalize the first word and all important words in the titles of chapters, magazine articles, short stories, essays, poems, and songs or short pieces of music.

Chapter title: Chapter 10, "The Industrial Revolution"
Magazine article: "Improve Your Tennis Game"
Short story: "The Open Window"
Essay: "Self-Reliance"
Poem: "Spring Thunder"
Song: "Battle Hymn of the Republic"

Capitalize the first word and all important words in titles of books, newspapers, magazines, plays, movies, television programs, works of art, and long musical compositions.

Book title: *To Kill a Mockingbird*
Newspaper: *Knoxville News-Sentinel*
Magazine: *People*
Play: *The King and I*
Movie: *Raiders of the Lost Ark*
Television program: *Today*
Work of art: *Girl with Braids*
Long musical composition: *Messiah*

Exercise A   Capitalize these sentences correctly.

1. Many people subscribe to *the wall street journal*.
2. both *forbes* and *fortune* are business magazines.

3. ms. appleton read the poem "danny deever" to us.
4. I. major world religions
   a. buddhism
      1. origins
5. billy joel won an award for the song "just the way you are."
6. dear sir or madam:
   i would like to order four mezzanine seats for the *nutcracker suite.* a check is enclosed.

   sincerely yours,
7. "doris," asked sue, "will you save a place for me?"
8. "my term paper is due next week," said ken. "maybe i'd better go to the library tonight."
9. edgar allan poe wrote "the pit and the pendulum."
10. the painting *at the moulin rouge* is by toulouse lautrec.

Exercise B Follow the directions for Exercise A.

1. the sportscaster sang "take me out to the ball game."
2. miniver cheevy, child of scorn
      grew lean, while he assailed the seasons;
   he wept that he was ever born
      and he had reasons.
   —from "Miniver Cheevy," EDWIN ARLINGTON ROBINSON
3. our class read chapter two, "how painting began."
4. "if i take the bus," complained howard, "i'll be late."
5. dad watches *the evening news* when he gets home.
6. jason asked, "who has my copy of *life* magazine?"
7. who played the title role in the movie *gandhi?*
8. the article "the two souls of peru" appeared in the march, 1982, *national geographic.*
9. the song "my way" was made famous by frank sinatra.
10. dear ms. schmidt,
    here are the two tickets to the play *west side waltz.*

    yours truly,

ADDITIONAL EXERCISES

Capitalization

A. Proper Nouns Number your paper from 1 to 10. Find the words in the following sentences that should be capitalized. Write the words beside the proper numbers. Capitalize the words correctly.

1. Was the soft drink dr. pepper named after an actual doctor?
2. My sister auditioned for the part of lady macbeth.
3. Margaret thatcher became prime minister of england in 1979.
4. This passage from the *bible* was written by st. luke.
5. Reverend elaine jones, rabbi samuel h. gelman, and father edward krause co-teach a course on the *old testament.*
6. Doesn't sgt. hays realize that i am on leave?
7. Your brother called while you were at work, grandpa.
8. Reg dwight changed his name to elton john.
9. Doesn't b. b. king call his guitar lucille?
10. At once, rep. garcia wired the president at the White House.

B. Capital Letters Copy the following sentences. Change small letters to capital letters wherever necessary.

1. the okefenokee swamp is in georgia and florida.
2. We drove south through brown county into kentucky.
3. The southwest can get very hot; its rivers sometimes dry up.
4. the coast of poland is on the baltic sea.

5. Penny worked at six flags, a park in magic mountain, california.

6. kay was used to swimming in the ocean and was surprised that the mediterranean had no tides.

7. one island in the west indies is st. vincent.

8. The swan islands are controlled by honduras.

9. The united states is on the south bank of rainy river; canada is on the river's north shore.

10. people who fear heights can ask a guard to drive their cars across chesapeake bay bridge.

C. Proper Nouns and Adjectives
Number your paper from 1 to 10. After each number, copy the words from each sentence that should be capitalized. Use the necessary capital letters.

1. Students in spanish III can earn extra credit by going to special sessions on thursdays.

2. The scanners at many food stores are made by ibm.

3. Uncle gene owns a '63 chevy that is in mint condition.

4. My cousin graduated from roberto clemente high school last june.

5. Since 1800, the president of the united states has lived in the White House, which was rebuilt after the war of 1812.

6. Our american history class toured the headquarters of the united nations.

7. The public schools as well as the catholic schools are closed on good friday.

8. The jewish holiday of yom kippur is celebrated in autumn.

9. Students in ms. holden's office machines II class learn to use a computer.

10. The mayans in yucatán devised an extremely accurate calendar around 300 b.c.

D. Titles, Outlines, and Letters Number your paper from 1 to 10. Find the words in the following sentences that should be capitalized. Write the words after the proper numbers, using the necessary capital letters.

1. the television comedy *after M*A*S*H* is a spinoff from *M*A*S*H*.

2. "*the moonlight sonata* is too difficult for you now," said the piano teacher. "maybe next year you can try it."

3. ms. mihalos assigned an article from *business week*.

4. dear madam or sir:
   have you often asked yourself, "is there any way that i can earn money at home?"

5. for my report, i read *let the circle be unbroken*, a novel by mildred d. taylor.

6. it was the summer of the sequels: *grease 2, rocky III,* and *star trek II: the wrath of khan.*

7. the state song of georgia is "georgia on my mind."

8. "can't you think of a better title for your essay," asked pat, "than 'how to make good pancakes'?"

9. my mother looked through the job ads in the *houston chronicle.*

10. II. superstitions
    a. good-luck charms
       1. rabbit's foot

MIXED REVIEW

Capitalization

A. Using capitalization correctly Number your paper from 1 to 10. Copy the following sentences, using the correct capitalization.

1. the dancer ronald perry trained at the dance theatre of harlem.
2. dear ms. allegretti,
      thank you for the cassette of christmas songs. my sister and i especially like "silent night" and "we three kings."
3. i think that the first woman to fly an aircraft across the english channel was an american, harriet quimby.
4. ross perot, jr. and s. w. coburn were co-pilots of the *spirit of texas*, the first helicopter to fly around the world.
5. my grandfather plays bagpipes with the shannon rovers band.
6. slowly grandfather said, "you may have heard about that battle in your history class."
7. after the battle of yorktown, general cornwallis refused to surrender his sword; the general ordered an irish soldier to do it for him.
8. on monday in world history II, i gave a report on the mali empire.
9. according to *information please almanac*, chief sitting bull was born in the west, on grand river, south dakota.
10. katherine d. ortega became treasurer of the united states on october 3, 1983.

B. Using capitalization correctly in proofreading Proofread the following paragraph. Rewrite it, using correct capitalization.

"peace" is a word rich in meaning, as a look at some recent recipients of the nobel peace prize will show. rev. dr. martin luther king, jr. was honored for leading a nonviolent movement for equal rights for all people in the united states. the co-winners mairead corrigan and betty williams worked toward a nonviolent solution to the problems between catholics and protestants in northern ireland. a nun, mother teresa of calcutta, won the prize for her care of the poor in india. For their efforts to promote disarmament, alfonsa garcia robles of mexico and alva myrdal of sweden shared the award. a polish labor leader, lech walesa, won for founding a union called *solidarity,* which seeks to achieve fair treatment for workers. the many kinds of work recognized by the nobel committee suggest that peace is much more than the absence of war.

USING MECHANICS IN WRITING
Capitalization

A. Your class has decided to publish a school *Who's Who.* Every student will be included, and each student will write one of the biographies. Interview a friend and then write a paragraph about your friend that could be included in the *Who's Who.* Be sure to include all the following information.

- your friend's full name
- the city and state (or country) of your friend's place of birth
- the names of places where your friend has traveled or would like to travel
- the names of clubs or other organizations to which your friend belongs
- the names of schools that your friend has attended
- the names of your friend's favorite book, movie, television program, and song

Check your work to be sure that the capitalization is correct. Underline each capital letter.

B. You have landed a job at a travel agency. This agency organizes group tours of major cities. Your first job as a trainee is to write a brochure about a city that you would like to visit. What city would you like to visit? How would you convince other people that they would like to visit it?

Write a paragraph that will help attract people to your favorite city. Before you begin writing, do some research to learn more about the city. Be sure to include historic sites, homes of famous people, and other attractions. Mention them by their proper names. Be careful to follow the rules for capitalization.

Punctuation

When you speak, you pause, you stop, and you raise or lower your voice at certain points. However, when you read and write, how do you show where to pause, stop, or raise or lower your voice? **Punctuation marks** serve this purpose. They show how a sentence should be read.

This section will review all the punctuation marks. Refer to these pages whenever you have a question about punctuation.

End Marks

End marks are the punctuation marks that indicate the end of a sentence. The three kinds of end marks are the **period,** the **question mark,** and the **exclamation point.**

The Period

Use a period at the end of a declarative sentence.

A **declarative sentence** is a sentence that makes a statement. You use declarative sentences when you tell something.

The meeting ended at noon.

Use a period at the end of most imperative sentences.

An **imperative sentence** is a sentence that orders or requests someone to do something.

Please pass the mustard.

At times, imperative sentences express strong excitement or emotion. Then an exclamation point, rather than a period, is used at the end of the sentence.

Stop that!   Wake up!

Use a period at the end of an indirect question.

An **indirect question** tells that someone asked a question. However, it does not give the exact words of the question.

The waiter asked if we had enjoyed our dinner.

Notice how a **direct question** differs:

The waiter asked, "Did you enjoy your dinner?"

A direct question shows the exact words of the person asking the question. A direct question ends with a question mark.

Use a period after an abbreviation or an initial.

An **abbreviation** is a shortened form of a word. An **initial** is a first letter that stands for a word.

Dr. Orville N. Boynton   3 A.M. on Sept. 13

Maj. Jacob M. Levine   8 lb., 13 oz.

Certain abbreviations do not use periods. To check whether or not to use a period with an abbreviation, look up the abbreviation in your dictionary.

CIA (*Central Intelligence Agency*)
CB (*Citizens' Band*)
UN (*United Nations*)

Use a period after each number or letter for an item in an outline or a list.

(An Outline)

I. Foods

    A. Fruits

       1. Peaches

(A List)

1. beach towel

2. suntan oil

3. sunglasses

Use a period between dollars and cents and before a decimal.

$42.91   2.36

The Question Mark

Use a question mark at the end of an interrogative sentence.

An **interrogative sentence** is a sentence that asks a question.

Who was at the door?

The Exclamation Point

Use an exclamation point at the end of an exclamatory sentence.

An **exclamatory sentence** expresses excitement or other strong emotion.

That's wonderful!✓   How lucky you were!✓

Use an exclamation point after an interjection.

An **interjection** is one or more words that show strong feeling. Sometimes the interjection is a sound.

Hurrah!✓   Yuck!✓   Oh, no!✓   Great!✓

Exercise A Copy the following sentences, adding the necessary punctuation. Be prepared to tell what punctuation marks you used and why you used them.

1. Has anyone seen Col Harms
2. Mona said that she wants a watch for her birthday
3. Incredible That micrometer measures up to 0001 of an inch
4. Does your plane leave at 6:00 AM or 6:00 PM
5. Ouch That plate is hot
6. I Types of fabric
    A Natural products
       1 Cotton
7. The initials NAS stand for the National Academy of Sciences
8. Address the invitation to Dr Jacob Morton, Jr, PO Box 1200, Nashville, Tennessee
9. Did Rev JT Smith give the sermon
10. The USS *Arizona* was sunk at Pearl Harbor

Exercise B Follow the directions for Exercise A.

1. Karen asked what UNICEF means
2. The book was published by Random House, Inc in 1968
3. Have you heard the new FM station
4. Is Sally an LPN or an RN
5. Oh, no He struck out
6. Dr O'Donnell's business card reads, "Mary O'Donnell, MD"

7. Does school end at 11 AM on Friday
8. The IRS audited his financial records
9. Dan handed the customer $237 change from the five-dollar bill
10. Stop Did you bring the tickets for the concert

The Comma

A comma is used to separate words that do not go together. When you are speaking, you can pause. When you are writing, you use commas for breaks in thought. In this way, commas help you to communicate clearly.

Using Commas in a Series

Use a comma after every item in a series except the last one.

A series is three or more items of the same kind. Your writing may contain a series of words, phrases, or clauses.

Words: Clair ordered soup, a salad, and milk.

Phrases: The cross-country team ran down the street, through the park, and into the forest preserve.

Clauses: The tour guide explained who founded Dallas, how it grew, and why it is an important city today.

Use commas after *first, second, third,* and so on, when these adverbs introduce a series.

There are four stages for writing a paper: first, pre-writing; second, writing a first draft; third, revising; and fourth, writing a final copy.

When there are two or more adjectives before a noun, use commas between them.

The weather reporter predicted another hot, humid day.

Exercise A Number your paper from 1 to 10. Copy the following sentences and add commas where necessary.

1. Skiing tobogganing and ice skating are winter sports.
2. Julie goes to dance lessons on Monday Wednesday and Friday.
3. Mexican food is known for its hot spicy flavors.
4. Craig started the car put it in gear and backed out of the driveway.
5. The soldier told his captors three things: first his name; second his rank; and third his serial number.
6. The Christmas stocking was filled with fruit nuts and candy.
7. Jerry struck a match turned on the gas and lit the camp stove.
8. Cheryl learned three swimming strokes: first the crawl; second the backstroke; and third the butterfly.
9. The baby waved his arms kicked his legs and talked to the stuffed animal.
10. Laura asked Barb where she bought the album how much it cost and whether she could borrow it.

Exercise B Follow the directions for Exercise A.

1. The mechanic listed the car's problems: first faulty transmission; second weak brakes; and third bald tires.
2. Streamers paper flowers and balloons decorated the gym.
3. To make vanilla frosting, mix butter powdered sugar vanilla and milk.
4. The radio announcer gave an accurate informative report of the game.
5. Marti saddled the horse mounted it and rode off down the trail.

6. Lush green tropical foliage had overgrown the path through the hot steamy jungle.
7. Seven-layer salad contains lettuce peas bacon hard-boiled eggs onions mayonnaise and cheese.
8. We visited cathedrals art museums and historical monuments on the tour.
9. First I planned the menu; second I went to the grocery store; third I prepared the dinner; and fourth I served it.
10. The waves roll in crash on the beach and roll out again.

Using Commas with Introductory Words

Use a comma to separate an introductory word, long phrase, or clause from the rest of the sentence.

Yes, I'd like a glass of water. (introductory word)

After three weeks without rain, the lawn became very dry and brown. (prepositional phrases)

Breathing hard, the runner kept walking after the race. (verbal phrase)

If it rains, the picnic will be postponed. (adverb clause)

As you can see, commas are used after introductory words like *yes* and *no*. They are also used after prepositional phrases, verbal phrases, and adverb clauses that begin sentences.

Sometimes the comma may be left out. When there would be little pause in speaking, no comma is used.

At midnight the band stopped playing.

Using Commas with Interrupters

Use commas to set off one or more words that interrupt the flow of thought in a sentence.

The defendant, I believe, is innocent.

Kevin, for example, plays two sports.

The price of gas, in fact, has gone down.

Mildred, of course, wants to be on the committee.

The following words are additional examples of interrupters. In a sentence, set them off with commas.

therefore	in any event	however
moreover	by the way	furthermore
I suppose	I think	nevertheless

Exercise A Number your paper from 1 to 10. Copy the following sentences. Add commas where necessary.

1. No *On Golden Pond* did not win the Oscar for best movie.
2. Before opening the door Brad knocked.
3. Waxing the car Tony found some rust spots.
4. Martin however refused to go.
5. Yes Myrna accepted the job.
6. Exhausted from fighting the brush fire the volunteers returned to town.
7. You know my brother I believe.
8. To be honest with you I really don't like that song.
9. After he had made the announcement the President left the room.
10. If the Lakers win this game they will win the championship.

Exercise B Follow the directions for Exercise A.

1. The finale was I think the best part of the show.
2. George on the other hand prefers bluegrass music.
3. Yes that is Lill's responsibility.
4. Miriam however walks to school.

5. After the last game of the season the team has an awards dinner.
6. Although Cathy moved to Florida we still call each other and write letters.
7. Worried about his final exams Joe couldn't sleep.
8. When Bill cooks dinner he always makes chili.
9. That book by the way is by Robert Peck.
10. Because Eddie had missed two practices the coach wouldn't let him play in the game.

Using Commas with Nouns of Direct Address

Use commas to set off nouns of direct address.

Sometimes when you speak or write to someone, you use the person's name. The name of someone directly spoken to is a noun of **direct address.**

> Betsy, type this letter.
>
> On the table, Mom, is a note from Dad.
>
> Are there any messages, Lloyd?
>
> When you finish the test, class, turn your booklets over.

As in the last example, nouns of direct address may be common nouns.

Using Commas with Appositives

Use commas to set off most appositives.

An **appositive** is one or more words that explain or identify another word. The appositive directly follows the word it explains.

> Marcel Marceau, a mime, appeared in the movie *Silent Movie*.

Our dance teacher, Miss Eden, took us to a ballet.

Rugby, a form of football, is played with no time-outs or substitutions.

As in the final example, an appositive may contain a prepositional phrase.

A noun used as an appositive is called a **noun in apposition.** When the noun in apposition is a single name, it is not usually set off by commas.

My cousin Sally lives in Denver.

Using Commas with Quotations

Use commas to set off the explanatory words of a direct quotation.

The explanatory words are the statements like *he said, Greg replied,* or *Sheila asked.* They are not part of the quotation.

Explanatory words often come before the quotation. Use a comma after the explanatory words.

Carol said, "Meet me at the corner of State and Adams."

Now look at this quotation:

"Meet me at the corner of State and Adams," Carol said.

In the sentence above, the explanatory words come after the quotation. Notice that the comma belongs at the end of the quotation inside the quotation marks.

Sometimes a quotation is broken into two parts. The explanatory words separate the two parts. Here is an example of a *divided quotation.*

"Meet me," Carol said, "at the corner of State and Adams."

In a divided quotation, a comma is used within the quotation marks at the end of the first part of the sentence. A comma is also used after the explanatory words.

Indirect quotations do not tell the speaker's exact words. No commas are used.

> Carol said that we should meet her at the corner of State and Adams.

Using Commas in Compound Sentences

Use a comma before the conjunction between the two main clauses of a compound sentence.

> The temperature was ten degrees below zero, but the car started with no problem.

The comma is not necessary when the main clauses are very short and are joined by *and*.

> We danced and we sang.

Sometimes very short main clauses are joined by *but* or *or*. A comma is used since the words *but* and *or* mark a change in the flow of thought.

> Ann eats, but she doesn't gain weight.

Don't confuse compound sentences with compound subjects or compound predicates. There is no comma before the *and* that joins a compound subject or predicate.

> Tom parked the car and dropped some change into the parking meter.

Exercise A Copy these sentences. Add commas as needed.

1. Pac Man a video game has become very popular.
2. The doctor a specialist in plastic surgery examined the scar.
3. Mr. Wilson I'd like to introduce my brother Fred.
4. Did you water the plants Sylvia?
5. The dune buggy a fiberglass shell with a Volkswagen engine drove down the beach.

6. Mr. Schmidt the building superintendent will make minor repairs in the apartment.
7. Paul said "The golf match is on TV at 1:00 P.M."
8. "I ordered four tickets for the concert" said Dad.
9. "That ball" said the angry tennis player "was in bounds."
10. Amy was nervous before the play but she remembered all her lines.

Exercise B Follow the directions for Exercise A.

1. Is Sandy still attending the junior college or did she transfer to the state university?
2. Jack cleaned out the leaves from the gutter and then he painted it with rust-proof paint.
3. Milton Friedman a well-known economist won the Nobel Prize.
4. Nora reported on the Middle East and Peter discussed the problems in South Africa.
5. Ralph asked "Who is going to the banquet tomorrow night?"
6. "Sewing on a button is not that difficult Marty" explained Debby.
7. "Your donations for the flood victims will be put to good use" said Father McDonald.
8. The sandwiches were made with pita a Middle-Eastern flat bread.
9. "It is your turn" reminded Mom "to do the dishes."
10. "Girls let's meet by the south tennis courts before the match" said Ms. Snyder.

Using Commas in Dates

In dates, use a comma between the day of the month and the year.

September 4, 1982   July 20, 1947

When a date is part of a sentence, a comma follows the year.

The Tiffany Exhibit opened on June 10, 1982, in Chicago.

Using Commas in Place Names

Use a comma between the name of a city or town and the name of its state or country.

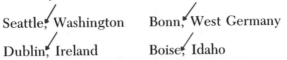

Seattle, Washington   Bonn, West Germany

Dublin, Ireland   Boise, Idaho

When an address is part of a sentence, use a comma after each item.

Simon addressed the letter to Mr. Edgar Evans, 1602 Fairview Road, Juneau, Alaska 99801.

Note that you do not put a comma between the state name and the ZIP code.

Using Commas in Letters

Use a comma after the salutation of a friendly letter. Use a comma after the closing of a friendly letter or a business letter.

Dear Margaret,   Yours truly,

Using Commas with Nonrestrictive Clauses

Use commas to set off nonrestrictive clauses.

A **nonrestrictive clause** is a clause that merely adds an idea to the sentence. The sentence would be complete without it. The meaning would be definite without it.

A **restrictive clause** is a clause that is essential to the meaning of a sentence. The clause is needed for the sense of the sentence. If a restrictive clause is dropped from a sentence, the meaning of the sentence changes.

Nonrestrictive clause: Mr. Murphy, *who is the new coach of the team,* held a press conference.
Mr. Murphy held a press conference.
(The clause could be dropped from the sentence.)

Restrictive clause: Mr. Murphy is the coach *who held the press conference.*
Mr. Murphy is the coach.
(The clause cannot be dropped from the sentence.)

To see if a clause is nonrestrictive, read the sentence without the clause. If the meaning doesn't change, the clause is nonrestrictive. Use commas before and after it.

Restrictive clauses are often used to identify or to point out the person or thing they modify. Without this identification, the meaning of the sentence would not be clear. Nonrestrictive clauses, on the other hand, add no essential meaning to the sentence.

Restrictive clause: Mr. Greenberg is the instructor who taught me to drive. (The clause tells which instructor.)

Nonrestrictive clause: Mr. Greenberg, who is very patient, taught me to drive.
Mr. Greenberg taught me to drive. (The clause could be dropped.)

Restrictive clause: This is the theater that shows double features. (The clause tells which theater.)

Nonrestrictive clause: This theater, which has a balcony, holds 2,000 people.
This theater holds 2,000 people. (The clause could be dropped.)

Using Commas To Avoid Confusion

Use a comma whenever the reader might otherwise be confused.

Sometimes no rule applies, but a sentence might be misread if the commas weren't there.

Without commas, the following sentences could be misunderstood.

Outside Mike barbecued chicken.
Whoever knocked knocked loudly.

With commas, the sentences are clearer.

Outside, Mike barbecued chicken.

Whoever knocked, knocked loudly.

Exercise A Copy the following sentences. Add commas where necessary.

1. Dear Alice
   I will be moving soon. Please write to me at 102
   Woodland Court Nashville Tennessee 37115.
   Yours truly
Margie
2. On March 4 1933 President Roosevelt closed every bank in the country.
3. The letter was postmarked from Paris France on June 10 1982.
4. Gary Indiana has many steel mills.
5. Johnny Morris who used to play football for the Chicago Bears is now a sports broadcaster.
6. On November 11 1918 the Armistice ending World War I was signed.
7. The plane made intermediate stops in Huntsville Alabama and Memphis Tennessee.
8. Ms. Bercher was stationed in Honolulu Hawaii from May 1 1980 to September 1 1982.

9. Send your application to Mr. Thomas Beale at the Beale Corporation 200 South Michigan Avenue Chicago Illinois 60025.

10. Inside Dad made a fire in the fireplace.

Exercise B Follow the directions for Exercise A.

1. On August 3 1923 Calvin Coolidge was sworn in as President of the United States.

2. Dear Mike
   My sister's new address is P.O. Box 1978 Monterey California 93940.

   Sincerely
Nick

3. On July 16 1945 the first atomic bomb was exploded in the desert near Los Alamos New Mexico.

4. The electrician you called called back.

5. The South surrendered to the North on April 9 1865 at Appomattox Virginia.

6. The house is at 691 Gilmore Street Long Beach California.

7. Are you from Hollywood Florida or Hollywood California?

8. Whoever screamed screamed loudly.

9. My sister who is sometimes called the family firecracker was born on July 4 1975.

10. This china which my grandmother brought back from Vienna Austria is extremely fragile.

The Semicolon

Use a semicolon to join the parts of a compound sentence if no coordinating conjunction is used.

We were bored with the programs on TV; we decided to write a play of our own.

When there are commas in the first part of a compound sentence, use a semicolon to separate the main clauses.

The corner store sells bread, milk, and some canned goods; but it does not carry fresh fruit, vegetables, or meat.

When there are commas within parts of a series, use semicolons to separate the parts.

The items we will make in woodshop this term are first, a chopping block; second, a tool box; and third, a footstool.

Use a semicolon before a conjunctive adverb that joins the clauses of a compound sentence.

You have learned that the parts of a compound sentence are sometimes joined by such words as *therefore, however, so, consequently, besides, nevertheless, then, yet,* and *moreover.* These words, called **conjunctive adverbs,** follow a semicolon.

The food in that restaurant is good; however, the service is slow.

The Colon

Use a colon after the greeting in a business letter.

Dear Mr. Blake: Dear Sir or Madam:

Use a colon between numerals indicating hours and minutes.

6:20 P.M.   7:10 A.M.

Use a colon to introduce a list of items. The colon indicates a pause before the items that follow.

Our high school has girls' teams for most sports: track, basketball, swimming, volleyball, tennis, and softball.

Do not use a colon if the list immediately follows a verb or a preposition.

Scholarships are given for academic achievement, athletic ability, and financial need.

Exercise A   Copy the word before and after each missing semicolon or colon. Add the correct punctuation mark.

1. Dear Sir
   The position that you inquired about has already been filled.
2. The customer gave her order to the waitress French onion soup, spinach salad, and iced tea.
3. The villain appeared on the stage the crowd booed.
4. Holiday traffic and road construction caused travel delays it was not a good weekend for taking a trip.
5. On the hanger, the dress looked great however, on me, it looked like a slipcover.
6. The play was supposed to start at 8 00 however, the curtain did not go up until 8 20.
7. Barb packed the following items hiking boots, mosquito repellent, a poncho, and a change of clothes.
8. Snow fell all night consequently, we had to dig our way out in the morning.
9. The tour stopped in these cities Florence, Italy Barcelona, Spain and Lisbon, Portugal.
10. Karen does not enjoy chemistry nevertheless, she does well in the course.

Exercise B   Follow the directions for Exercise A.

1. Kent broke his leg therefore he had to learn to use crutches.
2. The junk shop was filled with old, broken-down chairs rickety, wobbly tables and dozens of useless items.
3. The fog is really bad therefore all flights to and from the airport have been canceled.
4. Tex made some hot, spicy chili and he served it with grated cheese, onions, and sour cream.

5. Her wallet contained the following items ten dollars, two credit cards, a driver's license, a Social Security card, and several pictures.
6. Dear Reader
   It's time to renew your subscription.
7. I enjoy watching the Academy Awards however, I do not usually agree with the selection of winners.
8. The fireworks start at 9 00 PM on July 4.
9. The beaches are closed temporarily the pollution level of the water is too high.
10. Indoor tennis has the following advantages over outdoor tennis games are never canceled because of rain, there is no wind, and the sun doesn't get in the player's eyes.

The Dash

Using Dashes with Interrupters

You have learned about using commas with words or short phrases, such as *however* and *I think*, that interrupt a sentence. A **dash** is used with a long explanation that interrupts the thought.

The deluxe pizza—thin crust topped with double cheese, tomato sauce, pepperoni, sausage, green peppers, onions, and mushrooms—tasted delicious.

The microwave oven—it can cook a baked potato in minutes—has revolutionized cooking.

Using the Dash Before a Summary

Use a dash after a series to indicate that a summary statement will follow.

Spiders, termites, ants, and rodents—these are all household pests.

Fruits, vegetables, beans, nuts, and whole grains—this is the diet of many vegetarians.

Exercise   Copy these sentences. Insert dashes as needed.

1. School closings one district closed four schools in the last ten years are a result of the lower birth rate.
2. Bond paper, carbon paper, envelopes, and paper clips these items were ordered from the stationery store.
3. Gila monsters, tarantulas, jellyfish, stingrays all of them are venomous animals.
4. The state fair it is usually held during the first two weeks in August will feature live entertainment daily.
5. The James E. Sullivan Memorial Trophy an award given to the amateur athlete who has done the most to promote sportsmanship was given to Eric Heiden in 1980.
6. The young man wanted fame, wealth, and power goals most successful business people have in common.
7. Azaleas, jasmine, camellias, and roses all of these grew in the garden.
8. We can skip lunch unless you are really hungry and go shopping instead.
9. Golf, tennis, swimming, and sailing this park has something for everyone.
10. The town newspaper there were not enough ads to help pay printing costs printed its last edition today.

The Hyphen

Use a hyphen if part of a word must be carried over from one line to the next.

Words are separated by hyphens only between syllables.

The factory was patrolled by security guards.

Only words having two or more syllables can be broken by a
hyphen. Never divide one-syllable words, like *growl* or *weight*,
at the end of a line. Check your dictionary if you are not sure of
the syllables in a word.

A single letter should not be left at the end of a line. For
instance, this division of *election* would be wrong: *e- lection*. A
single letter should not begin a line either. This division of
ordinary would be incorrect: *ordinar- y*.

Use a hyphen in compound numbers from twenty-one to ninety-nine.

fifty-two pencils   twenty-six cars

Use a hyphen in fractions.

a three-fifths share   one-sixth of the pie

**Use a hyphen in certain compound nouns, such as *brother-in-law*,
drive-in, and *commander-in-chief*.**

My sister-in-law is a vice-president of the company.

**Use a hyphen or hyphens between words that make up a compound
adjective used before a noun.**

The radio announcer gives a play-by-play account of the
game.
but: The radio announcer describes the game play by play.

When compound adjectives are used after a noun, they are
not usually hyphenated.

A dictionary will tell you if a word needs a hyphen. These are
some examples of compound adjectives:

four-year-old girl   matter-of-fact approach
short-term loan   best-selling novel
well-used book   off-white paint
three-ring circus   half-baked idea

Exercise Number your paper from 1 to 15. After the proper number, write the word or words that should be hyphenated. Add the necessary hyphens. Use your dictionary if necessary.

1. This is an up to date version of the *World Almanac*.
2. Brad made a half hearted attempt to fix the lawnmower.
3. My three year old cousin got lost at the fair.
4. Check out time at the hotel was noon.
5. Chuck Brown was on the city all star football team.
6. The well to do executive donated large sums of money to her favorite charities.
7. My great grandmother only made forty five dollars a month at her first job.
8. One half of the students have part time jobs.
9. The newspaper reported the mayor's off the cuff remarks.
10. About forty nine out of every 100 babies born each year are girls.
11. Fewer than one third of the students ate a well balanced diet.
12. The two for one sale was very successful.
13. Doug wrote a letter to his brother in law.
14. The executive wore a three piece suit.
15. The quarterback asked for a time out.

The Apostrophe

The apostrophe is frequently used to form the possessive of nouns. To use the apostrophe correctly, you should know whether a noun is singular or plural.

To form the possessive of a singular noun, add an apostrophe and an s.

athlete + 's = athlete's   Cas + 's = Cas's
lady + 's = lady's   Jessica + 's = Jessica's

To form the possessive of a plural noun that does not end in s, add an apostrophe and an s.

children + 's = children's   men + 's = men's

To form the possessive of a plural noun that ends in s, add only an apostrophe.

runners + ' = runners'   surfers + ' = surfers'
Masters + ' = Masters'   drivers + ' = drivers'

To form the possessive of indefinite pronouns, use an apostrophe and an s.

somebody + 's = somebody's   anyone + 's = anyone's

Do not use an apostrophe with a personal pronoun to show possession.

hers   ours   yours   its   theirs

The sailboat was blown off *its* course.

Use an apostrophe in a contraction.

In contractions, words are joined and letters are left out. An apostrophe replaces one or more letters that are left out.

we'll = we will   hadn't = had not
they've = they have   won't = will not
it's = it is   I'll = I will

Use an apostrophe to show the omission of numbers in a date.

the winter of '78 (the winter of 1978)
an '82 Mercury (a 1982 Mercury)

Use an apostrophe and s to form the plurals of letters, figures, and words used as words.

ABC's   two 3's   five *i*'s   *but*'s and *and*'s

Exercise A   Insert apostrophes where they are needed.

1. Where is the childrens section of the library?
2. Im going with Besss cousin.

3. Shes bringing the 72 yearbook to the reunion.
4. Thats Tricias favorite song.
5. Theres a beautiful view of the Gilberts apartment.
6. Someones umbrella is in the closet.
7. Im going to test drive that sports car.
8. Theyve realized that the problem is theirs.
9. Mimis name has two *ms* and two *is*.
10. Mr. Elliot couldnt attend the mens luncheon meeting.

Exercise B   Follow the directions for Exercise A.

1. Is that our neighbors hammer youre borrowing?
2. The 1950s are sometimes called the Eisenhower years.
3. There were too many *wells* and *you knows* in your speech.
4. The childrens puppy was a gift from their aunt.
5. The class of 83 planned its prom.
6. Doesnt the Barkers car have a muffler?
7. Isnt Cathys party from 8:00 until 11:00?
8. The two coaches game plans were entirely different.
9. The toddler cant say *ths* or *ls* yet.
10. It is nobodys fault but yours.

Quotation Marks

Use quotation marks at the beginning and at the end of a direct quotation.

Quotation marks tell your reader that a speaker's exact words are being given. Here is an example:

Craig said, "Something is wrong with the radio."

Quotation marks are *not* used with indirect quotations. An indirect quotation does not tell the speaker's exact words.

Craig said that something was wrong with the radio.

At the beginning of a sentence there are often explanatory words. Use a comma directly after these words. Then begin the quotation with quotation marks. A period at the end of a sentence belongs *inside* the quotation marks.

The conductor said, "All aboard."

Sometimes explanatory words end the sentence. Then the quoted statement at the beginning of the sentence is followed by a comma. The comma belongs inside the quotation marks.

"All aboard," said the conductor.

Using Divided Quotations

Sometimes a quotation is divided into two parts by explanatory words. In that case, each part of the quotation is enclosed by quotation marks.

"A great city to visit," Roger said, "is Toronto."

In the example above, the divided quotation is a single sentence. The second part begins with a small letter. At times, however, the second part begins a new sentence. Then capitalize the first word of the second part.

"Let's go get some refreshments," Joy suggested. " The band is taking a break."

The first part of the divided quotation is followed by a comma. Commas always appear inside quotation marks.

"Your mail," Terry said, "is on the hall table."

The explanatory words in the middle of a divided quotation are followed by either a period or a comma. Use a period if the first part completes a sentence. Use a comma if the sentence continues after the explanatory words.

"In Florida," Don said, "we visited the Everglades."

"I want to go downtown today," Leslie explained. "I have to do some shopping."

Exercise Write each of the following sentences three ways as a direct quotation.

Example: I want a steady job.
a. "I want a steady job," he said.
b. He said, "I want a steady job."
c. "I want," he said, "a steady job."

1. Try snorkeling if you go to the Bahamas.
2. No, Robert Redford was not in the movie *Ordinary People*.
3. I wish that I could go to the concert.
4. After all that planning, we still forgot a flashlight.
5. In the second period, the Blackhawks were leading.

Using Punctuation with Quotation Marks

Place question marks and exclamation points inside the quotation marks if they belong to the quotation itself.

Katie asked, "Where can I find that information?"
Larry screamed, "Watch out!"

Place question marks and exclamation points outside the quotation marks if they do not belong to the quotation.

Did Kelly say, "Wait for me outside the cafeteria"?
How happy I was when Ms. Piley said, "You got an A"!

Commas and periods, as you have seen, always appear within quotation marks.

Exercise A Copy the following sentences. Punctuate them correctly with quotation marks, end marks, and commas. (There are three indirect quotations that need only end punctuation.)

1. Stay back ordered the fire chief
2. May I borrow your blue sweater asked Sue
3. Oh no said Pat I think I did the wrong exercises

4. Mr. Hardin explained how the clutch works in a car with standard transmission
5. My dog Grover is going to obedience school said Mark
6. The crowd shouted loudly We're number one
7. Eve said that she was going to summer school
8. The car started fine last night said Fran Why won't it start now
9. Did Ellen say that she would be on the clean-up committee
10. Did the doctor say I think we should X-ray your arm

Exercise B Write each of the following sentences as a direct quotation. In some examples, put the quotation first. In others, put the quotation last. Also, for variety, divide some quotations.

1. What language is spoken in Brazil?
2. Stop that!
3. I changed that flat tire on Denise's car.
4. There's a stream behind the cabin.
5. Can we join your book club?
6. After the Fourth of July, stores begin their summer clearance sales.
7. We hiked in the foothills.
8. Watch out!
9. Was that spider a black widow?
10. This afternoon I have to go to the orthodontist.

Using Long Quotations

You may wonder how to use quotation marks for quoting two or more sentences by the same speaker. Look at the following example.

"Once you have made a list of their birthdays, bring it to me," said the manager. "I want to ensure that everyone gets a card."

Using Quotation Marks for Dialogue

Dialogue is conversation between two or more people. It is punctuated in a special way. Begin a new paragraph each time the speaker changes.

"I am trying to limit my TV watching," said Anne.

"Well, I worked out a deal with my brother," replied Angela, "to try and cut down."

"What did you do, Angela?" asked Tom.

"I promised him that each week that I watched more TV than he did, I would do his chores."

"Did it work?" asked Anne.

"No!" exclaimed Angela. "Now we just watch TV together."

Exercise Rewrite the following conversation. Make correct paragraph divisions, and use the right punctuation.

What is the value of sports Mr. Munz asked. Well answered Dick I think team sports like football or basketball help the players to learn cooperation. Jim added I think sports are valuable because they keep you fit. I agree with you said Frank. I also think that individual sports like golf or tennis are important. That's a good point agreed Tim. I'll probably be playing tennis long after I've put away my football helmet.

Punctuating Titles

Use quotation marks to enclose the titles of magazine articles, chapters, short stories, essays, poems, songs, and short pieces of music.

Magazine article:	"Careers in Retailing"
Chapter title:	Chapter 5, "The Louisiana Purchase"
Short story:	"The Ransom of Red Chief"
Essay:	"Self-Reliance"
Poem:	"Fire and Ice"
Song:	"Hello, Dolly"

Underline the titles of books, newspapers, magazines, plays, movies, television programs, works of art, and long musical compositions.

In writing or typing, such titles are underlined, like this: <u>The Chocolate War</u>.

In print, these titles appear in italics instead.

Book title:	*Great Expectations*
Newspaper:	*Orlando Sentinel-Star*
Magazine:	*Sports Illustrated*
Play:	*The Wiz*
Movie:	*Rocky III*
Television program:	*Great Performances*
Work of art:	*American Gothic*
Long musical composition:	*Carmen*

Exercise A Copy the following sentences, adding quotation marks or underlining titles where necessary.

1. The story Blue Tea appeared in the June issue of Red-book magazine.
2. The band played Dixie.
3. Kathy read Jane Goodall's article about chimps, Life and Death at Gombe.
4. Custard and Company is a book of poems by Ogden Nash.
5. The TV show Hill Street Blues is about a police precinct.
6. One of Barry's favorite movies was Chariots of Fire.
7. The Washington Post is the only newspaper that thoroughly investigated the Watergate break-in.
8. Ms. Avery played some of the music from the Nutcracker Suite during the Christmas holidays.
9. The play The King and I is based on a true story.
10. The Spring House and Milk Cans are two paintings by Andrew Wyeth.

Exercise B Follow the directions for Exercise A.

1. Marcy read us Robert Frost's poem Birches.
2. Bill titled his research paper for economics class Inflation: What Causes It.
3. Dionne Warwick sang the song Do You Know The Way to San Jose?
4. The song Raindrops Keep Falling on My Head is from the movie Butch Cassidy and the Sundance Kid.
5. Did you read Chapter 1, The New World?
6. The community theater produced the play Annie Get Your Gun.
7. The Brethren is a book about the Supreme Court.
8. James Thurber, who wrote the story The Secret Life of Walter Mitty, was a cartoonist for The New Yorker magazine.
9. The story was printed in The Detroit Free Press.
10. Brain, Coma, and Fever are all books by Robin Cook.

ADDITIONAL EXERCISES

Punctuation

A. Punctuation Copy these sentences, adding the necessary punctuation.

1. How thin you are
2. How thin are you
3. Mr and Mrs Antonelli are having a party at 8:00 P M on Saturday; RSVP was written on the invitation
4. Dr Tucker asked if her patient had been X-rayed yet
5. Sal is 715 inches tall, just half an inch under six feet
6. John W Campbell, Jr wrote the story on which the movie *The Thing* was based
7. Oh, no Didn't Spencer tell you to keep the cage closed
8. The FBI trailed the suspect to St Louis
9. The bus to Washington, D C, is now boarding
10. II Relief programs of UNICEF
    A African drought
       1 Food supplies

B. Commas Copy the following sentences. Add commas where necessary.

1. Carol asked if she should bring her own pliers wrench or hammer.
2. Georgia looked in her address book rummaged through a stack of old mail and finally found the address.
3. Friday Saturday and Sunday have been the warmest most beautiful days this spring.
4. Gerrie put on her headphones closed her eyes and shut the world out.
5. Kip and Chad played chess Mel and Al argued over a ping-pong score and Esther leafed through an old magazine.

6. Playing Pac-Man trying to solve the Rubik's cube and watching cable TV were popular pastimes that year.
7. Bits of glass glittered like tiny brilliant diamonds scattered in the alley.
8. Do the Rabbit the Lynx the Mustang and the Cougar really move like the animals that they are named after?
9. First most of the streetlights were broken; second few houses had porch lights; third it was a foggy night.
10. These are standard rules for cooking: first read the entire recipe; second gather all utensils and ingredients; third clean up as you work.

C. Commas Number your paper from 1 to 10. Copy the following sentences, adding commas where necessary.

1. After Robin bought the ticket she put it in her pocket.
2. Well the problem isn't really that simple.
3. Although the subway goes to Coney Island many New Yorkers have never seen the ocean.
4. Really I'm sure that I'm right.
5. Guinea pigs to tell you the truth are not much fun.
6. That plant I'm sure is poison ivy.
7. The wheelbarrow however was too heavy to be pushed up the ramp.
8. Almost everybody in town in fact was at the game.
9. Left in the hot car the dog began barking and whining.
10. Amazingly enough Syl missed the free throw.

D. Commas Copy the following sentences, adding commas where they are needed.

1. Skates became more popular and skateboards were almost forgotten.
2. Joan of Arc the French heroine was declared a saint in 1920.
3. Yes Mel I remembered to buy Doritos and ginger ale.

4. My sister Carlene sang "Swing Low, Sweet Chariot."
5. He applied for a job at the post office but he mailed his application to the wrong address.
6. Denny said "I've started lifting weights."
7. "Whatever you do" said Nina "don't look down."
8. James have you seen my math book the one with the red cover?
9. Ms. Willis the career counselor said that we should always be on time for job interviews.
10. "I tried and I succeeded" said Vince.

E. Commas Copy the following sentences. Use commas where necessary. Write *Correct* if no comma is necessary.

1. On March 13 1852 the first newspaper cartoon of Uncle Sam appeared.
2. Dear Sandy
   My vacation address is 215 Main Street Carthage Illinois 62321.
   Your friend
   Luke
3. Mardi Gras which is the day before Lent begins is celebrated with a carnival in New Orleans Louisiana.
4. What clubs are you in in which you take an active part?
5. Otis who really doesn't believe in horoscopes said that he was born on May 3 1967 around noon.
6. If Beth drives over Vic will have a ride home.
7. The baseball player who broke Babe Ruth's record was Hank Aaron.
8. The pyramids near Cairo Egypt are all that are left of the Seven Wonders of the Ancient World.
9. The 1982 World's Fair which was not officially recognized was held in Knoxville Tennessee.
10. Bronko Nagurski who worked as a lumberjack to get in shape for football was a legendary Bears fullback.

F. Semicolons and Colons Copy the word before and after each missing punctuation mark and add the correct punctuation mark. If necessary, replace a comma with a semicolon.

1. Donna can remember everything that she hears furthermore she has a photographic memory.

2. Most of the students listed these goals more education, an interesting job, and a happy family life.

3. Dear Madam
   We have received your letter, it will be published in next week's column.

4. My grandmother likes songs by Hank Williams, Sr., who died in 1953, I prefer Hank Williams, Jr.

5. Doctors now say that these activities cannot cause colds sitting in a draft, getting one's feet wet, or swimming in chilly weather.

6. Please arrive promptly at 7 00 A.M. and bring the following items a sleeping bag, a ground cover, a mess kit, and a canteen.

7. People from many parts of the world live in Brazil some came to work in the rain forests.

8. Some of the amusement parks that Sheila visited were Old Country in Williamsburg, Virginia, Kennywood Park in Pittsburgh, Pennsylvania, Kings Island in Cincinnati, Ohio, and Astroworld in Houston, Texas.

9. Jackie had cut a lot of tape with the scissors therefore, the blades were sticky.

10. The beach was hot, however, the lake was freezing.

G. The Dash and the Hyphen Copy these sentences. Insert dashes and hyphens where they are needed.

1. At eighty six, my great grandmother still has a happy go lucky view of life.

2. The commander in chief, the general, and the prime minister these people will arrive at noon.

3. About two thirds of the students will buy yearbooks.
4. Perhaps half of the student body and that is just a rough guess have long term goals.
5. A green eyed cat crouched on the railing.
6. Simms parked the car in an out of the way spot.
7. The ten year old boy was half asleep.
8. Kenwood, St. Mel's, Lane Technical these schools have low drop out rates.
9. Wild burros the miners let them loose after the gold rush was over still roam California.
10. Sue wore a nineteenth century wedding gown, but her hairstyle was from the twenty first century.

H. Apostrophes Copy the following sentences. Add apostrophes where they are needed.

1. Rachel likes the TR-7s made in the early 1970s.
2. The students theme for their dance hasnt been chosen.
3. Swing was dance music popular in the 30s.
4. Its somebodys problem, but not yours.
5. Chriss laces are flapping because he cant tie his shoes.
6. All three teachers classes discussed the womens movement.
7. The Hesses cat batted the bee with its paw.
8. Youre making your *rs* look almost like *vs.*
9. His *Im sorrys* didnt change the jurys verdict.
10. Thats true. The Celtics chances dont look good.

I. Quotation Marks Number your paper from 1 to 10. Copy the following sentences. Add the necessary quotation marks and other punctuation marks. Two sentences need only end punctuation.

1. I don't see that article in this magazine said Beth Maybe it's in last week's issue
2. Have you included an outline with your term paper asked Ms. Stranskey

3. Heidi said The police photographer made a videotape of the scene of the crime
4. Shawn said I think that I know why Pac-Man is popular He looks like Charlie Brown
5. Did Holly ask if Claire had called
6. Max asked Does anybody have a pair of tweezers
7. Didn't the bus driver say There's no more room
8. Help shouted George Where's the emergency brake
9. I said that I had cleared the calculator
10. Cheerful songs Ms. Gaspar told us were popular during the Depression.

J. Quotation Marks and Underlining Copy the following sentences. Add quotation marks around titles or underline titles, where necessary.

1. The teacher assigned Tillie Olsen's story I Stand Here Ironing.
2. David won the oratory contest by reciting Claude McKay's poem If We Must Die.
3. Janine learned the words to the song Sweet Home Chicago from the movie The Blues Brothers.
4. The red hair of the child in Mary Cassatt's painting Picking Flowers in a Field blends with the flowers.
5. Karl shouts advice at the TV screen when The Guiding Light is on.
6. Juanita got some of the facts for her essay Where Did the Family Car Go? from a business newspaper, The Wall Street Journal.
7. Grease had a slightly longer run on Broadway than Fiddler on the Roof had.
8. Mother Goose Suite is a children's ballet.
9. Please read Chapter 15, The Power of Ice, in Physical Geography Today.
10. Mimi got a subscription to Sports Illustrated.

MIXED REVIEW

Punctuation

A. Using punctuation correctly Copy these sentences, adding the correct punctuation.

1. Ouch Did You have to use iodine
2. The address of the Sports Car Club of America is 6750 S Emporia Englewood Colorado 80112
3. Yes Mr Barnes Dr Flores will see you right away
4. Spartacus who was a slave and a gladiator led a revolt against the Romans in 71 B C however it failed
5. Has everyone here Bill asked met Shondra
6. If youre using an out of date I D card please get a new one before 8 30 A M tomorrow
7. Weve just received twenty five pairs of mens boots
8. The bandannas theyre very popular cost $175 each

B. Using punctuation in proofreading Proofread the following letter. Rewrite it, adding correct punctuation marks.

Dear Mr Mrs or Ms Occupant

Stop Youre probably asking yourself what you should stop Well stop worrying about what to get those hard to please people on your shopping list

Everyone who appreciates natural beauty would be overjoyed to receive a gorgeous healthy orchid plant for the holidays When they open these original gifts how delighted your friends will be

To make the holiday season of 90 one to remember fill out the order form below

If your order is mailed before December 5 1990 you will receive a surprise too

Very sincerely

USING MECHANICS IN WRITING
Punctuation

A. You are a proofreader for a local newspaper. One day, the typesetting equipment goes haywire. The following article is an example of the results. Proofread the article. Make all necessary corrections in punctuation.

WHATS HAPPENING IN PORT CITY

there will be an exhibit of rare books at port City Public Library in steep street? The exhibit will be open daily from 9 am " 8 pm!

at The Seaside Museum on River Street! there will be on exhibit of Whale photographs? Don/t miss it; Admission will be #1.50 for Adults and 75$ for children

Port City art association, on Harbor Walk, will be exhibiting work by local artists. The Exhibition opens on Thurs? at 9,30. . . .

B. Imagine this scene from a situation comedy program. On another planet, scientists have perfected a way to send beings over long distances. A visitor from that planet is sent to Earth. The alien visitor arrives in an average American apartment. It is empty except for a talking parrot. The visitor believes that the parrot is a typical inhabitant of Earth. Write a short conversation between the alien and the parrot. Include at least one divided quotation and at least one indirect quotation. Be sure to punctuate correctly.

Spelling

Your written work may give people a first impression of you. One of the things that people will notice is whether or not you spell words correctly. Good spelling is a valuable skill that you will use all of your life.

Becoming a good speller, however, is not easy. Words in English often are not spelled the way they sound. Also, it seems that there are many exceptions to every spelling rule.

This section will help you become a better speller. First, it will present steps for improving your spelling and for learning to spell new words. Also, it will explain the spelling rules and the exceptions to them.

How To Improve Your Spelling

1. Locate and conquer your own specific spelling problems.
What spelling errors do you make over and over? Study your
past written assignments. Make a list of words you misspelled on
them. Work on mastering those words.

2. Pronounce words carefully. Are you misspelling words
because you aren't pronouncing them correctly? If you are writing *famly* for *family*, for instance, you are probably mispro-
nouncing the word. Try to pronounce your words more
precisely.

3. Try to remember the letters in unfamiliar words. Do you
really look at the spelling of an unfamiliar or difficult word? That
habit can help you to remember how to spell the word. Write
the correct spelling of the word several times.

4. Always proofread your writing. Are some of your misspell-
ings careless mistakes? By examining your writing, you may
catch such errors. Read your work slowly, one word at a time.

5. Look up difficult words in a dictionary. Do you reach for
the dictionary when you're unsure of a spelling? Get into the
habit of letting the dictionary help you to spell well.

**6. Learn the few important spelling rules explained in this
section.**

How To Spell a Particular
Word Correctly

1. Look at the word and say it to yourself. Make sure to
pronounce it correctly. Say it twice, looking at the syllables as
you say them.

2. Look at the letters and say each one. Sound out the word
from its spelling. Divide the word into syllables and pronounce
each syllable.

3. Write the word without looking at your book or list.

4. Check to see if you spelled the word correctly. Look back at your book or list. If you spelled the word correctly, repeat the process.

5. If you made an error, note what it was. Then repeat steps 3 and 4 until you have written the word correctly three times.

Spelling Rules

Adding Prefixes

When a prefix is added to a word, the spelling of the word remains the same.

im- + patient = impatient   ir- + regular = irregular
re- + apply = reapply   mis- + lead = mislead
inter- + lock = interlock   de- + frost = defrost
dis- + respect = disrespect   il- + legible = illegible

Suffixes with Silent e

When a suffix beginning with a vowel is added to a word ending in a silent e, the e is usually dropped.

bake + -ing = baking   love + -able = lovable
style + -ish = stylish   like + -ing = liking
space + -ious = spacious   separate + -ion = separation

When a suffix beginning with a consonant is added to a word ending in a silent e, the e is usually retained.

face + -less = faceless   loose + -ly = loosely
love + -ly = lovely   place + -ment = placement
lame + -ness = lameness   care + -ful = careful

The following words are exceptions. Study them.

truly   argument   ninth   wholly

Exercise A Find the misspelled words. Spell them correctly.

1. John was stareing at the strangely dressed clown.
2. Jan is eraseing that mispelled word.
3. Craig's handwriting is definitly illegible.
4. The Dodgers were loseing in the nineth inning.
5. Many people dissagreed with Darwin's theory of createion.
6. The reporter missquoted the fameous writer.
7. These arguements are wholly unecessary.
8. Takeing the bus is unrealiable because the schedule is so iregular.
9. The detective rexamined all the likely suspects.
10. Translateing that story from Spanish to English was confuseing.

Exercise B Add the prefixes and suffixes as shown and write the new word.

1. save + -ing
2. mis- + treat
3. im- + material
4. tote + -able
5. ir- + rational
7. hope + -ing
8. un- + necessary
9. un- + waxed
10. mis- + spell
11. re- + arrange
12. race + -ing
13. re- + align
14. amaze + -ment
15. pace + -ing
17. retire + -ment
18. value + -able
19. dis- + agree
20. dis- + appear

Suffixes and Final *y*

When a suffix is added to a word ending in *y* preceded by a consonant, the *y* is usually changed to *i*.

heavy + -er = heavier   study + -ous = studious
cry + -ed = cried   twenty + -eth = twentieth
frilly + -est = frilliest   tiny + -est = tiniest

Note the following exception: When *-ing* is added, the *y* does not change:

worry + -ing = worrying   curtsy + -ing = curtsying
carry + -ing = carrying   fly + -ing = flying

When a suffix is added to a word ending in *y* preceded by a vowel, the *y* usually does not change.

pray + -ing = praying   employ + -er = employer
relay + -ed = relayed   annoy + -ing = annoying

Exercise   Add the suffixes as shown and write the new word.

1. crazy + -ness   8. sixty + -eth   15. lazy + -er
2. rally + -ing   9. employ + -able   16. library + -an
3. ready + -ness   10. play + -ed   17. play + -ful
4. carry + -er   11. purify + -ing   18. enjoy + -able
5. tricky + -est   12. sleepy + -est   19. holy + -ness
6. hurry + -ing   13. decay + -ed   20. try + -ed
7. marry + -age   14. fury + -ous

Adding the Suffixes *-ness* and *-ly*

When the suffix *-ly* is added to a word ending in *l*, both *l*'s are kept. When *-ness* is added to a word ending in *n*, both *n*'s are kept.

mental + -ly = mentally   open + -ness = openness
federal + -ly = federally   mean + -ness = meanness

Doubling the Final Consonant

In words of one syllable that end in one consonant preceded by one vowel, double the final consonant before adding *-ing*, *-ed*, or *-er*.

dig + -ing = digging   mar + -ed = marred
trap + -ed = trapped   grip + -ing = gripping
win + -er = winner   hop + -ed = hopped

In words of one syllable that end in one consonant preceded by two vowels, the final consonant is not doubled.

pour + -ing = pouring   read + -er = reader
thread + -ed = threaded   cool + -ing = cooling

Exercise A Find the misspelled words. Spell them correctly.

1. The child gleefuly riped open his birthday packages.
2. Joan stoped writing and taped her eraser on the desk.
3. The fox cruely attacked the traped rabbit.
4. Dad's hair is thining, and his waist is thickening.
5. The federaly funded program was ended last month.
6. The sterness of their leadder strengthened the pioneers.
7. Waitresses know that students are generaly poor tipers.
8. Is the water runing?
9. The leaness of veal makes it especialy good for dieters.
10. Are you bragging, or did you realy do that?

Exercise B Add the suffixes as shown and write the new word.

1. mean + -ness
2. rip + -ed
3. zoom + -ed
4. tag + -ed
5. sip + -ed
6. careful + -ly
7. slim + -est
8. fearful + -ly
9. drag + -ing
10. even + -ness
11. look + -ed
12. skip + -ed
13. get + -ing
14. drip + -ed
15. open + -ness
16. joyful + -ly
17. moan + -ing
18. zip + -ed
19. drop + -ing
20. loop + -ing

Words with the "Seed" Sound

There is only one English word ending in *sede: supersede.* Three words end in *ceed: exceed, proceed, succeed.* All other words ending with the sound of *seed* are spelled *cede:*

recede   precede   concede   secede

Words with *ie* and *ei*

There is a general rule for words with the long *e* (*ē*) sound. The word is spelled *ie* except after *c*.

I before E

field	grief	chief	piece	fierce
niece	reprieve	retrieve	believe	relief

Except after C

deceit	ceiling	receipt	perceive
conceit	receive	deceive	conceive

The following words are exceptions to the rule. Study them.

either	weird	leisure
species	seize	neither

Exercise Find the misspelled words in these sentences and spell them correctly.

1. I could not beleive the grief they experienced after the tragedy.
2. The cheif explained that federal law superceeds state law.
3. The reporter conseded that she had decieved her editors about the source of her story.
4. The proceeds from the fund-raising carnival exceded all expectations.
5. Niether of them noticed the weird speceis of bug crawling on the cieling.
6. Jim, I believe, is the most concieted person I know.
7. My neice offered me a piece of her three-teired wedding cake.
8. The store detective siezed the thief.
9. In her liesure time Sandy rode her horse through the fields.
10. Good greif! I lost my reciept.

A List of Commonly Misspelled Words

abbreviate
accidentally
achievement
across
address
all right
altogether
always
amateur
analyze
anonymous
answer
apologize
appearance
appreciate
appropriate
argument
arrangement
associate
awkward
balance
bargain
beginning
believe
bicycle
bookkeeper
bulletin
bureau
business
cafeteria
calendar
campaign
candidate
certain
changeable
characteristic
column

committee
courageous
courteous
criticize
curiosity
cylinder
dealt
decision
definitely
despair
desperate
dictionary
dependent
description
desirable
different
disagree
disappear
disappoint
discipline
dissatisfied
efficient
eighth
eligible
eliminate
embarrass
emphasize
environment
enthusiastic
equipped
especially
exaggerate
excellent
exhaust
expense
experience
familiar

fascinating
February
financial
foreign
fourth
fragile
generally
government
grammar
guarantee
guard
gymnasium
handkerchief
height
humorous
imaginary
immediately
incredible
influence
intelligence
interesting
knowledge
laboratory
lightning
literature
loneliness
maintenance
marriage
mathematics
medicine
minimum
mischievous
missile
misspell
mortgage
municipal
necessary

nickel
ninety
noticeable
nuclear
nuisance
obstacle
occasionally
occur
opinion
opportunity
original
outrageous
parallel
particularly
permanent
permissible
persuade
picnicking
pleasant
pneumonia
politics
possess
possibility
practice
prejudice
preparation
privilege
probably
professor
pronunciation
propeller
psychology
quantity
realize
recognize
recommend
reference

referred	separate	syllable	transferred
rehearse	sergeant	sympathy	truly
repetition	similar	symptom	Tuesday
representative	sincerely	temperament	twelfth
restaurant	sophomore	temperature	undoubtedly
rhythm	souvenir	thorough	unnecessary
ridiculous	specifically	throughout	vacuum
sandwich	strategy	together	vicinity
schedule	strictly	tomorrow	village
scissors	success	traffic	weird
secretary	surprise	tragedy	writing

ADDITIONAL EXERCISES

Spelling

A. Prefixes Find the misspelled words. Spell them correctly.

1. The audience sounds disatisfied and disappointed.
2. The driver missjudged the distance and braked unecessarily.
3. The unumbered pages contained many mispelled words.
4. You are misstaken about Tony's reaction to the unarmed robber.
5. That interrsection is at an inconvenient location.

B. Suffixes Add the suffixes as shown. Write the new word.

1. zone + -ing
2. advertise + -ment
3. pollute + -ion
4. argue + -ment
5. believe + -able
6. care + -less
7. take + -ing
8. waste + -ful
9. space + -ious
10. complete + -ly

C. Suffixes Add the suffixes as shown. Write the new word.

1. pity + -ful
2. early + -er
3. dusty + -est
4. study + -ing
5. happy + -ly
6. study + -ed
7. vary + -ous
8. employ + -ment
9. angry + -er
10. cry + -ed

D. Suffixes Find the misspelled words. Spell them correctly.

1. She defended her boss loyaly, despite his meaness.
2. The watertable was continualy dropping, especialy in the West.

3. The fire crew quickly chopped down the door.
4. The roaring maching suddenlly whimpered pitifuly.
5. The goalie had only the slimmest chance of stopping the puck.
6. Gus usualy arrived punctualy; his latness puzzled us.
7. Kevin looked around fearfuly, but Craig chatted cheerfully.
8. Claire was running to the bus stop when she nearly tripped over the curb.
9. Abby grinned happilly as the judges studied her painting.
10. Jeremy's height realy made shopping for clothes a problem; finaly, he learned to sew.

E. Spelling Find the misspelled words. Spell them correctly.

1. The cheif gave the brave a reprieve.
2. Some commercials are meant to decieve us.
3. Unbeleivable! Judy has kicked the ball across the field.
4. The states that had seceded were recieved back into the Union.
5. The dog was niether feirce nor friendly.
6. This reciept looks wierd to me.
7. Perhaps we have succeded in saving some endangered species.
8. Sam conceeded that his niece had deceived him.
9. Pieces of plaster fell from the cieling.
10. Everyone was releived when the flood waters receeded.

MIXED REVIEW

Spelling

A. Spelling words correctly Number your paper from 1 to 15. Correct the words that are spelled incorrectly.

1. He looked disappointed when the scores were tallyed.
2. The libraryian made a puzzleing announcement.
3. The mules wearily plodded across the feild.
4. Cy traced the drawing onto a thiner peice of paper.
5. Her puzzlement seemed completly unbelievable.
6. Niether of the babies has a carryage.
7. Andrew cheerfully recopied his composition.
8. The puck skided into the defenseive zone.
9. The opposing team recieved two penaltys.
10. Somebody is pageing the chief.
11. Betty is taller, but Joan is heavyer.
12. The puppies cryed continueously.
13. The workers are laying the foundation for the pavment.
14. Her statement realy endded the arguement.
15. I concede that, by misstake, I misspelled the word.

B. Using spelling in proofreading Proofread the following paragraph. Rewrite it, spelling all the words correctly.

I was siting in a chair in the dining room with my foot propped up because of a skating injurey. The phone in the liveing room started ringing. I waitted, hoping ilogically that the phone could percieve my feelings. However, it continued. I was becoming nerveous. Surelly the caller must have something really important to say. Painfully I got up and succeded in hopping to the phone. I seized the reciever. My niece was calling. She sayed that she was worrying about my foot. I impatiently reassured her and slamed the phone down. Struggling back to my chair, I steped onto a splinter of wood.

USING MECHANICS IN WRITING
Spelling

A. Write a review of a humorous movie. Choose any movie to review, but choose one that you found at least fairly funny. Use one of the following pairs of words in each sentence. At least one of the words in each pair is misspelled. Correct the misspelled words. Use all six pairs.

excelent performance stronglly reccomend
amuseing scenes unnusual situations
enthuseiastic audience hilarious writeing

B. The following paragraph from an article for a magazine contains many misspelled words. Proofread the paragraph for spelling errors. List the misspelled words, spelled correctly.

Genrally, the high school years are years of opportunity and acheivement. However, they are also years of incredable stress. Most students have busy scedules at school. They also have to make importent desisions about the future. Many work after school, either for pay or as volonteers. For busy students, liesure time is important. Students should be sure to get the necesary rest and relaxation. Everyone needs a break ocassionally.

C. Write a story about an acrobat on a bicycle. Use as many of the following words as you can. Be sure to spell each word correctly.

accidentally, across, awkward, balance, bicycle, certain, courageous, definitely, desperate, humorous, immediately, incredible, mischievous, obstacle, outrageous

The Correct Form for Writing

What you wear and how you speak give people an impression of you. Also, the way your papers look can give people a first impression. Content is the most important element of a paper. However, the form of your paper is important too. A paper that is carelessly written or difficult to read will probably affect your reader's attitude toward your work.

Care, neatness, and consistency are all part of good writing form. Your school may have specific rules for the correct form for written work. In this section you will learn about the kind of form that is accepted by many schools.

Guidelines for Clear Writing

Neatness

A neat, legible paper can be read easily. Neatness also suggests that the writer cares about what he or she is writing. There are several ways to give your papers a neat appearance.

Legible Writing

Typewritten papers are usually more legible than handwritten ones. However, if you do not have a typewriter, make your handwriting clear and legible. Always use ink. Blue or black ink is easiest to read. Make sure that letters are distinct, since some letters look similar. For example, *a*'s and *o*'s can be confused unless they are formed carefully. So can *e*'s and *i*'s.

The First Draft and the Final Copy

You cannot expect the first draft of a paper to be in perfect form. You write a first draft from your pre-writing notes or an outline. You then correct or revise the first draft. You may have to change words and sentences or rearrange whole sections.

Afterward, make your final copy. Proofread this new copy. You may find errors or words left out. To insert a word, write it above the line. Use a caret ($\wedge$) to show where the word belongs. To change a word, draw a line through it and write the correction above it. If you have made more than about three corrections on a page, you should recopy the page.

Acceptable Form

The correct form for writing means more than a neat appearance. In a paper with acceptable form, the various parts are positioned correctly. Headings, titles, margins, and spacing should be in the correct form.

The Heading

A heading identifies your paper. It is usually placed in the upper right-hand corner of the first page. Place your name on the first line. Write the name of your class on the second line. Write the date on the third line. In a paper with a title page, place the heading in the upper right corner of that page.

Each page, except for page one, should be numbered. Beginning with page two, place the page number in the upper right-hand corner. To identify all pages, you might want to put your name under the page number.

Some teachers may require a different form for labeling your paper. Follow any special instructions you are given.

The Title

The title of a paper should appear near the top of the first page. In general, place the title two lines down from the last line of the heading. Begin the first line of your paper two lines below the title.

Correct form for a title also means proper capitalization. The first word and all important words in the title should be capitalized. Use capitals for only the first letters of words, not for every letter. Do not underline your title or place it in quotation marks.

When a paper is more than three pages long, sometimes a title page is used. This page precedes the paper.

Margins and Spacing

Use correct margins and spacing to achieve an attractive appearance. Margins of one inch at the top, bottom, and left side of the paper look pleasing.

Try to keep the right-hand margin fairly even. Do not break too many words with hyphens, though, in order to keep the margin straight. A safe rule is to avoid hyphens in more than two lines in a row.

Double-spacing makes typed papers look neat. Paragraphs are usually indented five spaces. Skip two spaces after the punctuation mark at the end of a sentence.

Writing Numbers

The form for writing numbers should be consistent. Numbers under 100 are usually spelled out. Larger numbers are written in figures.

> The nursery charged *thirty-five* dollars to trim the tree.
> We need at least *eleven* more chairs.
> The sticker price on the car was *$8,175*.
> Over *350* invitations to the reception have been sent.

A number at the beginning of a sentence is always spelled out.

> *One million* people live in the New Orleans area.
> *Twenty-eight thousand* students attend the university.
> *Five hundred* dollars was the prize.

Figures rather than spelled-out words are used for these numbers: dates, street and room numbers, telephone numbers, temperatures, page numbers, decimals, and percentages.

> Humans first walked on the moon on July 20, 1969.
> The Marquette Building is at 140 South Dearborn.
> Dr. Blake is in Room 210.
> Jill's phone number is 555-5372.
> The high temperature today was 87 degrees.
> The map of China is on page 327.
> Scott ran the mile in 4.7 minutes.
> The current interest rate is 13½ percent.

In large sums of money or expressions of large quantities, commas are used to separate the figures. Commas are not used in dates, serial numbers, page numbers, addresses, or telephone numbers.

Correct: That mansion costs $350,000.
Correct: In 1980, the population of the United States was 226,504,825.
Incorrect: The stock market crash was in 1,929.
Correct: The stock market crash was in 1929.

Exercise Copy these sentences, correcting any errors in the writing of numbers.

1. Between 1970 and 1979, one thousand one hundred and forty-three law enforcement officers were killed in the United States.
2. The Thompsons live in apartment number six hundred and eighty-four.
3. 2nd prize is five hundred dollars and third prize is two hundred dollars.
4. The interest rate for home loans hasn't been below ten percent for over 4 years.
5. The temperature on the lakefront was 76 degrees, but in the western suburbs it was eighty-six degrees.
6. The author agreed to give 10 percent of the earnings to his agent.
7. 2 packages were delivered to 2,525 Harlem Avenue by mistake.
8. 1 gallon weighs eight and thirty-three hundredths pounds.
9. On December fourteenth, 1,911, Roald Amundsen reached the South Pole.
10. 400 students attended the convention which was held at three hundred and twenty-nine South Lakewood Avenue.

Using Abbreviations

Abbreviations are shortened forms of words. In formal writing, abbreviations are usually not acceptable.

Abbreviations, however, may be used for most titles before and after names. Abbreviations may also be used for government agencies and for time.

Titles before proper names:	Mrs., Mr., Ms., Gen., Dr., Rev., Sgt., Sen.
Titles after proper names:	Jr., M.D., D.D.S., Ph.D.
Government agencies:	FBI, VA, EPA, FTC
Dates and times:	A.M., P.M., B.C., A.D.

Notice that periods are not used in the abbreviations of government agencies.

A title is abbreviated only when it is used with a person's name, as in *Dr. Lauren Sherwood*. The following, for example, would not be acceptable: The dr. found a cure for the disease.

Abbreviations are not used for certain titles. *Honorable* and *Reverend* are not abbreviated when preceded by *the: the Reverend Lee Withers*. Abbreviations are not used for the titles of the President and Vice-President of the United States.

In most writing, abbreviations are not acceptable for the following: names of countries and states, months and days of the week, addresses, and firm names.

Incorrect:	Hebrew and Arabic are the official languages of Is.
Correct:	Hebrew and Arabic are the official languages of Israel.

Incorrect:	N.Y., N.Y., is called "The Big Apple."
Correct:	New York, New York, is called "The Big Apple."

Incorrect:	Sat., Sept. 25, is the homecoming dance.
Correct:	Saturday, September 25, is the homecoming dance.

Incorrect: The Baxter Co. headquarters are on Wacker Dr.
Correct: The Baxter Company headquarters are on Wacker Drive.

When you write paragraphs and compositions, abbreviations are not acceptable for the following: names of school courses, and the words *page*, *chapter*, and *Christmas*. Abbreviations for measurements, like *ft.*, *in.*, *hr.*, *oz.*, *qt.*, *mi.*, are also unacceptable.

Exercise Correct the errors in abbreviations in these sentences.

1. The baby gained three lbs. in one mo.
2. The Rev. Charles Potter is a chaplain with the U.S.A.F.
3. Last Sat., Pres. Reagan attended a Xmas party for sr. citizens.
4. The Proctor & Gamble Co. is located on 6th St. in Cincin., OH.
5. Dr. Greg Bradley, Ph.D., is teaching at the U. of Ill.
6. John R. Block is the Secy. of the Dept. of Agriculture.
7. William H. Webster was appointed to a ten-yr. term as Dir. of the FBI on Feb. 23, 1978.
8. Homework for Hist. of World Civ. is to read p. 300–315 of Ch. 28.
9. Buddhism was founded in the first cent. B.C. in Ind.
10. Many drs. work in govt. hospitals.

ADDITIONAL EXERCISES

The Correct Form for Writing

A. Numbers in Sentences   On your paper, correct any errors in the writing of numbers. Write *Correct* if a sentence has no errors.

1. The Cubs made 7 runs in the 4th inning.
2. The volcanic dust made the temperature one degree lower for months and caused an early 1st frost.
3. The summer of 1,816 was cold; on July Four, the temperature in Savannah, Georgia, was 49°.
4. 116,000 recreation workers had jobs in nineteen-eighty.
5. I paid twenty-four dollars for that sweater.
6. About forty-two percent of the land in Jamaica is used for agriculture.
7. Square roots are listed on page 33.
8. In 1980, the resident population of the United States was 226504825.
9. $5 is all that I paid for my 2nd bike.
10. That river is eight hundred and sixty-nine miles long.

B. Abbreviations   Correct the following errors in abbreviation.

1. American Samoa sent its first rep. to Congress in 1981.
2. Many drs. in the Lee Bldg. do not have Wed. office hrs.
3. Mr. Rios has worked for H.U.D. since last Oct.
4. Has the sgt. asked the Rev. Yeaglin to speak?
5. The Pres. signed the bill at 9:00 A.M.
6. The phys. ed. class did exercises for twenty mins.
7. The prof. told the class to read p. 205.
8. The labs. and the hosp. of NIH are located between Old Georgetown Rd. and Rockville Pike.
9. Cadets at West Point Military Acad. are in the Army.
10. Nancy worked in a dept. store during Xmas.

MIXED REVIEW

The Correct Form for Writing

Using the correct form for writing The following composition contains errors in writing form and in the use of abbreviations and numbers. Copy the composition, correcting any errors.

Water: Heading for the Shallow End

Remember the lines "Water, water, everywhere,/Nor any drop to drink" from lit. class? Well, we might see that situation someday. Although almost ¾ th's of the earth is water, not even three % of that water is fresh. Fresh water equals about one-thirtieth of our aprox. 300000000 cubic mi. of saltwater. More-over, ⅔'s of the fresh water is frozen in glaciers and polar ice. The largest supply of fresh water, nearly 2% of the world's total is in the Antarctic Icecap, which covers 6000000 sq. miles. We can actually use less than 1% of our water.

The U.S. spends more than $3,000,000,000 every yr. to pro-vide its population with water. Drs. suggest that we drink a qt. a day. Each person in the U. S. averages 90 gallons daily to clean and garden. 2 more are used for drinking and cooking.

More than 4 ×'s as much water as we use directly is used for farming. 115 gallons are needed to grow wheat for 1 loaf of bread. Producing one lb. of beef takes 4000 gallons.

Industry uses 5 times as much as people do. Sixty-thous. gallons are needed to make one ton of steel. Industry not only uses a lot; it pollutes even more. Since the govt. passed the Clean Water Act in nineteen hundred and seventy-three, corps. have kept surface water cleaner. The EPA, however, expresses concern about the growing pollution of ground water.

Our consumption of water is increasing faster than the no. of humans. In Ariz., for instance, ground water is being used 8 ×'s faster than it can be replenished by the natural water cycle. In summary, unless we become more careful, we might find our-selves "sinking" for lack of water.

USING MECHANICS IN WRITING
The Correct Form for Writing

Following is the beginning of a report about the interesting origins of some American businesses. The passage needs editing to put it in the correct form. Rewrite the passage, making all the necessary corrections.

Lisa Perkins
February 1

HOW IT ALL BEGAN

in Nov.,1,902 Pres. Theodore Roosevelt went on a hunting trip. He refused to shoot a baby bear that he saw. Reporters heard the story, and soon a cartoon showing the incident appeared in newspapers. Morris Michtom, who owned a smll shop in N.Y., saw the cartoons showing the cub. He made stuffed copies and called them "Teddy's Bear." He started a business that later became the Ideal Toy Corp., one of the largest toy business in this country.

CUMULATIVE REVIEW

Capitalization, Punctuation, and Spelling

A. Using capitalization, punctuation, and spelling correctly Copy the following sentences, correcting the errors in capitalization, punctuation, and spelling.

1. the editor in chief of the chicago sun times a well known newspaper resigned

2. "Is it ilegal to make a U-turn on castro street asked gordon

3. Clair who will be leaveing soon tryed out for the feild hockey team

4. the beginning of standard time in the united states was at noon on november 18 1883

5. "did your aunt visit the ship the *queen mary* when she was in long beach california asked hank

6. what truely amazeing architecture the city of chicago has

7. there are three steps to makeing ice cream pie first mix chocolate cookie crumbs and melted butter to make the crust second pour in softened ice cream and third put the pie in the freezer until it hardens

8. didn't I leave a copy of that new book blue highways on your desk asked ms castino

9. there are twenty two trophys on carls shelf

10. robert frost a new england poet wrote the poem mending fences

B. Using proofreading skills Proofread the following paragraph. Copy it, correcting the errors in capitalization, punctuation, and spelling.

Have you ever ridden a train. Well the Orient Express is no ordinary train. On october 4 1883 the most fameous train in history made it's first trip from paris france to giurgiu romania. the idea for the orient express known as "Train of Kings, the King of Trains" was concieved by Georges Nagelmakers a belgian banker. he wanted his train to link the republics kingdoms and empires of europe in luxuryous fashion. what style the train had. The dineing car had cieling paintings waiters in tailcoats and french crystal. The train carryed all of the crowned heads of europe as well as other fameous people. the actress sarah bernhardt the dancer anna pavlova the magician harry houdini and the spy mata hari all rode it. the orient express developed a legend of mystery and intrigue. this legend is carried on in books and movies. agatha christies murder on the orient express and ian flemings from russia with love are two examples. as one passenger on the new orient express said, this is not just a train . . . it is a state of mind.

A

origin of word in, 28
part of speech listed in, 28
plurals in, 28
principal parts in, 485
pronunciation in, 28
slang in, 29
special forms or endings in, 28
syllables in entries, 28
synonyms in, 29
types of, 26
unabridged, 26
See also Words *and* Vocabulary.
Directions
following, 308–309
giving (in a speech), 372
for reading forms, 360–362
Direct objects, 398–400
compound, 407, 584
definition of, 398
diagraming, 401, 605
infinitive phrase as, 559
nouns as, 435–436
predicate words or, distinguish-
ing, 404–405
pronouns as, 452
recognizing, 398–399
Direct quotations, 651
Discovery draft. *See* First draft.
Divided quotation, 651
Double negatives, 518–520
Drawing conclusions, 284–285

E

ei/ie, 704
Empty sentences, 52–53
Encyclopedia, 300–302
Ending compositions. *See*
Conclusions in compositions *and*
Compositions, conclusions.
Ending sentences in paragraphs,
100–101

English language
formal, 38–39
informal, 38–39
jargon, 42–43
nonstandard, 35–37
number of words in, 2
regional, 44–45
slang, 29, 40–41
standard, 35–37
English language words. *See*
English language *and* Words.
Entry words in dictionary, 28
Envelope, addressing, 331–332
Errors in reasoning, 280–283
Essay tests, 320–322
Examples
as context clues to word
meaning, 2
to develop a paragraph, 78–79,
94–95
Exclamation mark, or point
with exclamatory sentences, 409,
662–663
with interjections, 543–544
with quotation marks, 685–686
Exclamatory sentences
definition of, 409, 662–663
punctuation of, 662–663
Explanatory compositions, 211–239
explaining a process, 211–219
planning, 212–213
revising, 218–219
step-by-step order, 214–215
transitions in, 216–217
presenting an opinion, 221–229
developing an opinion,
222–223
first draft of, 226–227
organizing an opinion,
224–225
revising, 228–229
using transitions in, 226–227

F

G

Graphic aids, 316–317
Greek word roots, 14–15
Group discussions, 378–381
Guide cards, 298
Guidelines for writing
  compositions, 182–183
Guide words
  in dictionary, 26–27
  in encyclopedia, 300

H

have as helping verb, 479–480
Heading in letters, 328, 334
hear/here, 626
Hearing words, 20
Helping verbs, 392–393, 479–480
here/there, 517
Hyphen, 679–681

I

I
  capitalization of, 644
  with first-person point of view,
    118–119, 190–191, 253–255
ie/ei, 704
Imaginary narrative compositions
  (stories), 186–189
Imaginary subjects for paragraphs,
  114–115
Imperative sentences
  definition of, 409–410
  period with, 409, 661
  you as understood subject in,
    396–397
Importance of reasons as method
  of organization, 96–97, 150–151,
  224–225
in/into, 635
Indefinite pronouns, 460–461,
  574–575
Incidents in paragraphs, 78–79

Indenting first line of paragraphs
  in letters, 328–329
Indirect objects, 400–402, 452
Indirect question, 661
Inference, as context clue, 4–5
Infinitive, 557–561, 562–563
  phrase, 558–560
  split, 559
Informal English, 38–39
Initials,
  capitalization of, 643
  periods with, 661–662
Inside address of business letters,
  334–335
Interjections, 542–544, 662–663
Interrogative pronouns, 460
Interrogative sentences
  definition of, 409, 662
  period with, 661
  question mark with, 409, 662
Interviews and discussions,
  86–87
Interview, job, 354–359
Intransitive verbs, 399–400
Introductions
  in compositions, 168–169,
    192–193, 204–205, 214–215,
    226–227
  in speeches, 372
  in research papers, 253–255
Invitations. *See* Letters.
Irregular verbs, 484–490
  using a dictionary to find
    principal parts, 485
  and helping verbs, 485
  is, are, was, were, 479
  list of principal parts,
    485–486
  rules for, 485–490
  troublesome pairs of, 629–633
Italics, underlining for, 687–688
its/it's, 626

method of organization, 96–97
Multiple-choice tests, 320–321

N

Narrative compositions, 184–199
  choosing point of view in,
    190–191
  chronological order in, 196–197
  conflict in, 188–189
  dialogue in, 194–195
  first draft of, 192–193
  planning a story, 186–187
  plotting a story, 188–189
  point of view in, 190–191
  revising, 198–199
  transitions in, 196–197
Narrative paragraphs, 80–81,
  113–123
  choosing point of view in,
    118–119
  chronological order in, 116–117
  definition of, 80–81
  developing, 114–115
  first draft of, 120–121
  revising, 122–123
  transitions, 120–121
Nationalities, capitalization of, 649
Negatives
  double, 518–520
  n't not part of verb, 392–393
Nonfiction books, 294–295
Nonrestrictive clause, 672–673
Nonstandard English, 35–37, 625
Note cards, 245–247
Notes, social. *See* Letters.
Notetaking, 245–247, 312–313
Nouns, 431–446
  capitalization of, 432–433, 643
  clauses, 603–606
  as compound objects, 406–407
  as compound subjects, 406–407

common, 432–433
definition of, 432
as direct objects, 435–437
as indirect objects, 436–437
as objects of prepositions, 452,
  528–529, 605
plural forms of, 439–441
possessive forms of, 441–442
predicate, 403–404, 437–438
proper, 432–433, 643
in sentence patterns, 410–412
singular forms of, 439–441
as subjects, 390, 434–435
nowhere, 634
no words, *not* words. *See*
  Negatives.
Number of the verb, 571
Numbers in writing, 714–715
N LV Adj. sentence pattern, 411
N LV N sentence pattern, 411
N V sentence pattern, 410–411
N V N sentence pattern, 411
N V N N sentence pattern, 411

O

Objective tests, 318–321
Object of the preposition, 452,
  528–529, 605
Object of the verb, 605
Object pronouns, 449–450, 452
of, 636
Omniscient point of view, 190–191
Only-cause reasoning, 282–283
Opinion
  definition of, 274
  and facts, 274–275
  judgments, 276–277
  prediction, 276–277
  statement of obligation, 276–277
  supporting, 274–275
  in compositions, 222–225

there/here, extra in sentence, 517
Third-person limited point of view, 118–119
Third-person omniscient point of view, 118–119
Third-person point of view
in compositions, 190–191
in paragraphs, 118–119
those/them, 466–467, 517
Time sequence. *See* Chronological order.
Title card, 297–298
Titles
capitalization of, 644, 652
of compositions, 180–181, 713
of persons, 644
of written works
quotation marks with, 687–688
underlining for italics, 687–688
to/too/two, 627
Topic, choosing, 86–87
Topic, narrowing the
in compositions, 170–171
in paragraphs, 88–89
in research paper, 242–243
Topic sentence
in compositions, 174–175
in paragraphs, 76–77, 92–93
in research papers, 248–249
Touch words, 21
Transitions
showing chronological order, 96–97, 116–117, 120–121, 196–197
in compositions, 178–179, 196–197, 216–217, 224–227, 234–235
showing order of importance, 96–97, 150–151, 224–225

in paragraphs, 120–121, 132–133, 142–143
showing spatial order, 96–97, 128–129, 132–133, 202–203
showing step-by-step order, 140–143, 214–215
Transitive verbs, 399–400
True-false tests, 320–321
two/to/too, 627

U

Underlining titles for italics, 687–688
Understood subject (*you*), 396–397
Unity in paragraphs, 74–75
Using grammar in writing. *See* end of each lesson.
Using mechanics in writing
capitalization, 659
punctuation, 697
spelling, 720

V

Verb (simple predicate), 389–390
Verbals, 549–553, 556–557, 562–563. *See also* Gerunds, Participles and Infinitives.
Verbs, 475–499
action, 476
active, 491–492
after *there*, 394
agreement with subject, 570–581
be, 402–403, 476. *See also* State-of-being verbs, Linking verbs, *and* Irregular verbs
compound, 406–407
with compound subjects, 573–574
contractions, 463–464, 682
definition of, 476

diagraming, 390–391
using dictionary to find principal parts of, 485
direct objects of, 398–400
future tense, 481
future perfect tense, 482
helping, 392–393, 479–480
indirect object of, 400–402
intransitive, 399–400, 477–478
irregular, 484–490
linking, 402–405
main, 392–393, 479–480
in negative contractions, *n't* not part of, 392–393
number, definition of, 571
object of, 398–402
parts of, 392–393
passive, 491–492
past participle, 483–484
past tense, 481, 483–484
past perfect tense, 482
perfect tense, 482
plural forms of, 570–581
present tense, 480–481, 483
present perfect tense, 482
principal parts of, 483–484
regular, 483
in sentence patterns, 410–412
separated parts of, 392–393
singular forms of, 570–581
state-of-being, 389–390, 402–403, 476
subjects of, 390
tenses, 480–483
transitive, 399–400, 477–478
troublesome, 629–633
See also Irregular verbs.
Vertical file, 303
Vocabulary, 1–23. *See also* Words *and* Dictionary.

W

ways, 636
we/us, 465
weather/whether, 628
well/good, 517
whether/weather, 628
who/whom, 464–465
Word endings in dictionary, 28
Word parts, 8–15
Words, English language
  antonyms, 16–17
  base, 6–7
  combinations from Greek, 14–15
  context clues to meanings of, 1–5
  entry words in dictionary, 28
  as different parts of speech, 544–545
  guide words, 26–27
  hearing, 20
  jargon, 42–43
  Latin roots of, 12–13
  purr, 278–279
  regional, 44–45
  sight, 20
  smell, 21
  snarl, 278–279
  for special fields, 22–23
  synonyms, 16–17
  slang, 29, 40–41
  taste, 21
  touch, 21
  transitional
    in compositions, 178–179, 196–197, 216–217, 224–227, 234–235
    in paragraphs, 120–121, 132–133, 142–143
Writing
  choosing point of view, 118–119, 190–191

Photographs

Jim Whitmer, ii, 24, 34, 156, 166, 184, 230, 306, 326, 366, 382; Tom McCarthy/Hillstrom Stock, xviii; James L. Ballard, 46, 58, 292; Jacqueline Durand, 70, 82, 136, 200, 240, 340; Brent Jones, 104; Ray F. Hillstrom, 112; Bob Adelman/Magnum, 124; Sylvia Johnson/Woodfin Camp, 146; Michael Hayman/Click Chicago, 210; A. Devaney/Gartman Agency, 220.

Cover

Sinjerli Variation II, 1977. Frank Stella. Petersburg Press, London and New York. © Vert Fonce, 1977.